CHRIST IN THE PSALMS

CHRIST
IN THE
PSALMS

PATRICK HENRY REARDON

CONCILIAR PRESS
BEN LOMOND, CALIFORNIA

PUBLISHED BY:
Conciliar Press
P.O. Box 76
Ben Lomond, CA 95005-0076

Printed in Canada

Cover and interior design by Sam Torode

LIBRARY OF CONGRESS CATALOGING-IN-PUBLICATION DATA:

Reardon, Patrick Henry, 1938-
    Christ in the Psalms / by Patrick Henry Reardon.
        p. cm.
    Includes bibliographical references.
    ISBN 1-888212-21-7 (pbk.)
    1. Bible. O.T. Psalms—Meditations. I. Title.
BS1430.4 .R43 2000
223'.206—dc21
                        00-060289

Uxori,

Filiae,

Filioque

FOREWORD

BY BISHOP DEMETRI OF THE ANTIOCHIAN
ORTHODOX CHRISTIAN ARCHDIOCESE

The Psalms run like a golden thread through the beautiful garment of Orthodox worship. They form the core of Vespers, Matins and the other services of the Daily Office. They are found in the Divine Liturgy, Marriage and the other Sacramental services of the Church. They provided the inspiration for many of the prayers and hymns of Orthodox worship. The Psalms are so important that ancient tradition has decreed that the entire Book of Psalms must be read every week during Daily Offices. In addition to inspiring the public prayer of the Church, the Psalms are an indispensable part of the private devotions of all who seek a closer relationship with God.

The Psalms are important because they express in divinely inspired language the innermost thoughts and even fears of humanity. The Psalms express the wonder felt by those who gaze at the glory of God's creation. They give words to the intense sorrow for sin. They profoundly express the horror of loneliness and alienation. No matter how deeply invaded by sentiments of despair, one finds these feelings echoed in the Psalms themselves, and, more important, finds them answered by the glorious message of the love of God.

Most important, however, the Psalms point toward the ultimate liberation of humanity from sin, death, and despair through Jesus Christ. Indeed, it is only through Christ that we can understand the poetic language of the Psalms. From the first to the last Psalm, these ancient writings tell us in the language of prophecy that God will intervene through Christ to deliver us from the plight inflicted by our sins. It is most significant that, when He hung on the Cross, Our Lord quoted from the Psalms.

The Rev. Father Patrick Reardon, Pastor of All Saints Antiochian Orthodox Church in Chicago, Illinois, has done a great service to all who desire a deeper relationship with God by preparing these meditations on the Book of Psalms. Drawing on his long experience first as an Episcopal pastor and then as a priest of the Orthodox Church, Fr. Patrick has produced a work of depth and devotion. He rightly understands that one cannot truly probe the deep meaning of the Psalms unless one understands them in the light of the redemption brought by Christ. Although he is well qualified to apply the insights of modern scholarship to his work, having been a professor at one of the most prestigious Protestant seminaries in the United States, he does not yield to the temptation to treat the Holy Scriptures as merely human works that has so marred the works of many modern scholars. Instead, he always remembers the unique character of these sacred writings. Although Fr. Patrick frequently invokes the glorious traditions of the Fathers when studying the Psalms, his work is much more than a mere collection of Patristic commentaries. Instead, he provides the fresh and intensely personal insight of a pastor to the study of the Book of Psalms.

Thus I can recommend this book without hesitation. Those who study it will be edified by the scholarship and devotional quality of Fr. Patrick's writings on this important subject. One will read it again and again, gaining each time new and nourishing perspectives on the Book of the Psalms.

+ Demetri

ABOUT THIS BOOK

Preaching and public verbal instruction have always been an important, even major component of my ministry as a priest. As an Episcopal clergyman more than twenty years ago, I also took to composing a regular column in the parochial bulletin as an added forum of pastoral instruction for the congregation that I was then pastoring in Oklahoma City. It endured. Except for the few years when service on the faculty of an Episcopal seminary largely removed me from the parochial ministry, I have been writing that modest column ever since. Eventually the articles became uniform in length, exactly filling a legal-size page, and somewhere along the line the name "Father Pat's Pastoral Ponderings" was adopted as a title for the effort.

For a long time there was not much system to the thing. I simply wrote down the theological and spiritual ideas I happened to be thinking about at the time, ideas drawn from books I was reading, or such pastoral concerns as seemed needful and opportune. I commented on all manner of topics, from literature to the state of the Episcopal Church.

On becoming the pastor of St. Anthony's Orthodox Church in Butler, Pennsylvania, a few years ago, I continued this particular writing ministry to the folks in that parish. About the same time, someone introduced me to the art of e-mail, and I commenced sending these articles out to a few friends over the internet. While it is possible that the effort has cost me a friend or two over the years, my computer now holds seventeen different lists of those who receive these weekly "Pastoral Ponderings."

Then, in 1997, deciding to put a touch of structure into the project, I resolved to write a series of reflections on the Psalms. Even when I left Pennsylvania, I continued writing them for All Saints' Orthodox Church in Chicago, where our beloved Metropolitan Archbishop assigned me the following year. Each of these meditations, including the Introduction to this book, first appeared in an ordinary parish bulletin. Now, three years after their inception, at the rate of exactly one psalm per week, these meditations are finished, and you have them here in hand.

As it turned out, sometime after I had begun writing this series, I was assigned to translate and annotate the Book of Psalms for the Old Testament project of the Orthodox Study Bible, a task I have been at for about two years. Most often, therefore, the translations of various quoted verses of the Psalms that you will find in these pages are my own rendering from the Greek. Indeed, this is almost always the case, though I hasten to add that this translation work is ongoing, so the renderings contained herein are not in their final form. There is still a great deal to be done with this translation, especially to make it suitable for liturgical use.

Even though these reflections are tied together by the Psalter, they do not seem to be tied together in any other way, certainly not by approach, method, or style. Indeed, if there is any real *method* to my reading of Holy Scripture, I have never identified what it is. So you will find that each psalm is approached individually, in some fashion that happened to appeal to me at the time. Nor did I write the reflections in the order in which they appear here; I jumped all over the place during their composition, picking this or that psalm as I was disposed, my choice very often determined by seasonal liturgical usage, until they were all finished.

No one, I think, can sit down and at one reading exhaust the depths of meaning contained in a single psalm. What I find in a certain psalm on a certain day may be very unlike what I will find in that same psalm on a different day, and there is not the slightest doubt in my mind that, were I to write this book a dozen times over the next twenty years, it would be substantially different each time. Nor, even then, would I have even begun to sound the depths of the Psalter. All of this is to say, of course, that what you have here falls very short of being an adequate introduction to the Psalms.

Likewise, there is not the faintest trace of biblical scholarship anywhere in these pages. I am a simple parish priest who likes to read the Bible and spends some time each day thinking about what it says. For that reason, I have no doubt that some of the following pages may prompt Scripture scholars to wince and shake their heads. However, since this is exactly my own response when I read contemporary critical scholarship with respect to the Psalms, I suppose turnabout is fair play.

Nor, except for the once or twice that I consulted St. Augustine's great *Enarrationes in Psalmos* (a work most important to the contents of my head and heart since the mid-1950s), have I researched the Fathers of the Church while writing these reflections. If I do quote a Church Father here and there in these pages (as I vaguely recall having done), it is quite a matter of happenstance. Usually the quotation in question just happened to be in my mind at the time. After nearly a half-century of heavy reading of the Fathers of the Church, I could not begin to account for my debt to them. I do believe and hope, nonetheless, that those of you who have done the same reading will recognize the thought and inspiration of the Church Fathers all through this book.

At the same time, none of this book was written off the top of my head. Whether or not they show it in the final result, each reflection contained herein received great care. Nor were any of these pages rushed in composition. I usually had them completed a long time, even months, before they appeared in our parish bulletin.

Still they are only "pastoral ponderings," which is to say that they are thoughts about the Psalms that a parish priest, with no particular talents that would otherwise warrant the work, has shared with the people he pastors. I suspect that many priests, should they take up this book, may think that they could have written a better one. And I do not doubt that this thought would be correct. Indeed, I hope these are the kinds of ideas that any Orthodox priest normally shares with his people.

All I have done here is to try to look at the Psalms through the lens of Christ, especially as contoured through the rest of the Bible and the liturgical worship of the Church. Whenever this or that verse of the Psalter is explicitly interpreted in the New Testament, this fact has determined my line of interpretation. When Holy Church has chosen some psalm for a special day or season, or for a particular canonical Hour, I made a point to consult the propriety suggested by this usage, with a view to the explanation of that psalm. The whole idea here is to pray the Psalms with what St. Paul calls "the mind of Christ," which means the life of divine grace, the mystery of our redemption, the guidance of the Holy Spirit, the nourishing breasts of Holy Mother Church. From these rich blessings the lines of the Psalter never stray.

Now, how should someone go about reading this book? Well, everybody is different, so a formal rule is impractical. I will say this much, nonetheless. This book took three years in the writing, and I believe that it should take no less in the reading. Perhaps the best way to get through these pages with profit would be to take one psalm per week, meditating on it daily, and using these pages to aid in the meditation. This is my counsel. In any case, I suggest going slowly, for that is how it was written.

The foregoing comments lead naturally to some consideration of the best way to go about praying the Psalms themselves. I have given this quite a bit of thought over the years, especially in the context of spiritual direction. Having prayed various of the Psalms daily since childhood, and now having prayed through the entire Psalter each week for many years, I would offer the following suggestions for how to get started in this matter.

First, pick one translation and stick with it (at least until my new translation comes out in the Orthodox Study Bible!). One should not, normally, change the wording of his prayers anyway, not without very good cause. The entire business of praying with words is to put the words themselves deeply in the heart, so that the reflecting mind descends into the heart with the words of the prayer. This is what it means to learn the Psalms *by heart*. It involves memory, to be sure, but also a great deal more than memory. I think of it as a kind of kneading of leaven into the dough of the mind. The goal is to make the words, images, ideas, and sentiments of the Psalms part of our own inner world of thought and resolve. So, in general, stick with one translation. (If, however, someone can pray the Psalms in the canonical Greek, or even the original Hebrew, there is obviously a special blessing involved in doing so. I will often appeal to both of these languages in the pages that follow.)

Second, do not, at the beginning, try to pray all the Psalms, or even a very big portion of them. Better to start with a few favorites and gradually commit them to memory. As you do so, you will find that you can pray them at times when it is not possible to have a book open before your eyes. For many years, for example, I have been singing the "psalms of ascent" (these psalms to be explained herein when you come to them) while driving around in my car on pastoral visits and so forth. I regularly sing other psalms in the shower.

As often as I can, I sing the psalms, each psalm in a particular one of the eight tones, a method that helps a great deal with the memorization. Indeed, each of these that I regularly sing is associated in my mind with one of the eight tones. Thus, by long custom, I happen to sing Psalm 93 (Hebrew 94) in the second tone; I doubt that I could, by memory, sing it in any other, so strong is the force of habit. Psalm 149 I invariably sing in the seventh tone, and so forth.

The goal of this sort of practice should be, I submit, to have the words of the Psalms almost always on our lips, when walking down the street, driving to work or to the grocery store, going to or coming home from church, and so on. This is surely what the Psalter itself means when it says that the mouth of the just man shall meditate wisdom. The psalms become our basic internal text, as it were, the underlying preoccupation of our minds, the thematic source to which we spontaneously return when no other thoughts are forced upon us by the various duties that otherwise occupy our days.

But one is never going to memorize the various psalms, much less learn them *by heart*, unless he prays them very often. So, it is not a good idea to try to start by praying all the psalms over a longer period of time. If, say, someone is going to pray a psalm only once or twice a month, that psalm will simply never enter deeply into his mind and heart. So, my counsel is to go slowly at first.

If one is just getting started in this, I recommend the psalms that are already interpreted in the New Testament. Psalm 2, for instance, as it is interpreted in Acts 4, or Psalm 8, as it is explained in Hebrews 2. With respect to the use of the Psalter in the writings of the New Testament, the following pages will offer numerous suggestions.

I do not recommend that an ordinary Christian (as distinct from a monastic) immediately assume the burden of praying the whole Psalter weekly, nor ever do so except under the supervision of a wise spiritual father. There are simply too many dangers of overburdening one's soul in the attempt, neglecting one's other responsibilities, and becoming discouraged in the effort. Praying the Psalms, according to St. Benedict, is *opus*, "work"! Anyway, praying parts of the Psalter is usually part of a person's *daily rule*, which in the Orthodox Church means that it is done with the blessing and guidance of a spiritual father. Third, pick psalms that are appropriate to certain days or particular times of the day. For this reason, I often comment in these pages about the special use that Holy Church makes of individual psalms at the particular canonical Hours. Some psalms are more appropriate to the morning hours, some to the evening, and so forth. I often remark on this feature, drawing guidance from both the East and the ancient West. One will doubtless detect in these pages a predilection for the scheduling of the Psalms in the sixth-century Rule of St. Benedict of Nursia, a predilection to which I plead guilty.

In general, finally, a note on the numbering of the Psalms. In this book the Psalms are numbered according to the canonical Greek text or Septuagint (and the Latin Vulgate), which is the same as the Hebrew numbering in only 11 of the 150 Psalms! As each psalm is introduced, however, the Hebrew numbering will be listed in parentheses, just so that one can keep track of the business. Mine is the traditional numbering used in the Orthodox Church, nor is there any compelling reason to change it. At the same time, it is recognized that most English-speaking Orthodox Christians probably still use some Protestant version of the Psalms, which follows the numbering in the traditional rabbinical text. This volume includes a chart showing how these two numbers of the Psalter are related to one another.

INTRODUCTION

The Church's full format of prayer includes, among many other components, the weekly recitation of the entire Book of Psalms. Indeed, "among" is scarcely an adequate preposition in this case because of the very special place that psalmody holds in the Christian life of prayer. From the very beginning of her history, when the Church of God turns to Him in love and devotion, the words of the Psalter form the expressions that spontaneously, as by an impulse of her nature, rise from her heart and take shape in her mouth. The psalms find their truest context in the heart and on the lips of the Church. Those whose lips constantly move with the syllables of the Psalter give living expression to the deepest being of the Church.

Considered simply as a fact of history, the primacy of the Psalter in Christian prayer seems very clear. Thus, when Saint Benedict of Nursia, in the sixth century, prescribed the weekly reciting of the Book of Psalms as the barest monastic minimum, he lamented the inability of his contemporaries to perform that task *every day*, as earlier generations of monks had done. Likewise, those modern Protestant pocketbook Bibles, containing only the New Testament and the Psalms, embody a very ancient and deep insight of the Christian faith that sees the Psalter almost as part of the New Testament itself. When the Orthodox in this country published their first volume of the Orthodox Study Bible, the Book of Psalms was appropriately placed with the New Testament.

One of my former professors speculated a few years ago that in "Christian worship the psalms were first used at the end of the second century" (Norbert Lohfink, "The Psalter and Christian Meditation," *Theological Digest* 40:2, Summer 1993). Well, close, but not close enough. With all due respect to my justly esteemed and warmly remembered teacher, I think Father Lohfink's calculation here to be off the mark by more than a century. Already in the most primitive period of Christian history—indeed, in Jerusalem itself and prior to the conversion of Saint Paul—we have our first extant example of the use of a psalm in Christian worship. The relevant text is Acts 4:24–30, where we find Christians, evidently within the first months of Christian history, praying a section from Psalm 2.

Moreover, there is something beyond mere history to be learned from this passage in Acts; it also addresses the essentially theological question of *why* Christians pray the Psalter. This apostolic prayer quotes the first line of the second psalm: "Why have the gentiles raged, and the people imagined vain things? The kings of the earth rose up, and the rulers have conspired together against the Lord, and against his Anointed One." Then the prayer paraphrases that line of the psalm by pointing to its properly Christian meaning: "For of a truth, against Your holy child Jesus, whom You have anointed, both Herod and Pontius Pilate, together with the gentiles and the people of Israel, are gathered together." It is clear in this apostolic text that the psalm is being used in Christian prayer because of its reference to Christ Himself. In fact the prayer ends "through (*dia*) the name of Your holy child Jesus" (Acts 4:30).

By the way, one may observe that virtually all modern translations of Acts 4:30 miss this important point, by making "through the name" refer to the "signs and wonders." "Through the name of Your holy child [*pais*] Jesus" refers, rather, to the prayer itself and is an extremely primitive formula often found at the end of early Christian prayers. Because Christians change the words of their prayers only with the greatest reluctance, we find certain primitive expressions in solemn liturgical settings long after they have disappeared otherwise. (Historians call this trait Baumstark's Law, by the way.) The expression "Your child [*pais*]," as a reference to Jesus, is found in prayers as late as those of Hippolytus at the beginning of the third century, long after the Christians had stopped using that expression in other Christological contexts. This "through" [*dia* in Greek, *per* in Latin], as a reference to the mediation of Christ in Christian prayer, has remained to the present day. It is more common in the West, where believers normally end their prayer by adding something along the lines of "in Jesus' holy name," or *per Christum Dominum nostrum*. In the Orthodox East we find it in the Divine Liturgy, at the end of the litany just before the Creed: "*through* [*dia*] the compassions of Your only begotten Son." Anyway, the "through the name of Your holy child Jesus" in Acts 4:30 refers to the prayer itself; the Christians were asking that the prayer be heard in Jesus' name. They were doing exactly what Jesus commanded— praying to the Father, asking the Father, in Jesus' name.

It is the profound Christian persuasion that Christ walks within the psalms, and this is the reason that the Book of Psalms is the Old Testament book most often quoted in the New Testament. When He opened their eyes to the meaning of Holy Scripture, the risen Lord explained to His disciples the things concerning Himself "in the Law of Moses, in the prophets, and in the psalms" (Luke 24:44). Immediately after His ascension, when the Church gathered prayerfully in the upper room to await Pentecost, the brethren chose a replacement for the fallen Judas by having recourse to the Book of Psalms (Acts 1:20).

Then, when the pentecostal Spirit descended upon them and they began to preach, their first sermon was an exegesis of two psalms (Acts 2:25–35).

Christians have always sung the psalms (James 5:13). Properly to pray the psalms is to pray them in Jesus' name, because the voice in the Psalter is Christ's own voice. Christ is the referential center of the Book of Psalms. Even in speaking to one another, Christians invoke the psalms (Ephesians 5:19; Colossians 3:16). Christian lips readily break forth with the words of the Psalter, because the Christian heart meditates on the psalms day and night. Ultimately the words of the psalms are the mighty name of Jesus broken down into its component parts. Thus has it always been.

PSALM 1

BLESSED IS THE MAN

Each week the Church recites her way through the Psalter, section by section, at the various canonical Hours throughout the days and even nights. Each section is called a *kathisma,* the word indicating that one may be seated for the recitation. This recitation begins on Saturday evening, at the "first Vespers" for Sunday, when we chant the first *kathisma* (Psalms 1—8).

Thus, the Church's liturgical week normally begins with the opening words of Psalm 1: "Blessed is the man who walks not in the counsel of the godless, nor stands in the path of sinners, nor sits in the seat of the scornful." Like the Sermon on the Mount, the Book of Psalms commences with a "beatitude," a pronunciation of the blessings of God on the just man. The original Hebrew is delicious to pronounce at this point—"oh, the blessings of the man who walks not. . . ."—*'ashrei ha'ish 'asher lo halak.*

Three postures are considered: walking, standing, and sitting. There are three places the just man will not be found: following the counsel of the godless, standing in the way that sinners go, seated among the scoffers. Warnings against these three categories are found all through the Bible's wisdom literature, but the scoffers (*letsim*) appear here as the very climax of evil. Outside of this verse and Isaiah 29:20, "scoffer" is found only in the Book of Proverbs (14 times) and is a synonym for the consummate fool.

What is warned against in verse 1 is evil counsel (*etsah*), an idea that appears all through Proverbs, Isaiah, Jeremiah, and Job, as well as in many narrative passages, such as "the counsel of Ahithophel" in 2 Samuel 16—17, the "counsel of the young men" in 1 Kings 12:14, etc. Many individuals in the Bible are led astray by following evil counsel: Absalom, Rehoboam, Sennacherib (cf. 2 Kin. 18:20; Is. 36:5), Zedekiah, Ahaziah (2 Chr. 22:5), Amnon (counseled by Jonadab in 2 Sam. 13), the Sanhedrin under Caiaphas, and so on.

It is significant, then, that the Book of Psalms (and hence the liturgical week) commences with a consideration of certain wisdom themes. So far, the emphasis is entirely negative—that is, we are told what the just man does *not* do. Now just what does the just man *do*?

"He delights in the law of the Lord, and on that Law does he meditate day and night." Here is our program for the week: at various times during the day and even the night to enjoy (*hepets*) meditation on God's Law. (St. Paul also speaks of "delighting" in the Law of the Lord—Romans 7:22). The "medi-

1

tation" could also be translated as "musing," and it is a source of pleasure—"amusing." This is how the week of prayer will be spent, our psalm is saying: in the enjoyment of meditation.

And to what does this constant meditation lead? "And he shall be like the tree planted by the rivers of water, that brings forth his fruit in his season." Already, in the opening lines of the liturgical week, we are told that this is a matter of observing seasons. The habit of prayer, this incessant meditation on God's Law, is not supposed to be something immediately useful. Trees do not bear fruit right away. They first must eat amply of the earth and drink deeply of its water. Such nourishment must serve first to build up the tree. The fruit will come later on, when it is supposed to. The life of Christian prayer and meditation knows nothing of instant holiness; it is all a matter of perseverance and patience. Some trees do not even begin to bear fruit for many years.

The idea of the fruit-bearing tree as image of the just man is found elsewhere in the Bible, particularly Psalm 91 (92):13–15. By way of comparison, we observe that the latter psalm, like this one, portrays a contrast between the wicked who perish and the just who abide. Thus, the liturgical week begins with a wisdom format.

But there is a great deal more here. Just who is this "blessed man" of whom the psalmist speaks? It is not man in general. In truth, it really is not simply a "human being." The underlying words, here translated as "man," are emphatically masculine—that is, gender specific—in the original Hebrew (*ish*), as well as the Greek (*aner*) and Latin (*vir*) versions. They are not the Hebrew (*adam*) and Greek (*anthropos*) nouns accurately translated as "human being." The "man" of reference here is a particular man. According to the Fathers of the Church, he is the one Mediator between God and man, the Man Jesus Christ. The Law of the Lord, which is to be our delight and meditation day and night, finds its meaning only in Him. Christ is the one who fulfills it, and He is the key to its understanding.

PSALM 2

WHY DO THE NATIONS RAGE?

The Book of Psalms, having begun on a theme associated with Wisdom, next turns to messianic considerations. Psalm 2 commences: "Why do the heathen rage, and the people imagine something vain." The "blessed man" introduced in Psalm 1, Jesus our Lord, is an affront to the wisdom of this world. The powers of this world cannot abide Him. The moral contrast described in Psalm 1 thus becomes the messianic conflict narrated in Psalm 2.

A king of this world, Herod, immediately felt threatened at the birth of God's Anointed One. Well he should, for there can be no compromise nor compatibility between the wisdom and power of this world and the wisdom and power of God. They are at deep enmity (cf. 1 Cor. 2:4–14), and our second psalm is concerned with this historical conflict. Psalm 2 is a Christological interpretation of history.

Psalm 1 had spoken of the "counsel of the godless," and now Psalm 2 will go on to describe that counsel: "The kings of the earth took their stand, and the rulers were gathered in counsel, against the Lord and against his *anointed* [Messiah in Hebrew, Christ in Greek]." The counsel of this world will not endure the reign of God and Christ. "Let us break their bands asunder, and cast away their cords from us," they say.

The early Christians knew the meaning of these words, and they included them in one of their earliest recorded prayers: "Lord, You are God, who made heaven and earth and the sea, and all that is in them, who by the mouth of Your servant David have said: 'Why did the nations rage, and the people plot vain things? The kings of the earth took their stand, and the rulers were gathered together against the LORD and against His Christ." And about whom are these things being said? The prayer goes on: "For truly against Your holy Servant [*pais*, also meaning 'servant' or 'boy'] Jesus, whom You anointed, both Herod and Pontius Pilate, with the Gentiles and the people of Israel, were gathered together" (Acts 4:24–27).

The context of this prayer was the persecution of the Church by the authorities at Jerusalem (cf. all of Acts 3—4). That is to say, the psalm's meaning, to those Christians, was not something in the distant past; it was something contemporary to ongoing Christian history.

This psalm is not impressed by all the sinful revolution against the reign of God and his Christ. Like the first psalm, Psalm 2 will finish on the theme of the divine judgment, which blesses the just and condemns the wicked. Both psalms end much like the Creed: "He will come again in glory to judge."

Indeed, the parallels of Psalm 2 with the "last days" described in the Bible's final book, Revelation, are quite remarkable: the anger of the nations and the wrath of God (Rev. 11:18), the political conspiracy against God (19:19), the Messiah's "rod of iron" inflicted on His enemies (2:27; 12:5; 19:15).

God, meanwhile, may laugh at His enemies: "He that thrones in the heavens shall laugh; the Lord will hold them in derision." His Chosen One and Heir is already anointed. In the verse that explains the Church's partiality to this psalm at Christmas time, the Messiah proclaims: "The Lord said unto Me: 'You are My Son; this day have I begotten You." These words, partly reflected at the Lord's Baptism (Matt. 3:17) and Transfiguration (Matt. 17:5; 2 Pet. 1:17), came to express the essential Christological faith of the Church. This verse is cited explicitly in the apostolic preaching (cf. Acts 13:33; Heb. 1:5; 5:5; also 1 John 5:9) and directly answers the major question posed by Christian evangelism in every age: "What do you think of the Christ? Whose Son is He?" The (most likely) earliest of the Gospels thus commences: "The beginning of the Gospel of Jesus Christ, the Son of God" (Mark 1:1).

"This day," God says, "today have I begotten You." So early in the Book of Psalms is the Christian mind elevated to eternity, that undiminished "today" of Christ's identity—"Jesus Christ is the same yesterday, today, and forever" (Heb. 13:8). No one knows the Father except the Son and he to whom the Son chooses to reveal him (Matt. 11:27). That "blessed man" introduced in the first psalm is now proclaimed in the second psalm to be God's only-begotten Son, the sole Mediator between God and man, the Man Jesus Christ. His is the only name under heaven given men by which we may be saved. Therefore, "Be wise now, you kings; be instructed, you judges of the earth. . . . Blessed are all that put their trust in Him."

PSALM 3
LORD, HOW INCREASED ARE THEY
❧

Psalm 3 is the first of those especially useful for particular times of the day—
in this case, just after rising from sleep. Thus, in Eastern Orthodox practice this
psalm is prayed, not only at Saturday Vespers as part of the first *kathisma*
(Psalms 1—8), but also daily (and very first) in the Hexapsalmos, that special
selection of six psalms prayed each morning at the beginning of Orthros
(Matins). Similarly, in the West, the sixth-century monastic Rule of Saint
Benedict prescribes Psalm 3 everyday as the first psalm of Vigils, even prior to
the Invitatory. Thus, in these ancient liturgical traditions of the Church,
believers start their daily round of prayer by proclaiming: "I laid me down and
slept; I awaked, for the Lord sustained me."

For the believer in Christ, the very act of rising from sleep is full of significance. Sleep itself is symbolic of (among other things) death, and to arise from
sleep, unto the praise of God, is a kind of first taste of that final and definitive
rising that sustains our hope: "Awake, you who sleep, arise from the dead, and
Christ will give you light" (Eph. 5:14).

And just what is wrong with sleep? Very simply, that it normally renders
prayer impossible. As the one virtually insuperable obstacle to constant prayer,
sleep has often been a bit vexing, as it were, a sort of mild embarrassment for
those who take seriously the biblical mandate that they pray without ceasing.

Obviously, one must sleep. It is a debt that we owe to our nature. Yet, like
any other debt, there can be something burdensome about the thing, and a
number of the saints seem to have felt toward sleep a kind of resentment, the
impatient reluctance that one might feel toward any other demanding credi-
tor. This slight pique they felt toward their obligation to sleep doubtless explains why some of the saints have been so begrudging about it, so stingy in
the matter, handing it only such minimum payment as would suffice to settle
an inconvenient debt.

So we begin the day. Psalm 1 has already contrasted the lots of the just and
the unjust, and Psalm 2 indicated the battle between the two sides. Now, in this
third psalm, there cries out the just man engaged in that battle: "Lord, how
increased are they that trouble me; many are they that rise up against me. Many
there be that say of my soul: 'There is no help for him in God'."

Conflict we have here, and the distress that conflict brings, for fighting
battles is one of the major motifs of the Book of Psalms. This is not a prayer

book for the noncombatant, and unless a person is actually engaged in hostilities it is difficult to see how he can pray Psalm 3: "Arise, O Lord, save me, O my God; for You have smitten all my enemies on the jaw; You have broken the teeth of the ungodly."

This warfare has to do with the themes already inaugurated in the two preceding psalms—God's Wisdom against wickedness in Psalm 1, and the Messiah against ungodly mutiny in Psalm 2. The first tells us that the Psalter's battle is moral; the second tells us that it is theological. Thus, the many conflicts described in the psalms are engagements of the spirit, struggles of the heart, wrestlings of the mind.

To pray the psalms correctly, then, it is very important that we properly identify the enemies. Some modern Christians, not understanding this, have even gone so far afield as to exclude certain of the psalms from their prayer, attempting to justify the exclusion by an appeal to Christian charity and the spirit of forgiveness.

This is unmitigated nonsense. The enemies here are the real enemies, the adversaries of the soul, those hostile forces spoken of in the very first verse of the Book of Psalms—"the counsel of the ungodly." "For we do not wrestle," after all, "against flesh and blood, but against principalities, against powers, against the rulers of the darkness of this age, against spiritual hosts of wickedness in the heavenly places" (Eph. 6:12). To relinquish any one of the psalms on the excuse that its sentiments are too violent for a Christian is a clear sign that a person has also given up the very battle that a Christian is summoned from his bed to fight. The psalms are prayers for those engaged in an ongoing spiritual conflict. No one else need bother even opening the book.

And what are our resources in the discord? "But You, O Lord, are a shield to me, my glory and my head's support. I cried unto the Lord with my voice, and He heard me from His holy hill. . . . I will not fear the thousands that confront me round about. . . . Salvation is of the Lord, and Your blessing rests upon Your people."

PSALM 4
HEAR ME WHEN I CALL

Like Psalm 3, the fourth psalm is particularly associated with a special time of the day, in this instance the final moments just before retiring for the night. In the sixth century, when the Rule of St. Benedict first prescribed the canonical Hour of Compline as the day's final prayer, it also established Psalm 4 as the first of the psalms to be prayed at that time. This arrangement was amply justified by a couple of lines in the psalm: "Commune with your own heart upon your bed and be still. . . . I shall both lay me down in peace, and I will sleep; for You alone, O Lord, make me dwell in safety."

Like Psalm 3, which commences the day, this final prayer is also set in the context of moral and spiritual strife. The man of faith begins and ends his day on the battlefield; warfare attends him everywhere. Since the very first verse of the very first psalm, the just man has found himself in conflict with the counsel of the ungodly, the way of sinners, the seat of the scornful. In Psalm 4 these latter are described as the "sons of men" who "turn my glory into shame."

The reason for this battle is that the just man has been chosen and set aside. He walks not in the counsel of the ungodly. He stands not in the way of sinners. He does not sit in the seat of the scornful. He is not of the world, just as Christ is not of the world. "But know," says the psalmist, "that the Lord has set aside the godly for Himself." The servants of God are to be holy, just as their Father in heaven is holy. This is the meaning of the biblical doctrine of the divine election: the service of God in holiness of life. Thus, there are certain things the godly man does not do; there are certain places he must not be found. Holiness means separation from what is sinful.

The Hebrew term here, translated as "godly," is *hasid* (*hosios* in the Greek, *sanctus* in Latin). That is to say, the life in Christ is the life of the "holy ones," the *hasidim*; it is the "hasidic" life, the life of separation from the sinful standards of the world. This adjective, *hasid*, is used in the Hebrew Old Testament 32 times, of which 21 are found in the Book of Psalms, a proportion strongly suggesting that the prayer and praise of God are a major component of the biblical doctrine of holiness. One cannot live a worldly life and still expect to be able to pray the psalms. The Psalter has nothing to say to the worldly; it is not for the unconverted, the unrepentant. It is, rather, the prayer book of those who strive for holiness of life and the unceasing praise of God.

This separation of the godly for the service of the Lord is likewise the

7

source of the conflict that we find all through the Psalter. Thus said the "blessed man" who is the key to the psalms: "If the world hates you, you know that it hated Me before it hated you. If you were of the world, the world would love its own. Yet because you are not of the world, but I chose you out of the world, therefore the world hates you" (John 15:18, 19). Such are the Christological dimensions of the conflict that we have seen in each of the first four psalms.

Some measure of anger normally attends conflict, and there is ever the danger that such anger can become sinful. So our psalm (in the traditional liturgical versions, Greek, Latin, Arabic, and Slavonic) contains the warning: "Be angry and sin not," a very useful counsel inasmuch as sinful anger itself can be a great detriment to healthy sleep. Later on, the Apostle Paul will cite this verse of our psalm within the course of several moral exhortations relative to the life in Christ: "Be angry and do not sin; do not let the sun go down on your wrath, nor give place to the devil" (Eph. 4:26, 27). Prior to retiring for the night, then, the just man endeavors to put away from himself the passion that tends most tenaciously to endure, the passion of anger. This psalm of the evening tells him: "Commune with your own heart upon your bed, and be still."

The traditional time for this psalm (whether at Western Compline or in the first *kathisma* at Saturday Vespers) is the coming of night, the approach of darkness, and in such a context the psalmist remembers the true light, the light of glory that shines from the face of the Lord: "The light of Your countenance has been signed upon us, O Lord." Here we touch the deepest level of desire in the Book of Psalms—the longing for the glory of God, and the psalmist announces that this glory has already been "signed [or sealed] upon us" (*esemeiothe* in Greek, *signatum est* in Latin).

This verse reminds us that the Book of Psalms is not a universally available text, in the sense that just anyone can pick it up and make it his own at will. It is, rather, the prayer book of the Church, that assembly of those who, with faces unveiled, behold the glory of God shining on the face of Christ and are being transformed from glory to glory by the Spirit of the Lord (cf. 2 Cor. 3:18—4:6). As such the Psalter is a kind of first-fruits of the very prayer of heaven, and the transforming light of God's face will continue to be spoken of in various psalms: "God is the Lord who has shown us light"—"May God cause His face to shine upon us, and have mercy on us"—"Approach to Him and be illumined"— "Show forth Your face, and we shall be saved." Such are the closing thoughts of the Christian's day.

8

PSALM 5
GIVE EAR TO MY WORDS
~

Whereas in the East Psalm 5 is chanted at Vespers on Saturday evening, the West has traditionally preferred to pray it in the morning. For example, the sixth-century Rule of St. Benedict prescribes it for Monday Matins, or Orthros. The propriety for this is suggested in an early verse: "My voice will You hear in the morning; in the morning will I stand before You and keep watch."

The Hebrew verb (*'arak*), translated here as "stand," bears the root sense of "setting in order." Used without direct object here, it is very succinct, so succinct that English translators have sometimes felt the need to expand on it. Thus, the KJV paraphrases it as "I direct my prayer unto Thee," and the NIV as "I lay my requests before You."

The Greek (*parastesomai*) and Latin (*astabo*) versions used in the Christian liturgical traditions better preserve the original sense of simply standing in proper order in the presence of God. To this is added a certain note of vigilance, "keep watch." These two verbs, to take one's stand and to keep watch, set the tone for how to begin the day of prayer.

It is important that this tone be set early in the morning, the hour of rising. Over and over the psalms speak of prayer as the day's first task: "Rise up, my glory; awaken, lute and harp; I myself will awaken the dawn—I will sing aloud of Your mercy in the morning—In the morning shall my prayer come before You—To show forth Your loving kindness in the morning" and so forth. This early morning prayer is also mentioned elsewhere in Holy Scripture (Ex. 29:39, 40; Lev. 6:12; Num. 28:4; Dan. 6:10; Mark 1:35, etc.) and across a wide area by several early Christian sources (Hippolytus in Rome, Origen and Clement in Egypt, Tertullian and Cyprian in Latin Africa, Basil in Cappadocia, and so forth). The spirit of this morning prayer was well summed up by the Book of Wisdom: " . . . to make it known that one must rise before the sun to give You thanks, and must pray to You at the dawning of the light" (16:28).

Once again, then, it is clear that the proper praying of the psalms is related to a certain regular and disciplined style of life. The Christian, by preference, rises early and stands in vigilance in the presence of God. When the sun rises, it shines on the believer already at prayer. This is normally how the day begins. It is also the essential meaning of those later lines in the psalm: "I will enter into Your house in the multitude of Your mercies; in the fear of You will I bow myself down toward Your holy temple." To pray is to enter the house of God.

9

The context for this worship, nonetheless, is still the life of struggle with evil. When the Christian rises, it is always on the battlefield. Thus, most verses of this psalm explicitly refer to the workers of iniquity, and the psalmist prays fervently against them: "Destroy them, O God; let them fall by their own counsels; cast them out in the multitude of their transgressions, for they have rebelled against You."

"They have rebelled against *You*," the psalm says. Sin is abhorrent to God. He not only loves justice; he also hates iniquity. "Fools shall not stand in Your presence," our psalm goes on, "You hate all workers of iniquity." When the psalmist prays for the destruction of the wicked, this is not his personal sentiment, so to speak. It is not a prayer of private vindictiveness but of foundational justice. It is a plea that God vindicate His own moral order. When Jesus refused to "pray for the world" (John 17:9), He was recognizing the existence of those who, willfully unrepentant and deliberately hard of heart, have placed themselves beyond hope. Inveterate sinning against the light—unrepented evil—does exist in human hearts, and God hates it. He hates it vehemently. Jesus on the Cross had not one word to say to the blasphemous, unrepentant thief.

Some modern Christians are tempted to see in such sentiments only a lamentable vestige of Old Testament negativity and judgmentalism, now appropriately surpassed by a New Testament emphasis on God's mercy and compassion. The idea is abroad these days that, whereas the Old Testament God was a no-nonsense Divinity, the God of the New Testament is quite a bit more tolerant.

Such an idea would have surprised the Apostles. Romans 3:10–18, for instance, which is a mélange of various psalm verses describing the evil of sin, cites a rather violent line from our present psalm with reference to evildoers: "Their throat is an open sepulcher." Indeed, the descriptions of sin in Romans 1 and 3 make a good commentary on many verses of Psalm 5.

Similarly, when the Book of Wisdom says that "equally hateful to God are the ungodly man and his ungodliness" (14:9), its thesis is hard to distinguish from certain verses in the New Testament, such as "I never knew you; depart from Me, you who practice lawlessness" (Matt. 7:23; cf. 25:41) and "You hate the deeds of the Nicolaitans, which I also hate" (Rev. 2:6; cf. 21:8; 22:15). The loving mercy of God must never be thought of or described in ways suggesting that Christianity is less morally serious than Judaism. The moral sentiments of the psalms are, in this respect, Christian sentiments, and they are highly appropriate in Christian prayer.

PSALM 6

O LORD, DO NOT REBUKE ME

Psalm 6 is the first and shortest of what are popularly known as the Seven Penitential Psalms, canticles of contrition and lamentation accompanied by pleas for the divine forgiveness.

This psalm begins with a forceful recognition of the divine wrath. It is the second time that God's wrath is mentioned in the Book of Psalms; Psalm 2 had already spoken of God's anger toward the rebellious. In the present psalm, however, it is the psalmist himself who fears this wrath of God and prays to be delivered from it: "O Lord, do not rebuke me in Your anger, nor chasten me in Your fierce displeasure." Such a prayer suggests that only the grace of God can deliver us from the wrath of God.

The divine wrath is not some sort of irritation; God does not become peeved or annoyed. The wrath of God is infinitely more serious than a temper tantrum. It is a deliberate resolve in response to a specific state of the human soul. In Romans, where the expression appears twelve times, the anger of God describes His activity toward the hard of heart, the unrepentant, those sinners who turn their backs and deliberately refuse His grace, and it is surely in this sense that our psalm asks to be delivered from God's wrath. It is important to make such a prayer, because hardness of heart remains a possibility for all of us to the very day we die.

Perhaps the seriousness of such a prayer will appear more clearly if we reflect on exactly what Holy Scripture says about the divine wrath. The latter pertains, after all, to the divine revelation itself: "For the wrath of God is *revealed* from heaven" (Rom. 1:18, emphasis mine). God's wrath is not something we need to guess about. It is revealed. And how revealed? "Against all ungodliness and unrighteousness of men, who suppress the truth in unrighteousness." This deliberate hardness of heart, this radical recalcitrance to grace, is the sin that calls down the wrath of God. "So that they are without excuse, because, although they knew God, they did not glorify Him as God, nor were thankful" (Rom. 1:20, 21).

Three times in this passage, the Apostle Paul pounds the point home: *paredoken autous ho Theos*—"God gave them up . . ." (Rom. 1: 24, 26, 28). In this, then, consists the wrath of God: that He turns man loose, that He lets man go, hands him over, that He abandons man to his own choice of evil. The full context of this passage deserves deep reflection, because the moral evils to which God delivers the hard of heart appear to be the very vices characteristic of our own times (cf. Rom. 1:24–32). These verses describe in graphic detail exactly what happens when "God *gives them up*," and no attentive reader of this text will fail to recognize in it a description of the world in which we live today.

Every deliberate and willful sin is a step in the direction of hardness of heart. Psalm 6, as a penitential psalm, takes sin very seriously. The sin spoken of here is deliberate, willful. It is not just a mistake; it is not something for which we simply apologize. It is, rather, a voluntary affront to God's image in us. The taking away of sin required the shedding of Christ's blood on the Cross. This fact itself tells us how serious is this whole business of sin.

Sin has entered deeply into human experience, and it has left human beings in a very weakened state. It is felt in our inner frame, our very bones, as it were. The psalm goes on: "Have mercy on me, O Lord, for I am weak; O Lord, heal me, for my bones are troubled. My soul also is greatly troubled, but You, O Lord . . how long? Return, O Lord, deliver me. Oh, save me, for Your mercies' sake."

The psalmist then speaks of death, for by sin death entered into the world. Death is sin rendered visible. What we see death do to the body, sin does to the soul. Death is the externalizing of sin. Death is no friend. Apart from Christ, the Bible sees death as the realm where God is not praised. As the bitter fruit of sin, death is the enemy; indeed, it is the "last enemy," says 1 Corinthians 15:26. When the psalmist, then, prays for deliverance from death, he is talking about a great deal more than a physical phenomenon. Death is the "last enemy," the physical symbol of our sinful alienation from God: "For in death there is no memory of You; in the grave, who will give You thanks?"

Sin and death, then, form the context of this psalm, and these are the forces of Satan. Sin, death, and Satan—such are the enemies of which the psalmist speaks: "My eye wastes away because of grief; it grows old because of all my enemies. Depart from me, all you workers of iniquity. . . . Let all my enemies be ashamed and greatly troubled."

Even as he makes this plea for mercy, nonetheless, the man of faith already knows that God hears him: "For the Lord has heard my supplication; the Lord will receive my prayer."

PSALM 7

O LORD, MY GOD, IN YOU I PUT MY TRUST

It has long been common to remark that the Book of Psalms is a most "human" book, in the sense that its various prayers cover a wide range of emotions and sentiments, that there are virtually no situations in the moral life for which the psalmist provides no appropriate words of prayer, that the Psalter is a veritable mirror, as it were, of the human spirit facing the manifold and varying conditions of our destiny.

All this is true, of course, but taken without further qualifications it may represent a truth easily misunderstood. For the humanism found in the Psalter is not based solely on the universality of its human aspirations and sentiments. The Psalter is not human in merely the same sense that the *Iliad* is human, say, or the *Upanishads*, or *The Pickwick Papers*. These works, after all, do likewise cover the multiple range of emotions, sentiments, and convictions with respect to man's situation, his moral freedom, his duty, and his destiny. It is important to stress, nonetheless, that the Psalter is human in a far deeper and more properly theological sense.

The humanism of the Psalter is a humanism rooted in the Incarnation. The Psalter is not human merely because it speaks for man in general, but because it speaks for Christ. The underlying voice of the Psalms is not simply "man," but *the* Man. To enter into the prayer of this book is not merely to share the sentiments of King David, or Asaph, or one of the other inspired poets. Indeed, in a theological sense the voices of these men are secondary, hardly more important than our own. The foundational voice of the Psalms, the underlying bass line of its harmony is, rather, the voice of Jesus Christ, the only Mediator between God and man. The correct theological principle for praying the psalms is the Hypostatic Union, the ontological and irreversible coalescence of the human and the divine, "the synthesis achieved by God, which carries the name of Jesus Christ" (Hans Urs von Balthasar).

It is not surprising, then, that we will on occasion come across certain sentiments in the Psalms that are difficult to appropriate as our own. It does not take me long to discover that some of the lines of the Psalter are impossible to pray in my own person. There are cases in which my own "voice" is inadequate to express the sense of the psalm itself.

Psalm 7 provides an early example of this phenomenon. How many of us would feel comfortable claiming for ourselves the moral innocence expressed in this psalm? This is the prayer of someone whose hands are clean and mind undefiled, a man whose conscience finds nothing for which to reproach him. The voice of this psalm is His of whom St. Peter wrote that He "committed no sin, nor was deceit found in His mouth" (2 Pet. 1:22).

This is supremely a psalm of the Lord's redemptive sufferings at the hands of injustice. Line by line it inscribes the mounting drama of the Passion. Day by day it chronicles the sentiments of Holy Week: the official plot against the Lord's life, the growing tension as He daily parries the hostile interrogations, His early anointing in preparation for His burial, the bribe accepted by Judas to betray Him to His enemies, the heavy air enveloping that supper in which He washes the feet of His friends and identifies His betrayer, the prolonged prayer in the garden and its bloody sweat, the lengthy nocturnal trial during which He is thrice denied by yet another of the Twelve, the spittings and the mockery in the court of the high priest, the hailing before the cowardly Pilate, the humiliation at the cruel hands of Herod, the fickle crowd seeking the release of Barabbas and calling down His own blood on their heads and the heads of their children, the brutal scourging at the pillar and the crowning with thorns, the carrying of the Cross and the encounter with the women of Jerusalem, the stripping and distribution of His clothing, the fierce driving of the nails through His hands and feet, His raising on the Cross and the forgiveness of His persecutors, the excruciating distension of His joints and the racking of His entire body, the thirst, the agony, and the death.

Such is the proper setting for Psalm 7, as mankind's single just Man suffers and dies to atone for the sins of the rest. To pray this psalm properly is to enter into the mind of the Lord in the context of His redemptive Passion. It is not to give expression to our own personal feelings, but to discover something of His. It is to taste, in some measure, the bitterness and the gall.

PSALM 8

O LORD, OUR LORD, HOW EXCELLENT IS YOUR NAME

From the very earliest translations of the Creed into the English language, the mystery of the Incarnation has been expressed in a rather puzzling way, even if our long familiarity with the words has reduced our sense of their grammatical enigma. We say of the Son of God that He "became [or "was made"] man."

The puzzle posed by this construction is exactly how to classify the predicate nominative "man" in this instance. Is the sense of the expression indefinite—"*a* man," much as we might say that "Fred became *a* farmer"? But if so, why didn't the translators simply say that? "He became *a* man" would not only make sense; it would be both grammatically and theologically correct.

Or is the meaning of the expression merely descriptive—"he became human," much as we might say "Fred became agrarian"? Here again, the translators could easily have said that, if that is what they meant, because God's Son most certainly did become human.

No, neither of these translations was deemed adequate. Rendering very literally from the underlying Latin (and not directly from the original Greek, by the way), the translators said that He "became man," leaving us with this stylistic puzzle. One can hardly think of an occasion, after all, in which we might properly say "Fred became farmer."

What the translators gave us here is an idiom, which is to say a form of expression unique to a particular setting and standing outside of expected usage. On reflection, their recourse to idiom in this case is hardly surprising, for the event under discussion, the Incarnation, is itself "idiomatic" in the extreme, in the sense of being completely unique, utterly unexpected, and standing free of normal patterns of acquiescence. How better, after all, to speak of an incomparable and unparalleled event than by recourse to an idiomatic improvisation?

God's Son did not only "become human," though it is true that He did. Nor did He simply "become *a* man," though this likewise is a correct statement of the fact. He "became man," rather, in a sense defying grammatical precision as thoroughly as it confounds also the expectations of biology, psychology, metaphysics, and other aspects of the human enterprise, thereby shocked and left reeling, all its vaunted resources now massively strained and overcharged at the infusion of unspeakable glory.

The most correct formulation of the Incarnation is the one to which we are accustomed: "He became man." Christ is the archetype of man, bearing all of humanity in Himself. "It was for the new man that human nature was established from the beginning," wrote St. Nicholas Kavasilas; "the old Adam was not the model of the new, it was the new Adam that was the model of the old."

The wise English translators of the Creed were taking their cue here from Psalm 8: "What is man (*'enosh*) that You are mindful of him? Or the son of man (*adam*) that you care for him?" According to Hebrews 2, which is our oldest extant Christian commentary on Psalm 8, the word "man" in this text refers to Christ our Lord, and the entire psalm is a description of His saving work.

By the Incarnation, our psalm says to God, "You have made Him a little lower than the angels, and You have crowned Him with honor and glory," in explanation of which Hebrews replies that "we see Jesus, who was made a little lower than the angels, for the suffering of death crowned with glory and honor" (2:9).

When God gave our forefather Adam dominion over the earth and its fullness, that act was a prophecy of the universal subjection of creation to the reign of Christ. Such is the true meaning of Psalm 8: "You have made Him to have dominion over the works of Your hands; You have put all things under His feet."

Christ is no afterthought; He is the original meaning of humanity. Christ is what God had in mind when He reached down and formed that first lump of mud into a man. Again in the words of St Nicholas Kavasilas: "It was towards Christ that man's mind and desire were oriented. We were given a mind that we might know Christ, and desire, that we might run to Him; and memory, that we might remember Him, because even at the time of creation it was He who was the archetype."

The mystery of the Incarnation is the theme of Psalm 8. Christ is the reason for our singing out: "O Lord, our Lord, how sublime is Your name in all the earth, for You have set Your glory above the heavens."

PSALM 9 (9 & 10)

I WILL PRAISE YOU O LORD

The text of Psalm 9 (Hebrew 9 & 10) is notoriously spoiled, but it is clear that this was originally an "alphabetical" psalm—that is to say, a psalm in which each verse began with a letter of the Hebrew alphabet in immediate succession. Consequently, we also know that this was originally a single psalm (as in the canonical Greek text of the Church), not two different psalms (as in the traditional Masoretic Hebrew text and the modern translations based thereon). It is beginning from Psalm 9, therefore, that we are obliged to list two numbers when referring to each psalm. The first number given here will designate the canonical Greek version; the number in parentheses will refer to the psalm as it appears in the rabbinical text.

As the first psalm of the second *kathisma,* Psalm 9 is prayed in the Orthodox Church during Sunday Matins, a custom also observed in the West until the Council of Trent. This usage, however, was determined by the simple fact that this psalm is found so early in the Psalter, not because of any perceived propriety with respect to the hour. Still, it is curious that, though other ancient liturgical traditions prescribe Psalm 9 for different days of the week, invariably it is assigned to the morning.

The opening lines of this psalm introduce two ideas crucial to the praying of all the psalms: the heart and storytelling—"I will praise You, O Lord, with my whole heart, I will narrate all Your wonders."

First, the heart: "I will praise You, O Lord, with my whole heart." The key to the proper praying of the psalms is purity of heart. Psalmody involves prayer from one's central core, a heart characterized by wholeness. In Psalm 100 we will say to the Lord: "I will sing (*psalo*), and I will understand (*syneso*) in the blameless path." To pray with understanding in the deeper spirit of the psalms requires walking "the blameless path," living with an undivided heart. To give oneself over to psalmody as the skeletal frame of the life of prayer, therefore, is inseparable from the life of sustained spiritual effort to purify one's heart. All prayer is a struggle to see God, after all, and we have it on very strong authority that only the pure of heart will see God.

Second, storytelling: "I will narrate all Your wonders." A major motif of the Psalter is formed of the *magnalia Dei,* the great wonders that God has wrought. These wonders are forever set in review throughout the psalms: our creation from nothingness, the Lord's constant provision for our lives, His

17

promises with respect to our final destiny, His covenant with our forefathers and its fulfillment in Christ the Savior, our liberation from bondage to the satanic pharaoh through the shedding of the paschal blood of Jesus, our passage through the Red Sea of baptism, our journey through the wilderness where we are nourished with living water and the bread of angels. The "all Your wonders," then, has reference to the great mysteries of our redemption: the Incarnation, the atoning Passion and Death, the glorious Resurrection and Ascension, the sending forth of the Holy Spirit, and the founding of the Church. These manifestations of God's grace are the substance of the narrative inherent in the psalms.

Among the other ideas to be remarked on in Psalm 9, particular attention should be paid to that of the "name": "I shall sing to Your *name*, O Most High," and "Let all those who know Your *name* hope on You." This, of course, is that name of which St. Peter said that "there is no other name under heaven given among men by which we must be saved" (Acts 4:12). This, truly, is "the name which is above every name, that at the name of Jesus every knee should bow" (Phil. 2:9, 10). The praying of the Psalter, in fact, pertains to our sharing in that universal genuflection "of those in heaven, and of those on earth, and of those under the earth." As the only name by which we have access to God, the name of Jesus is the proper exegetical key to praying the Book of Psalms.

Finally, Psalm 9 is dominated by the image of the divine throne: "You have sat upon Your throne, O You who judge in righteousness," and "the Lord abides forever; You have prepared Your throne for judgment." In this psalm the judgment throne of God is the real and final arbiter before which all events in this world, especially the great moral and spiritual conflicts of man's history, are summoned with a view to their final assessment. Obviously a psalm about struggling with enemies, Psalm 9 has no doubts about the resolution of this struggle.

PSALM 10 (11)

IN THE NAME OF THE LORD I PUT MY TRUST

One may safely argue that the most important line of Psalm 10 (Hebrew 11), the sentence sustaining its message as a whole, is the one that says: "The Lord is in His holy temple. The Lord! His throne is in heaven." In a prayer that deals largely with the soul's experience of turmoil and dissolution, God's throne is the source of our stability and the foundation of our hope. As we invariably chant at the end of the Divine Liturgy and the various Church offices, "Glory to You, O Christ, our God and our hope, glory to You." If there is any firmness for our lives, any steadfastness for our souls, the cause of such constancy is the immovable throne of Christ our God. Consequently, in the history of Christian prayer this line has often served as the interpretive antiphon for Psalm 10, especially on the Feast of our Lord's Ascension.

Perhaps a good place to start thinking about this psalm is the drama described in Genesis 19, the destruction of Sodom and the flight of Lot. The similarities are striking. Consider the psalm: "Snares will He rain upon the sinners—fire, brimstone, and windstorm—these are their portion to drink." And Genesis: "Then the Lord rained brimstone and fire on Sodom and Gomorrah, from the Lord out of the heavens" (19:24).

Or, again, in the psalm: "In the Lord have I trusted. How say to my soul, 'Fly to the mountains like a sparrow'?" And the angels say to Lot in Genesis: "Escape for your life! Do not look behind you nor stay anywhere in the plain. Escape to the mountains, lest you be destroyed" (v. 17). To which Lot answers: "I cannot escape to the mountains, lest some evil overtake me and I die" (v. 19).

And yet again in our psalm: "For the Lord is just, and justice He loves. His face beholds what is upright." But according to the Apostle Peter, this explains precisely what transpired in Genesis 19, where God, "turning the cities of Sodom and Gomorrah into ashes, condemned them to destruction, making them an example to those who afterward would live ungodly; and delivered righteous Lot, who was oppressed by the filthy conduct of the wicked (for that righteous man, dwelling among them, tormented his righteous soul from day to day by seeing and hearing their lawless deeds)" (2 Pet. 2:6–8).

And the psalm once more: "The Lord is in His holy temple. The Lord! His throne is in heaven. His glance regards the poor man; His eyes will examine the sons of men. The Lord will test the just man and the unjust. The lover of evil hates his own soul." And once again Peter, commenting on Genesis 19: "The

Lord knows how to deliver the godly out of temptations and to reserve the unjust under punishment for the day of judgment" (2 Pet. 2:9).

Similarly, when Jesus would tell us of the final and catastrophic times, it is to Sodom that He sends us: "Likewise as it was also in the days of Lot: They ate, they drank, they bought, they sold, they planted, they built; but on the day that Lot went out of Sodom it rained fire and brimstone from heaven and destroyed them all. Even so will it be in the day when the Son of Man is revealed" (Luke 17:28–30).

Yes, "even so," for we too yet abide in the cities of the plain, "as Sodom and Gomorrah, and the cities around them in a similar manner to these" (Jude 7). Living in the world where injustice thrives and the wicked flourish, daily our prayer rises to God with the sentiments of Psalm 10.

This is a psalm, then, about the plight of the upright, the overthrow of the earth, the crumbling of foundations hitherto fixed: "For behold, sinners bend the bow, their arrows stand ready in the quiver, to shoot down in darkness the upright of heart. For they pull down what You established, and what has the just man done?" The "just man" of Psalm 10 is ultimately Jesus the Lord, that Righteous One of whom it is said: "We indeed [suffer] justly, . . . but this Man has done nothing wrong" (Luke 23:41).

Our psalm, then, bears a special relevance to the day of the Lord's sufferings, that hour of the earth's consummate injustice. In truth, this whole psalm may be prayed against the backdrop of Holy Friday. And what of the setting that is envisioned here, where the bow is bent against the righteous? It is "the great city which spiritually is called Sodom and Egypt, where also our Lord was crucified" (Rev. 11:8).

The idea is now common that the primary purpose of speech is communication, the sharing of ideas, impressions, and feelings with one another. Language is currently considered to be, first of all, social and therefore completely subject to social control. Human speech is widely interpreted as a matter of arbitrary and accepted fashion, subject to the same vagaries as any other fashion. Thus, the senses of words can be changed at will, different meanings being imposed by the same sorts of forces that determine whatever other tastes happen to be in vogue. Words become as alterable as hemlines and hats.

According to this view, words are necessarily taken to mean whatever the present living members of a society say that they mean, so that the study of language really becomes a branch of sociology. In fact, sociology textbooks themselves make this claim explicitly. Moreover, this notion of speech is so taken for granted nowadays as nearly to assume the rank of a self-evident principle. Nonetheless, it is deeply erroneous.

It is also egregiously dangerous to spiritual and mental health, for such a view of language dissolves the relationship of speech to the perception of truth, rendering man the lord of language without affirming the magisterial claims of truth over man. Declared independent of such claims, language submits to no tribunal higher than arbitrary social dictates. Human society, no matter how sinful and deceived, is named the final authority over speech, which is responsible only to those who use it, subject to no standards above the merely social. That is to say, in this view words must mean what people determine them to mean, especially such people as cultural engineers, political activists, feminist reformers, news commentators, talk-show hosts, and other professionals who make their living by fudging the truth.

This current notion of language was well formulated in the declaration of the proud and rebellious in Psalm 11 (Hebrew 12), in a passage manifestly portending the mendacious times in which we live: "With our tongue we will prevail. Our lips are our own; who is lord over us?"

How different is the view of the Bible, where speech is not regarded, first and foremost, as a form of communication among human beings. In fact, Adam was already talking before ever Eve appeared. Human speech, that is to say, appears in Holy Scripture earlier than the creation of the second human being, for we find Adam already naming the animals prior to the arrival of the marvelous creature that God later formed from his rib.

At the beginning, before the Fall, Man was possessed of an accurate perception into reality. He was able to name the animals because he could perceive precisely what they were. His words expressed true insight, a ravishing gaze at glory, a contemplation of real forms, so that the very structure and composition of his mind took on the seal and assumed the formal stamp of truth. Human language then was a reflection of that divine light with which heaven and earth are full. The speech of unfallen man was but the voice of vision.

This primeval human language, the pure progeny of lustrous discernment, flowed forth already from the lips of Adam prior to the creation of Eve, who heard it for the first time when her husband, awaking from his mystic sleep, identified her and told her exactly who she was: "You are bone of my bone, and flesh of my flesh." Human speech was already rooted in the vision of truth before it became the expression of human communication.

Moreover, the Fall itself, when it came, derived from that demonic disassociation of speech from truth that we call the Lie: "You will not surely die." Eve's acquiescence in that first lie was mankind's original act of metaphysical rebellion. It had more to do with the garbling of Babel than with the garden of Eden. It was human language's first declaration of independence: "Our lips are our own; who is lord over us?"

Just as truthful speech streams forth from vision, springing from the font of a pure heart, so lying is conceived in the duplicitous heart before it issues from the mouth. Says Psalm 11: "Each one has spoken follies to his neighbor, deceitful lips have spoken with divided heart." The situation described here is so bad that one despairs of finding any truths left in human discourse: "Save me, O God, for the godly man has disappeared, because truths are diminished among the sons of men. . . . The wicked prowl on every side."

In contrast to these varied, seemingly universal lies of men stand the reliable words of God: "The words of the Lord are pure words, smelted silver purged of dross, purified seven times." In this very unveracious world we yet trust that, though heaven and earth pass away, His words will never pass away.

PSALM 12 (13)

HOW LONG, O LORD?

The Christians of the East, along with many Christians of the West, are accustomed to praying Psalm 12 (Hebrew 13) at the canonical hour of Compline, just before retiring for the night. Throughout this prayer there lurks the threatening presence of an Enemy, symbolized in the growing darkness. Thus, as one is about to fall asleep, this psalm beseeches God that it will not be a sleep unto death. We likewise praise the Lord in this psalm for all the good things we have received during the day that is now coming to an end. Considered simply in terms of our human needs and dispositions, this is a fine psalm to be prayed just before going to bed.

Nonetheless, Psalm 12 yields a yet more ample understanding if we hear it on the lips of the Lord Jesus during the night of His agony and betrayal. That overcast night was the encroaching hour of which He said to His enemies: "But this is your hour, and the power of darkness" (Luke 22:53). As He enters the garden on that night to do battle with the Enemy, Jesus prays what may be taken as the cry of humanity itself, expelled from God's presence in that original garden where we fell victim to the same Enemy: "How long, O Lord? Will You abandon me forever? How long will You turn Your face away from me? To what purpose these worries in my soul, these sorrows in my heart, day and night?"

This was the night in which Jesus said to His disciples: "My soul is exceedingly sorrowful, even to death" (Matt. 26:38). In this exceeding sorrow of the soul He prays to His Father: "How long will my Enemy be exalted over me? Look upon me and answer me, O Lord, my God." Such was the petition made "in the days of His flesh, when He had offered up prayers and supplications, with vehement cries and tears to Him who was able to save Him from death, and was heard because of His godly fear" (Heb. 5:7).

In the enlarged darkness of the garden Jesus awaits with prayer the return of His betrayer, the Judas described by St. John: "Having received the piece of bread, he then went out immediately. And it was night" (John 13:30). Truly, night it was, and a dense darkness of the spirit, because Jesus, like Jacob in contest with His own wrestling angel, assumes humanity's place facing the Enemy, in the deeper shadows of the orchard trees so well known to those ancient transgressors of Eden: "Enlighten my eyes," He prays, "lest I slumber unto death, lest my Enemy ever say, 'I have prevailed over him'."

The "first blood" of the Lord's Passion, we recall, was that shed in the garden, where, "being in agony, He prayed more earnestly. Then His sweat became like great drops of blood falling down to the ground" (Luke 22:44). As it was in the garden that we first fell beneath the power of darkness, entirely proper it was that the redeeming blood of our true Adam should fall first on the earth of the orchard, in the shadows of the garden trees, those dear and lovely trees, of whose fruit, He told us, we might freely eat. His blood puddled on the very ground where we contemned His gracious trees, and where the earth had been cursed, and where the ancient serpent was condemned to crawl across it on his belly.

The Lord's prayer concludes in tones of His final victory over these ancient enemies of the race: "Those who vex me will exult, if I should be shaken; but I have hoped in Your mercy. My heart will rejoice in Your salvation. I will chant to the Lord, so generous to me, and I will sing to the name of the Lord most high."

What is described in Psalm 12, then, is the Lord's struggle with Satan, sin, and death, nor is it entirely proper that Christians should retire for the night without giving thought to Him who contended with the powers of darkness on their behalf and thus brought to pass their return to paradise. Every night has something about it of Gethsemane and the dark salvific drama that unfolded amidst the witnessing trees.

That nocturnal engagement of Jesus in the garden is repeated, too, in the souls of those He has reconciled to God, for they also are summoned to the bearing of His cross, warring against the devil, sin, and death. Jesus' persistence in the combat is held out to our studied emulation: "For consider Him who endured such hostility from sinners against Himself, lest you become weary and discouraged in your souls. You have not yet resisted to bloodshed, striving against sin" (Heb. 12:3, 14).

PSALM 13 (14)

THE FOOL SAYS IN HIS HEART

Psalm 13 (Hebrew 14) is almost identical with Psalm 52. The Book of Psalms shows several signs of including earlier collections of psalms, and this duplication of a single psalm is doubtless the result of some ancient confluence from two different collections.

Psalm 13 begins with what "the fool has said in his heart: 'There is no God.'" Taking this verse as thematic, we may say that the present psalm explores the relationship of atheism to folly.

"Fool" in Holy Scripture is a word rather of moral than of purely intellectual reference. Biblical "folly" is not a matter of being endowed with a hockey-score IQ. It would be inaccurate to describe the biblical fool as merely "a slow learner" or someone "intellectually challenged." The latter folk, after all, may well be pitied, but the Bible has no compassion for the fool. When it comes to suggest possible remedies for his problem, Scripture mentions a good, robust caning.

Folly, in the Bible, is a thing deliberately chosen. What is wrong with the biblical "fool" is always a matter of his heart. He is the man obdurate in evil. If the fool does not understand, it is because he is intentionally blind; he is hard of heart.

So what does this fool say in this hardened heart of his? *'Ein 'Eloim—Ouk estin Theos*—"There is no God." In the Bible, that is to say, atheism is a sort of ultimate folly, a denial of what is virtually self-evident.

There are two places where biblical literature explicitly discusses the natural evidence for God's existence: Wisdom 13 and Romans 1. Though both texts are directly concerned not with atheism, strictly speaking, but with idolatry, both passages are worth a quick glance, for they do bear indirectly on the subject of this psalm.

Wisdom 13 stresses the structured order of the world, wondering why some people are unable to perceive this order or to draw therefrom the correct inferences about the work of its Maker. They make the wrong identification of certain phenomena in nature with respect to the origin or governance of the universe. That is to say, they are idolaters rather than atheists, deeming "either fire, or wind, or the swift air, or the circle of the stars, or the violent water, or the lights of heaven, to be the gods which govern the world."

The author of Wisdom is of two minds regarding such folk. He speculates that perhaps they are "less to be blamed; for they peradventure err, seeking God and desirous to find Him." Still, he goes on, he is unable completely to absolve their blindness: "Howbeit neither are they to be pardoned. For if they were able to know so much, that they could study the world, how did they not sooner find out the Lord thereof?"

In Romans 1 St. Paul is certainly not of two minds on this point, and his criticism is less qualified or muted than those in Wisdom 13. For the Apostle, those who do not recognize the true God from the study of His works in nature are possessed of no reasonable appeal for pardon: "For since the creation of the world His invisible attributes are clearly seen, being understood by the things that are made, even His eternal power and Godhead, so that they are without excuse" (v. 20). He then goes on, like the author of Wisdom, to enumerate the sorts of idolatry resulting from this failure to recognize the Creator in His works.

Now if Holy Scripture speaks in such minatory tones about those who, failing to recognize the Creator of the world, become sidetracked or short-circuited into idolatry, how much worse will be the condemnation of the atheist. Recognizing no obligation to worship at all, the atheist is more corrupt than the poor idolater, who may be overly excited by the brilliance of the sun and so calls upon Apollo, or excessively impressed with the grandeur of the sea and thus prostrates himself before Neptune.

In our present psalm, indeed, the reasoning of the atheist is actually a mere contrivance for corruption—the atheist does not *want* to know God. By way of explaining the motive for saying that "there is no God," our psalmist continues: "They are corrupt. They have done abominable works. There is none who does good."

The folly of the fool, then, is not born of atheism. On the contrary, the atheism is born of the folly. The atheist does not know God, because he has *chosen* not to seek God: "The Lord looks down from heaven on the children of men, to see if there are any who understand, who seek God. They have all turned aside; they have together become corrupt." The constant, unreversed cultivation of sin leads in due course to total blindness, even blindness to what is self-evident.

PSALM 14 (15)

In Psalm 14 (Hebrew 15), man puts to God that most essential and burdened of questions: "Lord, who will abide in Your tabernacle, or who shall rest on Your holy mountain?" This is the same query found in various forms in other parts of Holy Scripture: "Who shall ascend the mountain of the Lord, or who may stand in His holy place?" (Psalm 23:3); "Sirs, what must I do to be saved?" (Acts 16:30); "What shall I do, Lord?" (Acts 22:10); "Good Teacher, what shall I do to inherit eternal life?" (Luke 18:18; 10:25); "What shall we do, that we may work the works of God?" (John 6:28); "Men and brethren, what shall we do?" (Acts 2:37).

A first feature to be noted about this repeated query is the implied supposition that there really does exist some kind of moral program to be followed. That is to say, this is an ethical inquiry by which man seeks to identify the nature of the dark, haunting, and native imperative that stalks his soul. Man cannot help but sense that, in order to abide in God's tabernacle and to rest on His holy mountain, there truly is something that he must "do." (One remembers here the final petition to exit the lips of the dying Goethe: *"Mehr Licht! More light!"*)

A second feature of this moral question is what we may call its implied eschatology. That is to say, the inquiry infers that man is supposed to *end up* somewhere other than where he is now. His life is to be lived as a journey toward some determined destination, and his question has something to do with making sure that he is pointed toward that destination. At the base of his soul he senses that it would be life's greatest tragedy if he should, at the end, fail to abide in God's tabernacle and to rest on His holy mountain.

A third feature of this biblical question is that it is invariably answered with some kind of command: "Believe," "repent," "love justice and hate iniquity," "be baptized," "sell all you have and give to the poor," "take up your cross." In other words, since God puts the moral, eschatological question into the human heart, it is a justified question and is always answered.

A fourth feature of this query is its implication of an ascent. God's tabernacle is to be found on His holy mountain, and mountains must be mounted. If the goal described is one of abiding and resting, the process thereto is called climbing: "Who shall ascend the mountain of the Lord?" The same haunting sense that prompts the inquiry also informs man that he is supposed to scale to that pinnacle, and he requests directions thereto: "Which way is up?"

Because we surmise it to involve an ascent, a climbing, a resolute resistance to the force of gravity, there is an aspect of the answer already contained in our question. That is to say, *a priori* we know that going *up* is more difficult than going *down*. Therefore we would be rightly suspicious of any response suggesting acquiescence in the aboriginal gravity of our fallen state. "Doing what comes naturally" is scarcely the path to ascent. To "go with the flow" is invariably to go lower. Whatever the answer to the moral question, then, we can be certain that it will involve stern effort, struggle, adherence to irrevocable duty.

So it is not surprising that in Holy Scripture the mountain of God is spoken of in terms of distinct moral obligations. It is on stones quarried from the *top* of God's holy mountain that we read the tenfold directions for ascending thereto. It is from the *top* of the mountain that the voice of Jesus declares the conditions necessary to its climbing—certain statutes with respect to poverty of spirit, meekness, mourning, mercy, peacemaking, purity of heart, as well as hungering, thirsting, and suffering persecution for the sake of righteousness (see Matt. 5:3–10). It is from this very mountain, finally, that the Lord sends out His preachers to tell all nations "to *observe* all things that I have commanded you" (Matt. 28:20).

From the holy mountain of the Lord, then, and from the tabernacle that Moses inspected atop thereof, there come forth the remaining lines of this Psalm 14 in answer to its original question: "He who walks blamelessly, and works righteousness; who speaks the truth in his heart, nor deceives with his tongue; who does no evil to his neighbor and brings no disgrace on his friends; before whom the vile person is scorned, but who honors those who fear the Lord; who pledges to his neighbor and does not fail him; who gives no money at interest, and takes no bribes against the innocent—he who does these things shall never be shaken."

PSALM 15 (16)
PRESERVE ME, O GOD
☙

In addition to showing His disciples the truth of His Resurrection "by many infallible proofs, being seen of them for forty days, and speaking of the things pertaining to the Kingdom of God" (Acts 1:3), the newly risen Lord took special care likewise to explain to the Church the authentic meaning of Holy Scripture. Indeed, we know that the day of Resurrection itself was partly devoted to this task (cf. Luke 24:25–27, 44, 45).

Thus, the Church's proper interpretation of Holy Scripture down through the centuries is rooted in what the Lord Himself taught her during those forty days spoken of in Acts 1:3. The correct—that is to say, the *orthodox*—understanding of the Bible is based on what the Church learned directly from the risen Christ. Her interpretation of Holy Scripture is inseparable from the hearing of the living Lord's voice (John 20:16), the handling of His flesh (Luke 24:39, 40; 1 John 1:1), the touching of His wounds (John 20:27). The Church's experience of the risen Christ is the source of all correct understanding of Holy Scripture.

These considerations, moreover, bear a special relevance to the interpretation of the Book of Psalms, for this section of the Bible, which became the Church's official prayer book for all times, was singled out for specific consideration (Luke 24:44). On Pascha, the Sunday of the Resurrection, when the Lamb came forward and "took the scroll out of the right hand of Him who sat on the throne" (Rev. 5:7) and began forthwith to open its seals (6:1), the Church commenced likewise her understanding of the psalms. From that day forward, the prayer of the Church would be rooted in the vision that the Lord gave her in His opening of the Psalter.

We may be sure that Psalm 15 (Hebrew 16) was among the psalms interpreted to the Church by the risen Christ, for this was the first psalm that she exegeted in her very first sermon when she came rushing with power from the upper room on Pentecost. According to the Apostle Peter, who preached that sermon, Psalm 15 describes the Resurrection of Christ:

> Men of Israel, hear these words: Jesus of Nazareth, a Man attested by God to you by miracles, wonders, and signs which God did through Him in your midst, as you yourselves also know—Him, being delivered by the determined purpose and foreknowledge of God, you have

taken by lawless hands, have crucified, and put to death; whom God raised up, having loosed the pains of death, because it was not possible that He should be held by it. For David says concerning Him: "I foresaw the Lord always before my face, / For He is at my right hand, that I may not be shaken. / Therefore my heart rejoiced, and my tongue was glad; / Moreover my flesh also will rest in hope. / For You will not leave my soul in Hades, / Nor will You allow Your Holy One to see corruption. / You have made known to me the ways of life; / You will make me full of joy in Your presence" (Acts 2:22–28).

Even though it was King David saying these things, the voice speaking more deeply in Psalm 15, according to St. Peter, is the voice of Christ. As the forefather and type of Christ, David was speaking in the tones of prophecy. Peter goes on to explain:

Men and brethren, let me speak freely to you of the patriarch David, that he is both dead and buried, and his tomb is with us to this day. Therefore, being a prophet, and knowing that God had sworn with an oath to him that of the fruit of his body, according to the flesh, He would raise up the Christ to sit on his throne, he, foreseeing this, spoke concerning the resurrection of the Christ, that His soul was not left in Hades, nor did His flesh see corruption. This Jesus God has raised up, of which we are all witnesses (Acts 2:29–32).

Since Psalm 15 speaks of the Lord's Resurrection in terms of a future hope, rather than of an accomplished fact, there would seem to be a special propriety in praying this psalm on Saturday, the very day that the Lord's body lay in the grave and His soul was in Hades. It may thus serve to prepare for the celebration of the Lord's Resurrection each following Sunday, when the Lamb begins to open the seals.

And as David prayed Psalm 15 *in persona Christi*, looking forward to the one who was to come, so do Christians, when they pray this psalm, identify themselves in hope with the risen Christ, for we too will rise with Him: "And God both raised up the Lord and will also raise us up by His power" (1 Cor. 6:14); "He who raised up the Lord Jesus will also raise us up with Jesus" (2 Cor. 4:14); "He who raised Christ from the dead will also give life to your mortal bodies" (Rom. 8:11).

PSALM 16 (17)

Like the psalm immediately before it, Psalm 16 (Hebrew 17) pertains to the hope of Christ in the context of His death and burial. Its final line is the key to its interpretation: "But I will appear before Your face in righteousness; at beholding Your glory will I be satisfied." Such was the hope of Jesus, "who for the joy that was set before Him endured the cross, despising the shame" (Heb. 12:2).

The Gospel of John especially portrays Jesus as God's perfect servant, doing "always . . . those things that please Him" (8:29). He could assert, therefore, in full serenity of soul, "I love the Father, and as the Father gave Me commandment, so I do" (14:31). Such obedience was the very reason for His journey to earth: "For I have come down from heaven, not to do My own will, but the will of Him who sent Me" (6:38). Furthermore, this sustained obedience to the Father was for Jesus the very channel of His sustenance: "My food is to do the will of Him who sent Me, and to finish His work" (4:34). At all times, then, was He able to say: "I do not seek My own will but the will of the Father who sent Me" (5:30).

This obedience to the Father was, of course, costly. As Jesus prays to Him in this psalm, "Because of the words of Your lips, I have adhered to the hard ways." And just what were these *words* of God for which Jesus adhered to the *hard ways*? Surely they were the words of "all that the prophets have spoken," for "ought not the Christ to have suffered these things and to enter into His glory?" (Luke 24:25, 26).

These, then, were the words that governed the life of Jesus: words about Isaac's burden of wood in Genesis, words about the paschal lamb in Exodus, words about atonement for sin in Leviticus, words about Samson giving his life for the people in Judges, words about David suffering opprobrium in Second Samuel, words about being pierced in Zechariah, words about the Lord's Suffering Servant in Isaiah, and, indeed, these very words of the suffering just man in the Book of Psalms.

When Jesus took up Isaac's wood on His shoulders, and became the paschal lamb, and made atonement for sins, and gave His life for His brethren, and suffered opprobrium, and was pierced with a spear, and all the rest—in doing all these things, "Christ died for our sins according to the Scriptures" (1 Cor. 15:3). All of the Hebrew Bible consists of prophetic words about Jesus, for the sake of which He adhered to the "hard ways."

And just what were those *hard ways* to which our Lord adhered for the sake of God's words? They were the hard ways of obedience to the Father's will, for "He learned obedience by the things which He suffered" (Heb. 5:8). St. Paul, about two decades after Holy Friday, quoted a line from a very primitive hymn of the Church, according to which Christ "humbled Himself and became obedient to the point of death, even the death of the cross" (Phil. 2:8).

It was in His Passion, then, that Jesus was put to the trial, and Psalm 16 is one of those psalms expressing His supplication to the Father in that setting. Jesus suffered and died in the divine service, committing His entire destiny into the Father's hand: "You have proved my heart; You have visited me in the night. You have tried me with fire, nor was wickedness found within me."

As this last line shows, the prayer of Jesus was that of a righteous man. Indeed, Psalm 16 so stresses this quality of righteousness that no other member of the human race could pray this psalm in such literal truth. Jesus says to the Father: "Attend to My righteousness, O Lord; give heed to my supplication. Hear my prayer from lips that are not deceitful. Let my judgment come forth from Your face, and let mine eyes behold uprightness."

Becoming "in all things . . . like His brethren" (Heb. 2:17), Jesus prays for the Father's protection in words that we are correct and prompt to make our own: "Manifest the wonders of Your mercy, O You that save those who hope on You. But from those who resist Your right hand, guard me as the apple of Your eye. In the shelter of Your wings will You hide me, from the presence of the godless who oppress me."

Himself sinless, God's Son became one with us in our fallen humanity, knowing fear and dread, but likewise trusting in God as a man. He assumed all that we are, in order that we, by Him, may be partakers of who He is.

PSALM 17 (18)

I WILL LOVE YOU, O LORD

Second Samuel 22 gives a nearly identical version of Psalm 17 (Hebrew 18), similarly providing the historical context of David's deliverance from the unjust persecution of Saul.

In the ancient and inherited liturgical customs of the Christian Church, this is a morning psalm, divided in the West between Fridays and Saturdays at prime (first hour), and prayed in the East at third hour (Tierce). It was about this time of day, from sunrise through early morning, that Jesus our Lord was brought to trial before Pontius Pilate (cf. Matt. 27:1), and many Christians have seen fit, over the centuries, to pray Psalm 17 in the context of that trial.

Indeed, certain lines of the psalm lend themselves readily to such a reading: "With praise will I call upon the Lord, and I shall be saved from my enemies. . . . From my powerful opponents will He deliver me, and from those who hate me, for they were stronger than I. They confronted me on the day of my calamity, but the Lord became my champion. . . . The Lord will reward me according to my righteousness; for the purity of my hands will He repay me. For I have kept the ways of the Lord, nor have I strayed profanely from my God. For all His judgments are before me, nor have His decrees departed from me. In His presence will I be faultless, and I will preserve myself from rebellion. And the Lord will reward me according to my righteousness; for the purity of my hands will He repay me."

Jesus was subjected to trial under the two greatest legal codes of that day, those of Israel and Rome, and in neither could His innocence find vindication. Within the finest forensic systems of humanity then devised, the most just man in history could obtain no justice. Psalm 17 fits congruously into that dramatic context.

In the final analysis, nonetheless, the real villains in this psalm, those opponents against whom the Lord Jesus directs His prayer, are not the Sanhedrin and Pilate. These are but the agents of a higher intrigue, as St. Peter will afterwards affirm: "Yet now, brethren, I know that you did it in ignorance, as did also your rulers" (Acts 3:17). No, the far deeper malice of the hour is that of the satanic spirits, the true enemies who conspired against the Holy and Righteous One.

Consequently, it is the fallen angels that we should see referenced in so many lines of this psalm, for against them our Lord waged a combat without quarter: "I will pursue My enemies and overtake them, nor will I turn back until they are perished. I will crush them, and they will not stand; they shall fall beneath My feet. . . . Like dust before the wind will I thrash them, and trample them down like mud in the streets." This crushing of the Lord's demonic foes is vividly described in the Bible's final book: "And fire came down from God out of heaven and devoured them. The devil, who deceived them, was cast into the lake of fire and brimstone where the beast and the false prophet are. And they will be tormented day and night forever and ever" (Rev. 20:9, 10). Obviously, in the ongoing war of the spirit, neither this last book nor the Psalter was composed for noncombatants.

Many lines of Psalm 17, however, lay greater stress on the rich blessings of the Lord's triumph over evil. For example, the calling of the Gentiles to salvation. Rejected by the Jews at His trial (cf. Matt. 27:25; John 19:15), Jesus speaks of the other nations: "You will set me at the head of the nations. An unknown people have served me. . . . For I will confess You among the nations, O Lord, and praise will I sing to Your name." Later the Apostle Paul will quote this verse from our psalm by way of explaining his thesis that "the Gentiles [should] glorify God for His mercy" (Rom. 15:9).

The merciful calling of the Gentiles, in the wake of Israel's defection, is, of course, a large theme in much of the New Testament. It is John's Gospel, however, that most specifically joins this theme to the Lord's rejection by Israel at the time of His sufferings and death. Note, for instance, that it is in the context of the appearance of the "Greeks" that Jesus gives the most explicit prophecy of His death: "'Unless a grain of wheat falls into the ground and dies, it remains alone; but if it dies, it produces much grain. . . . And I, if I am lifted up from the earth, will draw all peoples to Myself.' This He said, signifying by what death He would die" (John 12:24–33).

PSALM 18 (19)

THE HEAVENS DECLARE THE GLORY OF GOD

The Christian faith recognizes two ways in which God has made His revelation to us: through nature and through grace. "Through Creation and through Holy Scripture" is another way of saying the same thing. These are the two means that God has given us through which to know Him.

Starting with the inspired Scriptures, sometimes Christians have reached back, as it were, to speak of nature itself as a sort of book, a sacred scroll in which God is revealed. Nature itself provides a "text," analogous to Holy Writ. For example, a twelfth-century Englishman, Alexander Neckam, said that "the world is inscribed with the pen of God; for anyone who understands it, it is a work of literature," while a contemporary, the Parisian master Richard of St. Victor, said that "the whole of this sensible world is like a book written by the finger of God." Similarly, Garnier of Rochefort, in the same century, said that God speaks to us through two books, nature and the Law (Torah).

Such writers found this idea of a double revelation in the Bible itself. It is the theme, for instance, of Psalm 18 (Hebrew 19), which begins with the testimony to God's truth in the work of creation and then goes on to speak of the further testimony to that same truth in God's law. These two revelations are the topics of the two halves of this psalm.

First, nature, given us by God that we may know Him. "The heavens declare the glory of God," our psalm begins, "and the firmament proclaims the work of His hands. Day speaks the word unto day, and night unto night proclaims the knowledge. There is neither speech, nor words, nor can their voices be heard; yet their sound has gone forth to all the earth, and their message to the corners of the world." That is to say, there is a message for us from God, inscribed in the structure of creation.

Second, the law, also given us by God that we may know Him: "The law of the Lord is pure, converting souls. The testimony of the Lord is sure, giving wisdom to little ones. The judgments of the Lord are right, rejoicing the heart. The commandment of the Lord is bright, enlightening the eyes. The fear of the Lord is holy, enduring for ever and ever." Such is the reciprocity between the Creation account in Genesis and the Sinai event in Exodus. What God reveals in nature, He also reveals in His law. Thus, whether he turns to God's Word in nature or to God's Word in the Torah, man finds order and truth and justice and wisdom and holiness.

It should not surprise us, then, that the Apostle Paul should see in God's revelation in nature a foreshadowing of His revelation in the Gospel, for the universality of God's witness in the works of creation is to be matched in the universal character of the Gospel's proclamation. Speaking of the missionaries who proclaim God's Word to the ends of the earth, Paul compares their witness to that same wisdom in which "day speaks the word unto day, and night unto night proclaims the knowledge." He comments in Romans: "So then faith comes by hearing, and hearing by the word of God. But I say, have they not heard? Yes indeed: 'Their sound has gone out to all the earth, and their words to the ends of the world'" (10:18). Paul is saying that the Gospel is as cosmic as the cosmos.

Just as the Gospel is God's fulfillment of the Torah, so it is God's answer to the hope that lies at the heart of nature. Each morning we behold how God "set His tent in the sun, and he goes forth as a bridegroom from his wedding chamber; he rejoices as a giant to run his race. His going forth is from the furthest heaven, and his setting is at the other extreme, nor can anything be hidden from his heat."

Such is the daily promise proclaimed from the blue vault that arches over us, that firmament of which our psalm says that "the firmament proclaims the work of His hands." It is heaven's daily exhortation to hope. The rising of the sun, which the high poetry of the Bible regards as an exultant bridegroom and a racing giant, is itself a law and a Gospel, announcing the godly order of the one and the godly promise of the other. From the beginning of His Word to us, when His hands spread out the heavens above us, until that end when He will roll them up as a scroll, God's message is a unified poetic text of order, promise, and hope.

PSALM 19 (20)

MAY THE LORD HEARKEN TO YOU

In the Eastern Orthodox liturgical tradition, Psalm 19 (Hebrew 20) is recited each morning at Matins as a sort of blessing that Christians invoke on one another at the day's commencement: "May the Lord hearken to you on the day of affliction; may the name of the God of Jacob be your shield. May He send forth help to you from His holy place; and from Zion may He uphold you."

The history of Christian piety knows another way of praying this psalm, however—namely, as a prayer of the Church addressed to Christ Himself, who on her behalf mounts the hill of Calvary "on the day of affliction." The whole psalm thus becomes an "Amen" to the redemptive work of Christ.

Understood in this sense, our Lord's voluntary immolation on the Cross is the point of reference in the line that reads: "All Your sacrifice may He remember, and accept Your whole burnt offering." Prayed in this way, our psalm is the "Amen" of the Church to the pouring out of the redemptive blood, when "Christ was offered once to bear the sins of many" (Heb. 9:28).

Thus, too, when we say, "May He give you according to Your heart's desire, and fulfill Your every counsel," it is once again the "Amen" of the Church to the prayer Christ makes for her benefit: "I do not pray for these alone, but also for those who will believe in Me through their word. . . . I desire that they also whom You gave Me may be with Me where I am" (John 17:20, 24).

In like manner, when we say, "May the Lord fulfill all your requests," it is especially the "Amen" of the Church to such petitions as, "Father, forgive them, for they do not know what they do" (Luke 23:34) and, "Holy Father, keep through Your name those whom You have given Me" (John 17:11).

It is to the redemption wrought by Christ our Savior that we refer when we say to Him: "We shall exult in Your salvation, and in the name of our God shall we be exalted." The Church exults in His salvation whenever she gathers to worship in His name. And thus does she exult: "Worthy is the Lamb who was slain / To receive power and riches and wisdom, / And strength and honor and glory and blessing" (Rev. 5:12).

In the name of our God, moreover, is the Church herself exalted. And thus is she exalted: "You . . . have redeemed us to God by Your blood / Out of every tribe and tongue and people and nation, / And have made us kings and priests to our God; / And we shall reign on the earth" (Rev. 5:9, 10).

In contrast to the worship of the Church, who trusts thus in the blood of the Lamb, there are those who place their confidence elsewhere: "Some trust in chariots, and some in horses." This horse-trusting appears likewise in the prophets (e. g., Is. 31:1; 36:9) as a metaphor for man's placing his assurance in such human forces as military might.

These "horses," in which men put their trust, represent the designs of the worldly and powerful, but they are profoundly vain. Holy Scripture will finally describe these horses as white and carrying a conqueror, as red and bearing a warrior, as black and transporting famine, as pale and ridden by Death. These horses and their riders represent the forces of the world in its opposition to God, and "power was given to them over a fourth of the earth, to kill with sword, with hunger, with death, and by the beasts of the earth" (Rev. 6:1–8). That is to say, these horses, in which men put their trust, will return to exact their toll on human happiness and human history.

But has not the saving work of the Christ already been accomplished? Is it not a fact that already Jesus has "entered the Most Holy Place once for all, having obtained eternal redemption" (Heb. 9:12)? And is it not the case that even now "He always lives to make intercession" (Heb. 7:25)? Truly, these things are already so, and our psalm confesses them: "Now I know that the Lord has saved His Christ; He will hear Him from His holy heaven. In deeds of might is the salvation at His right hand."

Yet it still remains for Christ finally to triumph in our lives. Hitherto, after all, "it has not yet been revealed what we shall be" (1 John 3:2). There is still a future tense to the Christian life. "We *shall be* magnified in the name of the Lord, our God," says our psalm. Until that magnification be finally done, each of us must confess, "Not that I have already attained, or am already perfected" (Phil. 3:12). We continue, then, to plead: "O Lord, save the King," "and hear us on the day we call upon You."

PSALM 20 (21)

O LORD, THE KING WILL REJOICE IN YOUR STRENGTH

❧

Holy Church, both East and West, rather early decided that Psalm 20 (Hebrew 21) is best prayed during the earliest hours of Sunday morning, the Resurrection day of her Lord Jesus Christ. Indeed, traditionally it was chanted during the night's vigil between Saturday and Sunday, the weekly nocturnal watch commemorative of the Passover, wherein God's Church celebrates her freedom from the bondage of sin, death, and hell. (That weekly service is referred to in Acts 12:5, 12; 20:7–11 and slightly later in a letter of Pliny to Trajan.) This traditional liturgical context of Psalm 20 provides the proper interpretation of its final line: "Rise up, O Lord, in Your strength; we will sing and praise Your deeds of power."

The voice of the Church herself is the voice of this psalm, glorifying the Father for the Son's paschal victory over sin, death, and hell. The proper sense of Psalm 20 may be summarized as: "Blessed be the God and Father of our Lord Jesus Christ, who has blessed us with every spiritual blessing in the heavenly places in Christ. . . . In Him we have redemption through His blood, the forgiveness of sins, according to the riches of His grace" (Eph. 1:3, 7).

The psalm begins then, "O Lord, the King will rejoice in Your strength, and greatly will He exult in Your salvation." This is the rejoicing of "Jesus, the author and finisher of our faith, who for the joy that was set before Him endured the cross, despising the shame, and has sat down at the right hand of the throne of God" (Heb. 12:2).

The paschal victory is God's response to Christ's own prayer: "You have given Him His heart's desire, nor have You denied Him the request of His lips." The Gospels themselves suggest that the passing hours of our Lord's suffering were a period of His intense prayer, indicated by His several audible prayers that were recorded during that time (cf. Matt. 26:39, 42, 44; 27:46; Luke 23:34, 46). With respect to this prayer of Jesus during His sufferings we are told that "He was heard because of His godly fear" (Heb. 5:7).

And for what did Jesus pray during His Passion? "He asked life of You," answers our psalm. And what sort of life? The mere survival of his earthly body? Hardly. The object of Jesus' prayer was, rather, the total life that stands forever victorious over death, the irruption of the divine life into the world by reason of His own passage through death to glory.

The true *eternal* life is not a simple continuation of man's earthly exist-

39

ence. It is something new altogether: "He asked life of You, and You gave Him length of days unto ages of ages." This is the divine life given in the Resurrection, of which Jesus said: "Amen, Amen, I say to you, the hour is coming, and now is, when the dead will hear the voice of the Son of God; and those who hear will live. For as the Father has life in Himself, so He has granted the Son to have life in Himself" (John 5:25, 26).

This eternal life is joy forever in God's presence, "where the forerunner has entered for us" (Heb. 6:20): "Great is His glory in Your salvation; You will bestow glory and majesty upon Him. Blessing will You give Him forever and ever; You will gladden Him with joy in Your presence."

By reason of His Resurrection, says this psalm, Jesus reigns as King, the very title that Pilate, in God's providential irony, affixed to the Cross itself: "O Lord, the *King* will rejoice in Your strength." And because He is King, He is crowned: "For You have poured upon Him the blessings of goodness. A crown of precious stones have You placed upon His head."

Once again, this was the glorification for which Jesus prayed as He commenced the unfolding of His Passion: "Father, the hour has come. Glorify Your Son, that Your Son also may glorify You. . . . And now, O Father, glorify Me together with Yourself, with the glory which I had with You before the world was" (John 17:1, 5).

Many lines of this psalm (pretty much its entire second half) are devoted to the enemies of Christ, who are enemies of Christ precisely because they are the enemies of man. That enemy called sin, overcome by the atoning grace of His blood. That enemy called death, which He trampled down by His own death. That enemy called hell, which found itself unable to hold the Author of life.

Psalm 20 thus celebrates the victory of Him who proclaims: "Do not be afraid; I am the First and the Last. I am He who lives, and was dead, and behold, I am alive forevermore. Amen. And I have the keys of Hades and of death" (Rev. 1:17, 18).

PSALM 21 (22)

MY GOD, MY GOD, WHY HAVE YOU FORSAKEN ME?

Of all the psalms, Psalm 21 (Hebrew 22) is *par excellence* the canticle of the Lord's suffering and death. In Matthew and Mark, Jesus is described as praying the opening line of this psalm as He hangs on the Cross: "My God, My God, why have You forsaken Me?" (Matt. 27:46; Mark 15:34). In Luke, on the other hand, the last recorded words of Jesus on the Cross are a line from Psalm 30 (Hebrew 31): "Into Your hands I commit My spirit" (23:46). From a juxtaposition of these two texts there arose in Christian sentiment the popular story that Jesus, while He hung on the Cross, silently recited all the lines of the Psalter that lie between these two verses.

Whatever is to be said of that story, there is no doubt about the importance of Psalm 21 in reference to the Lord's suffering and death. Not only did Jesus pray this psalm's opening line on His gibbet of pain; other lines of it are also interpreted by the Church, even by the Evangelists themselves, as prophetic references to details in the drama of Holy Friday.

Consider, for instance, this verse of Psalm 21: "All who gazed at Me derided Me. With their lips they spoke and wagged their heads: 'He hoped on the Lord. Let Him deliver him. Let Him save him, since He approves of him.'" One can hardly read this verse without recalling what is described in Matthew: "And those who passed by blasphemed Him, wagging their heads and saying, . . . 'If You are the Son of God, come down from the cross.' Likewise the chief priests also, mocking with the scribes and elders, said, . . . 'He trusted in God; let Him deliver Him now if He will have Him'" (27:39–43).

The Gospels likewise tell of the soldiers dividing the garments of Jesus at the time of His Crucifixion. St. John's description of this event is worth considering at length, because he actually quotes our psalm verbatim as a fulfilled prophecy:

> Then the soldiers, when they had crucified Jesus, took His garments and made four parts, to each soldier a part, and also His tunic. Now the tunic was without seam, woven from the top in one piece. They said therefore among themselves, "Let us not tear it, but cast lots for it, whose it shall be," that the Scripture might be fulfilled which says: 'They divided My garments among them, / And for My clothing they cast lots'" (19:23, 24).

Moreover, if Holy Church thinks of the Lord Himself as praying this psalm on the Cross, such an interpretation is amply justified by a later verse that says: "Like a potsherd has my strength been scorched, and my tongue cleaved to my palate." Hardly can the Church read this line without calling to mind the Lord who said from the Cross: "I thirst" (John 19:28).

And as she thinks of the nails supporting the Lord's body on the tree of redemption, the Church recognizes the voice that speaks yet another line of our psalm: "They have pierced my hands and feet; they have numbered all my bones."

In addition, according to St. John, at the foot of the Cross stood the Mother of the Lord, a loyal disciple to the last, her soul transfixed by the sword that aged Simeon prophesied in the temple when she first presented the Child to God. To her the Lord Himself now makes reference in this psalm. Speaking of that consecration, Jesus says to His heavenly Father of his earthly mother, "You were He that drew me from the womb, ever my hope from my mother's breasts. To You was I handed over from the womb. From the belly of my mother, You are my God."

Outside of the Gospels, the New Testament's most vivid references to the Lord's Passion are arguably those in Hebrews, which speaks of the Lord's sharing our flesh and blood so that "through death He might destroy him who had the power of death" (2:14). Quoting Psalm 21 in this context of the Passion, this author tells us that Jesus "is not ashamed to call them brethren, saying: 'I will declare Your name to My brethren; / In the midst of the assembly I will sing praise to You'" (2:11, 12).

Finally, just as each of the Lord's three predictions of the Passion ends with a prediction of the Resurrection (cf. Mark 8:31; 9:31; 10:34), this psalm of the Passion appropriately finishes with the voice of victory and the growth of the Church: "My spirit lives for Him; my seed will serve Him. The coming generation shall be herald for the Lord, declaring His righteousness to a people yet unborn, whom the Lord created."

PSALM 22 (23)

THE LORD IS MY SHEPHERD

One has the strong impression—strong to the point of certitude—that the "Good Shepherd Psalm" is the best-known, most frequently prayed and the most widely memorized psalm of the Bible. This psalm, traditionally Psalm 22 from its numbering in the Septuagint and Vulgate, but now popularly known as the Twenty-third Psalm from its numbering in the Masoretic Hebrew text, is particularly popular in the King James version. Both of my children could recite it by heart at age three, an accomplishment that one suspects is not uncommon in Christian homes. Many believers pray it daily.

The popularity of this psalm is doubtless related to the traditional attraction of the image of Jesus as the Good Shepherd, the latter a fact readily demonstrable from the New Testament and the very earliest Christian art.

This attraction, still very widespread, was absolutely universal among the first Christians. For instance, in Matthew, written in Syria, the theme of Jesus as the Good Shepherd was especially related to that of evangelism and the sending out of the Apostles (9:36–38). This emphasis is consonant with the parable of the Shepherd's searching for the lost sheep, preserved in 18:12–14.

In Mark's Gospel, written in Rome, the theme of the Good Shepherd was especially associated with the Multiplication of the Loaves (Mark 6:34). Here one sees Jesus making his flock recline on the green grass (6:39), an image clearly drawn from our psalm. Evidently this became a favorite image among the Christians at Rome, for pictures of Jesus as the Good Shepherd appear everywhere in the catacombs and other early art in that city. Another New Testament work written at Rome twice refers to Jesus as the shepherd (1 Pet. 2:25; 5:4), and the image likewise appears in Hebrews (13:20), which also seems to be connected with Rome (13:24). Moreover, a second-century Christian of Rome, named Hermas, made this the major image of Jesus in a lengthy work that is called, in fact, *The Shepherd*.

Besides Syria and Rome, the symbol of Jesus as Good Shepherd was also clearly a popular one among the Christians in Asia Minor. For example, in the mid-second century the Bishop of Smyrna, Polycarp, refers to our Lord as "the Shepherd of the Church" (*Martyrdom of Polycarp* 19:2). Much earlier, however, that theme was already recorded in the Gospel of John, written in the Asian capital of Ephesus. At the very end of this Gospel, Jesus refers to "My lambs" and "My sheep" (John 21:15–17), but the longer development of this idea is in chapter 10. In this chapter several aspects of the image are treated: the sensitivity of the sheep to the Shepherd's voice (vv. 3–5, 8, 14, 16, 27), the utter uniqueness of the Shepherd in contrast to the hireling or the robber (vv. 1, 2, 8–10, 12, 13), the Shepherd's giving of His life for His sheep (vv. 10, 11, 14, 15, 17, 18), the gathering of the lost sheep into a single flock (v. 16) and their total security (vv. 28, 29).

In the traditional exegesis of the Church, this psalm bears special reference to the Sacraments of Initiation: Baptism, Chrismation, and the Holy Eucharist.

Thus, it is the baptismal font that the psalmist has in mind when he proclaims: "He leads me beside the still waters; He restores my soul."

Thus, too, it is the outpouring of the Holy Spirit in Chrismation that is referred to when the psalm says: "You anoint my head with oil."

Thus, likewise, it is the Altar of the Messianic Banquet that the psalm means when it says: "You prepare a table before me in the presence of mine enemies; . . . my cup brims over."

This interpretation is already clear in Mark 6, the earliest written account of the Multiplication of the Loaves. Above, we noted Mark's insertion, in 6:34, of a passage from Ezekiel on the theme of the Good Shepherd; also we saw his reference to the crowds reclining "on the green grass" (even though the event takes place in the desert!), the latter detail surely taken from our psalm. But in this same passage, Mark likewise regards the Multiplication of the Loaves (and, hence, of the Good Shepherd) through the lens of the Eucharist. Note, for instance, Mark's use of the four "eucharistic verbs," in verse 41, to describe how Jesus "took" the bread, "blessed," "broke," and "gave" it to the believers. Such is the mystic table that the Good Shepherd, having led us safely through the valley of the shadow of death, prepares before us, beside the still waters, our heads anointed with oil.

PSALM 23 (24)

THE EARTH IS THE LORD'S

As indicated in the New Testament, the recorded testimony of eyewitnesses is the basis for the Church's proclamation of the Gospel and, consequently, for the articles of the Creed (cf. John 1:14; Acts 1:21, 22; 1 Cor. 15:1–8; 1 John 1:1–3). Certain specific events, occurring within time and space, were both the direct objects of empirical observation and the topics of apostolic preaching: "For we cannot but speak the things which we have seen and heard" (Acts 4:20).

There are exceptions to this rule, nonetheless, for certain other events, though central to both the Gospel and the Creed, were neither seen nor heard by anyone on the earth; they were not empirically available within time and space, for the simple reason that they did not take place in this world. Such events include the conquering descent of Christ into Hades (cf. Eph. 4:9; 1 Peter 3:19) and His glorious entrance into heaven. These two events are celebrated on Holy Saturday and Ascension Thursday, respectively, the days at either side of that period during which the risen Lord "presented Himself alive after His suffering by many infallible proofs, being seen by them during forty days and speaking of the things pertaining to the kingdom of God" (Acts 1:3).

Relative to the Lord's Ascension, we may say that the Church saw Him "going" (Luke 24:51; Acts 1:9) but not "arriving." That triumphant arrival in heaven, nonetheless—Jesus' crowning as "Lord of all"—is explicitly affirmed in the New Testament (cf. Mark 16:19; Phil. 2:9; 1 Tim. 3:16).

The heavenly glorification of our Lord Jesus Christ is not simply an aftermath to our redemption, but rather an essential component of the very sacrifice of the Cross. His Ascension is integral to our Lord's priesthood. Indeed, if Jesus simply "were on earth, He would not be a priest" (Heb. 8:4). The atoning sacrifice of Christ did not end on Golgotha, but was rendered perfect and complete by His definitive entrance into the eternal Holy of Holies: "But Christ came as High Priest of the good things to come, with the greater and more perfect tabernacle not made with hands, that is, not of this creation. . . . For Christ has not entered the holy places made with hands, which are copies of the true, but into heaven itself, now to appear in the presence of God for us" (Heb. 9:11, 24).

Psalm 23 (Hebrew 24) is a celebration of the Lord's entrance into that heavenly sanctuary and royal court: "Who may ascend into the hill of the

Lord? Or who may stand in His holy place? He who has clean hands and a pure heart, who has not lifted up his soul to an idol, nor sworn deceitfully. He shall receive blessing from the Lord, and righteousness from the God of his salvation."

This "blessing from the Lord," this "righteousness from the God of his salvation" is the eternal redemption won for us by the sacrifice of Jesus at His heavenly glorification: "Not with the blood of goats and calves, but with His own blood He entered the Most Holy Place once for all, having obtained eternal redemption" (Heb. 9:12); "But this Man, after He had offered one sacrifice for sins forever, sat down at the right hand of God" (10:12).

This King of Glory comes to the entrance of heaven with the blood of the conflict still fresh upon Him (cf. Is. 63:1–6; Rev. 19:13), and a kind of dialogue takes place as the angels call for the opening of the portcullis at the approach of the returning Warrior: "Lift up your heads, O you gates! And be lifted up, you everlasting doors! And the King of glory shall come in. Who is this King of glory? The Lord, strong and mighty, the Lord mighty in battle."

The moment, however, is most special and most to be prolonged. Indeed, the moment is eternal, and the angelic dialogue goes on: "Lift up your heads, O you gates! Lift up, you everlasting doors! And the King of glory shall come in. Who is this King of glory? The Lord of hosts, He is the King of glory."

By virtue of the redemption, all of creation belongs to this Jesus, King and Priest, for God "raised Him from the dead and seated Him at His right hand in the heavenly places, far above all principality and power and might and dominion, and every name that is named, not only in this age but also in that which is to come. And He put all things under His feet, and gave Him to be head over all things to the church, which is His body, the fullness of Him who fills all in all" (Eph. 1:20–23). Thus, our psalm begins: "The earth is the Lord's, and all its fullness, the world and those who dwell therein."

PSALM 24 (25)

TO YOU, O LORD, I LIFT UP MY SOUL

In the original Hebrew text, Psalm 24 (Hebrew 25) is an alphabetical psalm; that is to say, each verse begins with the next letter of the Hebrew alphabet. It is the second such in the Book of Psalms.

(We may also note in passing that this curious device, the abecedarian form or alphabetical acrostic, did not die out with the ancient Hebrews, and there are numerous Christian examples of it in liturgical hymnography, using the Greek or Latin alphabet. Among the Greeks, for instance, it has been employed in numerous canons, such as in the Octoechos. It also appears in ancient Latin hymns; the venerable Matins hymn for Christmas, *A Solis Ortu Cardine*, comes to mind. Sometimes these compositions are quite ingenious. For instance, the Greek canon for the Feast of St. John on September 26 performs the feat backwards!)

But let us return to Psalm 24. "To You, O Lord," it says, "I lift up my soul; in You, my God, I put my trust." Truly, the rest of this psalm, concerned entirely with prayerful trust, may be read simply as commentary on the first verse.

At each service of the Divine Liturgy, going back at least to the *Apostolic Tradition* of St. Hippolytus near the beginning of the third century, when the priest commences the central eucharistic benediction (corresponding to the Hebrew *berakah*), he turns to the congregation to exhort them to intensify their prayer: "Let us lift up our hearts!" (*Ano skomen tas kardias* is the lovely Greek original.) In the ancient Latin version, this exhortation becomes more succinct: *Sursum corda*, "Hearts up!" A congregation of elevated hearts is the proper context for that great act known simply as "The Thanksgiving," *Eucharistia* (the priest's next line being "Let us *give thanks* to the Lord our God!").

Psalm 24 begins with such a "lifting up" of our inner being to God, and it is significant that we Orthodox daily pray this psalm right before the beginning of the morning work, at the Third Hour (Tierce). (In traditional usage, both East and West, this is likewise the canonical hour that immediately precedes the Eucharist on Sundays and feast days.) We commence our labor each day, that is to say, by raising our hearts and mind to God. If we want to "pray always," as Holy Scripture tells us to do, it is important to raise our souls to God right away as we face the day's labor. Otherwise, there is great likelihood

47

that our occupations will involve us in endless distractions that blind us to the thought of God's presence.

But this is also a prayer for the Lord's guidance throughout the rest of the day: "Show me Your ways, O Lord, and teach me Your paths. Lead me by Your truth." And also a prayer for deliverance during the day: "My eyes are ever turned unto the Lord, for He will snatch my feet from the snare." And for protection against the many enemies that afflict the soul: "Behold how many are my enemies, and with an unjust hatred have they hated me. Guard my soul and deliver me, that I may not be put to shame, for in You have I placed my hope."

If this is a good psalm with which to commence the activities of the day, nonetheless, it is also an excellent psalm with which to close them. In fact, besides its use at daily Third Hour, the Orthodox Church also prays this psalm at Great Compline, at the day's end. In this respect, several lines of Psalm 24 beseech the mercy of God for those many sins and failings with which our conscience is invariably stricken as we look back over the previous activities of the day. Mindful of our numerous offenses, we pray at nightfall, "Remember Your compassion, O Lord, and Your mercy, for they are eternal. Remember not the sins of my youth nor my stupidity; but remember me in Your mercy— in Your compassion, O Lord."

And if with such a supplication we end the day, it is with such a supplication that we should likewise finish our lives: "Remember not the sins of my youth nor my stupidity." We pray to be remembered only with the divine compassion. Having no righteousness of our own, having "done no good deed upon the earth" (as the Liturgy of St. Basil says it), possessed of no other ransom note in our favor, this will be our prayer: "Remember me, O Lord, when You come in Your kingdom." Thus our psalm ends, "Deliver Israel, O God, from all his afflictions."

PSALM 25 (26)

VINDICATE ME, O GOD

❧

Psalm 25 (Hebrew 26) has long been used in the Church to accompany the priest's ritual washing of hands, either before or during the Sacred Mysteries. This custom is explained, of course, by the lines that say: "I shall wash my hands among the innocent, and make procession about Your altar, O Lord, that I may listen to the sound of Your praise, and recount all Your wonders."

In the measure that the voice of this psalm is the voice of innocence, it is a psalm most properly heard from the lips of Christ our Lord, who alone is truly innocent. The deepest sense of Psalm 25 is Christological.

Nonetheless, there is also a moral sense to this psalm, for we Christians too are called to live in some measure of innocence, in contrast to the world around us. Thus, St. Paul wrote to the Philippians: "Do all things without complaining and disputing, that you may become blameless (*amempti*) and harmless, children of God without fault (*amoma*) in the midst of a crooked and perverse generation, among whom you shine as lights in the world" (2:14, 15). In this context, Christian "blamelessness" is not an abstract or general ideal. It has to do, rather, with the avoidance of antipathy and unnecessary strife within the local church. Earlier in the same chapter the Apostle had exhorted that Macedonian parish to do nothing from ambition or conceit, but always to regard the interests of others, with fellowship, affection, and mercy (2:1–4); and later he will remind two women in that church of their specific duty with respect to such things (4:2).

In Psalm 25 as well, the innocence at issue is related to one's relationship to the Church, particularly in the context of worship: "I have loved, O Lord, the splendor of Your house, and the dwelling place of Your glory. . . . My foot stands firm in integrity; in the churches will I bless You, O Lord."

The aspired-to innocence of the Christian has chiefly to do, then, with his relationship to those with whom he worships in communion. It is to be determined by evangelical love. Thus, St. Paul prayed for another Macedonian congregation: "And may the Lord make you increase and abound in love to one another and to all, just as we do to you, so that He may establish your hearts blameless (*amemptous*) in holiness before our God and Father" (1 Thess. 3:12, 13). Paul himself had given them the proper example: "You are witnesses, and God also, how devoutly and justly and blamelessly (*amemptos*) we behaved ourselves among you who believe" (2:10). Once again, this innocence has to do with the behavior of Christians to one another.

In yet a deeper sense, however, Christian blamelessness is to be understood as far more than simply a moral quality. It is also a blamelessness *before God*, manifestly a state that none of us can attain on his own. Such innocence is the fruit of cleansing redemption, of which the Lord's washing of the Apostles' feet is perhaps the Bible's most striking symbol: "If I do not wash you, you have no part with Me" (John 13:8).

This Christian innocence is not simply a forensic verdict. We are more than merely *declared* innocent. We are *made* innocent. Christian blamelessness is not simply imputed; it is infused. Something actually happens to us; something real is effected in our souls. It truly make us clean. The blood of Christ really washes us from our sins (cf. Rev. 1:5). St. Paul wrote thus to the Colossians: "And you, who once were alienated and enemies in your mind by wicked works, yet now He has reconciled in the body of His flesh through death, to present you holy, and blameless (*amomous*), and above reproach in His sight" (Col. 1:21, 22). This, ultimately, is the innocence that we bring to God's holy altar, that we may listen to the sound of His praise, and recount all His wonders, loving the splendor of His house, and the dwelling place of His glory.

But none of this is our doing. Even as we say to God (twice in this psalm), "I have walked in my innocence," it is still necessary to add, "Redeem me and have mercy on me." Innocence is not to be claimed except through repentance: "If we confess our sins, He is faithful and just to forgive us our sins and to cleanse us from all unrighteousness" (1 John 1:9). It is from the altar of repentance that we are rendered innocent, purged by a coal so ardent that not even the fiery seraph dares to take it except with tongs.

PSALM 26 (27)

THE LORD IS MY LIGHT AND SALVATION

Although we have no reason to believe that it ever existed as such, it is not difficult to picture Psalm 26 (Hebrew 27) as two discrete psalms, so easily can each of the two parts stand on its own. In the first part God is spoken *about* ("The Lord is my illumination and my savior"); in the second He is spoken *to* ("Hear my voice, O Lord, when I call"). The first has to do with blessings already received, the second with blessings yet sought.

The voice in this psalm is the voice of the Church, who cries out with respect to Jesus Christ: "The Lord is my illumination and my savior; whom shall I fear? The Lord is the safeguard of my life; of whom shall I be afraid?"

(There is in the original Hebrew text a delicate pun involving *'ori* ["my illumination"] and *'ira'* ["shall I fear"]. No attempt was made to duplicate this paronomasia in the canonical Greek.)

"The Lord is my illumination (*photismos*)," we pray, using a word that has long borne special reference to our baptism in Christ (cf. Heb. 6:4; 10:32). This is the "light of the knowledge of the glory of God in the face of Jesus Christ" (2 Cor. 4:6). It is in this context of illumination that the Lord is also called "savior" (*soter*), inasmuch as "there is also an antitype which now saves us—baptism" (1 Peter 3:21).

This assurance—"whom shall I fear? . . . of whom shall I be afraid?"—is that which asks: "If God is for us, who can be against us? . . . Who shall bring a charge against God's elect? . . . Who shall separate us from the love of Christ?" (Rom. 8:31, 33, 35). Like Romans 8, our psalm then takes several verses to revel in the powerlessness of our spiritual enemies.

Psalm 14 had asked: "Lord, who will abide in Your tabernacle, or who shall rest on Your holy mountain?" and Psalm 23 had inquired: "Who may ascend into the hill of the Lord? Or who may stand in His holy place?" It is the same here in Psalm 26: "A single thing have I sought of the Lord, and this will I pursue—that I may abide in the house of the Lord all the days of my life, that I may gaze upon the gladness of the Lord, and tarry in His holy temple." In this verse our psalm touches on the deeper longing of all prayer, the desire to live in intimacy with God, to find joy in His worship, to abide in the consolation and light of His sanctuary: "Lord, it is good for us to be here; if You wish, let us make here three tabernacles" (Matt. 17:4). These are metaphors for that intimate concord with God that is the quest of all our prayer.

We pray for this union with God, but we also actively follow after it, says our psalm. Closeness to the Lord is inseparable from the doing of His will, love itself involving chiefly a union of wills. Thus, union with God comes of both pure grace ("A single thing have I sought of the Lord") and strenuous effort ("and this will I pursue"—*ekzeteso*). Such things as fasting, self-denial, patience, kindness, obedience to the Lord's commandments, and the disciplined exercise of the virtues are all components of this pursuit.

In this psalm the Lord's sanctuary is chiefly pictured as a place of refuge: "For He screened me in His tabernacle in my day of adversities; in the hidden recess of His tent did He shelter me and lift me high upon a rock."

Then, evidently in a sequence not decided by logic, we ask in the psalm's second part those blessings that we celebrated in the first. We ask, that is, for the grace of illumination: "To You my heart has spoken; my face has sought You out. Your face, O Lord, will I seek. Turn not away Your face from me; be not averted in anger from Your servant."

This is the final grace of prayer, of course, to gaze upon the face of God. On the mountain Moses asked to see the face of God (cf. Ex. 33:17–23), but it was more than a thousand years later when, on yet another mountain, his petition was finally granted (cf. Matt. 17:3). For our Lord Jesus Christ is the face of God, "the brightness of His glory and the express image of His person" (Heb. 1:3). To seek the face of God, then, it is imperative to seek it where it is definitively and forever revealed.

To Him we pray, therefore, "Be my helper, and reject me not. Do not forsake me, O God my savior." Once again, as at the psalm's beginning, this same expression "my savior," the knowledge of whom is everlasting life. For Him we wait in longing hope: "I believe that I shall see the good things of the Lord in the land of the living."

PSALM 27 (28)

Psalm 27 (Hebrew 28) is among those traditionally associated with the early morning of Sunday, because the Church has long interpreted it as a psalm of the Lord's Resurrection. Some lines of it tend to make that association inevitable: "My helper and protector is the Lord; in Him my heart hoped, and I was helped. And my flesh took life again, so I shall praise Him with ready will."

This revival of the very flesh of Christ was not a simple return to a life in the flesh, for the risen body of our Lord is saturated with the transforming energies of the Holy Spirit. It is a spiritual and heavenly body, not in the sense of being immaterial, but in the sense that its material composition is itself completely filled with, and inwardly transformed by, God's definitive out-pouring of the divine life. The risen flesh of Christ is thus the first fruits of the new creation, the root and initial installment of that universal transformation by which God will make things new.

The Apostle Paul wrote of this sacred mystery of the Resurrection during the paschal season of the year 55. He was addressing the church at Corinth sometime during the fifty-day interval between Pascha and Pentecost, and, even as he wrote, he referred to the extended paschal season that the Christians were observing: "Christ, our Passover, was sacrificed for us. Therefore let us keep the feast" (1 Cor. 5:7, 8). He wrote these words from Ephesus, where he was planning to stay until Pentecost, which would come presently (16:8).

Writing during that paschal season, St. Paul used the occasion to expound on the meaning of the Resurrection of Jesus, particularly with respect to the new quality of the risen body. The resurrection of the dead, he insisted, is not a simple return to the corruptible life of the body that all men know. It is something marvelously different, analogous to the transformation that takes place when the sown seed rises to new life in the growing plant: "So also is the resurrection of the dead. The body is sown in corruption, it is raised in incorruption. It is sown in dishonor, it is raised in glory. It is sown in weakness, it is raised in power. It is sown a natural body, it is raised a spiritual body. There is a natural body (*soma physikon*), and there is a spiritual body (*pneumatikon*)" (15:42–44).

The spiritual body of the Resurrection is not some kind of "shade." Jesus is no ghost. "Handle Me and see," says the risen Christ, "for a spirit does not have flesh and bones as you see I have" (Luke 24:39). The risen body is still a body, which is to say that it is still composed of matter. To say that the risen body is spiritual does not mean that it is immaterial, but that it is incorruptible. Indeed, in order to emphasize the point that His risen body is still a reality composed of matter, the Lord insisted on actually eating a honeycomb and a piece of fish in the presence of the Church (24:42, 43).

Therefore, the contrast involved here is not one of matter and immateriality, but of two different states of matter: matter subject to corruption, or matter suffused with the Spirit-given dynamism of immortality—matter that is subject to death and corruption, or matter that can never again die.

Our corruptible bodies were descended from Adam; our new bodies are derived from Christ: "And so it is written, 'The first man Adam became a living being.' The last Adam became a life-giving spirit. . . . The first man was of the earth, made of dust; the second Man is the Lord from heaven. As was the man of dust, so also are those who are made of dust; and as is the heavenly Man, so also are those who are heavenly. And as we have borne the image of the man of dust, we shall also bear the image of the heavenly Man" (1 Cor. 15:45–49).

Such is the divine mystery celebrated in our psalm. The resurrection of the Lord ("my flesh took life again") is contrasted with the lot who simply go down unto death: "O my God, be not silent to me, for if you are silent to me, I shall be like unto those that descend unto Hades."

Our psalm also teaches that the life of the Resurrection is a life of divine praise. Indeed, the Church's praise of God is rooted in the Resurrection of Christ: "The Lord is the strength of His people, and the protector of His anointed one's salvation."

PSALM 28 (29)

BRING TO THE LORD, YOU SONS OF GOD

Because its literary style includes some sonorous features dependent on specific Hebrew words, Psalm 28 (Hebrew 29) tends to suffer more in translation than is the case with many other psalms. For example, the Hebrew noun found most frequently in this psalm is *qol*, meaning "voice." Pronounced with the full glottal shock of the letter "q," the word mimics the sound of thunder, which is, in fact, what the noun refers to in this psalm. (This rhetorical device, in which a word imitates the thing to which it refers, is called onomatopoeia. Words like "crash" and "bump" and "scream" are examples in English.) The expression *qol Adonai*, found seven times in this psalm, conveys the impression of a repeated thunder roll, not entirely expressed in the softer English equivalent, "the voice of the Lord." Nor perhaps does even the canonical Greek *phone Kyriou* do the thing full justice, though the Latin version, *vox Domini*, may come closer.

The same sort of guttural sonority is likewise exemplified in another Hebrew word in this psalm, *kavod*, "glory," which occurs twice near the beginning and then again close to the end. Psalm 28 features several additional examples of this technique, for it is a poem describing a thunderstorm, and in the original Hebrew it really does sound like a thunderstorm. (It has thus always reminded me of Beethoven's musical portrayal of a storm in the *Pastorale*.)

The setting of this tempest is a giant cedar forest, whose overarching branches assume the contours of a vaulted temple, and through this lofty sylvan shrine the booming voice of God comes pounding and roaring with a terrifying majesty, accompanied by the swishing of the wind and rain, while flashing bolts of lightning split the very trunks of the towering trees: "In His temple everything speaks glory."

This is a psalm about God's "glory" (*kavod*) and "holiness" (with a couple of plays on the corresponding Hebrew root *qodesh*—note, for instance, the "wilderness of *Kadesh*"). In any language, this is most certainly a psalm to be prayed out loud, allowing its words to come rumbling through the soul. Recited properly, it becomes a literary extension and re-living of that ancient storm which was the psalmist's original inspiration.

This is a very active piece of poetry. After calling on the sons of God to bring Him glory and honor, the psalmist begins to describe that glory as it is revealed in the storm. Calling all God's sons to "give glory to His name," the psalmist immediately speaks of "the voice of the Lord upon the waters. The God of glory thunders." This is the same thunderous voice that in the Gospel of John tells of the glory of God's name: "'Father, glorify Your name.' Then a voice came from heaven, saying, 'I have both glorified it and will glorify it again.' Therefore the people who stood by and heard it said that it had thundered" (John 12:28, 29).

This divine and thunderous voice is heard exactly seven times in our psalm, seven being the number of fullness and perfection. These seven thunders of God represent the summation of unspeakable mysteries heard by the Apostle John: "I saw still another mighty angel coming down from heaven, clothed with a cloud . . . and [he] cried with a loud voice, as when a lion roars. When he cried out, seven thunders uttered their voices. Now when the seven thunders uttered their voices, I was about to write; but I heard a voice from heaven saying to me, 'Seal up the things which the seven thunders uttered, and do not write them'" (Rev. 10:1–4). Such too was the awesome experience of the Apostle Paul when he "was caught up into Paradise and heard inexpressible words, which it is not lawful for a man to utter" (2 Cor. 12:4).

If most of this psalm is rather loud and active, however, its ending is decidedly peaceful, for it closes with God serene upon His throne, reigning eternally over His Church: "The Lord puts away the storm (*kataklysmon*, "cataclysm," in the Greek); the Lord thrones as king forever. The Lord will give strength to His people; the Lord will bless His people in peace." This people blessed with strength and peace at the ending of the psalm are those very "sons of God" summoned to worship Him back at its beginning. The thunderstorm now come to an end, there remains in the temple of the cedar forest only the everlasting reign of the heavenly throne.

PSALM 29 (30)

I WILL EXTOL YOU, O LORD

Psalm 29 (Hebrew 30) bears a curious title that tells us something interesting of this psalm's use in ancient Judaism: "A Psalm of David. A Song at the dedication of the House of David."

First, it is ascribed to King David, nor is it difficult to think of him praying this psalm of thanksgiving for the Lord's deliverance. After all, David came to the throne of Israel after years of oppression and exile under Saul, and these are the sentiments we would expect on his being delivered from those hard times.

Second, however, besides its individual and personal use in the case of David, this psalm was later sung as part of a communal, liturgical festival celebrated every year—the Dedication (*Hanukkah*) of the temple. This was a winter feast (cf. John 10:22) dating from 165 B.C., and Jews around the world continue to celebrate it even today, long after their temple has disappeared from history.

This twofold historical use of our psalm already suggests more than one layer of meaning. First, there is the remembrance of David's years of oppression and exile, followed by a final deliverance: "I will extol you, O Lord, for You have lifted me up, and have not let my foes rejoice over me."

But the second half of the title, which tells us of its use at the feast of Hanukkah, indicates its communal use. David's personal sentiments of gratitude and praise to the redeeming God became incorporated into Israel's restoration to her temple after years of oppression and strife. This history is narrated in chapters 1—4 of 1 Maccabees. When Antiochus Epiphanes IV came to the throne of Syria in September of 175 B.C., it was the beginning of very hard times for the Chosen People. Their oppression by this ruthless overlord included even the desecration of the temple. At the end of this decade of terror (175–165), when Judas Maccabaeus rededicated the temple at Jerusalem, Israel felt it could now, with unburdened heart, make its own the ancient sentiments of David: "I will extol you, O Lord, for You have lifted me up, and have not let my foes rejoice over me."

But both David and the temple were "types" of Him who was to come, and the deeper, truer voice in this psalm is Christ our Lord on the day of the Resurrection: "O Lord, you have brought my soul up from the grave; You have kept me alive, that I should not go down into the abyss." The time of suffering was followed by the morning of the paschal deliverance: "For His anger is but for a moment, His favor is for life." The dark hour of the Passion (cf. John 13:30) gave way to the dawn of victory.

In the Garden, on the night in which He was betrayed, the Lord had prayed for this deliverance: "You hid Your face, and I was troubled. . . . I cried to You, O Lord; and to the Lord I made supplication: 'What profit is there in my blood, when I go down into the pit? Will the dust praise You? Will it declare Your truth? Hear, O Lord, and have mercy on me; Lord, be my helper'."

The New Testament describes that Garden prayer of the Lord "who, in the days of His flesh, when He had offered up prayers and supplications, with vehement cries and tears to Him who was able to save Him from death, *and was heard* because of His godly fear" (Heb. 5:7). And on the dawning of the day of Easter victory, our psalm refers back to God's *hearing* of that vehement prayer of tears: "Weeping may endure for a night, but joy comes in the morning. . . . You have turned for me my mourning into dancing; You have put off my sackcloth and clothed me with gladness."

Christ is the true David, the new Israel's sweet Psalmist, our songmaster in the eternal praise of God: "Sing praises to the Lord, you saints of His, and give thanks to the remembrance of His holy name. . . . To the end that my glory may sing praise to You and not be silent. O Lord, my God, I will give thanks to you forever."

Old Israel's winter Feast of Dedication (*Hanukkah*) is now the new Israel's spring feast of Pascha, for Christ is the true Temple, of which St. John wrote: "But I saw no temple in [heaven], for the Lord God Almighty and the Lamb are its temple" (Rev. 21:22). When the Lord told His enemies: "Destroy this temple, and in three days I will raise it up," they misunderstood him, not aware that "He was speaking of the temple of His body. Therefore, when He had *risen from the dead*, His disciples remembered that He had said this to them" (John 2:19–22).

For this reason, following an ancient custom of the Church (as, for example, in the Rule of Saint Benedict), Psalm 29 is most appropriately prayed on Sunday, the day of the Lord's Resurrection, the day of the vindication of the new David and the consecration of the true Temple.

PSALM 30 (31)

IN YOU, O LORD, I PUT MY TRUST

The correct sense of Psalm 30 (Hebrew 31) is indicated in verse 5: "Into Your hand I commend my spirit." This verse, according to Luke 23:46, was the final prayer of our Lord from the Cross, and I take it to indicate the proper "voice" of this whole psalm. It is the prayer of "Jesus, the author and finisher of our faith, who for the joy that was set before Him endured the cross, despising the shame" (Heb. 12:2), speaking to His Father in the context of His sufferings and death. This psalm is part of His prayer of faith.

In making this psalm our own, we Christians are subsumed into the voice and prayer of Christ. We partake of His own relationship to the Father. No one, after all, knows the Father except the Son and the one "to whom the Son wills to reveal Him" (Matt. 11:27). Our only access to God is through Christ and the mediation of His atoning blood. Our incorporation into Christ is the foundation of all our prayer. Only in Christ do we call God our Father. The only prayer that passes beyond the veil, to His very throne, is prayer saturated with the redeeming blood of Christ. This is the prayer that cries out more eloquently than the blood of Abel.

In this psalm, then, the voice of Christ becomes our own voice: "In You, O Lord, I put my trust, let me never be put to shame. Deliver me in Your righteousness. . . . You have redeemed me, Lord God of truth. . . . But I trust in the Lord. I will be glad and rejoice in Your mercy. . . . But as for me, I trust in You, O Lord; I say 'You are my God.' . . . Oh, how great is Your goodness, which You have laid up for those who fear You, which You have prepared for those who trust in You." The righteousness of God is our salvation in Christ, "whom God set forth as a propitiation by His blood, through faith, to demonstrate His righteousness" (Rom. 3:25). Likewise, this trust in God is the source of our sanctification, as in the words of the standard Orthodox prayer: "O God . . . who sanctify those who put their trust in You."

This committing of our souls to God in loving trust is not just one of the various things we do as Christians; it is the essential feature of our life in Christ: "Therefore let those who suffer according to the will of God commit their souls to Him in doing good, as to a faithful Creator" (1 Pet. 4:19).

In this psalm we enter into the sentiments and thoughts of Jesus in His sufferings. We see the Passion "from the inside," as it were. There is the plot, recorded in the Gospels, to take His life (cf. Mark 3:6; 14:1): "Pull me out of the net that they have secretly laid for me. . . . Fear is on every side; while they take counsel together against me, they scheme to take away my life." There are the false witnesses rising against Him (cf. Mark 14:55–59): "Let the lying lips be put to silence, which speak insolent things proudly and contemptuously against the righteous." We learn of the flight of His friends and the mockery of His enemies (cf. Mark 14:50; 15:29–32): "I am a reproach among all my enemies, but especially among my neighbors, and am repulsive to my acquaintances; those who see me outside flee from me. I am forgotten like a dead man, out of mind." There is, moreover, that awesome mystery by which God "made Him who knew no sin to be sin for us, that we might become the righteousness of God in Him" (2 Cor. 5:21), "so the Scripture was fulfilled which says, 'And He was numbered with the transgressors'" (Mark 15:28): "For my life is spent with grief, and my years with sighing; my strength fails because of my iniquity, and my bones waste away."

The reason that the voice of Christ in His Passion must become our own voice is that His Passion itself provides the pattern for our own lives: "But beware of men, for they will deliver you up to councils and scourge you in their synagogues" (Matt. 10:17). "Then they will deliver you up to tribulation and kill you, and you will be hated by all nations for My name's sake" (24:9). We are to be baptized with His baptism; the bitter cup that He drinks we too are to taste in our own souls. The prayer of His Passion becomes our own, because "all who desire to live godly in Christ Jesus will suffer persecution" (2 Tim. 3:12).

Throughout this psalm there is also an ongoing changing of tenses, back and forth between past and future. We have been redeemed, but we still pray for our final deliverance. Even as we taste the coming enjoyment of God's eternal presence, hope's struggle in this world goes on: "For we were saved in this hope, but hope that is seen is not hope" (Rom. 8:24).

PSALM 31 (32)

Psalm 31 (Hebrew 32) is the second of the traditional "penitential psalms," which express the themes of sin, repentance, mercy and forgiveness.

The correct interpretation of certain psalms comes more readily than others, and the task is rendered easier still if a psalm's meaning has already been made plain in the New Testament. The New Testament is, after all, the key to the full (that is to say, Christian) understanding of the Old. When the New Testament tells us the meaning of some passage in the Old Testament, then the matter of authentic interpretation, for us Christians, is settled.

Such is the case with Psalm 31, which begins: "Blessed is he whose transgression is forgiven, whose sin is covered. Blessed is the man to whom the Lord does not impute iniquity." Saint Paul explicitly quotes these lines near the beginning of Romans 4 to illustrate "the blessedness of the man to whom God imputes righteousness apart from works" (v. 6). The apostle's thesis here, as in Romans generally, is that we believers are not justified before God by our own merits, by the effort of our "works," by a correct and meticulous observance of the Mosaic Law, but by receiving, in faith, God's gracious justification of us for the sake of Christ our Redeemer. Psalm 31, then, is the prayer of those who, standing at the foot of the Cross and forswearing all righteousness of their own, commit their lives and entrust their destinies entirely to God's forgiving mercy richly and abundantly poured out in the saving, sacrificial blood of His Son, because "God was in Christ reconciling the world to Himself, not imputing their trespasses to them" (2 Cor. 5:19).

Such is the key to the proper understanding of Psalm 31; such is the correct context for praying the rest of the psalm: "I acknowledge my sin to You, and my iniquity I have not hidden. I said: 'I will confess my transgressions to the Lord,' and You forgave the iniquity of my sin."

Our justification by God is no contrivance, no legal fiction. It truly renders us holy, even glorious, in His sight: "whom he justified, these He also glorified" (Rom. 8:30). Thus, Psalm 31 speaks of the justified as "blessed," "godly," "righteous," and "upright in heart."

This forgiveness of God has ongoing implications for how we are to live. Inasmuch as we have been "bought at a price" (1 Cor. 6:20), we may no longer live as though we belonged to ourselves: "Do you not know that . . . you are not your own?" (6:19); "He died for all, that those who live should live no longer for themselves, but for Him who died for them and rose again" (2 Cor. 5:15).

Those who are justified in Christ will live quite differently, for Christ is our Lord and Teacher as well as our Savior: "God did not call us to uncleanness, but in holiness" (1 Thess. 4:7). Thus this psalm continues: "I will instruct you and teach you in the way you should go; I will guide you with My eye." How we walk in Christ is of critical importance. We are not to take this responsibility lightly, says Psalm 31: "Be not like the horse or like the mule, which have no understanding, which must be harnessed with bit and bridle, else they will not come near you."

Above all, the forgiveness that God grants us for Christ's sake is the source of our ongoing confidence, for this same God will never abandon us: "He who did not spare His own Son, but delivered Him up for us all, how shall He not with Him also freely give us all things?" (Rom. 8:32). Our psalm thus speaks of the constant refuge we have in this God of mercy, no matter the trials that face us: "For this cause everyone who is godly shall pray to You in a time when You may be found; surely in a flood of great waters they shall not come near him. You are my hiding place; You shall preserve me from trouble; You shall surround me with songs of deliverance. . . . Many sorrows shall be to the wicked; but he who trusts in the Lord, mercy shall surround him."

This psalm is likewise a call to gladness. Joy is not just an option for the Christian; it is an imperative. As well as a gift of God, joy is a sentiment that the believer is *commanded* to engage. From the bleakness of his prison cell Paul sent forth this order: "Rejoice in the Lord always. Again I will say, rejoice!" (Phil. 4:4). Thus our psalm, a canticle celebrating the divine forgiveness of our sins, closes on the theme of godly exultation: "Be glad in the Lord and rejoice, you righteous; and shout for joy, all you upright in heart!"

PSALM 32 (33)

Psalm 32 (Hebrew 33) begins exactly where the last verse of the previous psalm left off, with a summons to the righteous to sing with joy the praises of God: "Rejoice in the Lord, O you righteous! For praise from the upright is beautiful. Praise the Lord with the harp. Make melody to Him with an instrument of ten strings. Sing to Him a new song. Play skillfully with a shout of joy."

The present psalm may thus be read as a sort of continuation of the previous psalm. Even though they are distinct and individual poems, the sense of continuity between them is so pronounced that in some manuscripts they form a literary unity (which would also explain why, in the Hebrew text, this psalm has no title). Whatever may be said from a literary perspective, however, the two psalms are certainly joined from a theological viewpoint; the proper praise of God has to do with the forgiveness of our sins and the renewal of our life by divine grace.

Now then, for the first time, the Book of Psalms uses an important expression—"new song," *shir chadash*—which will later appear four more times in the Psalter and once in Isaiah: "Sing to Him a *new song*" (see Psalms 95:1; 97:1; 143:9; 149:1; Is. 42:10). The praise of the righteous, of the just man to whom the Lord imputes no guilt and in whose mouth is no deceit, is characterized by a particular kind of newness, of renewal, of new life, inasmuch as "He who sat on the throne said, 'Behold, I make all things new'" (Rev. 21:5). The song of the believers is always a new song, because it springs from an inner divine font. It is the song of those who are born again in Christ and therefore "walk in newness of life" (Rom. 6:4). The song of the Lord's redeemed is a new song, for they adhere to the new covenant in Christ's blood and "serve in the newness of the Spirit" (Rom. 7:6).

All Christian praise of God is a participation in the liturgy of heaven where the saints gather in glory about the Lamb in the presence of the Throne. According to Revelation 5:9, our "new song" has to do with the opening of the seals of the great scroll by the Lamb who gave His life for our redemption: "You are worthy to take the scroll, / And to open its seals; / For You were slain, / And have redeemed us to God by Your blood." The new song is for those who have been made "kings and priests to our God" (5:10). The new song is "the song of the Lamb" (15:3). The new song, according to Revelation 14:1–3, is sung by the redeemed as they gather about the Lamb on Mount Zion. This is the folk of whom our psalm says: "Blessed is the nation whose God is the Lord, the people He has chosen as His own inheritance."

Therefore, when the present psalm summons us to the "new" praise of God, it is to a newness that will never grow old. Indeed, it will grow ever newer as, day by day, we "are being transformed into the same image from glory to glory" (2 Cor. 3:18), and our "youth is renewed like the eagle's" (Psalm 102:5).

The call to God's praise in Psalm 32 looks explicitly to the absolute fidelity of His word and work: "For the word of the Lord is right, and all His work is done in truth." How mighty is God's word? "By the word of the Lord, the heavens were made. And all the host of them by the breath of His mouth. . . For He spoke, and it was done; He commanded, and it stood fast."

Throughout this psalm there is a sustained contrast between the reliability of the Lord and the unreliability of everything purely human: "The Lord brings the counsel of the nations to nothing; he makes the plans of the peoples of no effect." In contrast, "the counsel of the Lord stands forever, the plans of His heart to all generations." This "counsel of the Lord," these "plans of His heart," are the contents of that great and mysterious scroll opened by the Lamb who was slain. This is "the mystery of Christ" (Eph. 3:4), "the mystery of His will, according to His good pleasure which He purposed in Himself" (1:9). By divine grace we redeemed share in "the fellowship of the mystery" (3:9).

Thus, there is also a contrast between two kinds of hope, a deceptive confidence (*sheqer*) in man or a lasting trust (*yachal*) in God: "No king is saved by the multitude of an army. A mighty man is not delivered by great strength. A horse is a vain hope (*sheqer*) for safety; neither shall it deliver any by its great strength." By way of contrast, "the eye of the Lord is on those who fear Him, on those who hope (*lamyachlim*) in His mercy. . . . Our soul waits for the Lord; He is our help and our shield. For our heart shall rejoice in Him, because we have trusted in His holy name. Let Your mercy, O Lord, be upon us, just as we hope (*yichalnu*) in You."

PSALM 33 (34)

I WILL BLESS THE LORD AT ALL TIMES

⤫

Summarizing an entire Wisdom theme of Holy Scripture with a single question, Psalm 33 (Hebrew 34) asks: "Who is the man who desires life, and loves many days, that he may see good?" At first the question may appear merely rhetorical. After all, doesn't everyone desire life? Would anyone intentionally choose or prefer death over life?

Oh? Really? The Bible is not so confident on this point. Deuteronomy distinguishes a true choice between life and death. It really is a matter of choosing, and some people do, in fact, prefer death over life (Deut. 30:19). That person shows little familiarity with history, or even his own soul, who would deny this deep, inveterate death-wish at work in the human heart. Our psalm's question, then, is well directed; in very truth, just who *is* the man who desires life?

By "life" we mean, of course, much more than material, animal survival, for man does not "live" by bread alone. True human life is a far more ample thing, a matter of the soul's relationship to God; true life involves living in a particular way. The psalmist goes on, then, to answer his own question: "Keep your tongue from evil, and your lips from speaking deceit. Depart from evil and do good; seek peace and pursue it."

Our choices really do count in the sight of God. Even though He causes His rain to fall on both the just and the unjust, it would be a serious mistake to suppose that God has no regard for the difference between a just and an unjust man. God actively resists the proud man and gives His grace to the humble (Prov. 3:34; James 4:6). God really does discriminate, and our psalmist elaborates the consequences of this discrimination: "The eyes of the Lord are on the righteous, and His ears are open to their cry. The face of the Lord is against those who do evil, to cut off the remembrance of them from the earth."

These verses of Psalm 33 are later paraphrased in 1 Peter 3:10–12—"He who would love life / And see good days, / Let him refrain his tongue from evil, /And his lips from speaking deceit. / Let him turn away from evil and do good; / Let him seek peace and pursue it. / For the eyes of the Lord are on the righteous, / And His ears are open to their prayers; / But the face of the Lord is against those who do evil." For the Apostle Peter, these lines of our psalm provide an outline for how the Christian is to live. He comments on them: "Finally, all of you be of one mind, having compassion for one another; love as brothers, be tenderhearted, be courteous; not returning evil for evil or reviling for reviling, but on the contrary blessing, knowing that you were called to this, that you may inherit a blessing" (3:8, 9).

Choosing life over death clearly has a great deal to do with the discipline of one's mouth: "*Keep* your tongue . . . and your lips," says the psalmist, for "if anyone does not stumble in word, he is a perfect man" (James 3:2). Seeking and pursuing peace is nine-tenths a matter of keeping bad things out of one's mouth.

And how does one accomplish this difficult vigilance? By constantly, over and over, putting the words of prayer into his mouth, and this was how the psalm began: "I will bless the Lord at all times; His praise shall continually be in my mouth." This ceaseless prayer, manifestly a standard teaching of the New Testament, is also a theme in our psalm: "This poor man cried out, and the Lord heard him. . . . The righteous cry out, and the Lord hears."

This life of constant, sustained calling on God involves also a certain cultivation of "taste" that leads to vision: "Oh, taste and see that the Lord is good." Once again, it is 1 Peter that comments on our psalm by contrasting the sins of the tongue with the godly discipline of the Christian mouth: "Therefore, laying aside all malice, all deceit, hypocrisy, envy, and all evil speaking, as newborn babes, desire the pure milk of the word, that you may grow thereby, if indeed you have tasted that the Lord is gracious" (2:1–3; see also Heb. 6:5).

Finally, in Psalm 33 the context for this continual effort of prayer is the experience of various trials suffered in the service of God. The dominant sentiment is one of trust in God: "I sought the Lord, and He heard me, and delivered me from all my fears. . . . The young lions lack and suffer hunger; but those who seek the Lord shall not lack any good thing. . . . Many are the afflictions of the righteous, but the Lord delivers him out of them all. He guards all their bones; not one of them is broken. . . . The Lord redeems the soul of His servants, and none of them who trust in Him shall be condemned."

PSALM 34 (35)

JUDGE THOSE WHO HARM ME, O LORD

❧

The meaning of Psalm 34 (Hebrew 35) is not difficult to discern, because it is one of those psalms for which the New Testament explicitly provides the proper "voice" and setting. The voice speaking in Psalm 34 is the voice of our Lord Jesus Christ Himself, and the psalm's theological context is the drama of His Passion and death.

Among the many truths that the Lord taught the fledgling Church on the night of His betrayal was the very sobering truth that believers would suffer persecution just as He did: "If the world hates you, you know that it hated Me before it hated you" (John 15:18). Thus began that night's prediction of the coming sufferings of the Church for His sake. The Lord went on to say: "If they persecuted Me, they will also persecute you" (15:20).

The Passion of the Lord and the subsequent suffering of His Church are not mere historical phenomena, He told us; they are rooted, rather, in a point of theology—man's deliberate ignorance of, even his resolved hatred of, God: "But all these things they will do to you for My name's sake, because they do not know Him who sent Me. . . . He who hates Me hates My Father also. . . . but now they have seen and also hated both Me and My Father" (John 15:21, 23, 24).

At this place in His discourse our Lord explicitly appealed to our psalm, Psalm 34, to show that this hatred and this persecution by the world are a realization of prophecy: "But this happened that the word might be fulfilled which is written in their law, 'They hated Me without a cause'" (15:25). Thus Jesus Himself gave us His own interpretation of our psalm. Indeed, He here indicated the proper meaning of several psalms, because the reference to His being "hated without cause" appears two other times in the Psalter (68:4; 108:4).

These, then, are psalms in which the praying voice is that of Christ Himself, and, by reason of her sharing in the sufferings of Christ, the Church prays these psalms in His Person. Psalm 34 is a prayer of the Lord's Passion and death, and it is therefore the prayer of anyone who in truth can say: "Yet indeed I also count all things loss for the excellence of the knowledge of Christ Jesus my Lord, for whom I have suffered the loss of all things, and count them as rubbish, that I may gain Christ and be found in Him, not having my own righteousness, which is from the law, but that which is through faith in Christ, the righteousness which is from God by faith: that I may know Him and the power of His resurrection, and the fellowship of His sufferings, being conformed to His death, if, by any means, I may attain to the resurrection from the dead" (Phil. 3:8–11).

Psalm 34, a prayer descriptive of this spiritual struggle, is much concerned that the ignorance and hatred of God not ultimately prevail. In line after line it is a prayer for vindication: "Let them be put to shame and dishonor who seek after my life! Let them be turned back and confounded who devise evil against me!" In all such lines it is important to remember that it is the voice of Christ. It is Christ who prays, "Let them be like chaff before the wind, with the angel of the Lord driving them on! Let their way be dark and slippery, with the angel of the Lord pursuing them!" The prayer of Christ here is a battle prayer, for He wages war on the forces of sin, darkness, and destruction: "Let ruin come upon them unawares."

The vindication sought by this psalm is not some sort of petty revenge. This is the prayer of Christ doing battle with the forces of sin and death, looking forward to the hour of His victory, when His very body, brought down to the grave, will rise again in the paschal victory: "And my soul shall be joyful in the Lord; it shall rejoice in His salvation. All my bones shall say, 'Lord, who is like You, delivering the poor from him who is too strong for him.'"

Salvation, as understood by Christians, is attained by God's vindication of His own righteousness in the Resurrection of Christ, "who was delivered up because of our offenses, and was raised because of our justification" (Rom. 4:25). This truth is the key to our psalm. It is the prayer of those, in Christ, still struggling as they fill up in their flesh what is lacking in the afflictions of Christ (Col. 1:24). In Christ theirs is this prayer for victory over sinful ignorance, hatred, and death: "Do not keep silence. O Lord, do not be far from me. Stir up Yourself, and awake to my vindication, to my cause, my God and my Lord. . . . And my tongue shall speak of Your righteousness and of Your praise all the day long."

PSALM 35 (36)

PLANNING SIN, THE LAWLESS MAN

Psalm 35 (Hebrew 36) is a meditative prayer contrasting man's wickedness with the mercy of God.

Though the Hebrew text of the opening is rather obscure and has probably suffered in transmission, the general sense is clear enough. The Greek text reads: "Planning sin, the lawless man converses within himself; there is no fear of God before his eyes."

Our psalm thus commences with the sinner's perverse delight in evil— those things traditionally called "the devices and desires of our own hearts." Man does not simply fall into evil. His perversity is a veritable project of his mind, the object of an intentional strategy. He can be said to lie awake at night figuring out new ways to work evil: "He devises wickedness on his bed."

Using seven expressions, the biblical number of totality, our text describes this man: (1) "There is no fear of God before his eyes;" (2) "He deceives himself;" (3) "The words of his mouth are wickedness and deceit;" (4) "He has ceased to be wise and to do good;" (5) "He devises wickedness on his bed;" (6) "He sets himself on a way that is not good;" (7) "He does not abhor evil."

The biblical view of sin includes, not just human weakness, but human rebellion. The one here called the "lawless man" (*paranomos*) is in revolt against God. He has willfully "deceived" himself (*edolosen*) that his "lawlessness (*anomia*) will not be found out and hated." This free agent has declared his moral independence.

The source of the problem is what the inveterate, unrepentant sinner does not have: the fear of God. The fear of the Lord, which a later psalm calls "the beginning of wisdom," is not part of his composition.

And just who is included here? Well, in some measure, all of us, says the Apostle Paul. Changing its reference to the plural, he quotes this line from our psalm in Romans 3:18: "There is no fear of God before their eyes." In the context of Romans 3, Saint Paul is saying that this rebelliousness is part of each of us; no one is exempt: "For there is no difference; for all have sinned and fall short of the glory of God" (3:22, 23). This passage stands as a warning to those of us disposed to regard our failings as merely symptoms of weakness. The Apostle is telling us, on the contrary, that human sinfulness is more profoundly rooted in the substance of our moral composition. More deeply than it is comfortable to think, we are all rebels against God. The contrast in Romans 3 is not between human evil and human goodness, but between human evil and divine mercy.

This is also true of Psalm 35. Here, the characteristics of the lawless man are contrasted, not with those of a just man, but with the boundless divine mercy (Hebrew *hesed*, Greek *eleos*): "Your mercy, O Lord, is in the heavens. . . . How precious is Your mercy, O God. . . . Oh, continue Your mercy to those who know You." This is not a psalm about human morality, but about the metaphysics of mercy.

The qualities of divine mercy in this psalm are indicated by the various words with which it is set in parallel—faithfulness, righteousness, judgments: "Your faithfulness reaches to the clouds. Your righteousness is like the great mountains; Your judgments are a great deep." Gazing out on the vast expanse of sky, mountains and sea, the psalmist contemplates the omnidimensional mercy of God: "that you, being rooted and grounded in love, may be able to comprehend with all the saints what is the width and length and depth and height—to know the love of Christ which passes knowledge; that you may be filled with all the fullness of God" (Eph. 3:17–19).

When we pray this psalm, therefore, we do not need to go outside of our own souls to discover the identity of the "lawless man," before whose eyes "there is no fear of God." That lawlessness is a deep dimension of ourselves that is recalcitrant to God's infinite mercy and the righteousness of His judgments. This lawless man lives in his own little world, its chief characteristic being that it is so terribly, so pitifully little.

The sole cure for this rebellion in our hearts is the divine gift of mercy. Only God can heal our blindness: "For with You is the fountain of life; in Your light we see light." (Traditionally this psalm has been assigned for Matins, as the dawn breaks on Monday mornings.) Knowing that all is His gift, we ask only the maintenance of God's mercy: "Oh, continue Your mercy to those who know You, and Your righteousness to the upright in heart."

PSALM 36 (37)

If we think of prayer as speaking to God, Psalm 36 (Hebrew 37) appears at first to challenge the very notion of the psalms as prayers, inasmuch as not a single word of it is explicitly addressed to God. It speaks about God, of course, but never to Him, at least not overtly.

Psalm 36 is also strangely constructed, even if the construction is rather simple. It is one of those twelve psalms built on what is known as an alphabetic acrostic pattern—that is to say: starting with the first letter of the Hebrew alphabet, *aleph,* each new line (in this case, every other line) of the psalm begins with the next successive letter of the alphabet. Thus, if one looks for some sort of logical or thematic progression in the course of the psalm, he may be mightily disappointed. The arrangement of the psalm's ideas is determined only by something so artificial and arbitrary as the sequence of the alphabet, so the meditation does not really progress. It is, on the other hand, insistent and repetitive.

It is obvious at once that Psalm 36 has close ties to the Bible's Wisdom tradition. If it were not part of the Psalter, we would expect to find it in Proverbs or one of the other Wisdom books. It appears to be a kind of discourse given by a parent to a child, or a wise man to a disciple. It is full of sound and godly counsel: "Fret not thyself because of evildoers . . . Trust in the Lord and do good . . . Cease from anger and forsake wrath . . . Wait on the Lord and keep His way," and so forth. Such admonitions, along with the psalm's allied warnings and promises, are stock material of the Wisdom literature.

So how does one pray such a psalm? To begin with, by respecting its tone, which is one of admonition, warning, and promise. Surely prayer is talking to God, but it also involves listening to God, and this is a psalm in which one will do more listening than talking. It is a psalm in which the believer prays by placing his heart open and receptive to God's word of admonition, warning, and promise.

One may likewise think of Psalm 36 as the soul speaking to itself: "Rest in the Lord, and wait patiently for Him . . . But the meek shall inherit the earth . . . The little that the righteous has is better than the riches of many wicked . . . The Lord knows the days of the upright . . . The Law of his God is in his heart," and so on. The human soul, after all, is not of simple construction. The great thinkers who have examined the soul over many centuries seem all to agree that it is composed of parts, and sometimes these parts are at odds one with another. This mixture of conflicting experiences in the soul leads one to utter such petitions as, "Lord, I believe. Help my unbelief." It is one part of the soul praying for the other.

In this psalm, one part of the soul admonishes the other, reminds the other, cautions the other, encourages the other. And this inner conversation of the human spirit all takes place in the sight of God, the Giver of wisdom.

This inner discussion is rendered necessary because of frequent temptations to discouragement. As far as empirical evidence bears witness, the wicked do seem, on many occasions, to be better off than the just. By the standards of this world, they prosper.

Our psalm is at pains to insist, however, that this prosperity is only apparent, in the sense that it will certainly be short-lived. As regards the workers of iniquity, "they shall soon be cut down like the grass, and wither as the green herb . . . For evildoers shall be cut off . . . For yet a little while, and the wicked shall not be . . . For the arms of the wicked shall be broken . . . The transgressors shall be cut off together."

The suffering lot of the just man is likewise temporary and of brief duration. He need only wait on the Lord in patience and trust: "Delight yourself also in the Lord, and He will give thee the desires of thy heart. Commit your way unto the Lord, and trust in Him, and He shall bring it to pass . . . But the salvation of the righteous is of the Lord; He is their strength in the time of trouble. And the Lord will help them and deliver them; He will deliver them from the wicked and save them, because they trust in Him."

This, then, is a psalm of faith and confidence in God, without which there is no Christian prayer. It is also faith and hope under fire, exposed to struggle and the endurance that calls for patience. After all, "faith is the substance of things hoped for" (Heb. 11:1), and "We were saved in this hope, but hope that is seen is not hope . . . But if we hope for what we do not see, we eagerly wait for it with perseverance" (Rom. 8:24, 25). Our psalm is a meditative lesson on not being deceived by appearances, and a summons to wait patiently for God's deliverance.

PSALM 37 (38)

LORD, REBUKE ME NOT IN YOUR WRATH

With its heavy emphasis on sin and suffering, Psalm 37 (Hebrew 38) is one of the rougher parts of the Psalter, and its thematic conjunction of sin and suffering is also the manifest key to its meaning.

Suffering and death enter the world with sin. To humanity's first sinners the Lord said: "I will greatly multiply your sorrow," and "Cursed is the ground for your sake" (Gen. 3:16, 17). So close is the Bible's joining of suffering to sin that some biblical characters (such as Job's friends and the questioning disciples in John 9:2) entertained the erroneous notion that each instance of suffering was brought about by certain specific sins.

Like Psalm 6, the present psalm commences with a prayer for deliverance from divine anger: "O Lord, do not rebuke me in Your wrath, nor chasten me in Your hot displeasure." Already the poet feels overwhelming pain which he describes, whether literally or by way of metaphor, in the most physical terms: "Your arrows [thunder bolts?] pierce me deeply, and Your hand presses me down." What he suffers comes from sin and the response of the divine wrath, from which he begs to be delivered: "There is no soundness in my flesh, because of Your anger, nor any health in my bones because of my sin." The equation: sin = wrath of God.

Whether physical, emotional, mental, or spiritual—or all of them together—what we suffer in this life are the incursions of death, and death is simply sin becoming incarnate and dwelling among us, for "through one man sin entered the world, and death through sin, and thus death spread to all men, because all sinned" (Rom. 5:12).

Such is the essential conviction of our prayer in this psalm: "For my iniquities are gone over my head; like a heavy burden they are too heavy for me. My wounds are foul and festering because of my folly."

The proper response to sin and suffering? Confession of sins and the sustained cultivation of repentance, for "if we say that we have no sin, we deceive ourselves, and the truth is not in us" (1 John 1:8). Thus we pray in this psalm: "For I am ready to fall, and my sorrow is continually (*tamid*) before me. For I will declare my iniquity; I will be in anguish over my sin." Notwithstanding a widespread heresy that says otherwise, repentance (*metanoia*) is not something done once, and all finished; according to one of the last petitions of the litany, it is something to be perfected (*ektelesai*) until the end of our lives. This sorrow for sin, says our psalm, is continual, ongoing (*tamid*). Every suffering we are given in this life is a renewed call to repentance. Every pain is, as it were, the accusing finger of Nathan: "You are the man" (2 Sam. 12:7).

Psalm 37 is not the happiest of psalms, but it is exceedingly salubrious to the spirit. If its message can be summed up in one line, that line may well be David's response to Nathan: "I have sinned against the Lord." These words make all the difference, because, as another psalm insists, "a broken and contrite heart, O God, You will not despise." Over and over the tax collector "beat his breast, saying, 'God, be merciful to me a sinner!'" (Luke 18:13).

Sin is also the great solvent of our relationships to one another. As is clear in the accounts of the first sins (Gen. 3:11–13; 4:12), sin means isolation and alienation. Sin separates us, not only from God, but also from one another. Our psalm speaks of this isolation: "My loved ones and my friends stand aloof from my plague. And my relatives stand afar off."

We are not talking about morbidity here. Contrition and sorrow in this psalm are accompanied by repeated sentiments of longing: "I groan because of the turmoil of my heart. Lord, all my desire is before You; and my sighing is not hidden from You. My heart pants, my strength fails me. . . . For in You, O Lord, I hope; You will hear, O Lord my God."

Finally, there are the enemies. As I have insisted all through these meditations, the demons are the only enemies of the man who correctly prays the Book of Psalms. Nowhere does Holy Scripture exhort us to forgive or pity the demons. They are the only true enemies that our prayer recognizes. Unlike human enemies who are to be prayed for, the demons are always to be prayed against. Our fight with them is unsleeping, as is their fight with us, plotting our ruin: "Those also who seek my life lay snares for me; those who seek my hurt speak of destruction, and plan deception all the day long."

PSALM 38 (39)

Not every day is Sunday, nor does even the holiest soul abide permanently on the mountain top. Rather our lives tend to be full of "weekdays," as we plod a humbler path down below, through the valleys, unable for a season to gain that greater overview of things that allows us to make better sense of them.

Prayer generally comes easier on Sundays, of course, and the sentiments of joy and rapture are almost natural on the mountain top. Who, indeed, would want to leave? "Lord, it is good that we are here. Let us make three tabernacles."

But we do leave, of course. A mountain without valleys is very difficult to picture, and a Sunday with no weekdays is simply not of this world.

It is imperative to rid ourselves, then, of the common notion that true worship must invariably be festive, and that notion certainly is common nowadays. Because Jesus our Lord has definitively triumphed over sin, suffering, and death, it is probably natural and certainly understandable that some Christians would reach the conclusion that sentiments of sadness, feelings of discouragement, despondency and dereliction have no proper place in Christian worship.

But who among us never sees a day when all is darkness? We struggle to hold such sentiments at bay, of course, and doubtless feel guilty that we have them, but can any of us claim fully to have purged our hearts of all despair? Are there no times when, if we gave voice to our sharpest impressions, we would not agree with the Buddha that our existence is ephemeral and impermanent (*anicca*) and our soul itself ultimately unreal (*anatta*) and destined to perish?

We wonder how we can, as Christians, express such non-Christian responses in our prayer, and perhaps we think it would manifest a lack of faith if we did so. Who are we, after all, to experience feelings of despair when Christ has conquered all evil? In consequence, such unredeemed feelings remain concealed in the caverns of the heart, not brought forth into the light, finding no portion in our prayer, assigned no part in the process of our salvation.

But does this need to be the case? Have we never considered that, in the Gospels of Matthew and Mark, the last recorded words of Jesus our Lord in His earthly life were a question and a cry? Or do we aspire to be more Christian than Christ?

If we do not venerate in the valleys—if we chant only on Sundays and on the mountain top—we will not be praying at all times, as Holy Scripture bids

75

us do. If we are to follow that injunction, then, it is important to learn the ways of workday prayer, worship down in the valleys. That is to say, we must find a prayer appropriate to those times when we do not enjoy the broad vista and brighter view. This is the reason that the Bible contains, not only the Song of Solomon, but also Ecclesiastes and the Book of Job.

This is also the reason that the Book of Psalms contains the likes of Psalm 38 (Hebrew 39). This is a valley supplication and one of the very few psalms ending on a tenebrous note: "Do not be silent at my tears; for I am a stranger with You, a sojourner as all my fathers were. Remove Your gaze from me, that I may regain strength, before I go away and am no more."

Yes, God permits us to say such things to Him, for these sentiments of profound despondency are also part of Sacred Scripture, inspired by the Holy Spirit. God would not have us hide from His gaze these dark places in the heart: "Certainly every man at his best state is but vapor. Surely every man walks about like a shadow [in the Hebrew, *kol hebel*, "all shadow"]; surely they busy themselves in vain . . . You make his beauty melt away like a moth; surely every man is vapor."

The psalmist himself is reluctant to say such things to God, afraid of sinning by doing so: "I will guard my ways, lest I sin with my tongue. I will restrain my mouth with a muzzle . . . I was mute with silence, I held my peace even from speaking good." But all this effort of restraint comes to nothing, for these sentiments only grow more fierce when thus confined: "And my sorrow was stirred up. My heart was hot within me; while I was musing, the fire burned. Then I spoke with my tongue."

"Hope that is seen is not hope," says St. Paul (Rom. 8:24), and here below, in the valley, on the workday, our prayer of hope must strive with other, darker voices rising from our hearts. But these honest voices too can be our prayer: "Lord, I believe; help my unbelief."

PSALM 39 (40)

The correct "voice" for Psalm 39 (Hebrew 40) is not in doubt. We know from Hebrews 10 that these are words springing from the heart of Christ our Lord and have reference to the sacrificial obedience of His Passion and death.

We may begin, then, by examining that interpretive context in Hebrews, which comes in the section where the author is contrasting the Sacrifice of the Cross with the many cultic oblations prescribed in the Old Testament. These prescriptions of the Mosaic Law, says Hebrews, possessed only "a shadow of the good things to come." Offered "continually year by year," they were not able to "make those who approach perfect" (10:1). That is to say, those sacrifices did not really take away sins, and their effectiveness depended entirely on the Sacrifice of the Cross, of which they were only a foreshadowing. Indeed, "it is not possible that the blood of bulls and goats could take away sins" (v. 4).

In support of this thesis, the author of Hebrews quotes our psalm: "Sacrifice and offering You did not desire / . . . In burnt offerings and sacrifices for sin / You had no pleasure" (vv. 5, 6). In fact, this theme appears rather often in the Old Testament itself. Isaiah, for example, and other prophets frequently attempted to disillusion those of their countrymen who imagined that the mere offering of cultic worship, with no faith, no obedience, no change of heart, could be acceptable to God.

The author of Hebrews, therefore, is simply drawing the proper theological conclusion when he writes: "And every priest stands ministering daily and offering repeatedly the same sacrifices, which can never take away sins" (v. 11). What God seeks, rather, is the perfect obedience of faith, and such an obedience means the total gift of self, not the mere sacrificial slaughter of some beast.

This obedience of Christ our Lord is a matter of considerable importance in the New Testament. He Himself declared that He came, not to seek His own will, but the will of the Father who sent Him (John 5:30). This doing of the Father's will had particular reference to His Passion, in which "He . . . became obedient to the point of death, even the death of the cross" (Phil. 2:8). This was the obedience manifested in our Lord's prayer at the very beginning of the Passion: "Take this cup away from Me; nevertheless, not what I will, but what You will" (Mark 14:36).

This spirit of obedience to God's will is likewise the essential atmosphere of Christian prayer. "Your will be done" is the spiritual center and major sentiment of that prayer that the Lord Himself taught us.

Christ's own obedience to God's will is also the key to the psalm here under discussion, and Hebrews goes on to quote the pertinent verses, referring them explicitly to the Incarnation and Sacrifice of Jesus the Lord: "Sacrifice and offering You did not desire, / But a body You have prepared for Me. / In burnt offerings and sacrifices for sin / You had no pleasure. / Then I said, 'Behold, I have come— / In the volume of the book it is written of Me— / To do Your will, O God'" (vv. 5–7).

The body "prepared" for Christ in the Incarnation became the instrument of His obedience to that "will" of God by which we are redeemed and rendered holy: "By that will we have been sanctified through the offering of the body of Jesus Christ once for all. . . . For by one offering He has perfected forever those who are being sanctified" (vv. 10, 14).

The various sacrifices of the Old Testament, which are spoken of from time to time throughout the Book of Psalms, have now found their perfection in the one self-offering of Jesus the Lord. Again the author of Hebrews comments: "Previously saying, 'Sacrifice and offering, burnt offerings, and offerings for sin You did not desire, nor had pleasure in them' (which are offered according to the law), then He said, 'Behold, I have come to do Your will, O God'" (vv. 8, 9).

The "He" of this psalm, then, according to the New Testament, is Christ the Lord. We pray it properly when we pray it as His own words to the Father. The "will" of God to which He was obedient was that "will" to which He referred when in the Garden He prayed: "Not my will, but Yours be done."

This self-oblation of our Lord's obedience to God is not simply a feature of this particular psalm; it is the interpretive door through which we pray all of the psalms. The "Your will be done" of the Lord's Prayer is likewise the summation of the entire Book of Psalms, and what ultimately makes Christian sense of the Psalter.

PSALM 40 (41)

BLESSED IS HE WHO CONSIDERS THE POOR

◌

In our consideration of the earthly life and work of Jesus, it is important not to separate into distinct categories the different components of the picture. It would be easy to think of each of the four Gospels as composed of two separable parts: (1) the earthly ministry of Jesus, with its teaching and miraculous healings; (2) the suffering and death of Jesus. Such a categorization would be easy, but it could also be inaccurate and misleading.

First, all of the Lord's earthly ministry is directed to, and preparatory for, the drama of His saving Passion. While this is clear in all four Gospels, it is probably most apparent in Mark, where the Lord very early refers to His coming death (2:20), and the plot of His enemies to kill Him follows almost immediately (3:6), providing the somber backdrop for the whole story.

Second, the compassion of our Lord throughout His earthly ministry, and most particularly His seeking out of sinners, is of whole cloth and single weave with the ensuing account of how He laid down His life to redeem sinners from their sins. The single theme in each Gospel is the redemptive mercy of Christ our Lord, whether exhibited in His teaching, or in His many healings, or in the shedding of His blood. It is all a single story.

By way of illustrating this unity of theme, we may observe how a single passage from Isaiah (53:4—"He Himself took our infirmities and bore our sicknesses" [LXX]) was interpreted by 1 Peter 2:24 to refer to the Lord's suffering on the Cross, and by Matthew 8:16, 17 to refer to the Lord's healing of the diseased and the driving out of demons. These are not separate nor separable things. The Lord's teaching and healings are not, as it were, "moral aspects" of His character, essentially unrelated to the Cross, but components of His one redemptive work, aspects of the single truth that "Jesus saves."

Psalm 40 (Hebrew 41), speaking of both aspects of the earthly life of Christ our Lord, likewise maintains their unity of theme. It begins with the Lord's compassion for the poor and sick: "Blessed is he who considers the poor; the Lord will deliver him in the time of trouble. The Lord will preserve him and keep him alive, and he will be blessed on the earth. You will not deliver him to the will of his enemies. The Lord will strengthen him on his bed of illness; You will sustain him on his sickbed." This is not simply a moral theme, as it were, but a matter of the divine salvation, for right away the psalm goes on to describe Christ's compassionate assumption of our sinful condition—the identification of the Sinless One with sinners: "I said: 'Lord, be merciful to me; heal my soul, for I have sinned against You.'" Here we have the voice of the one of whom St Paul said: "For He made Him who knew no sin to be sin for us, that we might become the righteousness of God in Him" (2 Cor. 5:21).

Christ's compassion for the poor and the infirm is not simply a moral quality of His character, so to speak. It is of a piece with that love that compelled Him to lay down His life for sinners, paying the price for their return to God. The voice of Psalm 40, then, is that of Christ our Lord, and its context is His saving Passion.

More specifically, this psalm's context is Christ's betrayal by Judas Iscariot. We know this because, on the very night of that betrayal, the Lord quoted this psalm with reference to it, saying that Judas's act of treachery happened "that the Scripture may be fulfilled, 'He who eats bread with Me has lifted up his heel against Me'" (John 13:18). (The Lord said this during the Last Supper, which thus seems to determine the "bread" in this psalm to be the Holy Eucharist.)

Other verses of the psalm go on to elaborate the setting of the Lord's Passion: "All who hate me whisper together against me; against me they devise my hurt." This "whispering together" (the very literal meaning of "con-spiracy") of the Lord's enemies is likewise recorded in the Gospels: "Then the Pharisees went out and immediately plotted with the Herodians against Him, how they might destroy Him" (Mark 3:6); "Then, from that day on, they plotted to put Him to death" (John 11:53). This psalm, then, narrates the prayer of Jesus in the setting of that unfolding drama of deceit and betrayal.

The psalm ends, however, on the note of His paschal triumph over death and the demons: "But You, O Lord, be merciful to me, and raise me up, that I may repay them. By this I know that You are well pleased with me, because my enemy does not triumph over me."

PSALM 41 (42)

AS THE DEER LONGS FOR THE WATER BROOKS

Showing a unified theme and sharing a common refrain, Psalms 41 & 42 (Hebrew 42 & 43) seem originally to have been a single psalm. This conjecture would explain also why Psalm 42 (43) has no title.

If such was the case, however, the two parts became divided very early (no later than the third century BC), because they stand as two different psalms in both the Hebrew and the Greek Bibles. This is also true of the liturgical traditions of the Church; moreover, in the Latin West these two psalms, never recited in sequence, were even assigned to two different days of the week. For all such reasons, they will be treated here as two psalms.

Psalm 41 is one of those psalms taking their rise from the grace-filled experience of the material creation. The poet is gazing at a formidable scene of rugged rock formations, with thundering cataracts of cold, clear water cascading down from pristine mountain springs and melting snow. He stands on the stony ascent of the Golan Heights, at the sources of the Jordan River, from which he looks up and sees nearby Mount Hermon, the loftiest peak of the region. No sound is heard but the loud pounding and roar of the rushing stream. Some deer come to drink from an eddying pool of the fresh water.

This stark, yet glorious scene before him becomes a sort of picture of the poet's very soul, simultaneously yearning and tumultuous, full of both dereliction and desire: "As the deer longs for the water brooks, so longs my soul for You, O God. My soul thirsts for God, the living God. When shall I come and appear before God? . . . O my God, my soul is cast down within me. Therefore, I think of You from the land of Jordan and Hermon. From this low summit, deep calls out to deep at the voice of Your waterfalls. All Your waves and Your billows have overwhelmed me."

God's roaring waterfalls, His overwhelming waves and billows, describe the infinite, frightful abyss of the longing that He evokes from the human spirit, the very depths of God calling out to the depths of the soul. The forlorn poet prays: "Why are you cast down, my soul? And so disquieted within me? Hope in God, for I shall yet praise Him, for my God is the salvation of my being."

From the depths of his dereliction in the belly of the whale Jonah prayed to God: "All Your billows and Your waves passed over me. / Then I said, 'I have been cast out of Your sight; / Yet I will look again toward Your holy temple.' /

81

. . . When my soul fainted within me, / I remembered the Lord; / And my prayer went up to You, / Into Your holy temple" (Jonah 2:3, 4, 7).

Likewise here in Psalm 41 our struggling poet, longing for God and deeply experiencing His apparent absence, recalls the joy of worshipping in His temple: "I remembered these things and poured out my soul within me—how I walked in the place of the marvelous tabernacle, even to the house of the Lord, with the voice of rejoicing and praise, the echo of festivity."

Though the soul longs for their return, the music of those happy days is for now but a distant memory. There sounds instead the incessant mockery of the unbelieving world that takes such longing as an illusion. The voice of a scornful and skeptical world taunts the God-afflicted soul: "My tears have become my bread day and night, while day by day they say to me: 'Where is your God?' . . . Within me is my prayer to the God of my life. I will say to God, 'You are my helper. Why are You hidden from me? Why do I go about in grief, while the enemy afflicts me?'"

What this psalm describes is a fairly common experience of the life in Christ. Our memory testifies to a sense of spiritual heights earlier attained, but now evidently lost to us. We recall "how things used to be" and sadly contrast them with our current trek through the lowlands. We find ourselves saying such things as, "I know a man in Christ who fourteen years ago . . . was caught up to the third heaven" (2 Cor. 12:2). Fourteen years ago, yes, but no third heaven for us now.

The message of this psalm is one of encouragement, an inner exhortation to trust the memory of earlier grace and to hope for its abundant return. Even if, like Jonah, our loss of the earlier heights is of our own fault and infidelity, God is yet merciful and can restore to us the joy of His salvation: "The Lord will command His mercy by day, and His song by night. . . . Hope in God, for I will yet praise Him, my God, the salvation of my being."

PSALM 42 (43)

Psalm 42 (Hebrew 43) was long used as a private preparatory prayer for the celebration of the Holy Eucharist, a usage easily explained by the line that reads: "I will go unto the altar (*thysiasterion*) of God." That devotional usage explains, in turn, how this psalm became part of "the prayers at the foot of the altar" in the Latin Mass, even until the 1960s. It still remains today an excellent prayer to be said before approaching the Blessed Sacrament of the Altar.

The attention of this psalm is directed to that altar of which Hebrews says: "*echomen thysiasterion*—we have an altar" (13:10). This altar is, first of all, the eucharistic table, whereon is laid the Lamb slain from the foundation of the world. To this eucharistic table St. Paul contrasted both ancient Israel's altar of sacrifice (1 Cor. 10:18) and the sacrificial altar of paganism, which he called "the table of demons" (10:20, 21). Ours is, rather, the altar at which we "proclaim the Lord's death till He comes" (11:26).

According to the Liturgy of St. John Chrysostom, however, this eucharistic table itself, on which "we perform the sacred Mystery of Your holy and immaculate Body and precious Blood," points to yet another altar far above itself: "Accept also the prayer of us sinners, and bear it to Your holy altar." We further pray that "the precious Gifts which have been spread forth and sanctified" may be received upon God's "holy, heavenly and ideal altar." The altar here on earth is linked to an altar in heaven, of which it is a type and symbol.

This is not an idea exclusively Eastern. The identical theology of the heavenly altar is likewise found in the ancient Latin Liturgy, where the priest prays God to "command these things [that is, the consecrated Gifts] to be carried up by the hands of Your holy angel to Your altar on high, in the sight of Your divine majesty."

This heavenly altar is found in both the Eastern and Western liturgical texts of the ancient Church because both are drawn from the same source: Holy Scripture. The heavenly altar is spoken of in the Book of Revelation, as the place where the prayers offered on earth are poured out with the incense in the sight of God (8:3, 4). This heavenly altar, too, is the sacred table to which we refer when we pray in our psalm: "I will go unto the altar of God." The definitive fulfillment of this prayer will be our participation in the worship that arises in the immediate presence of God's throne. All our worship on this earth is a preparation for the liturgy of heaven, because divine worship is the ultimate meaning of our human existence.

Meanwhile we pray for God's guidance that we may attain to that heavenly altar: "Send forth Your light and Your truth; they have guided me and brought me unto Your holy hill and unto Your tabernacles."

Both on earth and in heaven, the altar of God is surrounded by music. Indeed, in the Book of Revelation (5:8 [here with incense];14:2;15:2) the songs before the heavenly altar are said to be accompanied by the harp, and this harp of the heavenly worship is also spoken of here in our psalm: "I will praise You on the harp, O God, my God."

As in the previous psalm, in Psalm 42 God is called "*soterian tou prosopou mou*—the salvation of my being." Translated here as "being," the original and most literal meaning of *prosopon* is "face." If I am painted or photographed, it is invariably my face that is painted or photographed. My face is the place where "I" may be seen, where contact is made with "me." Thus this word is used in the conciliar and patristic Tradition of the Church to mean "person," or personal being. The *prosopon* is the "who" of one's identity.

When the psalmist says, then, that "my God is the salvation of my being," he goes to the heart of the mystery of redemption. In Jesus our Lord, salvation is offered to the identified human person as such: "The life which I now live in the flesh I live by faith in the Son of God, who loved *me* and gave Himself for *me*" (Gal. 2:20, emphasis added). That is to say, He died and rose again for "who I am." My very identity is redeemed by the God who was in Christ, reconciling the world to Himself (2 Cor. 5:19). This is why He is "my God."

When I go unto the altar of God, therefore, I go in the fullness of my redeemed personality. Such is the meaning of the expression, used here, "the God who gives joy to my youth." This is not my youth of yesteryear, but the new being that grows ever more new.

PSALM 43 (44)

Second Chronicles 20:1–19 describes a special liturgical service at the Jerusalem temple, in which King Jehoshaphat (873–849) led the people in a prayer of lamentation and intercession during a time of great crisis. He also proclaimed a period of fasting, for the plight of the people seemed desperate; their enemies were upon them, and "Judah gathered together to ask help from the Lord" (20:4).

There were many such occasions in biblical times, and many more since then, for the enemies of God's people are both numerous ("My name is Legion; for we are many," Mark 5:9) and powerful ("For we do not wrestle against flesh and blood, but against principalities, against powers, against the rulers of the darkness of this age, against spiritual hosts of wickedness in the heavenly places," Eph. 6:12). Indeed, we are continually at war, we children of God, and we sometimes feel simply overwhelmed, almost empty of hope.

Psalm 43 (Hebrew 44) was obviously written for such times: "You have given us as sheep to the slaughter and scattered us among the nations. You have bartered Your people for a pittance and made no profit on the sale." A useful prayer, this psalm of despondency, because the life of faith is not a sustained, uninterrupted series of triumphs.

The prayer begins, however, with an appeal to Tradition: "We have heard with our ears, O God; our fathers have told us." Such an appeal to the lessons of history is, of course, standard in the Bible, for the biblical God is, first and last, "the God of our fathers." Thus, the message of Genesis has to do with God's fidelity to Israel's patriarchs, while Exodus tells of Israel's redemption by that same patriarchal God. Other historical books of the Bible narrate the continued faithfulness of His promises to an unfaithful people. The prophetic literature, likewise, constantly looks back to God's redemptive work throughout Israel's history, as both paradigm and prophecy of what He will do for His people in the future.

A similar note is sounded strongly in the Wisdom literature of the Bible. The Book of Proverbs, for instance, is forever appealing to the moral lessons of history, that complex of disciplines and standards learned by experience, prescribed by the authority of Tradition and handed down through succeeding generations. In this case too, biblical religion is essentially an inherited religion, and its Lord is "the God of our fathers."

Tradition is also the note on which our psalm begins, then, almost its entire first half being taken up with a review of past experience. But God is not only the God of the patriarchs in the past; He is also our own God, one and the same: "You are my king and my God, You who command victories for Jacob."

Then suddenly the psalm's tone changes, for the reassuring lessons from the past are now being put sternly to the test: "But You have cast us off and put us to shame. You no longer march forth with our armies; You have turned us back from the foe, and our enemies plunder us at will."

The situation here may be likened to that of Job. He too had ever endeavored to be pleasing to the God of the fathers, steadfastly following the high moral precepts handed down from authorities of old. If one reads carefully what is said of Job in the first chapter of the book that bears his name, it is clear that he is a perfect embodiment of the traditional prescriptive norms treated in Proverbs and Israel's other wisdom literature.

Thus, when Job is undeservedly afflicted, his sentiments are very much what we find here in our psalm—shock, surprise, and disappointment. He complains to God, very much as this psalm complains: "You have made us the taunt of our neighbors, a derision and scorn to those about us." Such is the prayer of those who, like Job, feel overwhelmed by the sense that, in spite of His salvific deeds in the past and His promises for the future, God has simply forgotten. There are days when, if we are believers at all, we can only be described as "men of little faith."

Psalm 43 is the prayer of an individual, or a people, being sorely tried with respect to faith. Were it not for such experiences of being abandoned by God, there would be no test for the important proposition that the just man lives by faith. Whatever the trial (and its possible forms are manifold), it is finally the voice of faith—albeit, little faith—that prevails in this psalm. We pray to the Lord with those other men that our Lord describes as "of little faith," the frightened disciples on the stormy lake: "Awake! Why do You sleep, O Lord? Rise up, and do not cast us off forever. . . . Arise and come to our help; deliver us for the sake of Your name."

From Romans 8:35, 36 we know how the Apostle Paul prayed this psalm, seeing in its lament a reflection of the sufferings in his own soul by reason of his fidelity to Christ: "Who shall separate us from the love of Christ? Shall tribulation, or distress, or persecution, or famine, or nakedness, or peril, or sword? As it is written: /'For Your sake we are killed all day long; / We are accounted as sheep for the slaughter.'"

PSALM 44 (45)

MY HEART GAVE FORTH A NOBLE THEME

"The kingdom of heaven," we are told by a uniquely reliable source, "is like a certain king who arranged a marriage for his son" (Matt. 22:2), that marriage's consummation being the definitive aim of our destiny, and all of history constituting the courtship that prepares and anticipates the yet undisclosed hour of its fulfillment. Thus, the end of time is announced by the solemn proclamation: "Behold, the bridegroom is coming; go out to meet him!" (Matt. 25:6).

This interpretation of history as the preparation for a royal wedding ceremony is so pervasive and obvious in Holy Scripture that we Christians, taking it so much for granted, may actually overlook it or give it little thought. Indeed, in this modern materialistic world there is a distinct danger that we too may forget that the present life is but the preparation for another, its many and manifold efforts only a provisioning for the greater future, its varied blessings but rehearsals for the greater joy.

The modern materialistic world seems to know nothing of all this, believing in no future outside of its immediate and perceived needs. Its gross but unduly modest aspirations are well summed up by Dr. Johnson's bull: "Here is this cow, and here is this grass: what more could I ask?" Beyond these gratifications, the spokesman for the purely materialistic world nourishes no further hope.

To counter such forgetfulness of our future, therefore, God's Holy Writ repeatedly reminds us of that coming wedding day of the King's Son: "Let us be glad and rejoice and give Him glory, for the marriage of the Lamb has come, and His wife has made herself ready. . . . 'Blessed are those who are called to the marriage supper of the Lamb!'" (Rev. 19:7, 9).

Thus too we are warned against the grave danger courted by those who refuse their wedding invitations (Matt. 22:3–10; Luke 14:17–24), as well as the exclusion awaiting those improvident souls presumptuous of entrance without preparation (Matt. 22:11–14; 25:7–12).

Psalm 44 (Hebrew 45) is the psalm that anticipates and most descriptively foretells that future royal wedding. Its lines describe the "bride adorned for her husband" (Rev. 21:2): "The royal daughter is all glorious within the palace; her clothing is woven with gold. She shall be brought to the King in robes of many colors; the virgins, her companions who follow her, shall be brought to You.

With gladness and rejoicing they shall be brought; they shall enter the King's palace."

There is even more description of the King's Son, however, that Lamb of God who takes away the sins of the world: "You are fairer than the sons of men. Grace is poured out upon Your lips. Therefore God has blessed You forever. Gird Your sword upon Your thigh, O Mighty One, with Your glory and Your majesty. And in Your majesty ride victorious because of truth, humility and righteousness." This Son's riding forth in victory is similarly described in the Bible's final book: "Now I saw heaven opened, and behold, a white horse. And He who sat on him was called Faithful and True, and in righteousness He judges and makes war. His eyes were like a flame of fire, and on His head were many crowns. . . . And He has on His robe and on His thigh a name written: KING OF KINGS AND LORD OF LORDS" (Revelation 19:11, 12, 16).

We need not guess at the identity of this Bridegroom nor be in doubt of His divine dignity, for the New Testament quotes our psalm when it speaks of the Son's anointing by His Father: "But to the Son He says: / 'Your throne, O God, is forever and ever; / A scepter of righteousness is the scepter of Your kingdom. / You have loved righteousness and hated lawlessness; / Therefore God, Your God, has anointed You / With the oil of gladness more than Your companions'" (Heb. 1:8, 9). This 'anointed one' (for such is the meaning of the name Messiah, or Christ) is Jesus, of whom the Apostles preached: "God anointed Jesus of Nazareth with the Holy Spirit and with power" (Acts 10:38).

Inasmuch as "the form of this world is passing away" (1 Cor. 7:31), then, a certain measure of detachment is necessary to prepare ourselves for the wedding feast of the King's Son, a certain using of this world as though not using it, a refusal to take seriously its unwarranted claims on our final loyalty. So our psalm once again warns us: "Listen, O daughter. Consider and incline your ear; forget your own people also, and your father's house. So the King will greatly desire your beauty. Because He is your Lord, worship Him."

PSALM 45 (46)

Over the centuries Psalm 45 (Hebrew 46) has risen to God in a variety of forms from the lips of Christians. The Christian East, for example, has always followed the Greek reading in which the "our" modifies "God"—"our God is refuge and strength." This is identical to the Vulgate version of the Roman West, where this psalm inspired an old Leonine collect that begins with the very first line of this psalm: *Deus noster, refugium et virtus.* When the latter was translated into the St. Andrew's Missal, however, the "our" was shifted to "refuge and strength"—"Oh God, our refuge and our strength." This rendering is closer to the original Hebrew, "God is to us refuge and strength."

The same line of our psalm likewise inspired the opening of a popular hymn by Martin Luther: *Ein' feste Burg ist unser Gott.* This famous line of Luther, in turn, was to have an interesting history of its own, being translated over eighty times into fifty-three languages prior to 1900. Though all of them attempted to preserve Luther's meter, the English translations varied quite a bit. Just ten years after Luther published it, Miles Coverdale did the first English rendering, which read, "Oure God is a defence and towre." In England they yet seem to be content with Thomas Carlyle's version: "A safe stronghold our God is still," but other translations have been attempted. For instance, there were W. R. Wittingham's "A mountain fortress is our God" and H. J. Buckoll's "A tower of strength our God doth stand." The version to prevail in this country, however, was published by Frederic Henry Hedge in 1852: "A mighty fortress is our God." Anyway, this brief survey may suggest something of the importance of Psalm 45 in popular Christian piety over the years.

The psalm's structure is very easy to perceive, its two strophes each ending in the refrain, "The Lord of hosts is with us, the God of Jacob is our helper." The wording of this refrain accentuates what we may call its ecclesiological theme; that is to say, the voice in this psalm is the voice of the Church, the holy city, which is the dwelling place of God. Hence the importance of the first person plural all through this psalm: "we," "us," and "our." God is "our" refuge and strength, "we" shall not fear, The Lord of hosts is with "us," and so forth. This is the voice of God's people, the same voice that prays, "*Our* Father."

This is no modest or understated theme in Holy Scripture, this image of God's people as a holy city, the Church. Thus our psalm touches the rest of the

Bible at a hundred points, all the way to the Book of Revelation, where John's final vision is one of the holy city which is the definitive dwelling place of God: "God is in the midst of her; she shall not be moved."

As in the Book of Revelation, our psalm speaks of a stream of living water in connection with the holy city: "There is a river whose streams make glad the city of God, the holy place of the tabernacle of the Most High." This stream is at once the primeval river of Paradise, the holy font of Baptism and the water of eternal life.

The psalm's first strophe is concerned with God's protection of His Church in the midst of the conflict and instability of her life in this world, where "the nations raged, the kingdoms were moved." This section speaks of the very overthrow of the earth, the roaring of waters and the crashing down of mountains, but in all of this tumult the Church of God remains secure: "God will help her at the dawning of the day." That dawn and that day, of course, are the dawn and day of the Resurrection of Christ, God's consummate victory over chaos and death.

The second strophe of the psalm is, therefore, a vision of peace, in which God "makes wars to cease to the ends of the earth; He breaks the bow and cuts the spear in two; He burns the chariot in fire." This second part of the psalm reflects the rest and peace of heaven. Then God Himself speaks, and His words are a summons to inner quiet and rest in His presence: "Be still, and know that I am God, exalted among the nations, exalted on the earth."

The twofold refrain says that God is "with us," in Hebrew *'immanu* . A close look at that word shows it to be most of the name of the Messiah, "Immanuel," which literally means "with us God." "God with us" is, of course, Christ our Lord, abiding in our midst all days, even to the end of the world.

PSALM 46 (47)

ALL YOU NATIONS, CLAP YOUR HANDS

⚬

Its eternal, "heavenly" character is an essential and defining feature of the priest-hood of Christ our Lord. According to Hebrews, indeed, "if He were on earth, He would not be a priest" (8:4). We have been redeemed and justified by Jesus, our High Priest, not only by the shedding of His blood, but also by the power of His glorification over death, because He "was delivered up because of our offenses, and was raised because of our justification" (Rom. 4:25). Christ's re-demptive sacrifice on the Cross, by which He ransomed us and paid the pur-chase of our souls, was completed, fulfilled, brought to perfection by His Res-urrection and entrance into the heavenly holy of holies, that place "behind the veil, where the forerunner has entered for us, even Jesus, having become High Priest forever according to the order of Melchizedek" (Heb. 6:19, 20).

The Ascension of Christ is not, then, an afterthought, a sort of postlude to salvation. It is not merely an appropriate but optional parade celebrated in consequence of the victory. It is an integral part of the triumph itself; or more properly, it is the crowning moment of the Lord's priestly offering. The Lord's Ascension is a *ritus*, a liturgical event.

In this respect Hebrews contrasts the earthly tabernacle of the Old Testa-ment, the scene of the Mosaic sacrifices, with the eternal tabernacle of heaven, consecrated by the glorification of Jesus: "But Christ came as High Priest of the good things to come, with the greater and more perfect tabernacle not made with hands, that is, not of this creation. Not with the blood of goats and calves, but with His own blood He entered the Most Holy Place once for all, having obtained eternal redemption" (9:11, 12).

This Ascension of Christ into glory is likewise the object of biblical proph-ecy, especially in several places in the Book of Psalms. One of the more notable places is Psalm 46 (Hebrew 47): "God has ascended with jubilation, the Lord with the sound of the trumpet. Oh sing to our God, sing! Sing to our King, sing!" This is an invitation to us on earth, a summons to join our voices in jubilation with the angels on high. The Ascension of Christ is the event where heaven and earth are joined forever.

David's taking of the ark of the covenant into the Holy City may be seen as a figure and type of the Lord's entry into the heavenly Jerusalem, and that long-distant day was likewise marked with the rapture of happiness at God's approach: "Then David danced before the Lord with all his might; and David was wearing a linen ephod. So David and all the house of Israel brought up the ark of the Lord with shouting and with the sound of the trumpet" (2 Sam. 6:14, 15). Our psalm calls for similar marks of celebration at the coming of Christ into the Holy City on high: "Oh, clap your hands, all you peoples! Shout to God with the voice of triumph! For the Lord most high is awesome; He is the great King over all the earth."

What the Old Testament prophesied in narrative and psalm came finally to pass when God "raised Him from the dead and seated Him at His right hand in the heavenly places, far above all principality and power and might and dominion, and every name that is named, not only in this age but also in that which is to come" (Eph. 1:20, 21).

Our psalm of the Ascension, therefore, sends forth its invitation to all the peoples of the earth. By reason of His glorification, all of history and all of culture belong to Christ. All nations are summoned before His throne, to share His exaltation: "God reigns over the nations; God sits on His holy throne. The princes of the peoples are gathered together with the God of Abraham. For all the strong ones of the earth belong to God; they are greatly exalted."

The place on earth where heaven and earth meet is called the Church, which finds her very identity in the exaltation of Christ. The mystery of the Ascension leads immediately to the mystery of the Church, God's Chosen People: "He will subdue the peoples under us, and the nations under our feet. He has chosen us for His inheritance, the beauty of Jacob which he loves." *Christi ascensio, nostra provectio*, said Pope St. Leo the Great back in the fifth century: "The ascension of Christ is our advancement." In glorifying Christ, God also "raised us up together, and made us sit together in the heavenly places in Christ Jesus" (Eph. 2:6). Immediately after describing the Lord's Ascension, then, the Apostle Paul went on to speak of the role of the Church in that holy mystery: "And He put all things under His feet, and gave Him to be head over all things to the church, which is His body, the fullness of Him who fills all in all" (Eph. 1:22, 23).

PSALM 47 (48)

GREAT IS THE LORD AND GREATLY TO BE PRAISED

Most especially after the Assyrian Sennacherib's failure to capture Jerusalem in 701 (cf. 2 Kin. 19; 2 Chr. 32; Is. 37), many of its citizens came to believe that God's protection of the city would forever save it from such a fate. Their presumptuous confidence in this illusion grew into an arrogant, almost magical audacity at odds with an earlier warning they had received from the Prophet Micah. He had cautioned them that unrepented sin inevitably invites the judgment of God, even on His chosen city (Micah 3:12). Then, more than a century later, this warning of Micah was taken up by Jeremiah, when Nebuchadnezzar led his Babylonian army against Jerusalem. So strong and popular was their rash, magical presumption of Jerusalem's invincibility that Jeremiah's words fell largely on the deaf ears of a people not convinced of their need for conversion. God would protect His holy city, they were persuaded, so why repent? In consequence of this sinful attitude, the city fell in 586.

It would be rather easy to read Psalm 47 (Hebrew 48) as expressing the same unfounded presumption on the part of a sinful city. So many lines, on a first reading, would seem readily to bear such an interpretation: "God is in her palaces; He is known as her refuge. . . . In the city of our God; God will establish it forever. . . . Walk about Zion, and go all around her. Count her towers; mark well her bulwarks; consider her palaces."

Interpreted as referring to the earthly city of Jerusalem, however, such affirmations are surely wide of the mark, for that city has been conquered many times in the course of history.

But Jerusalem is vastly more than Jerusalem. Back in the late fourth century the Egyptian Abba Nesteros, in words recorded by St. John Cassian, distinguished four meanings of the name Jerusalem in Holy Scripture. "One and the same Jerusalem," he said, "can be taken in four senses: historically, as the city of the Jews; allegorically, as the Church of Christ; anagogically, as the heavenly city of God 'which is the mother of us all'; and tropologically, as the soul of man, which is frequently subject to praise or blame from the Lord under this title" (*Conferences* 14.8).

In which of these four senses, then, is Jerusalem meant in our present psalm? Certainly not in its literal sense, as we have seen, for Jerusalem has been captured by Babylonians, Romans, Arabs, and others.

Should Jerusalem be understood here, then, in what Cassian calls its tropological sense, as "the soul of man"? There is much to recommend such a reading, for God certainly does surround the souls of His servants with every manner of blessing and protection. The confidence expressed in this psalm seems identical with that of the Apostle Paul: "If God is for us, who can be against us? . . . It is God who justifies. Who is he who condemns? . . . Who shall separate us from the love of Christ?" (Rom. 8:31–35). Such sentiments express the consoling doctrine of the divine assurance, according to which no one can snatch our souls from the hand of Christ (cf. John 10:28).

This is a true and valid meaning of our psalm, I think, unless such confidence be understood in the same presumptuous sense condemned by the Prophets. On occasion one does discern such a sinful attitude among individuals deceived into believing that, once they have come to faith in Christ, they will inevitably be saved, even should they apostatize from that faith. The catch-phrase of these misdirected minds is "once saved, always saved," a very unbiblical notion entertained only unto grave spiritual danger.

Surely what Cassian calls Jerusalem's allegorical sense is also a proper understanding of our psalm, which speaks impressively of God's protection of His Church throughout the centuries: "For behold, the kings assembled, they passed by together. They beheld and marveled; they were disturbed and fled away." The Church of God has indeed beheld the rise and fall of empires, and this psalm is perhaps best prayed as an expression of gratitude to God for this fixed and lasting institution of His grace in this world: "We have received Your mercy, O Lord, in the midst of Your temple." This is the one, holy, catholic house of God's praise: "As is Your name, O God, so is Your praise to the ends of the earth."

PSALM 48 (49)

HEAR THESE THINGS, ALL YOU NATIONS

☙

Psalm 48 (Hebrew 49) is not a prayer in our usual sense, of words directed to God. It is, rather, a meditation on a theme having to do with the pursuit of wisdom. Its tone and direction are universal, characterized by a broad and general perspective. It is a philosophical psalm, making its appeal to the human mind as such, any human mind, in any time or place: "Hear these things, all you nations. Give ear, all you who dwell upon the earth."

Directed to all peoples at all times, it does not mention the specific events of the salvation history narrated in the Bible. It says nothing about the Exodus or the giving of the Law, nothing about the Covenant or Jerusalem, nothing about the Chosen People or the Messiah or salvation.

Rather, it calls upon the human mind, any human mind, to think deeply about certain universal facts and phenomena of human life. The poet invites all mankind to meditate with him on a specific but universal problem. He is also going to take his time with the matter, for this is a deep and enigmatic concern, not a subject to be hurried. No fewer than four times the psalmist declares what he is about to do: (1) "My mouth shall speak wisdom; [2] and the concern of my heart, understanding. [3] I will bend my ear to a puzzle; [4] I shall broach my riddle in a ballad."

Now the thing that most strikes the psalmist about human existence is that it ends in death, and he is a fool who forgets or neglects this truth. Human beings tend to take too seriously the wealth and other sorts of honor that this world gives, for death will make it all come to nothing. This ill-placed confidence is no basis for a wise life. Halfway through and again at the end, our psalm comes back to a refrain on this theme: "Abiding in honor, man has failed to understand. He has come to resemble the witless beasts, and to be compared with them."

Graves tending to be dug to roughly the same depth, death has been called the great leveler. Rich and poor, great and small, suffer an identical fate. Cemeteries are very democratic places, so this psalm is addressed to "wealthy and poor alike."

The psalmist is particularly struck by the irony that some individuals become so powerful and famous that regions of the world are called by their names. Whatever claim these folk make upon the earth, he says, the earth will eventually make its own claim on them: "Their graves are their homes forever,

95

their dwelling places from generation to generation."

Worldly power takes itself very seriously and throws its weight around, but no amount of prestige or riches can save a man from his appointed fate. So God's servant does not fear what such people may do to him. In contrast to the wealthy presumptuous man who "cannot redeem his soul," he sings out: "God will redeem my soul from the hand of Hades, when He receives me." This latter verb is the same used for God's "receiving" such just men as Enoch (Gen. 5:24) and Elijah (2 Kin. 2:9–11).

Psalm 48, then, is about the sad fate of those who substitute honor and wealth for the godly understanding of life and reality. Having taken their wealth and honor seriously, "like sheep they are herded in Hades; death becomes their shepherd."

This is the same spiritual descent described by Plato. Indeed, he uses the very same words. *Time*, honor or reputation, according to Plato, is the next step down from wisdom, and *plousia*, wealth, is yet a step lower. Wisdom, on the other hand, has to do with the pursuit of justice, and Plato's model, Socrates, accepting the unjust sentence of his enemies, proclaims that the difference between just and unjust men is well recognized at that high tribunal on the other side of death. Like our psalmist here, Socrates does not fear what his honored and wealthy enemies can do to him.

Indeed, our psalm is one of those places where the wisdom tradition of the Bible touches universal philosophy, mankind's perennial quest for understanding. Not once in this melodic poem does the psalmist refer to God's special revelation to the Chosen People. No appeal is made to the divine words spoken on Sinai or to the Prophets. Here we find, rather, the God-inspired thought of biblical man addressing the human mind on its own terms. This psalm is one of those places where the Bible forsakes, as it were, the greater heights of divine truth in order to concentrate man's attention on the lowest steps to its ascent. The fear of the Lord, the psalmist tells us elsewhere, is the very beginning of wisdom, and Psalm 48 is a plain, straightforward summons to a godly fear.

PSALM 49 (50)

THE GOD OF GODS HAS SPOKEN

If Psalm 48 can be said to embody ideas characteristic of the Bible's wisdom books, Psalm 49 (Hebrew 50) takes up a favorite motif of the prophetic books—God's displeasure at a mere external observance of religious practices, without true faith, inner repentance, moral responsibility, and the gift of the heart. The Book of Isaiah is big on this theme.

In either Testament, the Bible knows nothing of nonritual, nonceremonial religion. From the offering of animal and vegetable sacrifices among the earliest patriarchs, through the elaborate ceremonies of the Mosaic tabernacle and the Solomonic temple, all the way to the sacraments of the New Law, the religion of the Bible prescribes the use of ritual as an integral feature of worship. Knees and necks are to be bent, hands to be raised in prayer and extended in blessing. Moreover, the Christ who declared that the Father's true worshippers would worship in spirit and in truth is the same Lord who commanded His disciples to "baptize" new believers, to "anoint" them when sick, and to "do" the Eucharist for them.

Anything can be abused, however, and perhaps religion most of all, so no age has lacked individuals who, neglecting repentance and recalcitrant to moral standards, have restricted their religion to the bare maintenance of prescribed ritual, especially when the ritual's performance could be left to the care of a priest or some other religious professional.

Thus, on the appropriate day one could simply show up at the temple with his sheep or whatever, hand it over to the priest to be sacrificed, and then depart, under the illusion that God was thereby and of necessity pleased with the transaction.

Really? God needs sheep? Our psalm raises some genuine doubt on the point: "Should I be hungry, I would hardly tell you, for mine are the whole world and its fullness. Shall I eat the flesh of bulls, or drink the blood of goats?" The observance of ritual, any ritual, without true dedication to God is, at best, a waste of God's time, and more likely a form of magic.

Like Isaiah, our psalm stresses in particular the moral or ethical character required of the true worshipper. He may be a friend of the priest at the time of worship, but who are his friends otherwise? "If you saw a thief, you ran with him, and you kept company with adulterers. Your mouth gushed with evil, and your tongue fashioned deceits. You sat and spoke against your brother, and cursed your mother's son."

As with Isaiah again, one observes in such verses that the sin especially condemned in the false worshipper tends to be social sin, sin against other people in the outside, nonritual world. He offends his fellow man, whether by neglecting his duties of mercy, or by actively inflicting injustice. All the Bible cries out the impossibility of loving the God whom we do not see, without loving the brother whom we do see (cf. 1 John 4:20).

The Apostle Paul faced this problem at Corinth, where the Holy Eucharist itself, that supreme, definitive ritual of the biblical religion, was being desecrated by the participation of the uncharitable and unrepentant. Thus, since very early in Christian history, evidenced already in 1 Corinthians 10— 11, there have been worshippers who treated even the Lamb of God with the same moral insouciance that the Old Testament sinner sometimes showed to that ritual sheep that he handed over for sacrifice in the temple.

The sin of such a man comes from his inadequate, truly pathetic idea of God: "Wickedly you thought I was like you."

In fact, of course, God is not in the least like us, and the first part of the psalm graphically describes the awesome majesty of the God whom we approach in adoration. The worship of God is no place for moral or any other sort of nonsense: "Fire burns in His presence." Or, as Hebrews phrases it: "Let us have grace, by which we may serve God acceptably with reverence and godly fear. For our God is a consuming fire" (12:28, 29).

Yet once more our psalm is here reminiscent of Isaiah, who speaks of God repeatedly as "the Holy One of Israel." This title, used almost exclusively in Isaiah, is doubtless related to the Prophet's inaugural vision in the temple. Seeing "the Lord, high and lifted up," he thought it very sinful to attempt to bribe Him with a sheep or two.

For all its ritual and ceremony, the religion of the Bible is ultimately a matter of the heart. This theme in our present psalm prepares for that important line in the psalm which is to follow: "The sacrifice to God is a contrite spirit; a broken and contrite heart, O God, You will not despise."

PSALM 50 (51)

HAVE MERCY ON ME, O GOD

෧෧

It is not by accident nor without significance that Psalm 50 (Hebrew 51) is the only psalm prescribed to be recited in its entirety during every celebration of the Eastern Orthodox Divine Liturgy. Whether in the Liturgy of St. Basil or St. John Chrysostom, it is the prayer of a murderer and adulterer that the priest must pray when the congregation commences singing the Cherubic Hymn in preparation for the "Great Entrance" of the Holy Gifts. At that moment, the priest takes the censer and starts censing the entire sanctuary area. While he does this, he says (and is expected to know it by heart) the whole psalm that begins, "Have mercy on me, O God, according to Your great mercy." It is chiefly this eucharistic context, I submit, that provides the proper avenue to the deep meaning of that psalm popularly known (from the first word of its Latin version) as the *Miserere*. It is a psalm in which, using the words of that great sinner David, one prays for God's mercy and forgiveness.

At the Great Entrance, we stand at the threshold of theophany: "Let us, who mystically represent the Cherubim and sing the thrice-holy hymn to the life-creating Trinity, now lay aside all earthly cares, that we may receive the King of all, who comes invisibly upborne by the angelic hosts." At that point we are just moments away from chanting the hymn that Isaiah and St. John heard chanted by the seraphim ("fiery ones") at the throne of God: "Holy, holy, holy, Lord God of hosts . . ." It is at that awesome moment that we think of our sinfulness and say, as did Isaiah at that moment, "Woe is me, for I am undone! / Because I am a man of unclean lips, / And I dwell in the midst of a people of unclean lips; / For my eyes have seen the King, / The Lord of hosts" (Is. 6:5). The true sense of our sinfulness does not come from measuring the distance between our own conduct and the grandeur of the moral law. Oh no, it is only in the overwhelming presence of the Holy One Himself that we sinners know how utterly sinful we are.

Such a sinner was Job. In chapter after chapter of the dramatic book that bears his name, Job kept arguing that he was an innocent man, that he was suffering unjustly, that he did not deserve to be punished, and so forth. But then God abruptly reveals Himself to Job, who now finds himself standing naked in the presence of the Holy One, and suddenly Job is a man of altered mind. No more can he claim innocence. Never again can he point to some alleged purity of his conscience. The pretense is over. Job must simply repent:

"I have heard of You by the hearing of the ear, / But now my eye sees You. / Therefore I abhor myself, / And repent in dust and ashes" (Job 42:5).

This overwhelming holiness of God, the source of profound repentance, is particularly related to the coming of the Holy Spirit, for it is our pride and sinfulness that grieve and impede the operation of God's sanctifying Spirit.

Once again, the eucharistic context provides an illustration. The recitation of the *Miserere* is a preparation for the praying of the epiklesis, that solemn prayer for the sending down of the Holy Spirit to transform the bread and wine into the Body and Blood of the Lord. Before he ever begins that awesome invocation, the priest is made to say: "Create in me a clean heart, O God, and renew a steadfast spirit within me. Cast me not away from Your presence, and take not Your Holy Spirit from me."

In the Slavic tradition, these words are said again at the time of the epiklesis itself, used as the deacon's refrain to the priest's thrice-recited prayer: "O God, who did send down Your Holy Spirit upon Your disciples at the third hour, take Him not from us, O Good One, but renew Him in us who pray to You." In the Liturgy of St. Basil, the priest even prays that God will not, because of the priest's own sinfulness, "withhold the grace of Your Holy Spirit from these Gifts here spread forth."

It is this strong sense of the holiness of the face of Christ and the presence of the Holy Spirit that keeps the *Miserere* from being morbid or morose. "Wash me yet more from my iniquity, and cleanse me from my sin" is the proper concomitant to "Heaven and earth are full of Your glory." "Hide Your face from my sins, and blot out all my iniquities" is our condign answer to "God has sent forth the Spirit of His Son into your hearts." Continued repentance is the appropriate response to ongoing theophany. Since we are all "with unveiled face, beholding as in a mirror the glory of the Lord" (2 Cor. 3:18), we do not cease to pray, over and over: "Wash me, and I shall be whiter than snow."

PSALM 51 (52)

The title attached to Psalm 51 (Hebrew 52), whatever be said of its canonical authority (see commentary on Psalm 53), is most instructive, I think, in getting to the heart of the psalm's message: " . . . when Doeg the Edomite came and told Saul, 'David has come to the house of Ahimelech.'"

Strikingly at odds with today's popular bias against "demonizing the enemy," this psalm presents a simple but stark contrast between good and evil, in which the "bad guy" really does appear quite bad: "Why boast of your lawlessness, O man mighty in evil? All day long your tongue, like a sharp razor, plotted wickedness; you have devised guile. You have loved to speak evil rather than good, wickedness rather than justice. You have preferred every discourse of disloyalty, a mendacious tongue."

No wonder that the vicious man thus described in this psalm came to be identified with Doeg the Edomite, for the latter was arguably the worst, most unmistakably evil and reprobate man in all of Scripture. Doeg's story is told in 1 Samuel 21; 22. He it was who chanced to be privy to the assistance that young David, then in exile and pursued by Saul, received from Ahimelech, the priest at Nob. Later on, Doeg reported that incident to Saul, leading to the arrest of Ahimelech's priestly family and the charge of treason laid against them. When none of Saul's army proved willing to put the accused to death, Doeg volunteered to perform the task with his own hands. He then slaughtered eighty-five innocent people in cold blood.

Dante put Judas Iscariot at the very bottom of the Inferno, in the mouth of Satan (between Brutus and Cassius, by the way, a detail evidencing Dante's rather Romanocentric reading of history), thus suggesting that Judas was mankind's worst sinner. A better choice might have been Doeg the Edomite. Not that Holy Scripture excuses the Iscariot or displays doubt with respect to his final destiny (cf. Matt. 26:24; Mark 14:21; Luke 22:22; John 6:70, 71). No, the Bible affords us no room for "a reasonable and holy hope" with regard to Judas.

Still, that man's very despair, driving him to take his own life, was born of a certain sense of the evil he had done by his betrayal of the Lord. Judas's "I have sinned," while it bore quite a different meaning from the "I have sinned" of the repentant David, yet manifested some recognition of real moral evil. Even without a godly repentance, even perhaps in the very act of defying the mercy of God, Judas displayed the innate decency of avowing his own guilt. That is to say, even Judas himself does not appear to have been quite as bad as he might have been. In his very despair, he bore witness to some vestigial moral conscience within him. At least with respect to the treachery of his betrayal, he could still discern the difference between right and wrong.

No, with due reverence to the immortal Dante, if there is a lowest place in hell, it more probably belongs to the likes of Doeg the Edomite, a man of cultivated cruelty, an individual with a developed taste for evil and a singular delight in the shedding of blood, a callous villain of no remorse. Doeg's ethical stature did not rise so high as hopelessness. As a moral character Judas seems preferable. Doeg would never have been capable of a moral sentiment so "sensible" as despair, nor a moral statement so "principled" as suicide.

In truth, Judas surpasses Doeg also in terms of literary and artistic interest. Even if despair triumphs at the end, at least one is aware of a struggle taking place inside Judas, and inner moral struggles, whatever their outcome, are intrinsically interesting things. Judas Iscariot has thus never proved a boring subject. The problem with Doeg is that he is not only bad, but he is so evil as to be uninteresting—an utterly one-dimensional character. There is no struggle or doubt or despair inside Doeg. Those he does not cut down with the sword he bludgeons to death with boredom.

So Psalm 51, pointing to Doeg, paints evil as completely evil. The dialectic involved here is important, for if evil is not really evil, then good is not really good. In the final Throne-room analysis, there is no chance of confusion, and no third option. Evil is portrayed in all its ugliness, so that good may be pictured in all its glory. And our psalm is much more interested in the goodness of the good man and in the assembly of God's friends, who place their whole trust in the infinite goodness of the Lord: "But I am like a fruitful olive tree in the house of God. I have placed my hope in the mercy of God for ever, and unto ages of ages I will confess You forever, for You have done this, and I shall await Your name, for it is excellent in the sight of Your holy ones."

PSALM 52 (53)
THE FOOL SAYS IN HIS HEART
※

It has already been noted that the content of Psalm 52 (Hebrew 53) is nearly identical with that of Psalm 13 (Hebrew 14), a duplication probably best explained as the result of the joining of various collections of psalms in the primitive textual history of Sacred Scripture. We do not know when this conflation was made, but it clearly antedates our earliest extant version of the canonical Book of Psalms, that of the Septuagint, a Greek translation of the Old Testament crafted at Alexandria in the third century BC. This latter was the version habitually quoted in the New Testament and adopted among the first Christian churches.

Thus, the comments previously made with respect to Psalm 13 are also pertinent to Psalm 52.

In Romans 3:10–12 the Apostle Paul quotes this text (probably by heart, because he spontaneously adds lines from several other psalms in the following verses), with special emphasis on the universal need for salvation. His point is that, strictly speaking, there are really no just men in this world—men who are just in the sense that they are able, by the righteousness of their own works, to attain to the presence of God and stand innocent before him. Thus understood, who is a just man in this world? St. Paul's answer is emphatic—nobody, absolutely nobody, and he quotes our psalm text to prove the point: "There is none righteous, no, not one; / There is none who understands; / There is none who seeks after God. / They have all turned aside; / They have together become unprofitable; / There is none who does good, no, not one."

The Apostle is using our psalm here to address the major theme of Romans—that only God can justify man, and that God does so only in Jesus the Lord. Men are helpless, if left to their own capacities and accomplishments, and they are foolish to imagine otherwise. We human beings are so thoroughly infected by the results of sin that, unless God intervenes in our misery and takes a hand in our destiny, our inevitable lot is despair. None of us can measure up, no, not one. Whether Jew or Gentile, "there is no difference; for all have sinned and fall short of the glory of God" (Rom. 3:22, 23).

We Christians are not Buddhists nor Jains. We do not rely on our own resources and efforts. Nor is there is anything in common between the God of the Bible and that pathetic little divinity played by George Burns some years ago in that unbelievably abysmal movie entitled *Oh, God,* the old gentleman whose "good news" consisted in a call to greater reliance on our own lights and efforts. Ours is not a self-help religion. The Christian faith does not even commence except on the firm foundation of utter despair in purely human endeavor.

We do not have it within us to find God. We do not have it within us even to begin looking for God. We do not have it within us even to want to look for God. Adam and Eve, with the taste of the forbidden fruit still in their mouths, were not searching for God; they were hiding from Him, and so do we all. Left to our own resources, none of us can do better than to conceal ourselves in the bushes, with our bare behinds hanging out, hoping that God will pass us by.

This is a very important truth taught in Holy Scripture, and it stands foursquare against any optimism about "man's quest for God." Those optimists who entertain the notion that human beings are searching for God are simply neglecting the evidence. C. S. Lewis remarked that speaking of man's quest for God is something on the order of speaking of the mouse's quest for the cat.

Indeed, in the strict sense, the true God cannot even be searched for; He can be sought only in the measure that He reveals Himself in holy grace. Whatever searching for God is undertaken by sinful human beings when left to their own devices will invariably involve idolatry—the setting up of false gods in human resemblance, whether it be the high likeness of Apollo, or the rather pitiful portrait of that George Burns divinity who so loved the world that he sent forth John Denver.

This truth that the Epistle to the Romans finds in the Book of Psalms is central to our life of prayer. Christian devotion begins on the basis of God's own self-revelation in holy grace. Worship is our Spirit-given response to God's saving intervention in our destiny.

PSALM 53 (54)

SAVE ME IN YOUR NAME, O GOD

During the long time and probably complex process involved in the composition and arranging of the Book of Psalms, efforts were made by some anonymous editor to "place" a few of the psalms into plausible circumstances during the life and career of King David. In these cases the given psalm's title mentions some particular setting in David's life that is used to interpret that particular psalm. Thus, Psalm 50 is ascribed to David's repentance of his sin with Bathsheba, while Psalm 51, as we have seen, is related to his encounter with Doeg the Edomite. Similarly, the title of Psalm 58 places it in the context of Saul's pursuit of David, while Psalm 55 is ascribed to the time "when the Philistines captured him in Gath." Several of the psalms are so contextualized. Clearly the editor responsible for these notations had in mind to say that the life of David was the key to the understanding of the psalms.

We Christians, of course, know that the historical David was himself a prefiguration, a living prophecy, of the true King yet to come, and we believe that the divine promises made with respect to David's messianic throne are fulfilled in the Kingdom of Jesus, at once David's descendant and his Lord. Following the lead of Jesus Himself (cf. Luke 24:44), we interpret (and pray) the psalms in the light—the theological light—of this fulfillment of biblical prophecy. We come to the psalms completely with what Saint Paul called "the mind of Christ" (1 Cor. 2:16). Our interest in the psalms—or, indeed, in any part of the Bible—is solely a Christian interest. As we pray to Christ our Lord in one of the Resurrection troparia, "You are our God, and we know no other than You."

Psalm 53 (Hebrew 54) may serve to illustrate this interpretive principle. The title or inscription at the head of this psalm describes it with reference to the incident "when the Ziphites went and said to Saul, 'Is David not hiding among us?'" For an understanding of the psalm the reader is thus sent to 1 Samuel 23:14–20, which tells of the treachery of the Ziphites in betraying David to Saul. That is to say, this is a psalm about the betrayal of the messianic King.

The assiduous reader of the Gospel, therefore, should have no great trouble recognizing the correct interpretive setting of this psalm, or discerning the "voice" that prays it. This is a psalm properly understood from within "the mind of Christ," for it describes both His anguish at the betrayal that sent

Him to suffering and death, and His full assurance of final vindication in the paschal glory.

Each of these aspects of the Lord's Passion is narrated in the New Testament accounts. For example, the Lord's three predictions of His coming sufferings, while dwelling in detail on certain specific aspects of the pain, all finish with a prophecy of His Resurrection (cf. Mark 8:31; 9:31; 10:33, 34). Likewise, Hebrews speaks both of the Lord's distress and dereliction ("who, in the days of His flesh, when He had offered up prayers and supplications, with vehement cries and tears to Him who was able to save Him from death"—5:7) and also of His assurance of final vindication ("who for the joy that was set before Him endured the cross, despising the shame"—12:2).

Both these aspects of "the mind of Christ" in reference to the Passion are similarly present in our psalm. First, it speaks of how Jesus "endured such hostility from sinners against Himself" (Heb. 12:3): "For strangers are risen up against me, and the strong ones have sought my soul." But then the voice of Jesus, "the author and finisher of our faith" (12:2), proclaims His assurance of final vindication and victory: "For behold, God helps me, and the Lord is the receiver of my soul."

The theme of final victory over His enemies (who, in the Gospels, are ultimately the demonic powers) forms the final note of this psalm. It is in the assurance of this victory that Jesus, entering into Jerusalem on Palm Sunday to commence the definitive overthrow of Satan, prays to His Father: "Glorify Your name" (John 12:28). Our psalm expresses the generous spontaneity of His soul as He prepares to offer the one sacrifice that takes away the sins of the world: "Willingly will I offer sacrifice to You." He prepares to lay down His life that He may take it up again (cf. John 10:17).

PSALM 54 (55)

HEAR MY PRAYER, O GOD

As we have seen repeatedly, to pray the psalms as Christians means to pray them with reference to Christ. Just as Jesus was written of by the lawgiver Moses (John 5:46), and the prophet Isaiah (John 12:41), so was He spoken of by the psalmist David (Mark 12:35–37). Thus, when the risen Lord interpreted the Holy Scriptures to His first disciples, He explained to them how "all things must be fulfilled which were written in the Law of Moses and the Prophets and the Psalms concerning Me" (Luke 24:44).

In that same conversation during which the risen Jesus "opened their understanding, that they might comprehend the Scriptures" (v. 45), He went on specifically to relate the content of those Scriptures to His own Passion, death, and Resurrection: "Thus it is written, and thus it was necessary for the Christ to suffer and to rise from the dead the third day" (v. 46).

It should come as no surprise, therefore, that the praying of the psalms will bring us back repeatedly to considerations of the mystery of the Cross and of those deep sufferings by which the Lamb of God took away the sins of the world.

Now of all the things that the Lord endured in what Hebrews 5:7 calls "the days of His flesh," one of the most grievous seems to have been that betrayal from within the intimacy of the apostolic band. As we saw earlier, this betrayal by Judas Iscariot was itself a fulfillment of a prophecy given in the Psalter: "He who eats bread with Me has lifted up his heel against Me" (Psalm 40, quoted in John 13:18).

Indeed, references to the Lord's betrayal appear in several places among the psalms, one of which is Psalm 54 (Hebrew 55). Here our Lord prays in the setting of His Passion: "For if an enemy had cursed me, I could have borne it; or if someone who hated me had boasted over me, I could have hidden myself from him. But it was you, a man with whom I was one in soul, my companion and intimate friend, who enjoyed pleasant meals with me; we walked in harmony together in the house of God."

The context of this psalm, then, is the Lord's betrayal by someone with whom He had shared many a meal, even the miraculous loaves and fishes and, more recently, the Passover Seder, on the night before He died. We may see in this psalm, then, the Lord's sentiments in the agony at Gethsemane, as He awaited the arrival of the treacherous friend who would betray Him with a kiss and hand Him over to His enemies. Judas was a "companion" in the strict sense of someone with whom He had shared bread (*panis*).

The Gospels suggest that this experience of treachery from a special friend was among the deepest sufferings sustained by the One who became like unto His brethren in all things save sin. If the story of Judas is narrated in all four canonical Gospels, as well as Acts, the earliest Christians must have thought it singularly important.

In each of the Gospels, moreover, Judas is identified as the betrayer precisely during the Last Supper—that is to say, in a context recognized to be eucharistic. Nor is it incidental that the first occasion at which our Lord spoke of the coming betrayal was at the end of His own lengthy discourse about eating His body and drinking His blood (John 6:70, 71).

In addition, early, extremely early, some mention of the Lord's betrayal became part of the standard wording of the eucharistic liturgy. When St. Paul, during the eighteen months he spent at Corinth from late 49 to mid-51, had taught those Christians how to celebrate the Eucharist, the recognized formula already contained a reference to the betrayal: "For I received from the Lord that which I also delivered to you: that the Lord Jesus on the same night in which He was betrayed took bread . . ." (1 Cor. 11:23). Likewise, in our earliest extant full eucharistic formulary, the *Apostolic Tradition* (4.8) of Hippolytus of Rome (about A.D. 210), we find the same wording, as we do in both eucharistic liturgies of the Byzantine tradition.

It is not difficult to detect the reason for remembering the treachery of Judas in the context of the Holy Eucharist. It serves as a distinct warning, right at the Lord's own Table, of the extreme peril of sharing that most holy Meal without "discerning the Lord's body" (1 Cor. 11:29). Treachery, we are reminded, was already active at the first celebration of the Eucharist.

PSALM 55 (56)

HAVE MERCY ON ME, O GOD

⁂

Psalm 55 (Hebrew 56) is the prayer of a believer sorely tried but still trusting in God. It may easily be prayed as the prayer of Christ our Lord in the context of His redemptive sufferings, but it also expresses the feelings of those who have, like the Apostles, been counted worthy to suffer for the name of Jesus (cf. Acts 5:41). That is to say, this psalm is the prayer of Christ, and the prayer of the Church, and the prayer of any disciple of Christ within the Church.

What the Church suffers, after all, she suffers in communion with Christ, and what is suffered by individual members is part of that same mystic communion, of which the Apostle Paul wrote: "I now rejoice in my sufferings for you, and fill up in my flesh what is lacking in the afflictions of Christ, for the sake of His body, which is the church" (Col. 1:24).

The mandate laid on all believers, that they daily take up the cross and follow Jesus, is not a thing light or incidental to the living of the Gospel, for Holy Scripture affirms that "all who desire to live godly in Christ Jesus will suffer persecution" (2 Tim. 3:12).

Psalm 55 is a perfect prayer for all such folk: "Have mercy on me, O God, for man has trampled me down; all day long the belligerent man has afflicted me. My enemies trample me all day long, for many have warred against me since daybreak. . . . All day long they have scorned my words; all their machinations are directed to my hurt. They position themselves for ambush, setting a snare for my foot; they prowl for my soul."

Here in our psalm is described, first of all, the very situation we find with respect to Jesus in the Gospels. Early in Mark, for instance, there is a series of five episodes (2:1—3:6) in which the enemies of Jesus interrogate and investigate Him, spy on Him and finally reach their sinister resolve: "Then the Pharisees went out and immediately plotted with the Herodians against Him, how they might destroy Him" (3:6). There are five more such stories nearer the end of Mark's Gospel (11:27—12:34), leading at once to the conspiracy to put Jesus to death (14:1). The present psalm may certainly be prayed as the sentiments of our Lord in that context, revealing His trust in the Father even in the midst of the evil plots against Himself.

But much of this drama in the Gospels is repeated in the experience of the first Christians narrated in Acts and the various Epistles, where we likewise read repeatedly of persecutions, plots, lurking ambushes, false testimony, denunciations, floggings, imprisonment, and even death. In varying degrees, such was the lot of Stephen, James, Paul, and the other Apostles, one of whom wrote: "Rejoice to the extent that you partake of Christ's sufferings, that when His glory is revealed, you may also be glad with exceeding joy. If you are reproached for the name of Christ, blessed are you, for the Spirit of glory and of God rests upon you" (1 Peter 4:13, 14).

The more important sentiment in our psalm, however, is deep trust in God's abiding mercy and help. If God has numbered the hairs on our heads, how much more has He counted every tear falling from our eyes. Not a sigh uttered before Him will go unremembered: "Lord, I have recounted my life to You. You have placed my tears in Your sight, and in Your promise. My enemies shall be thrown back, on whatever day I shall call upon You. Behold, I know that You are my God."

Our trust in God is open-ended. It is not just a matter of trusting Him in our present trials, but of confiding to His care all that lies ahead, that future still unknown to us but for which God has already made provision. This is the God from whom nothing can separate us, "neither death nor life, nor angels nor principalities nor powers, nor things present nor things to come, nor height nor depth, nor any other created thing" (Rom. 8:38, 39).

In this psalm's act of trust, the future itself becomes a sort of narrative past: "You have delivered my soul from death, my feet from stumbling, so that I may rejoice before the Lord in the light of the living." Since nothing "shall be able to separate us from the love of God which is in Christ Jesus our Lord" (Rom. 8:39), we believers already know the final blessing of our destiny: "Moreover whom He predestined, these He also called; whom He called, these He also justified; and whom He justified, these He also glorified" (8:30). Such is the biblical doctrine of the divine election and assurance, the source of our hope and consolation in every trial that attends our faith. "Finally," says the believer in Christ, "there is laid up for me the crown of righteousness, which the Lord, the righteous Judge, will give to me on that Day, and not to me only but also to all who have loved His appearing" (2 Tim. 4:8).

PSALM 56 (57)

HAVE MERCY ON ME, O GOD, HAVE MERCY ON ME

Psalm 56 (Hebrew 57) is another of those instances of duplication in the Psalter, its last half being nearly identical with the opening lines of Psalm 107 (Hebrew 108).

It has long been prayed as a morning psalm; for nearly fifteen centuries (indeed, until just thirty years ago) in Western monasteries, for instance, it was chanted weekly at Tuesday matins, and Archbishop Cranmer assigned it for Morning Prayer on the eleventh day of each month in *The Book of Common Prayer*. The propriety of praying Psalm 56 in the morning is amply indicated by the lines that read: "I was disturbed in my sleep. . . . Rise up, my glory; rise up, harp and lyre. I will rise up early."

The psalm breaks neatly into two parts, each of which ends with the refrain: "Be exalted above the heavens, O God, and may Your glory be over all the earth." The dominant motif in the first half is trust in God, while the second half is chiefly a praise of God.

In the first part of the psalm God is sought as refuge in the day of distress. In lines that deserve to be fixed in memory and often invoked, we pray for God's mercy and put our confidence in His redemption: "Have mercy on me, O God, have mercy on me, for my soul confides in You, and in the shadow of Your wings will I hope, until the evil be past."

Twice in this half of the psalm we speak of God's redemption as a "sending forth" (*exsapesteilen* the verb in each instance): "He *sent forth* from heaven and saved me. . . . God *sent forth* His mercy and His truth." Does this double "sending forth" of God refer to the sending forth of the Son and the Holy Spirit into the world? Well, maybe so. Compare the wording here with that in Galatians 4:4–6, where the identical verb, *exsapesteilen*, is used twice—"When the fullness of the time had come, God *sent forth* His Son . . . And because you are sons, God has *sent forth* the Spirit of His Son . . ." Holy Scripture recognizes two "missions" coming from God, a "horizontal," historical revelation in the categorical, anamnetic order ("God sent forth His Son"), and a "vertical," internal revelation in the transcendent, epikletic order ("God sent forth the Spirit of His Son"). Is not this the same thing our psalm is saying?

Both the Second and Third Persons of the Holy Trinity have been sent into the world for its full salvation in mercy and truth: "he *sent forth* from heaven and saved me. . . . God *sent forth* His mercy and His truth." Indeed, our Father in heaven has no relationship with this world except through the Son and in the Holy Spirit, whom Irenaeus of Lyons called "the two hands of God." God's deliverance of His servants, the manifestation of His mercy and truth in this world, has to do with the "missions" of the Son and the Holy Spirit. Following the imagery of this psalm, we may want to speak of the Son and the Holy Spirit as the two "wings" of God, under which we believers take refuge.

The second half of our psalm is more directly concerned with the praise of God. This praise rises from the heart, which is here described as "prepared" (*hetoime*): "My heart is prepared, O God, my heart is prepared; I shall praise and sing." The proper praise of God requires such preparation of heart; the life of prayer is inseparable from the sustained efforts to purify our hearts of all that is resistant and inimical to the grace of God. To be convinced of this truth, one need only note how often we speak, in the psalms, of our hearts: "You have put gladness in my heart . . my heart shall rejoice in Your salvation . . may the meditations of my heart be acceptable in Your sight . . Your law is within my heart . . a broken and contrite heart You will not despise . . incline not my heart to evil. . . search me and know my heart. . . incline my heart to Your testimonies," and so on. The task of praying the psalms includes, then, the work of purifying our hearts, safeguarding our hearts, redirecting our hearts, receiving God's illumination into our hearts, for the pure of heart shall see God, and sing His praise.

Finally, like so many of the psalms, this one also calls on all nations to praise God. The praise of God is a catholic thing, not an individual enterprise. No matter how private the setting of our praying the psalms, the psalms themselves repeatedly speak of their native catholicity: "I will confess You among the peoples, O Lord, I will praise You among the nations." God has sent His Son and His Spirit to catholicize the heart in His praise.

PSALM 57 (58)

IF YOU SPEAK OF JUSTICE

Back in 1930 an English professor at Vanderbilt University, John Crowe Ransom, authored a book entitled, *God Without Thunder*. A poet and literary critic, Ransom was associated with a group of philosophers, historians, and other local scholars profoundly disturbed by the rampant materialistic consumerism that had become, even then, a predominant characteristic of American culture. Writers all, they attempted in various ways, depending on their separate disciplines (for example, two of them, Caroline Gordon and Robert Penn Warren, wrote novels), to examine the historical roots of what they agreed was a most grievous problem corrupting our nation's ethical core and, if left unchallenged, threatening its final moral decline. *God Without Thunder* was Ransom's major contribution to that discussion.

His thesis was fairly plain. Ransom argued that we had forsaken the God of our fathers, the biblical God who smote the hosts of Pharaoh and delivered his poor from the hand of the oppressor, the stern God of an unbending but therefore dependable moral purpose, and we had replaced Him with a more congenial divinity better seasoned to our modern and gentler tastes. We had graven with our thoughts, that is to say, and had fashioned forth unto ourselves a God without thunder.

This new divinity was broadminded, reasonable and, above all, nonjudgmental. Ransom wrote: "The God of the new religion is anthropomorphic. So doubtless are the gods of most other religions. But the present anthropomorphism is peculiarly tame and ingenuous. . . . The net result of holding by this religion is just to be encouraged in attending to one's own human concerns, secured of God's favour and finding no propriety in burnt offering and sacrifice."

A major problem spawned by this new religion, according to Ransom, was the loss of any sense that human existence is answerable to a higher moral throne that takes seriously such old-fashioned matters as doing justly, loving mercy, and walking humbly. Without that abiding sense that it must eventually render an account of its earthly stewardship to a God very serious on points of justice, mercy, and humility, our society was losing its way upon the earth. A chief deficiency of this new, completely benign godhead was that no one could any longer say of Him, for sure, that "He will come again in glory to judge." Transcendent moral judgment was a vanishing memory of yesteryear.

American society, thus cut loose from its moral mooring, now felt itself free to seek, not the Kingdom of heaven and its righteousness, but selfish materialism and other delights of the American dream.

Not enough people having bothered to read Ransom's book about him, this new god bereft of thunder is still with us, of course, and has his devotees. Those folk resolved to pay him their homage, nonetheless, should be cautioned, charitably, to avoid the undue stress likely to be brought on by opening certain sections of the Bible, those yet thunderous parts that enunciate unmistakable distinctions between the right and the wrong and make some mention of plagues affixed to the wrong.

Psalm 57 (Hebrew 58) may be counted one of these parts. This psalm is chock full of hatred—hatred of evil, arrogance, injustice, and hardness of heart. This is a very, very judgmental psalm. Over and over the evil man is criticized and cursed, because he refuses to judge uprightly, because his steps go astray even from his mother's womb, because he is full of venom and deaf to exhortation.

And just who is this evil man? Actually he is not hard to identify. He is very close to each of us. Indeed, we do not have to go outside of ourselves to find him, for from within, out of the heart of men, proceed evil thoughts, adulteries, fornications, murders, thefts, covetousness, wickedness, deceit, lewdness, an evil eye, blasphemy, pride, foolishness. All these evil things come from within and defile a man.

Christian struggle against evil in this world is not, in its first instance, political or social, but ascetical. It commences in the heart of man in the prayer of a warring faith. The inner warrior washes his hands in the blood of the wicked, attuning his ear to the voice of thunder: "Surely there is a God who judges the earth."

PSALM 58 (59)

SAVE ME FROM MY ENEMIES

The structure of Psalm 58 (Hebrew 59) is divided into halves, each of which contains, near its end, the refrain: "You, O God, are my helper." Each half also speaks of the psalmist's enemies as a pack of vicious dogs threatening to devour him.

The context of this psalm is that sacred Passion by which we were redeemed, and the psalm's voice is that of Christ our Lord, the only One who could make the claim of innocence found near the beginning: "For behold, they have stalked my soul, the powerful have assaulted me. Not for any wrongdoing of mine, nor for any sin in me, O Lord. Without wrongdoing have I run, and straight have I kept my course." Jesus said exactly the same thing to His enemies: "Which of you convicts Me of sin?" (John 8:46).

This innocence of Jesus appears rather frequently in the Book of Psalms, beginning as early as Psalm 7. It is one of the Christological themes shared by the Psalter and the New Testament. For example, the Apostle Paul wrote that God "made Him who knew no sin to be sin for us, that we might become the righteousness of God in Him" (2 Cor. 5:21).

Surely sinlessness, blamelessness, and innocence, as such words apply to Jesus, designate far more than a merely moral trait. Let us look again at that last text: "He made Him who knew no sin to be sin for us, that we might become the righteousness of God in Him." This is clearly a passage about the Lord's atoning death. To say that God made Jesus "to be sin" is a very strong way of saying what John the Baptist had already proclaimed: "Behold! The Lamb of God who takes away the sin of the world" (John 1:29). God's making Jesus "to be sin" means that He was God's chosen "sin offering," the sacrificial victim of the atonement. The innocence that Holy Scripture predicates of Jesus has to do with the efficacy of His redemptive suffering and death upon the Cross. His blamelessness, His freedom from blemish, is a quality of that oblation by which we have been delivered from the power of sin.

Those parts of Holy Scripture that speak of the qualities required in the victim slain in a sin offering lay special stress on its being "without blemish" (e.g., Lev. 4:3, 28, 32; 6:6). The oblation must be "clean," symbolizing the state attained by the removal of sin.

Ultimately, of course, all of those Old Testament sin offerings were but a prefiguring of the truly efficacious sacrifice of the Cross, "for it is not possible that the blood of bulls and goats could take away sins" (Heb. 10:4). But if the victims of those older, inefficacious sacrifices had to be without blemish, how much more that Lamb who takes away the sin of the world. It was because He was without sin that Jesus could take away our sins. Thus, it was with specific reference to the Passion of Christ ("Christ also suffered for us") that the Apostle Peter applied to Him a line descriptive of the Suffering Servant in Isaiah: "Who committed no sin, / Nor was deceit found in His mouth." He then went on to narrate the atoning sacrifice: "who Himself bore our sins in His own body on the tree, that we, having died to sins, might live for righteousness—by whose stripes you were healed" (1 Peter 2:21–24).

The four stories of the Passion not only describe the events that transpired on Holy Friday, but also reveal the theological meaning of those events. Thus, in the Gospel accounts of the Lord's trial before the Sanhedrin, it is made clear that His accusers were all false witnesses. Pontius Pilate, in reviewing the case, repeatedly declared the innocence of Jesus. Now the point of these reports was not simply to narrate a miscarriage of justice on the part of the Jewish leaders; it was to emphasize the blameless quality of the sacrificial victim, for a blemished victim could not have redeemed us. The biblical protestations of Jesus' innocence are integral to the theology of the redemption: Himself sinless, He became sin for us.

Each time he begins the preparation of the gifts for the celebration of the Divine Liturgy, the priest raises and kisses the *diskos* (or paten), saying, "You have redeemed us from the curse of the Law." Then, raising and kissing the chalice, he continues that prayer—"by Your precious blood." He finishes the prayer while kissing the other instruments used in handling the bread and wine: "Nailed to the Cross, pierced by the spear, You have poured forth immortality upon mankind." Drawn from several parts of the New Testament, that prayer is chiefly inspired by Galatians 3:13—"Christ has redeemed us from the curse of the law, having become a curse for us (for it is written, 'Cursed is everyone who hangs on a tree')."

Psalm 58 is a prayerful description of those sufferings of the Lord Jesus, innocent but hounded by His enemies, blameless but pursued unto death, trusting in the righteousness of a righteous God to vindicate His innocence by the acceptance of that unique sacrifice by which, as the unblemished Lamb of God, He takes away the sin of the world.

PSALM 59 (60)

O GOD, YOU HAVE REJECTED US

Psalm 59 (Hebrew 60) is a warfare psalm, full of the sorts of things we associate with doing battle, even a map to plan the campaign.

As the psalm commences, the situation is not good. God's people have just suffered a defeat, though it is not as bad as it might have been: "O God, You have rejected us and destroyed us. You have been angry with us, yet have you shown us mercy. You have shaken the earth and thrown it into disarray; repair what is left of it, for it trembles." The destruction is compared to an earthquake, the Greek word here for "shaken" (*syneseisas*) being of the same root as our English "seismic."

Saying that "the earth has been cut out from under us" is, of course, a poetic way of suggesting that we've been pretty badly shaken up. This idea continues in the next sensation, a feeling of stupor resulting from recent defeat: "You have shown Your people hard times; You have made us drink a numbing wine."

But then comes the prayer for deliverance, the rally cry, and the raising of the battle flag: "You have flown the ensign for those who fear You, to escape from the range of the bow. That Your beloved may be delivered, give salvation with Your right hand, and hear me." God Himself will wage war on behalf of His people. "God has spoken in His holy place," says our psalm, and there follows a list of all the things that God will do, all the enemies that He will defeat.

Someone has commented on the importance of knowing "the whole Bible, from Genesis to maps." The latter, of course, is a reference to the cartographic pages at the end of most modern editions of Holy Scripture. These are important, and those who never consult them will suffer disadvantage from the neglect. We Bible-believers do not worship some general, all-purpose divinity. On the contrary, we worship a very specific God who has revealed Himself in certain historical events. Now historical events happen within time and space, and this is the reason for binding maps, and sometimes historical charts, within the Bible itself, so that the reader may keep himself informed about the "places" spoken of in the sacred text. Indeed, some knowledge of geography must be presumed for a proper understanding of many parts of the Bible. Our psalm is certainly one of these.

When God arises and begins to do battle for His people, He provides a list of all the projected battlefields: Shechem, Succoth, Gilead, Manasseh, Ephraim, Judah, Moab, Edom, Philistia. These are real places, and one is much more likely to pray the psalm with understanding if he knows where these places lie in the Holy Land. All the names down through Judah, of course, refer to parts of Israel's traditional inheritance, whereas Moab, Edom, and Philistia came under Israel's control only with the ascendancy of David.

In fact, the line that says "Judah is my scepter" seems to place the context of Psalm 59 during the reigns of either David or Solomon, when a king of the tribe of Judah governed the whole of this area and all the places named in this psalm. Further attention narrows the time to the reign of David (1000–961), whom the Bible credits with conquering Moab, Edom, and Philistia. The very inscription of this psalm places it in the context of 2 Samuel 8, where David conquers the Edomites, and it is difficult to imagine a more probable setting or one that better explains all the particulars in these lines.

The conquest of Edom was particularly hard: "Who will bring me into the fortified city? Who will lead me even unto Edom?" From reading the notice in 2 Samuel 8:14 one would scarcely guess the great difficulty of defeating the Edomites, but it must have been among Israel's most hard-fought battles. The Edomite capital, Selah or Petra, is carved into the sides of an immense box canyon, offering access to an invading army (or today's tourist) only through a thin pass somewhat over a mile long and only about fifteen feet wide. The two sides overlooking this pass rise up to 300 feet. Narrow passes are notoriously easy to defend (cf. the example of Thermopylae in ancient times, or Burnside's Bridge at the Battle of Antietam Creek), but in this case the invader would be harassed by boulders that the defenders, all along that mile and more, could hurl down on the attackers some 300 feet below. Riding through there even now, it is difficult to imagine how the place was ever taken.

Our psalm commences on a note of near despair, but all things are possible to God. David's conquest of Edom will remain forever a symbol of what extraordinary things can be done when God fights on the side of His people: "In God shall we do valiantly, and He will bring our oppressors to naught." We can do all things in Him who strengthens us.

PSALM 60 (61)

ᘍ

Combining petition and confidence, Psalm 60 (Hebrew 61) is one of the simplest and easiest prayers of the entire Psalter.

"Hear my petition, O God," we begin, "attend to my prayer. From the ends of the earth I called out to you, when my heart was anxious." Already is introduced here the first part of a contrast between "far" and "near." In anxiety of heart we cry out to God "from the ends of the earth," but by the very act of doing so we then find ourselves saying: "I will abide in Your temple forever; I will be protected in the shadow of Your wings."

The movement from "far" to "near," which is the whole business of prayer, is a great deal more than a mere psychological experience. It has to do, rather, with the mystery of redemption: "But now in Christ Jesus you who once were far off have been brought near by the blood of Christ" (Eph. 2:13). It is not a matter here of our "feeling far off." Our feelings on the point are futile and unreliable. It is not a feeling but a fact that without Christ, we *are* far off, and the anxiety of heart, mentioned here as characteristic of our being far from God, is well founded: "At that time you were without Christ, being aliens from the commonwealth of Israel and strangers from the covenants of promise, having no hope and without God in the world" (Eph. 2:12).

Now classical paganism did think of itself as hopeful. Even when Pandora opened the jar and released the many plagues that beset the human race, wrote Hesiod, "hope alone yet remained . . . by the will of Zeus the aegis-bearer." This, said Pindar, is the "hope that principally governs the fickle mind of mortals," and Aristophanes spoke of "the great hopes stirred within us by longing." Rome had several temples dedicated to the goddess Hope, and its citizens celebrated her annual feast on August 1. As far as paganism could tell, there was every reason for continuing to hope. A certain healthy kind of hope, after all, is built into the very structure of the rational mind, and the saner sort of paganism, especially on the northern rim of the Mediterranean, paid that hope its proper heed.

Yet, in that text from Ephesians cited above, the Apostle Paul, unwilling to accept paganism's own assessment of its expectations, described those outside of Christ as "having no hope." Whatever classical paganism thought of itself, its prospects were really quite hopeless. Having been "brought near by the blood of Christ," the Christian is keenly aware that such a drawing near is quite beyond his natural ability even to hope.

Our true hope is founded, then, not in the native aspirations of the human spirit but in the redemption wrought by the God to whom we say in our psalm: "For You have become my hope." Our Christian hope is described as "a better hope, through which we draw near to God" (Heb. 7:19), and of the man who has this hope our psalm says: "He will live forever in the presence of God."

Our drawing near to God in prayer is based on His drawing near to us in Christ, who is the one place where God and man meet: "having a High Priest over the house of God, let us draw near with a true heart" (Heb. 10:21, 22). No prayer goes to God except through Christ. It is Christ who gives both foundation and form to our "drawing near" to God, for "we have peace with God through our Lord Jesus Christ, through whom also we have access by faith into this grace in which we stand, and rejoice in hope of the glory of God" (Rom. 5:1, 2). In Christ is "the hope set before us. This hope we have as an anchor of the soul, both sure and steadfast, and which enters the Presence behind the veil" (Heb. 6:18, 19).

Christ is the King, likewise, of whom this psalm says that He "will live forever in the presence of God." Indeed, this King has entered once into the Holy of holies, now to make intercession on our behalf and "whose years," our psalm says again, "will endure from generation to generation."

In one of the more tender sentiments of the Psalter, using an image that appears likewise in Psalms 16 and 90, this psalm tells God: "I will be protected in the shadow of Your wings." This is indeed "the inheritance of those who fear Your name." We finish on the resolve of praise: "So I will sing to Your name forever and ever, and pay my devotion day by day."

PSALM 61 (62)

SHALL NOT MY SOUL BE SUBJECT TO GOD?

Whereas Psalm 60 is concerned with drawing near to God in hope, Psalm 61 (Hebrew 62) is about clinging to God in patience. The address of the psalm goes in a variety of directions—we muse within ourselves, we address our enemies, we speak directly to God, we address one another. This is a psalm supremely useful for settling one's soul quietly in the presence of God.

"Shall not my soul," we ask, "be subject to God? because from Him comes my salvation. For He is my God and my salvation. He is my protector, and I shall be disturbed no more."

Salvation in this psalm, as frequently in the Bible, is something for which we wait in patience. In the grammar of Holy Scripture, salvation is very often spoken of in the future tense: "Whoever calls on the name of the Lord *shall be* saved" (Joel 2:32; Acts 2:21; Rom. 10:13 [also 10:9]). From heaven we "eagerly *wait for* the Savior, the Lord Jesus Christ" (Phil. 3:20), "*looking for* the blessed hope and glorious appearing of our great God and Savior Jesus Christ" (Titus 2:13).

This future perspective of salvation is especially true of the Epistle to the Romans: "Much more, then, having now been justified by His blood, we *shall be saved* from wrath through Him. For if when we were enemies we were reconciled to God through the death of His Son, much more, having been reconciled, we *shall be saved* by His life" (5:9, 10). The Apostle quotes Isaiah to the effect that "the remnant *will be saved*" (9:27), and he hopes that "all Israel *will be saved*" (11:26). Indeed, "our salvation is nearer than when we first believed" (13:11). Even when Romans speaks of salvation in a past tense, it is still a matter of hope for the future: "We were saved in this hope, but hope that is seen is not hope" (8:24).

This future perspective of salvation is certainly the one that dominates in the Psalms, where we are forever telling God such things as: "I will rejoice in Your salvation. . . . I have longed for Your salvation. . . . I hope for Your salvation. . . . My soul faints for Your salvation. . . . Let Your salvation come to me according to Your word. . . . My mouth shall proclaim Your salvation. . . ." and so on. This is also certainly the tone of our present psalm.

Awaiting God's salvation, the believer muses within himself: "Be subject to God, my soul, because from Him comes my patience. He is my God and my savior. He is my protector, and I will not wander. On God depends my salvation and my glory. He is the God of my help, and my hope is in God." The Epistle to the Romans, once again, provides the best commentary: "But if we hope for what we do not see, we eagerly wait for it with perseverance" (8:25). In Israel's darkest moment Jeremiah wrote: "It is good that one should hope and wait quietly / For the salvation of the Lord" (Lam. 3:26).

The life of faith is pretty much evenly divided between serving and waiting. (It is curious that we still call those who serve us "waiters.") These are the two activities of faith—"to *serve* the living and true God, and to *wait* for His Son from heaven" (1 Thess. 1:9, 10). The life of prayer in particular involves a great deal of waiting, while attempting to calm our souls in the presence of God. This is the exhortation of our psalm: "Hope in Him, every gathering of the People. Pour out your hearts before Him, for God is our help."

To this quiet waiting in the presence of God is contrasted the busy agitation of life without God, filled with vanity, dishonesty, lying, cheating, hypocrisy, cursing. In all these lines one recognizes themes from the Bible's wisdom literature. In accord therewith the servants of God are told that, even if from a worldly perspective things are going well, they must be careful not to lose the custody of their hearts: "If wealth increases, do not set your heart upon it."

In the final analysis, God has had only one message to the race of men ("God spoke but once"), containing a twofold truth. First, that power and mercy belong to God, and second, that He will render to each man according to his works. Yes, works. According to Romans, even while he awaits the salvation of God, the believer is supposed to continue working, "not lagging in diligence, fervent in spirit, serving the Lord; rejoicing in hope, patient in tribulation, continuing steadfastly in prayer; distributing to the needs of the saints" (12:11–13).

PSALM 62 (63)

O GOD, MY GOD, I RISE TO YOU AT THE BREAK OF DAY
❧

Psalm 62 (Hebrew 63) is the first of three more psalms long associated with prayer at the hour of dawn. In this case it is an association readily justified by the opening line: "O God, my God, I rise to You at the break of day," as well as a later verse: "I have been mindful of You on my bed, and I will meditate on You during the morning watch." Like Psalm 60, this psalm has recourse to the image of seeking shelter under the shadow of the Lord's wings.

Communion with God is the goal of all prayer, no matter how elementary, pedestrian, or dry. This psalm, in fact, speaks of the soul's sense of dryness, even as it aspires to divine union: "My soul thirsts for You, and in so many ways my flesh as well, in a desert land, trackless and without water; for Your mercy is better than life."

There is a communion with God expressed chiefly in rest and silence; such was the tone of the two previous psalms. In the present psalm, however, the emphasis lies rather on the rapture of blessing and praise: "My lips shall praise You; thus will I bless You. I will lift up my hands unto Your name. . . . My mouth will praise You with joyful lips."

Most men seem not to know it, but a longing for union with God is native to the human soul. Using images of both adherence and pursuit, our present psalm expresses this quality of the soul in a verse that largely defies condign translation into standard English—*ekollethe he psyche mou opiso sou*—*adhaesit anima mea post te*. This would literally read: "My soul stuck fast after You."

This natural, in-built longing within the human spirit to know, praise, and be united with God is that of which Saint Augustine spoke in the famous line in the beginning of his Confessions: "You move us to delight in praising You, for You have formed us for Yourself, and our hearts are restless until they find their rest in You. . . . And those who seek the Lord will praise Him. For those who seek will find Him, and those who find Him shall praise Him. Let me seek You, Lord, in calling upon You, and call upon You in believing in You."

This psalm's aspirations after God, nonetheless, express a more than human longing, for the desire of our hearts is itself transformed by the Holy Spirit. The inner activity of the Holy Spirit, in fact, is not something merely added to a human amorphous yearning. Only the Holy Spirit can turn the soul's innate thirst into a prayer pleasing to God: "Not only that, but we also who have the firstfruits of the Spirit, even we ourselves groan within ourselves.

. . . Likewise the Spirit also helps in our weaknesses. For we do not know what we should pray for as we ought, but the Spirit Himself makes intercession for us with groanings which cannot be uttered" (Rom. 8:23, 26).

Just as the Holy Spirit is the source of the Church's faith (cf. Rom. 8:14; 1 Cor. 12:3; Gal. 4:6) and her charity (cf. Rom. 5:5), so is He the fountain of her hope. This is truly the Spirit of longing, for He causes us to yearn for God well beyond even our own ability to aspire. The Spirit's prayer is the one that the Father reads: "Now He who searches the hearts knows what the mind of the Spirit is" (Rom. 8:27). As one of the Bible's most intense prayers of yearning, the words of Psalm 62 open the mind to what the Holy Spirit prays to God within our souls.

At the same time, the soul's spiritual enemies are ever present, and they, too, are referenced when our psalm speaks of "those who vainly seek my soul," those destined to be "delivered to the hands of the sword" and to become "the portion of foxes."

As a prayer of longing for communion with God, Psalm 62 is especially to be recommended as partial preparation for Holy Communion. Indeed, traditional liturgical usage prescribes this psalm for Matins on Sunday, the day of the celebration of the Holy Eucharist. That defining ritual of Holy Church, given to her in prescription by Christ our Lord, in which she offers to God the sacrifice of praise, and in which the Lord Jesus makes Himself known to His disciples in the Breaking of the Bread, is surely the most perfect context in which to pray such lines as, "So I have come before You in the holy place, to see Your power and Your glory. . . . Let my soul be filled as with marrow and fatness, and my mouth shall praise You with joyful lips." As the highest possible communion with God on this earth, the Holy Eucharist is the supreme fulfillment, this side of heaven, of the aspirations of Psalm 62.

PSALM 63 (64)

O GOD, ATTEND TO MY PRAYER WHEN I CRY

✦

From the earliest times of the Church, Wednesday has been a day of special observance. For instance, we know that it was one of the days on which Christians normally gathered for weekly common prayer, and even now, twenty centuries later, many Christian congregations still observe Wednesdays with something special, like Vespers (or, during Lent, Presanctified Liturgy), or some kind of worship service, or a Bible class, or even a parish supper.

Already in the *Didache* (8.1), at the end of the first century, Wednesday and Friday had been adopted as the two regular fasting days of the normal Christian week. There is other evidence for this primitive discipline, which is still that of the Holy Orthodox Church (cf. Tertullian, *de Jejunio* 14; Clement of Alexandria, *Stromateis* 7.12.75).

Both of these weekly fasting days, Wednesday and Friday, were chosen by reason of their special relationship to the Lord's redemptive suffering, Friday being the day that the Bridegroom was taken away (cf. Mark 2:20), and Wednesday being the day on which He was sold for thirty pieces of silver. It was of Wednesday that the Bible says, with respect to Judas Iscariot: "So from that time he sought opportunity to betray Him" (Matt. 26:16). For this reason the fourth day of Holy Week has long been known in the West as Spy Wednesday.

Wednesday's relationship to the betrayal of Judas seems to be the major reason that Psalm 63 (Hebrew 64) has been associated with that day for many centuries. The Rule of St. Benedict, in the sixth century, already testifies to what appears to have been the older custom of praying this psalm on Wednesday mornings at Matins.

Wednesday was the day before the Last Supper. It was the day on which the Lord said, "You know that after two days is the Passover, and the Son of Man will be delivered up to be crucified." This was the day on which "the chief priests, the scribes, and the elders of the people assembled at the palace of the high priest, who was called Caiaphas, and plotted to take Jesus by trickery and kill Him" (Matt. 26:2–4). On that same day, shortly after this resolve, these enemies of Jesus were approached by a traitor. Treachery and violent intent were everywhere in the air. Jesus Himself was "troubled in spirit" at the impending betrayal from within His own ranks (cf. John 13:21). Such was the setting in which one easily fits the prayer of Psalm 63: "O God, hear my voice when I pray to You; deliver my soul from the fear of the enemy. Protect me from the pack of wicked men, from the mob of those who work iniquity, who sharpen their tongues like a sword, who in ambush bend their bow to let fly the bitter word at a blameless man. Suddenly will they shoot at him without trepidation. They fortify themselves in an evil intent; they plot the concealment of traps, saying, 'Who will see them?'"

The traditional liturgical use of this psalm is a good reminder of the "chronological" structure normally and readily adopted in early Christian piety. Just as each Sunday was a kind of "little Easter," so the other days of the week provided distinct occasions to reflect on the saving mysteries that took shape during that last week of the earthly life of Jesus. Reading the four Gospels, it is striking to see how much space in each of them is devoted to those dramatic days: in Matthew, 8 of 28 chapters; in Mark, 6 of 16 chapters; in Luke, over 5 of 24 chapters; and in John, 11 of 21 chapters. The sheer amount of detailed information relative to that final week, as compared with the other parts of the Gospels, argues that these stories stood out with greater and more vivid precision in the minds of believers.

Moreover, one will hardly fail to notice how the various days of the week of the Passion, and even the times, are clearly indicated in the narrative—"the hour was already late" (Mark 11:11)—"the next day" (11:12)—"when evening had come" (11:19)—"in the morning" (11:20)—"after two days" (14:1)—"on the first day" (14:12)—"in the evening" (14:17)—"in the morning" (15:1)—"it was the third hour" (15:25)—"until the ninth hour" (15:33)—"when evening had come" (15:42)—"very early in the morning, on the first day of the week" (16:2). The different days of the Christian week, and even the various stages within those days, provide the occasions for godly reflection and prayer structured on the historical unfolding of that drama in which salvation was wrought in the midst of the earth.

PSALM 64 (65)

TO YOU A HYMN IS DUE, O GOD, IN ZION

Psalm 64 (Hebrew 65) is traditionally associated with new year's day—not January 1, but the beginning of the Church's new year on September 1. In the Orthodox Church this date is called "the crown of the year," an expression that comes, in fact, from Psalm 64: "You will bless the crown of the year with Your kindness."

Like the Jews, who also celebrate the new year in the autumn with a feast called Rosh Hashanah (literally, "the head of the year"), the Church senses that the closing of the old year has something to do with the bringing in of the late summer's harvest. When this culminating labor has been accomplished, the people of God feel that the year itself has come to completion, and it is time to begin anew.

Because of its connection to the harvest, Psalm 64 is emphatically fitting to the fall: "The sunrise and the evening You make delightful. You visit the earth and water it. You endow it in manifold ways. The river of God is filled with water. You prepare food for Your people, for this is Your provision. Oh, drench the furrows of the earth; increase her crops; budding forth will she dance in the downpour. You will bless the crown of the year with Your kindness, and Your meadows will bulge with Your bounty. Seasonal fruits will swell in the wild, and the hills will be girdled with joy. Thick coats will adorn the rams, and valleys stand deep with the grain. They will vow themselves over to ovations, and the chanting of hymns."

In a number of places, moreover, Holy Scripture (e.g., Matt. 13:30; Rev. 14:15) likens the final times themselves to a harvest, a theme that has found its way into much of the popular hymnody of autumn ("Bringing in the Sheaves," "For the Lord our God shall come, and shall take His harvest home," etc.). The tones of autumn, growing ever more sober through the season, tend to turn reflective minds to thoughts of the ultimate things: death, judgment, and eternity.

Psalm 64 touches also this eschatological aspect of the harvest: "To You a hymn is due, O God, in Zion, and devotion will be offered to You in Jerusalem. Hear my prayer; to You all flesh will make its way." This psalm's line about the final return of mankind ("all flesh") to God became part of the Introit of the Latin Funeral Mass: *Ad Te omnis caro veniet*, an affirmation immortalized in both a well-known Gregorian chant rendition and the polyphonic versions of

Mozart and other great composers. Thus, the abundant fruit for which we pray in this psalm should include also—indeed, most of all—the great harvest of godly lives.

For this reason, the holy city of this psalm, called Zion and Jerusalem, is best thought of here as that heavenly city that is both the goal of our pilgrimage and the garnering house of our harvest. Such seems to be the sense of the next lines: "Blessed is he whom You have chosen and taken to abide with You; he shall dwell in Your courts. We shall be filled with the delights of Your house. Holy is Your temple, magnificent in righteousness." This is that city of which it is said: "There shall be no night there: They need no lamp nor light of the sun, for the Lord God gives them light. And they shall reign forever and ever" (Rev. 22:5).

Prior to its heavenly reference, this coming of all flesh to God pertains likewise to our drawing near to Him in worship, especially in bearing gifts from the harvest. The underlying Hebrew expression here, 'adeka, very often has this meaning in the specifically liturgical literature of Holy Scripture. Just in the Hebrew text of Leviticus and Numbers, for example, the word is used in this sense 138 times. The worship of the Church, which is anticipatory of, and preparatory for, the worship in heaven, is the place where all flesh may draw near unto God, because His house is a house of prayer "for all nations" (Is. 56:7; Mark 11:17).

It is no surprise, then, that our psalm will emphasize this note of universalism, of fulfilled geographical catholicity: "Hear us, O God our Savior, the hope of all the far reaches of the earth, and in the distant sea. . . . The nations shall be in ferment, and those who dwell in the far reaches will be afraid of Your signs." These "signs" of God include the wonders by which He has endowed the world, "preparing the mountains in His strength, wrapped about with power, stirring the bowl of the sea, mastering its waves."

PSALM 65 (66)

SHOUT FOR JOY TO THE LORD, ALL THE EARTH

❦

The reference to the drying up of the waters in Psalm 65 (Hebrew 66) suggests that its original context was the celebration of the Passover and Israel's liberation from slavery in Egypt, themes manifestly understood in the New Testament as types of the new Christian Pascha: "He turns the sea into dry land; through the river they will walk on foot."

There is further reason for believing that Christian tradition has ever understood this psalm as referring to the mystery of Pascha. Most Greek biblical manuscripts of it add a single word supplementing the inscription. To the psalm's Hebrew title, which reads simply "To the choirmaster—a song—a psalm," the majority of Greek manuscripts adjoin the word *anastaseos*, "of the resurrection," a reading that is followed in the Latin tradition as well. Thus, according to the general Christian manuscript tradition of Psalm 65, it is "a psalm of the resurrection."

By way of explaining this tiny augment to the text, a note in the critical apparatus of Alfred Rahlfs's edition of the Septuagint says that "it is a Christian addition, teaching that this psalm was sung on the feast of the Resurrection in the second or the first century." And, by way of confirming this judgment, Rahlfs (a German Protestant) goes on to observe that the first four lines from Psalm 65 are still used in the Divine Liturgy for the Feast of Pascha.

Indeed they are. The opening antiphon of the Paschal Liturgy of St. John Chrysostom is sung with each of the first lines from Psalm 65: "Shout for joy to the Lord, all the earth. Sing to His name, give glory to His praise. Say unto God, 'How magnificent are Your works.' . . . Let all the earth worship You and sing to You, let them sing to Your name, O Most High."

(One may further remark that the very next psalm, Psalm 66, is chanted with the second antiphon at that same Paschal Divine Liturgy, and that the next psalm after that, Psalm 67, is sung on that same day at the very beginning of the Divine Liturgy, even prior to the Great Litany, along with the troparion: "Christ is risen from the dead, trampling down death by death." One is at a loss to cite any other feast during the liturgical year when three psalms sequential in Holy Scripture are chosen for use in the Divine Liturgy. This is truly remarkable and significant.)

The "works" of God being celebrated in this psalm, then, and for which we give thanks to His name, have to do with His accomplishing of our redemption in the paschal mystery, the death and Resurrection of Christ our Lord. These are the "works" of God celebrated in the Divine Liturgy: "Having in remembrance this saving commandment and all those things that have come to pass for us: the Cross, the grave, the third-day Resurrection, the Ascension into heaven, the sitting at the right hand, and the second and glorious coming— Your own, of Your own, we offer unto You on behalf of all and for all." To which the congregation responds, of course: "We praise You, we bless You, we give thanks unto You, O Lord. And we pray unto You, O our God."

Similarly the psalm's references to deliverance from enemies should be read in the context of the drama of Holy Week and the redemption thereby won. This is a psalm about the passage from death to life, for the enemies of the human race are sin and death. It is from these that Christ has set us free, restoring us to eternal favor with God: "He set my soul in life and does not let my footsteps falter. For You, O God, have tested us, You have smelted us as silver. You have brought us into a trap; You laid affliction on our back, and caused men to lord it over us. We passed through fire and water, but You have brought us back to life."

The sense and sentiment of this psalm, then, are identical to the victory canticles in Exodus 15 and Revelation 15, celebrating the destruction of oppressive and death-dealing forces at Israel's deliverance from slavery. Psalm 65 may be thought of as another "seaside psalm," but this sea is "mingled with fire" (Rev. 15:2). Beside it stand the redeemed of the Lord, and "they sing the song of Moses, the servant of God, and the song of the Lamb, saying: 'Great and marvelous are Your works, / Lord God Almighty'" (15:3). These are the "works" of our paschal redemption. "Christ, our Passover, was sacrificed for us. Therefore, let us keep the feast," wrote St. Paul at Passover season, only two decades or so into Christian history (1 Cor. 5:7).

PSALM 66 (67)

O GOD, HAVE MERCY ON US AND BLESS US

~

For many centuries, among Western Christians, Psalm 66 (Hebrew 67) was recited at the break of dawn each morning, invariably as the first psalm of Matins. Thus, just as the sunlight began to break through the darkness on the eastern horizon and to extend, bit by bit, its ever-ranging rays still further to lands in the distant west, holy Church employed this psalm to summon all these myriad peoples to proclaim the praises of God: "O God, have compassion on us and bless us, and let Your face shine upon us, to make known Your way upon the earth, and Your salvation to all the nations." Twice during this psalm will come the double refrain: "May the peoples bless You, O Lord, may all the peoples bless You." Just as God begins, at the opening of the day, to cause His sun to shine alike on both the just and the unjust, all the earth is invited to laud His universal mercy.

The God of the Bible, in the definitive covenant that He has given us in Christ, has brought to perfection and fulfillment the promises contained in all of the earlier, preparatory covenants of sacred history. One of the earliest of these was the covenant with Noah, that primeval compact of God with "every living creature of all flesh that is on the earth." This ancient arrangement of grace, described in Genesis 9:16 as *berith 'olam*, "a covenant forever," has never been abrogated, nor can it be, for it rests solely on the infallible promise of a gracious God. Using the specific technical expressions "give" (*natan*) and "establish" (*haqim*), Genesis describes this covenant as both gratuitous and permanent (cf. 9:9, 11, 12, 17).

Symbolized in that heavenly "sign" (*'oth*) of the rainbow, it is God's covenant with creation itself: "While the earth remains, / Seedtime and harvest, / Cold and heat, / Winter and summer, / And day and night / Shall not cease" (Gen. 8:22). As such, it is a universal covenant, for Noah is the father of us all. God's covenant with Noah, moreover, is universal in two ways—in space and in time.

First, space, and all that it contains. The covenant with Noah is the Lord's guarantee that His disposition toward His creation will forever stay gracious, that His grace will be hierarchically expressed in the very structure of the natural universe, linking higher and lower natures in a wise and eternal order, and placing all of it under the governance of a provident God.

In particular, the human being, who stands near the top of this covenanted hierarchy of natures, remains forever the special object of God's salvific attention, and the contract with Noah found its fulfillment in the Incarnation, the Redemption, and the preaching of the Gospel. The very movement of the sun across the sky was regarded by St. Paul as symbolizing the advance of the apostolic proclamation (cf. Rom. 10:18). God's everlasting mercy is written in the heavens. This was the persuasion that prompted St. Benedict of Nursia, in the sixth century, to prescribe the praying of Psalm 66 each morning at daybreak, that God would let His face shine on all peoples of the world and show them His way upon the earth.

Second, time. As we have seen, Genesis 9 lays particular stress on the permanence of God's covenant with Noah. It is the contract that binds each generation to both the generations gone before and those yet to appear. History itself thus becomes hierarchical, as each new generation, learning its language (and therefore the structured patterns of thought and evaluation) from the one preceding it, submits in faith to the accumulated wisdom of ages past, and then, it is hoped, enhances and further refines that wisdom for the children still to come. The covenant with Noah is, thus, our sacred partnership with history—what Edmund Burke calls "the contract of eternal society," extending down through the centuries, joining the living with those who have already passed on, with those yet unborn, but most of all with the God who wills all men to be saved and to come to the knowledge of the truth.

This permanent and universal covenant with Noah is the foundation for what the Romans called "piety," the cultivated, deep, heartfelt respect for our stewardship of tradition, for the ancestral associations whence derives our identity, and for the gracious God above who sanctions the order of the world and invests it with the majesty of His wisdom.

PSALM 67 (68)

The Book of Numbers 10:35 indicates what seems to have been the original context for Psalm 67 (Hebrew 68): "So it was, whenever the ark set out, that Moses said: 'Rise up, O Lord! / Let Your enemies be scattered, / And let those who hate You flee before You.'" This was the psalm chanted to accompany the movement of the ark of the covenant, as it was carried by the Levites from place to place during Israel's desert wanderings.

Reference is made to the central event of that wandering—Mount Sinai: "O God, when You went out before Your people, when You marched through the wilderness, the earth shook; the heavens also dripped rain at the presence of God. Sinai itself was moved at the presence of God, the God of Israel."

The enemies to be scattered, in that historical context, were those up-to-no-good Amalekites, Moabites, Amorites, Midianites and so forth, who did battle against the Chosen People on their way to the Promised Land: "Kings of armies flee, they flee. . . . But God will wound the head of His enemies, the hairy scalp of one who still goes on in his trespasses. . . . Scatter the peoples who delight in war."

This wandering of Israel through the desert was a kind of procession, in which the various tribes marched in set formation: "The chariots of God are twenty thousand, even thousands of thousands. . . . Bless the Lord in the congregations, the Lord from the fountain of Israel. There is little Benjamin, their leader, the princes of Judah and their company, the princes of Zebulun and the princes of Naphtali."

Other lines in the psalm make it clear, likewise, that it was later chanted to accompany liturgical processions in the temple at Jerusalem: "They have seen Your procession, O God, the procession of my God, my King, into the sanctuary. The singers went before, the players on instruments followed after; among them were the maidens playing timbrels. . . . Because of Your temple at Jerusalem, kings will bring presents to You."

Because of textual corruptions suffered over many centuries, some lines of this psalm are likely to remain forever obscure, but the general sense of it is clear enough. It is a psalm for God's people who have set out to accompany Him on the march.

The Christian sense of this psalm is abundantly clear in its traditional liturgical use, the best example being the rush procession of Holy Saturday night. In front of the church doors, after we have thrice marched around the building, we stand and listen to St. Mark's account of the myrrhbearing women coming to the empty tomb of the Risen Christ. Then, after that Gospel, we repeatedly chant the triumphant troparion of Pascha: "Christ is risen from the dead, trampling down death by death, and upon those in the tombs bestowing life." Between chantings of that great troparion we sing lines from Psalm 67: "Let God arise, let His enemies be scattered; let those also who hate Him flee before Him. As smoke is driven away, so drive them away; as wax melts before the fire, so let the wicked perish at the presence of God."

Here we have the deeper, more authentic sense of the psalm: Jesus, the author and perfecter of our faith, arising from the dead ("Let God arise"), triumphant over sin and death ("Let His enemies be scattered"), bringing His saints from the demonic depths of Hades ("I will bring back from Bashan, I will bring them back from the depths of the sea"), leading the Church in her journey through history ("O God, when You went out before Your people").

This is a psalm about the glorification of Christ, with particular accent on His ascent into heaven: "Sing to God, sing praises to His name; extol Him who rides on the clouds. . . . You have ascended on high, you have led captivity captive; You have received gifts among men. . . . Sing to God, you kingdoms of the earth; Oh, sing praises to the Lord, to Him who rides on the heaven of heavens, which were of old."

In Ephesians 4:8, our earliest Christian witness to this interpretation of Psalm 67, St. Paul actually changes its wording, so that the "gifts" refer to the various ministries in the Church: "When He ascended on high, / He led captivity captive, / And gave gifts to men." The Apostle explains in verses 9 and 10: "(Now this, 'He ascended'—what does it mean but that He also first descended into the lower parts of the earth? He who descended is also the One who ascended far above all the heavens, that He might fill all things.)" Paul then lists some of the major ministries in the Church, all of them "gifts" of the risen, glorified Christ.

PSALM 68 (69)

SAVE ME, O GOD

From the very beginning the Christian reading of Psalm 68 (Hebrew 69) has uniformly interpreted this prayer in the context of the Lord's suffering and death. "Save me, O God, for the waters have come even unto my soul. . . . I have come to the depths of the sea, and the flood has submerged me," prays the Man of sorrows who described His approaching Passion as the baptism with which He must be baptized (cf. Mark 10:38; Luke 12:50; Rom. 6:3).

This same Sufferer goes on to pray: "Zeal for Your house has consumed me," a verse explicitly cited in the New Testament with respect to the Lord's purging of the temple (John 2:17). In the context this consuming of the Lord was a reference to His coming Passion; He went on to say to those who were plotting to kill Him: "Destroy this temple, and in three days I will raise it up." In saying this, the evangelist noted, "He was speaking of the temple of His body" (vv. 19, 21).

The very next line of Psalm 68 says: "The reproaches of those who reproached You have fallen on me," a verse later cited in Romans as bearing on the sufferings of the Lord. The apostle's lapidary and understated comment was that "even Christ did not please Himself" (15:3). In this passage St. Paul could obviously presume a common Christian understanding of Psalm 68, even in a congregation that he had not yet visited.

Still later in our psalm stands the line: "Let their dwelling be deserted, and let no one live in their tabernacles." Even prior to the Pentecostal outpouring, the Church knew this verse for a reference to Judas Iscariot (cf. Acts 1:20), that dark and tragic figure who guided the enemies of Jesus and betrayed his Lord with a kiss.

Psalm 68 is the prayer of Him "who, in the days of His flesh . . . offered up prayers and supplications, with vehement cries and tears to Him who was able to save Him from death" (Heb. 5:7). The Christian Church has ever been persuaded that Psalm 68 expresses the sentiments of that soul "exceedingly sorrowful, even to death" (Matt. 26:38). In Psalm 68 we are given a vision into the very heart of Christ in the circumstances of His Passion: "Deliver me from those that hate me, and from the depths of the waters. Let not the flood of water submerge me, nor the depth swallow me down, nor the mouth of the pit close over me."

This is the Christ who in dereliction sought in vain the human companionship of His closest friends during the vigil prior to His arrest: "What? Could you not watch with Me one hour?" (Matt. 26:40). Psalm 68 speaks of this disappointment as well: "My heart waited for contempt and misery; I hoped for someone to share my sorrow, but there was no one; someone to console me, but I found none."

According to all four Gospels, the dying Christ was offered some sort of bitter beverage, *oxsos,* a sour wine or vinegar, as He hung on the Cross. This is the very word used at the end of the following verse of Psalm 68: "And for my food they laid out gall, and for my drink they gave me vinegar."

But there is another dimension to the Passion of the Lord—the resolve of His victory. Even as He was being arrested, His enemies were unable to stand upright in His presence (cf. John 18:6). This was the Christ, "who for the joy that was set before Him endured the cross, despising the shame" (Heb. 12:2). No man takes the Lord's life from Him, for He has power to lay it down and to take it up again (cf. John 10:18). This is the Christ whom death could not hold, who descended a very conqueror into hell to loose the bonds of them that sat in darkness, and who "went and preached to the spirits in prison" (1 Pet. 3:19).

This sense of Christ's victory also dominates the final lines of Psalm 68: "I am poor and distressed, but the salvation of Your face, O God, has upheld me. I will praise the name of God with song; and I will magnify Him with praise."

The victory of Christ is the foundation of the Church, those described when our psalm says, "Let the poor see and rejoice. Seek God, and your soul will live. . . . For the Lord will save Zion, and the cities of Judah will be built, and they shall dwell there and hold it by inheritance, and the seed of His servants will possess it."

PSALM 69 (70)

O GOD, COME TO MY ASSISTANCE

Except for a few very minor variations, Psalm 69 [Hebrew 70] is nearly identical to the final verses of Psalm 39. A plea for help in distress, it is a prayer appropriate to a great many circumstances in life. In fact, it is safe to say that the psalm's opening line—"O God, come to my assistance; O Lord, make haste to help me"—has been prayed, over the centuries, more than any other line of the Psalter. There is a reason for this. In the sixth century, the great monastic code of the West, the Rule of St. Benedict, prescribed that each of the seven "day hours" (as distinct from Vigils, the midnight service) should begin with this verse, thus guaranteeing that it would be prayed at least seven times each day.

This usage became common in the West, even for nonmonastics. One finds it in the traditional Roman Breviary, for example, and Archbishop Cranmer placed that verse at the beginning of the Anglican daily Evensong.

The roots of this usage, however, go back earlier to the Christian East, especially Egypt. A century before the Rule of St. Benedict, the popularity of this prayer among Egyptian monks was observed by St. John Cassian, a Romanian monk who traveled extensively around the Mediterranean and finally settled in southern Gaul. The tenth book of Cassian's great work, *The Conferences*, which is the second conference of Abba Isaac on prayer, most marvelously describes the efficacy of this psalm verse in all the circumstances of life. Whether in temptation or calm, says Abba Isaac, whether in fear or reassurance, whether in pain or pleasure, joy or sorrow, there are no circumstances in life when it is not supremely proper to pray: "O God, come to my assistance; O Lord, make haste to help me." This prayer, he goes on, should never be absent from our lips.

As a simple doubling and slight expansion of the "Lord, have mercy," this opening line of Psalm 69 became, then, one of the most important early formulas in the quest for constant prayer. It served as a kind of historical forerunner to the "Jesus Prayer" ("Lord Jesus Christ, Son of the living God, have mercy on me a sinner").

After stating that this formula—"O God, come to my assistance; O Lord, make haste to help me"—had been handed down through the Egyptian monastic tradition from its most ancient fathers, with a view to attaining purity of heart and constant prayer, Abba Isaac continues: "Not without reason has this verse been selected from out of the whole body of Scripture. For it takes up all the emotions that can be applied to human nature and with great correctness and accuracy it adjusts itself to every condition and every attack. It contains an invocation of God in the face of any crisis, the humility of a devout confession, the watchfulness of concern and of constant fear, a consciousness of one's own frailty, the assurance of being heard, and confidence in a protection that is always present and at hand, for whoever calls unceasingly on his protector is sure that he is always present. It contains a burning love and charity, an awareness of traps, and a fear of enemies."

Then several pages of Abba Isaac (as narrated by Cassian, in what may be counted among the most eloquent and carefully crafted paragraphs in all of Latin patristic literature), are devoted to the sundry and manifold circumstances in which it is proper to pray, "O God, come to my assistance; O Lord, make haste to help me." Prayed from the heart, it places the mind constantly in communion with God.

The quest of the ancient Egyptian tradition, Isaac insists, was to make this formula a permanent invocation: "This verse should be poured out in unceasing prayer so that we may be delivered in adversity and preserved and not puffed up in prosperity. You should, I say, meditate constantly on this verse in your heart. You should not stop repeating it when you are doing any kind of work or performing some service, or are on a journey. Meditate on it while sleeping and eating and attending to the least needs of nature. . . . Let it be the first thing that comes to you when you awake, let it anticipate every other thought as you get up, let it send you to your knees as you arise from your bed, let it bring you from there to every work and activity, and let it accompany you at all times."

PSALM 70 (71)

IN YOU, O LORD, I PUT MY TRUST

As a normal ending to most of the litanies of the Orthodox Church, her herald deacon, his summoning stole lifted before the icon of the Lord, exhorts the worshipping congregation, "Let us commend ourselves, and each other, and all our life unto Christ our God." "To You, O Lord," chants God's people in response.

"All our life" we thus commend—every single aspect of our lives—our economy and the labor of our hands, our culture and the striving of our minds, all that John Keats calls "those flowery bands that bind us to the earth," and most particularly the myriad mutual relationships ("and one another") in which we are to be sanctified.

"All our life" we commend—not just the present moment, which is still somewhat within our governance, but more especially those two other chronological blocks over which we have so little say, the past and the future; the past, remembered with both thanksgiving and remorse, and the future, dimly surveyed with hope as well as fear. To Christ our God, we commend "*all* our life."

In that brief commendation of our lives, so frequently heralded in our hearing by the Church's deacon, we are right to find a kind of summary of Psalm 70 (Hebrew 71): "For You are my patience, O Lord. From my youth the Lord has been my hope. I have leaned on You from my very birth; since my mother's womb have You been my defense. . . . Oh, forsake me not as the years advance, nor cast me aside when my strength is spent. . . . From my youth have You taught me, O God, and unto this day Your wonders I declare. And unto old age and hoary head, O God, forsake me not."

Those who pray the psalms are aware that, in spite of their own infidelities to God over the years, God has nonetheless remained faithful. Were that not the case, they would not be praying the psalms at all.

This sense of God's lifelong fidelity is at the heart of the Christian experience. In the middle of the second century, put on trial for his faith in Jesus and pressured either to renounce that faith or die a violent death, the venerable Polycarp, Bishop of Smyrna, responded to his judge: "For eighty-six years have I served Him, and He has done me no wrong. How can I blaspheme the King who saved me?"

Trial and trouble, nonetheless, shape the context of fidelity in this psalm, as they did in the long life of Polycarp: "My God, deliver me from the hand of the sinner, from the law-breaker and the wicked. . . . For mine enemies have spoken against me, and there is a conspiracy among those that stalk my soul. They say, 'God has forsaken him. Hound him down and catch him, for there is none to deliver him.'" This is the persecution of which our Lord spoke so often in the Gospels, saying that it would be the constant lot of those who bear His name.

The many trials mentioned in this psalm are well known to the servants of Christ, one of whom described himself as "in labors more abundant, in stripes above measure, in prisons more frequently, in deaths often. From the Jews five times I received forty stripes minus one. Three times I was beaten with rods; once I was stoned; three times I was shipwrecked; a night and a day I have been in the deep; in journeys often, in perils of waters, in perils of robbers, in perils of my own countrymen, in perils of the Gentiles, in perils in the city, in perils in the wilderness, in perils in the sea, in perils among false brethren; in weariness and toil, in sleeplessness often, in hunger and thirst, in fastings often, in cold and nakedness" (2 Cor. 11:23–27).

And what does the servant of God do in the midst of such trials? According to our psalm, he is chiefly engaged in praising God: "I will sing psalms to You on the harp, O Holy One of Israel. My mouth will proclaim Your righteousness, and all day long Your salvation. . . . My lips will exult when I sing to You, and my soul which You have redeemed. And all day long will my tongue meditate on Your righteousness." Once again the ministry of the Apostle Paul is most instructive in this respect. One remembers how Paul, after being beaten at Philippi, sang songs of praise during the night in his jail cell. One recalls that he uses words for "joy" in a letter that he wrote from a prison cell (that is, the Epistle to the Philippians) more often than in any other of his letters.

PSALM 71 (72)

Psalm 71 (Hebrew 72) is often referred to as a "messianic" psalm, in the sense that it is concerned with God's "anointed" king. Considering only the simplest reading of this psalm, it is difficult to escape the impression that it was composed for use at ceremonies of royal coronation, the ritual point of dynastic transition: "Grant Your justice to the king, O God, and Your righteousness to the king's son." The title added to this psalm does, in fact, ascribe it to Solomon, the first successor to the Davidic throne.

Two narrative sections of Holy Scripture readily come to mind in connection with the themes of Psalm 71. The first text is 2 Samuel 7, containing Nathan's great prophecy about the royal house of David, which now became the beneficiary of a special covenant to guarantee that his descendants would reign forever over his kingdom. A number of lines of our psalm, especially those pertaining to the permanence and extension of David's royal house, reflect that historical text.

The second pertinent passage is 1 Kings 3, which describes Solomon's prayer for the "wise heart" that would enable him to govern God's people justly. Repeatedly throughout this psalm mention is made of the justice and wisdom that would characterize God's true anointed one.

Both aspects of Psalm 71, as well as the two narrative texts that it reflects, proved to be more than slightly problematic in Israel's subsequent history. For example, Solomon's vaunted wisdom as a ruler, that for which he had prayed at Gibeah, didn't last even to the end of his own lifetime, and it was displayed among his posterity with (not to put too fine a point on it) a rather indifferent frequency. Similarly, what is to be said about the permanence of the reign of David's household over God's people? More than half of that kingdom broke away shortly after the death of David's first successor, nor was any Davidic king ever again to reign on his throne after the fall of Jerusalem in 586 BC. What, then, could be said for either the prophecy of Nathan or the prayer of Solomon? How were the promises in this psalm to be understood?

As Christians, of course, we believe that the inner substance of all these prefigurings finds its fulfillment in Jesus the Lord, the goal of biblical history and the defining object of all biblical prophecy.

The Archangel Gabriel announced the fulfillment of these ancient prophecies when he told the Mother of the Messiah that "the Lord God will give

Him the throne of His father David. And He will reign over the house of Jacob forever, and of His kingdom there will be no end" (Luke 1:32, 33). Yet other angels announced to the shepherds that "there is born to you this day in the city of David a Savior, who is Christ [Messiah] the Lord" (2:11). He was to be at once David's offspring and His Lord (cf. Mark 12:35–37).

As for Solomon, was he the wise king? Well, in measure, to be sure, but now behold, a greater than Solomon is here. If Solomon's wish was to rule God's people wisely and with righteousness (a word that comes repeatedly in our psalm), what shall we say of the One whom the New Testament calls our wisdom and our righteousness (1 Cor. 1:24, 30)?

The liturgical use of this psalm during the festal days of Christmastide suggests still further dimensions of its fulfillment, particularly the anticipated universality of the Messiah's Kingdom. For example, consider these lines: "The Ethiopians [usually meaning any of Africa south of Egypt] shall fall down before Him, and His enemies shall lick the dust. The kings of Tarses [in Spain] and the islands [Corsica, Sardinia, Sicily, Crete, Cyprus, Rhodes, etc.] shall offer gifts, and the kings of Arabia and Saba shall bring offerings. And all the kings shall bow down before Him, and all nations serve Him." Such lines must put one in mind of those wise kings who came to bow down before the Christ Child, especially in light of the psalm's later line that says: "And He shall live and shall receive the gold of Arabia" (cf. Matt. 2:9–11).

No matter how successful his reign, no other king in history fulfilled the hopes outlined in Psalm 71. The Kingdom here described is truly not a kingdom of this world.

PSALM 72 (73)

HOW GOOD GOD IS TO ISRAEL

While many of the psalms are congregational hymns manifestly composed for public worship, Psalm 72 (Hebrew 73) is one of those showing signs of a more private origin, taking its rise in the intimate reflections of the pondering heart. Psalm 72 is concerned with much the same moral problem as Job and Habakkuk—"If God is just and on the side of justice, and if also God is almighty, why do wickedness and injustice seem to prevail?"

Already in this, its most elementary moral presupposition—its basic sentiment of hope, expecting goodness and justice to prevail over evil and injustice—Psalm 72 stands radically at odds with much of our present popular philosophy. Indeed, one of the more characteristic features of the modern world is its growing inability to presume that the moral order, including the social order, is rooted in the metaphysical order, described by Colin Gunton as "the order of being as a whole." Relatively few people in today's culture seem any longer able to presuppose that they live in a moral universe where the differences between right and wrong, justice and injustice, are fixed in the composition of reality.

Like the ancient Sophists, those ethical relativists who perceived no essential relationship between objective reality and ethical norm, and thus no necessary association between nature and culture, many thinkers today, not viewing the universe in fixed moral terms, would find no reason for surprise at the apparent prevalence of evil.

For modern man, after all, as for those ancient foes of Socrates, justice is only what a given culture determines justice to be. Justice is configured only as a society decides to configure it. Thus, there is no way for injustice to prevail, for if a society approves or prefers a certain kind of behavior, then the latter conduct automatically becomes just.

Strictly speaking, then, since for modern man correct behavior consists solely in the acquiescence to purely cultural norms, there can really be no such thing as an unjust society. That is to say, whatever prevails in a society is necessarily just, because society is the sole and ultimate arbiter of justice. In contemporary sociology and other behavioral disciplines this presumption rises to the level of an axiomatic first principle, quite beyond academic controversy.

Moreover, in a world whose only presumed rule is the survival of the fittest, why would anyone anticipate that justice and goodness would prevail?

In short, a major conversion of mind would be required of modern man even to appreciate the moral problem posed in this psalm, much less to deal with that problem philosophically or, yet less, to make it the inquiry of prayer.

For Psalm 72, however, since it presupposes the identification of the world's Creator with the Author of the moral law, the prevalence of evil in the world is the stuff of a crisis. Even as the psalm begins, the crisis has already been worked through, so to speak, and the prayer simply reviews the reflective process that brought about its resolution. Even as we begin the psalm, then, we are ready to praise God.

First, the moral problem. There is the scandal at beholding the prosperity of the wicked, in contrast to the suffering of the just. Second, there is the temptation to envy or even emulate the wicked. After all, evil seems to provide a bigger payoff than good. This was the candid argument explicitly made by the Sophist Thrasymachus, who contended that, because injustice does a better job of "delivering the goods," only a dunce or weakling would prefer justice! Third, there is the believer's awareness that he is actually being tempted; he senses that, in permitting himself even to think such thoughts, he places his soul in moral peril. Thus, the believer takes stock of his thoughts before it is too late. Fourth, he takes stock of his thoughts by entering into the deeper presence of God: "So I tried to understand this, but it was too difficult for me, until I entered the sanctuary of God." (One may want to interpret this "sanctuary of God" as the loving intellect; Cicero thus speaks of the "temple of the mind.") Fifth, the believer reflects on the judgments of God, who knows how to deal with the unjust, and will, at the last, do so. Finally, the believer commits his own destiny to God, who will never abandon him, ever be with him, and, at the end, receive him into glory.

PSALM 73 (74)

WHY DO YOU UTTERLY ABANDON US, O GOD?

ℭ

It is sometimes imagined that Charles Darwin's *Origin of Species,* when it appeared in 1859, was generally shocking or took the intellectual world by surprise. In fact, however, his theory of radical randomness did not land on entirely unfavorable or even neutral ground. On the contrary, a lot of thinkers were ready for the notion and disposed to receive it favorably. It is more precise, rather, to think of Darwin's theory of evolution as promising a sort of scientific validation and framework for a cosmology already congenial to many minds.

During the half-century previous to Darwin, many philosophers and literary figures had entertained the idea that the universe did not point to anything beyond itself—that it really did not have anything intelligible to "say" to man—that the world was ultimately silent, without voice—that it embodied no "truth" that man could discover. Many thinkers had, thus, reached the conclusion that truth was not something to be discovered, but something to be invented. To such minds Darwin's theory seemed to lend scientific support.

The historical development of this line of thought is examined by an American philosopher, Richard Rorty. Near the beginning of the nineteenth century, says Rorty, "the idea that truth was made rather than found began to take hold of the imagination of Europe." Whereas former ages, he writes, had gone to the world's structure to find an abiding truth already concealed within it by its Creator, modern men could no longer make that presumption: "The suggestion that truth, as well as the world, is *out there* is a legacy of an age in which the world was seen as the creation of a being who had a language of his own." But modern men could no longer feel convinced on the point, nor does Rorty believe they should be: "The world does not speak. Only we do. The world can, once we have programmed ourselves with a language, cause us to hold beliefs. But it cannot propose a language for us to speak."

In such a view, intelligibility is not a characteristic of the world itself, but only of the human mind. Intelligibility, or "sense," implies structure, or knowable form. In contrast, the "random" is that which has no intelligible structure. This is why we say that accidents are "senseless." A random world, then, is necessarily a world without sense, a world devoid of knowable forms.

The foregoing considerations bear witness, of course, to the modern intellectual rebellion against the creating God who is described in the Bible.

Psalm 73 (Hebrew 74), for example, testifies to the God who structures the world and divides it from the chaotic and random: "In Your might You hold the sea; You have crushed the heads of the dragons in the waters. Crushing the dragon's head, You have fed him to the people of Ethiopia. You opened the springs and torrents, and You dried up the waters of Etham. The day is Yours, and Yours is the night; You prepared both the sun and the moon. You have fixed all the boundaries of the earth."

The God of Psalm 73 is the world's Creator, and His act of creation implies the imposition of limits: "You have fixed all the boundaries of the earth." To create a knowable world is to pattern it according to intelligible forms, and limit is essential to the very notion of form (limit being "this" and not "that"). To say that God has "fixed all the boundaries, the determined limits, of the earth" is to say that God has already attached meaning to the structure of the world. Truth is already in the world, awaiting man's discovery. The world already speaks the mind of God; man's task is to listen to what it says.

Psalm 73 also testifies, nonetheless, that the sinful human mind is disposed to rebel against the formal, noetic structure that God has given to the world. Indeed, this intellectual rebellion seems often to prevail on the earth: "Why do You utterly abandon us, O God? . . . Raise Your hands against all that the enemy has done in Your holy place, against their undying pride. . . . How long, O God, will the enemy taunt us? Will the adversary defy Your name forever? . . . Remember that the enemy blasphemes the Lord, and a foolish people defies Your name."

We modern men live late in an age of intellectual rebellion, when darkened, unrepentant hearts stand defiant before the plain speech that the Creator has placed in the very structure of the world. Such is the strife of which we pray in Psalm 73.

PSALM 74 (75)

၈

The structure of Psalm 74 (Hebrew 75) is unique in the Book of Psalms. While its opening and closing verses are expressions of praise, the entire central section is spoken by God Himself.

God is praised for His "marvelous deeds" (*thavmasia, mirabilia*), an expression normally referring to His works of redemption. In Holy Scripture, God's redemptive deeds are the basis of man's praise.

Now, if our redemption is the foundation of our prayer, there is some reason for supposing that our prayer may be improved by a better understanding of what is meant by redemption. Alas, the latter is a widely misunderstood theological category.

To begin with, much of later Christian thinking about redemption has tended to rely rather heavily on metaphors drawn from the world of commerce. Indeed, the Latin root of the word "redemption" (*re-emi*) means "to buy back," a notion certainly familiar to those obliged, on occasion, to make use of the services of pawnbrokers. Moreover, the New Testament most certainly speaks of redemption in terms of a "price" that was paid (cf. 1 Cor. 6:20; 7:23; Eph. 1:14).

Some Christians, however, understanding these metaphors rather literally, began to make more specific inquiries with respect to them, particularly asking: "To whom was the price paid?" Origen, a third-century heretic, suggested that the price was paid to the devil, while much of the West preferred to think of the "price" of redemption as being paid to God the Father on behalf of fallen humanity. One finds this interpretation in the Western liturgy, for instance, in the Paschal *Exultet*, and after the Great Schism it became the foundation for the theory of atonement devised by Anselm of Canterbury. According to his idea, our reconciliation to the Father involved some sort of legal transaction whereby Christ paid to Him the full price of our sins, so that we now stand before God debt-free.

There are (at least) four things wrong with this theory of redemption. First, it disregards the metaphorical quality of biblical language about redemption. It takes the imagery of commerce too literally, not respecting the specific ways in which the Bible uses such metaphors. For example, Scripture repeatedly says that God redeemed Israel out of Egypt. God did this, nonetheless, not by paying Pharaoh a legal price, but by slamming him upside the head with a series of plagues and then a tricky ruse at the Red Sea.

Second, understanding the commercial metaphor too literally, Anselm's theory goes on to ask (and then answer) inappropriate questions that the Bible never considers. For example, since "we were reconciled to God through the death of His Son" (Rom. 5:10), none of us doubts, surely, that the price of our sins was paid by Jesus. But why assume that this "price" is to be understood in a legal and commercial sense? When I was a boy, very many Americans were "paying the price" for my liberty by dying in combat in World War II. Everyone knew what this meant, and no one thought to ask "to whom" the price was being paid. To ask such a question would have betrayed a misunderstanding of the metaphor. There are any number of similar uses of this imagery, as when we say that tough exercise and a rigid diet are the "price to be paid" for staying healthy or being a good athlete, or that intense study is the price of a successful education. Similarly, to ask "to whom" Jesus paid the price of our redemption is an inappropriate question, giving rise to theories quite foreign to Holy Scripture.

Third, Anselm's theory of redemption leaves insufficient room for the biblical assertion that the Father Himself reconciled and redeemed us in Christ: "Now all things are of God, who has reconciled us to Himself through Jesus Christ, and has given us the ministry of reconciliation, that is, that God was in Christ reconciling the world to Himself, not imputing their trespasses to them, and has committed to us the word of reconciliation" (2 Cor. 5:18, 19).

Fourth, Anselm's theory reduces the work of redemption solely to the Cross, whereas Holy Scripture includes the Resurrection and glorification of the Lord among the deeds of redemption (cf. Rom. 4:24, 25; Heb. 9:11, 12). All of these things are included among the "marvelous deeds" of which Psalm 74 speaks. They are the basis of our continued praise of God.

Whereas later theology, particularly in the West, has been disposed to think of the Christian redemption chiefly in legal terms, favoring a rather literal interpretation of the commercial metaphors used in the Bible with respect to it (cost, purchase, price, debt, etc.), the older and more traditional texts of the Church, especially the liturgical texts, have tended to use exactly the same terms in an interpretive context of combat, defeat, and victory.

The contrast between these two perspectives will perhaps be made clearer by examining a single image very important to the biblical understanding of redemption: the shedding of the blood of Christ as the "price" of our salvation. The later (eleventh-century) Western view regards this expression in a kind of legal and commercial setting, understood rather literally. This view must then fit the concept of "price" into the full context of a legal and commercial transaction, a kind of business arrangement, as it were, involving a true *quid pro quo*, in which Jesus pays to His Father the debt of fallen humanity.

The older view, on the other hand, represented in patristic and liturgical texts (in both East and West), perceives this same image—the blood of Christ as the price of our salvation—in terms of combat, defeat, and victory. In this perspective, Jesus indeed "paid the price" for our sins, saving us by shedding His blood unto death, but He did so as a warrior doing battle with the devil, sin, and death on our behalf. He willingly laid down His life, accepting suffering and death, but then descending into the nether regions victorious, as the very Giver of life whom neither the grave nor hell could hold, and rising again for our justification, having trampled down death by death. Thus Jesus defeated sin by His dying, and death by His rising again.

Now such are the great redemptive acts of which the Bible speaks, those "marvelous deeds" of mortal strife, whereby salvation was wrought upon the earth and for which praise and thanksgiving rise to God as we pray through the Book of Psalms.

This concept of redemption as battle is found, for instance, in Psalm 75 (Hebrew 76), long used in the West at Matins on Friday, the day when the earth quaked as the Bridegroom was taken away, lowered from the Cross on the hill of combat. (Indeed, for many centuries it was customary to follow Psalm 75 with the great warrior scene from Habakkuk 3.) This majestic psalm evokes the memory of the defeat of Pharaoh's army in order to describe how the Lord, with fire and fury, shook the earth and overthrew His foes: "Wondrously You blaze forth from the eternal mountains, and all the foolish of heart are thrown into confusion. All the men of wealth slept their sleep, nor found ought left in their hands. At Your rebuke, O God of Jacob, the riders of horses were put to rest. For you are terrifying, and who can defy You, for such is Your wrath. From heaven You caused judgment to be heard. The earth trembled and became still, when God arose unto judgment, to save the meek of the earth."

Even as He dies on the Cross, the Church sees Jesus already victorious, descending with majesty and might to do battle with the demonic lords of the underworld. Such is the meaning of the great earthquake that accompanies His death. Indeed, according to the Lamentations of Holy Saturday Matins, the dying Lord violently shook the earth in order to loosen the grip of the grave, to facilitate the universal resurrection (cf. Matt. 27:51–53), thus "to save the meek of the earth."

One rarely hears modern Christians speak of Christ's redemptive work as an outpouring of the divine anger, but most assuredly it was. True combat always involves anger, and the redemptive deeds of Christ were the supreme and ultimate war ever waged in this world. Indeed, this truly was a war to end all warfare, for it graced human history with the key to its final peace: "God is known in Judah; His name is great in Israel. His dwelling is in peace, and His abode in Zion. For there did He break the power of the bow, the armor, the sword, and the battle." (The Greek translation "peace" [*eirene*] is based on an underlying Hebrew *shalom*. One may note, however, that the standard rabbinic text actually reads *shalem*, an ancient name for Jerusalem. Both ideas are doubtless included in the meaning of the reference, Jerusalem being the Bible's symbol of everlasting peace.)

PSALM 76 (77)
WITH MY VOICE I CRIED TO THE LORD

Some commentators treat Psalm 76 (Hebrew 77) as the meditation of an insomniac, the prayer offered by a man so afflicted with grief that he is unable to sleep. The case seems, however, quite the opposite. This is the deliberate vigil of a man who is fighting sleep precisely so that he can pray and meditate: "In the day of my trouble I sought God, my hands raised up to Him during the night. . . . My eyes stood sentinel through the watches. . . . I meditated in the night and communed with my heart and stirred up my spirit." This is the prayer of a man struggling to stay awake, not someone unable to fall asleep.

The psalm deals with a problem: "In the day of my trouble I sought God . . . My soul refused to take comfort . . . Will the Lord reject us forever, and never again be gracious? Or will He cut off His mercy forever? Has His everlasting promise come to an end?"

Burdened with such thoughts, a man may well be tempted to seek refuge in sleep, as we see in the case of Peter, James, and John. These three men the Lord took with Him to keep a prayerful vigil during the hours preceding His arrest, but the task proved too much, the flesh being weaker than the spirit was willing. So in their sadness they gave themselves over to slumber while the Lord Himself continued steadfast in prayer.

The keeping of prayerful vigil in the time of trial was also exemplified by the earliest believers in those days when "Herod the king stretched out his hand to harass some from the church. . . . Peter was therefore kept in prison, but constant prayer was offered to God for him by the church" (Acts 12:1, 5). Even as "Peter was sleeping, bound with two chains between two soldiers" (12:6), the Church maintained her prayerful vigil through the night.

And on what was the Church meditating as she prayed for Peter that night of trouble? We are not obliged to guess here. She was meditating on the Exodus. This we know for certain, because it was the night of Pascha, the night of salvation, the night that heralds the very dawn of deliverance (cf. Acts 12:3, 4). As she prayed for Peter chained in prison by Herod, the afflicted and saddened Church spent that night remembering the God who brought forth His people from the oppression and bondage of Pharaoh, and thus inspired she prayed for the renewal of God's wonders.

The situation and the prayer of the troubled Church that night were very much those of our psalm, which also seeks strength by turning to meditate on the mystery of the Exodus: "With Your arm You redeemed Your people, the sons of Jacob and Joseph. The waters saw You, O God, the waters saw You and whirled back in fear, and the depths stirred with trembling. Awesome was the roaring of the waters. The clouds gave forth their voice, as Your arrows transfixed them. The voice of Your thunder was in the whirlwind; Your flashings illumined the orb of the world; the earth shook and trembled. Your ways (*hodoi*) were in the sea, and Your paths in the mighty waters, and Your footsteps will not be known. Like sheep did You lead Your people, by the hand of Moses and Aaron."

The footsteps of the delivering God are covered over by the baptismal waters of the paschal mystery, and the praying Church seeks them again in meditation through the night: "Your way (*hodos*), O God, is in holiness. What god is as great as our God? You are the God who does wonders; You have made known Your power to the peoples."

In fact we know how God worked His wonders for the Church during that night she spent praying for the imprisoned Peter, for the story goes on to tell how he himself shared in the mystery of the Exodus. Like the tomb of his Lord, Peter was being guarded by soldiers when suddenly the cell was illumined at the appearance of the angel of the Resurrection telling Peter, "Arise quickly!" (Acts 12:7). As on the morning of the Lord's Resurrection, the whole scene appeared ethereal and unreal (12:9).

The artist Rafael caught this scene perhaps better than anyone else ever has, in his painting of it over the window in a room of the papal apartments called the Stanza of Heliodorus, skillfully using chiaroscuro to outline the figures of the soldiers and the rising Peter. Until one looks at it very closely, the painting easily passes for the scene of the Lord's Resurrection. It is God's answer to the Church's night of vigil, meditation, and prayer.

PSALM 77 (78)

Just as the early Christians saw the Passover and other events associated with the Exodus of the Old Testament as types and foreshadowings of the salvation brought by Jesus (cf. 1 Cor. 5:7; John 19: 36, etc.), so they interpreted the forty years of the Israelites' wandering in the desert as representing their own pilgrimage to the true Promised Land. Thus, the passage through the Red Sea became a symbol of Baptism, the miraculous manna was a foreshadowing of the Eucharist, and so forth. In particular did they regard the various temptations experienced by the Israelites in the desert as typical of the sorts of temptations to be faced by Christians. This deep Christian persuasion of the true significance of the desert pilgrimage serves to make the Books of Exodus and Numbers necessary and very useful reading for serious Christians.

In the New Testament there are two fairly lengthy passages illustrating this approach to the Israelites' desert pilgrimage. One is found in 1 Corinthians 10:1–13. In this text the Apostle Paul begins by indicating the sacramental meanings of certain components in the Exodus story: "All our fathers were under the cloud, all passed through the sea, all were baptized into Moses in the cloud and in the sea, all ate the same spiritual food, and all drank the same spiritual drink" (vv. 1–4). The Apostle's chief interest, however, is moral; by way of warning to the Corinthians he points to the sins and failures of the Israelites in the desert: "Now these things became our examples, to the intent that we should not lust after evil things as they also lusted. And do not become idolaters as were some of them. . . Nor let us commit sexual immorality, as some of them did, . . . nor let us tempt Christ, as some of them also tempted, . . . nor complain, as some of them also complained" (vv. 6–10). For Saint Paul the entire story of the Israelites in the desert is a great moral lesson for Christians: "Now all these things happened to them as examples, and they were written for our admonition, upon whom the ends of the ages have come" (v. 11).

The second New Testament text illustrating this theme is even longer, filling chapters 3 and 4 of Hebrews. The author of this book was much struck by the fact that almost none of those who had departed from Egypt actually arrived in the Promised Land. And why? Because of unbelief, disobedience, and rebellion in the desert: "For who, having heard, rebelled? Indeed, was it not all who came out of Egypt, led by Moses? Now with whom was He angry forty years? Was it not with those who sinned, whose corpses fell in the wilderness?" (3:16, 17). Here, as in 1 Corinthians, the story of the desert pilgrimage is remembered as a moral warning for those in Christ.

One of the longer psalms, Psalm 77 (Hebrew 78) is largely devoted to the same theme, which provides its proper interpretation. This psalm, which is a kind of poetic summary of the Books of Exodus, Numbers, Deuteronomy, and even some of Joshua, Judges, and 1 Samuel, concentrates on the Chosen People's constant infidelity and rebellion, but especially during the desert pilgrimage: "But they sinned even more against Him by rebelling against the Most High in the wilderness. . . . How often they provoked Him in the wilderness, and grieved Him in the desert! Yes, again and again they tempted God, and limited the Holy One of Israel. They did not remember His power: The day when He redeemed them from the enemy."

Quite a number of hours are required to read the whole story of the people's infidelity in the desert as it is recorded through several books of the Bible. Psalm 77, however, has long served as a sort of meditative compendium of the whole account. Its accent falls on exactly those same moral warnings that we saw in 1 Corinthians and Hebrews—the people's failure to take heed to what they had already beheld of God's deliverance and His sustained care for them. They had seen the plagues that He visited on the Egyptians, they had traversed the sea dryshod, they had been led by the pillar of cloud and fire, they had slaked their thirst with the water from the rock, they had eaten their fill of the miraculous bread, they had trembled at the base of Mount Sinai, beholding the divine manifestation. In short, they had already been the beneficiaries of God's revelation, salvation, and countless blessings.

Still, "their heart was not steadfast with Him, nor were they faithful in His covenant." And just who is being described here? Following the lead of the New Testament, we know it is not only the Israelites of old, but also ourselves, "upon whom the ends of the ages have come." The story in this psalm is our own story. So we carefully ponder it and take warning.

PSALM 78 (79)

༒

After the four horsemen had appeared, all carried on mounts distinctive in color, and the earth had been ravaged with their fourfold affliction, the Lamb of God reached forth to break the fifth seal of the great scroll. St. John tells us what he saw when that seal was opened: "I saw under the altar the souls of those who had been slain for the word of God and for the testimony (*martyria*) which they held" (Rev. 6:9).

These are the souls of the martyrs, which means "witness-bearers," and they are said here to be "under the altar" because their blood, poured out as in sacrifice, lies uncovered at the base of the altar. In the Bible, that is to say, the "soul [or "life"] is in the blood" (cf. Lev. 17:11, 14; Deut. 12:23). Their holy blood, unjustly shed, cries out to God "with a loud voice, saying, 'How long, O Lord, holy and true, until You judge and avenge our blood on those who dwell on the earth?'" (Rev. 6:10).

In a holy impatience that the truth of God should be vindicated, "How long?" is a cry and a question often enough heard from the lips of the psalmist (Psalms 73:10; 78:5; 88:46) and the Prophets (Is. 6:11; Dan. 8:13; 12:6; Hab. 1:2; Zech. 1:12), so it is not surprising that we should hear it too from those whose own lives were with violence cut short because of their witness to God.

"How long?" is not a petition for personal vengeance, of course, for the desire for personal vengeance is offensive to God and therefore forbidden to His servants. It is a prayer, rather, that God's own justice be validated by decisive fact and that a very important article of the Creed be vindicated with utterly determined finality: "He will come again in glory to judge."

Even as the saints wait for that hour, they pray with fervor that it might, please God, be hastened: "How long?" A certain impatience, after all, is an essential component of desire. No sincere prayer of faith says: "Lord, we want this very badly, You understand, Sir, but, really, do take Your time about it. We would hate to rush You. It's quite all the same to us."

God's answer to this prayer of the martyrs, nonetheless, is that He has much bigger plans in mind and does, in fact, intend somewhat to take His time in the matter, so they are exhorted to "rest a little while longer, until both the number of their fellow servants and their brethren, who would be killed as they were, was completed" (Rev. 6:11). In other words, there are more martyrdoms to come.

Similarly, Hebrews, after listing those who "died in faith, not having received the promises, but having seen them afar off" (11:13), says that even though they were "stoned, they were sawn in two, were tempted, were slain with the sword" (11:37), they are nonetheless obliged to wait still longer, "God having provided something better for us, that they should not be made perfect apart from us" (11:40).

This "How long?" prayer of Holy Church also finds expression in Psalm 78 [Hebrew 79]: "Help us, O God our Savior; for the sake of the glory of Your name, O Lord, deliver us, and forgive us our sins for the sake of Your name, lest the nations say: 'Where is their God?' Let the vengeance of the blood of Your servants, which was poured out, be known among the nations in our sight. Let the groaning of the prisoners come before You. With Your enormous arm take charge of the children of those who are slain. To our neighbors render sevenfold in their bosoms the contempt with which they have contemned You, O Lord."

The Bible gives us no reason to believe that a prayer for the vindication of God's judgment should be a particularly gentle prayer, for the judgment of God really is a judgment. It is not ambiguous or hazy. That is to say, it really does make decisions; it says, clearly and very emphatically, "this but not that." God's judgment really does know the difference between sheep and goats. There is no danger that God will mistake Abel for Cain.

Therefore, as our psalm surveys the ravages and wastes of our sinful history, with God's house laid in ruins and the holy city "reduced to a fruit market," with the corpses of God's servants given as food to the fowl of the air and the beasts of the field, and "their blood poured out like water round about Jerusalem," we join our voices with the martyrs who cry aloud "How long?" to the Lord holy and true.

PSALM 79 (80)

The situation in Psalm 79 (Hebrew 80) is pretty rough: "Will You feed us with the bread of tears, and give us only tears as our measure of drink? You have made us a contradiction to our neighbors, and our enemies regard us with scorn." The problem in this psalm is not private, so to speak; it has to do with afflictions brought upon the Church.

The remedy requested against this plight is the revelation of God's glory, a theme that appears early in our psalm: "You who sit upon the Cherubim, reveal Yourself to Ephraim, Benjamin, and Manasseh; stir up Your might and come to save us." Then, three times comes the refrain that makes the same prayer: "Convert (*epistrepson*) us; show forth Your face, and we shall be saved." The order in this refrain is important, in that God shows His face only to the converted—"when one turns [or "is converted" (*epistrepse*)] to the Lord, the veil is taken away" (2 Cor. 3:16). So the psalm prays for a conversion, a change in our hearts, that we may behold the glory of God and thereby be saved.

But it is important to note that this is a prayer of the Church, a petition for conversion made by those who are, presumably, already converted and already have been enlightened and tasted the heavenly gift, and already were made partakers of the Holy Spirit, and already have tasted the good word of God and the powers of the world to come. Even these, our psalm is saying, still need even further to be converted and further to be saved.

Neither conversion nor salvation is a once-and-for-all thing in Holy Scripture, where the often repeated command to "repent" appears invariably in the Greek present imperative tense. This grammatical form means something much closer to "keep on repenting." According to the sustained exhortation in Hebrews, those who have already repented should still be careful about "the sin which so easily ensnares us" (12:1). Similarly with respect to "being saved"; in the Bible words about salvation are more often used in the future tense than in a past tense. Thus, this prayer—"O Lord of hosts, convert us; show forth Your face, and we shall be saved"—is always appropriate to our state. The Church is the body of those who are constantly being converted and saved.

In Psalm 79 there are two chief metaphors for the Church: the flock and the vine. First, the Church is a flock. Thus this psalm commences: "Attend, O Shepherd of Israel, You who herd Joseph like sheep." Holy Church is called "the flock of God," awaiting the day "when the chief Shepherd appears" (1 Pet.

5:2, 4), who is elsewhere called "that great Shepherd of the sheep" (Heb. 13:20). Our psalm is the flock's prayer for the appearing of that Shepherd. Left to their own devices, sheep have been known to get themselves terribly lost, and, as our psalm suggests, they are vulnerable to many predators.

Second, the Church is a vine: "You transplanted a vine out of Egypt; You drove out the nations and planted it. You cleared the way before it; You planted its roots, and it filled the earth." It is a catholic plant, this vine, for its branches spread everywhere: "Its shadow covered the mountains, and its boughs the cedars of God. It stretched out its limbs to the sea, and its tendrils to the rivers."

The vine, however, is at least as vulnerable as a flock of sheep: "A boar from the forest has ravaged it, and a wild beast has eaten it up." Such things do happen to the Church, of course, whether from imprisonment at Philippi, beatings and dissensions at Corinth, heresy in Galatia, the synagogue of Satan at Smyrna, or the deeds of the Nicolaitans at Ephesus and Pergamum. It is against such beastly ravages that the Church prays this psalm.

The victory for which we pray, moreover, is the vindication of Christ our Lord in this world, the one referred to here as "the Man of Your right hand, the Son of man whom You have strengthened for Yourself." This is the same Man of which Psalm 1 had said, "Blessed is the Man," and of whom Psalm 8 had inquired, "What is Man that You are mindful of Him, or the Son of man that You care for Him?" This vine, this flock, belongs to Christ, and its cause in this world is His. The enemies of the Church are the enemies of Christ, and their final doom is described in some of the more colorful pages of 2 Thessalonians and Revelation.

PSALM 80 (81)

In the normal circumstances of our daily lives, the abrupt, loud blowing of a horn can serve as a notable stimulant to advertence, a feature that explains why we equip our automobiles, boats, and trains with such a device. This rousing quality of the horn is also the reason we sometimes introduce "events" with what is called a fanfare. Whatever the musical value of the thing, the shrill blast of a horn is likely to attract some measure of attention.

If, however, a number of other extraordinary, distracting phenomena are taking place at the same time, it is possible to miss even the loud sounding of a horn. Thus, when we read of all the marvels that accompanied Moses' reception of the Law on Mount Sinai, it is altogether possible for us not to notice the sustained and sonorous wail of a ram's horn. Nonetheless, it was not lost on the Israelites who were present (Ex. 19:16, 19) nor on the early Christian reader who commented on the "sound of a trumpet" that accompanied that event (Heb. 12:19).

Likewise, Psalm 80 (Hebrew 81), prescribing the blowing of this ram's trumpet in the context of liturgical worship, links this context to the singular events of the Exodus: "Rejoice in God our helper, raise an ovation to the God of Jacob. Raise the song and roll the drum; strum the dulcet lyre and play the lute. Intone the trumpet of the New Moon, the famed day of your feast. For a command is ordained unto Israel, a decree of the God of Jacob. He made it a statute to Joseph, when he went out of the land of Egypt and heard a tongue he did not know."

Literary historians still debate which specific liturgical feast day formed the original context of Psalm 80, since trumpets seem to have been played on many of ancient Israel's feast days (cf. Numbers 10:10). But this historical question is of no solid significance to the proper praying of this psalm. It suffices to know that our theme is the Exodus from Egyptian servitude.

All our prayer, after all, is the fruit of the Exodus. That is to say, all our worship of God is rooted in our deliverance from demonic slavery by His gracious redemptive hand. It is "to the praise of the glory of His grace" (Eph. 1:6) that He has saved us. Of each of us, then, it is proper to say that God "unfettered his back from the burdens, and took from his hands the basket of bondage."

According to Exodus (2:23–25; 3:8–10; 4:31, etc.), our deliverance is itself

God's response to prayer. Likewise in this psalm the Lord says: "You called upon Me in distress, and I delivered you. I answered you from the eye of the storm." These words, which resonate with the tempestuous scene in Exodus 19:18 and 20:18, are uniquely and perhaps more forcefully expressed in the original Hebrew: *'e'nka bseter ra'am*—"I heard you in the hiding place of thunder."

God then goes on to speak of His leading and feeding us in the desert of Sinai: "I tested you at the water of conflict. Listen, My people, and I will exhort you. O Israel, if only you would hearken to Me. You shall have no new god, nor shall you worship an alien god. For I am the Lord your God, who conducted you up from the land of Egypt. Open wide your mouth and I will fill it."

Israel's infidelity to the covenant during that lengthy desert wandering subsequent to her Exodus from Egypt remains the Bible's perpetual admonition to the Church (cf. 1 Cor. 10:1–11; Heb. 3:12—4:2). Therefore this psalm contains both promise and warning for God's people: "But My people heard not My voice, nor did Israel give heed to Me. So I dismissed them to their hearts' desires; they shall walk in their own pursuits. If only My people would hear Me, and Israel would walk in My ways, I would humble their enemies at once, and take in hand their tormenters. The foes of the Lord will fawn before Him, and their doom will be eternal. But these folk has He fed with the finest of wheat, and with honey from the rock has He filled them."

The sin to which we redeemed people are forever prone is that very idolatry from which the Lord has delivered us, that servitude to darkness from which "we have redemption through His blood, the forgiveness of sins" (Eph. 1:7). Those idols seem forever to call us back, even after we have turned away from them "to serve the living and true God" (1 Thess. 1:9).

PSALM 81 (82)

GOD STANDS IN THE ASSEMBLY OF THE GODS

In the Gospel of St. John (10:34, 35) our Lord gives us a key to understanding Psalm 81 (Hebrew 82), when He quotes and interprets a line therefrom: "Jesus answered them, 'Is it not written in your law, "I said, 'You are gods'"? If He called them gods, to whom the word of God came . . . .'" In context, those "to whom the word of God came" were the ancient judges and rulers of Israel. That is to say, the Bible actually uses the word "gods" to refer to certain men who exercised an exalted and godly office, human beings who, because the word of God came to them, served as judges to God's people.

It is a rather high thing to speak of judges as "gods," but the impulse to do so makes some sense if one bears in mind that judging is itself radically and ultimately a divine prerogative.

Indeed, this latter truth is the real point of the psalm: "God stands in the gathering (*synagoge*) of the gods. In their midst He judges the gods: 'How long do you judge unjustly, and respect the persons of the sinful? Give judgment for the orphan and the poor man, grant justice to the man meek and needy. Deliver the needy and poor man, save him from the hand of the sinner.' But they do not know nor understand; they walk about in the darkness. Let all the foundations of the earth be shaken. I said: 'You are gods, and sons of the Most High, all of you. You will die, nonetheless, like men, and fall like one of the princes.' Arise, O God, and judge the earth, for You will inherit all the nations."

It would be easy, one supposes, to read this psalm as a simple calling of human judges to task by reminding them that, at the end, they too will face the higher tribunal of the justice of God. Read in this way, the sense would be that of Socrates, at his trial, reminding his own judges that he was about to go to the gods above, who could distinguish between a just and an unjust man.

Such a consideration would not, however, exhaust the proper exegetical potential of this psalm, which is better understood, it is here suggested, by the psalm's most prominent place in the liturgical worship of Holy Church. For this entire psalm is chanted during the Divine Liturgy of the Great Vigil of Pascha, in lieu of the traditional Alleluia, just before the Resurrection account in the Gospel of the day (Matt. 28:1–20). During this psalm, the priest walks all around the church strewing handfuls of bay leaves over all the people as a sign of Christ's victory over sin and death. After each verse of the psalm the entire congregation sings, in the imposing seventh tone and with full-throated voice, the antiphon "Arise, O God, and judge the earth, for You will inherit all the nations." This is one of the most unique and memorable celebrations of the whole liturgical year, and those who have sung it in that context will forever pray Psalm 81 quite differently.

"Arise, O God, and judge the earth" is a cry for the Resurrection of Christ. All of the injustices of human history come from a single source, which is man's enslavement to the powers of darkness. This is the deeper root and more radical meaning of the line: "But they do not know nor understand; they walk about in the darkness." It is in the Resurrection of Christ, in the great earthquake that accompanied the rolling away of the heavy stone from the door of His tomb (cf., again, Matt. 28:2), that we find the real meaning of the line that reads: "Let all the foundations of the earth be shaken."

The divine judgment, manifest in the Resurrection of the Lord Jesus, is not a simple forensic decision, but a vindication of God's righteousness against the enslaving forces of demonic darkness. It was they who aspired to equality with God. The Christian sense of Psalm 81, then, is very much the same as Psalm 67: "Rise up, O Lord! Let Your enemies be scattered, and let those who hate You flee before You."

To pray for the vindication of God's righteousness, as we do in this psalm, is to make a distinctly political prayer. Indeed, true prayer is possessed of a certain political component. When Christians pray on earth, a kind of political interest, as it were, is stirred in the heavens. Our prayer ascends in God's sight as the incense, to the tone of trumpets, we are told, and God's angel pours on the earth "hail and fire . . . mingled with blood" (cf. Rev. 8:4–7). Pharaoh's throne is once again threatened. When we pray, God arises to judge the earth in His righteousness.

PSALM 82 (83)

WHO IS LIKE UNTO YOU, O GOD?

☙

Throughout the Book of Psalms is the constant mention of enemies. Indeed, it may occasionally cross one's mind that about half of the psalms are prayed *against* somebody or other, an impression that may be pretty close to accurate. There is a lot of strife in the Psalter.

Nonetheless, though the psalms make almost ubiquitous references to enemies, these are seldom identified very specifically. Psalm 82 (Hebrew 83) is an exception to the rule. Here, at least, the psalm points its finger and actually names the foes.

And just who are these enemies? Well, take your pick: "The tents of Edom and the Ishmaelites, Moab and the Hagrites, Gebal and Ammon and Amalek, and foreigners with the citizens of Tyre. For Assyria too has joined with them; they have come to the aid of the sons of Lot."

Now taken all together, this list would describe a pretty impressive coalition of adversaries. Such a confederacy, in fact, never really came together against Israel. Moreover, at no point in Israel's history did all of these forces even exist simultaneously. Our psalm is describing, rather, an ongoing general situation, not a specific historical event. Whoever the enemy happens to be at the moment, the servants of God live under constant threat of incursion. "Deliver us from the evil one" is ever a fitting petition.

In most of these names we recognize Israel's real military enemies. Such are Moab, Ammon, and Amalek (cf. Judg. 3:12–30). The first two of these are likewise identical with "the sons of Lot." Gebal was a city of the Philistines (cf. 1 Kin. 5:18), against whom Israel fought in many a battle. The Edomites are remembered in Holy Scripture for their participation in the fall of Jerusalem to the Babylonians (cf. Obadiah, *passim*), and we will meet them again in Psalm 137. Hagar being the mother of Ishmael, the Hagrites and the Ishmaelites are apparently the same folk (cf. 1 Chr. 5:10, 18–22). Assyria, finally, was one of the cruelest and most loathed of Israel's ancient foes (cf. Nahum, *passim*).

A special feature of this list, nonetheless, indicates that the enmity involved is more than simply military. That element is the mention of the Phoenician capital of Tyre. Although Israel's relationship with the Phoenicians may sometimes have been strained (cf. 1 Kin. 9:11–14), we have no evidence of any military hostility between them.

Nevertheless, from another and more spiritual perspective, it may be the case that Phoenicia, with its capitals at Tyre and Sidon, was the worst enemy that Israel ever had, because it was through the various economic and political alliances with the Phoenicians that Israel learned ever anew the ways of infidelity to God. Solomon's early pacts with this nation paved the avenue by which the likes of Jezebel and Athaliah traveled south to teach Israel to sin, and opposition to Phoenician influence was a sustained feature of the prophetic message, from Elijah's encounter with the servants of Baal (cf. 1 Kin. 18), through Amos's condemnation of the Phoenician slave trade (cf. Amos 1:9), to Ezekiel's lengthy tirade against their great economic empire (Ezek. 26—28).

The introduction of Tyre into our psalm's list of foes, therefore, shows that the threatened enmity is more than physical and military. Whether with hostility on the battlefield, or along the subtler paths of syncretism, materialism, idolatry, and cultural compromise, there is more than one way for the people of God to be destroyed. And the danger of destruction is the very theme and meat of this psalm.

The real threat to God's people, then, is one of spirit, because "we do not wrestle against flesh and blood, but against principalities, against powers, against the rulers of the darkness of this age, against spiritual hosts of wickedness in the heavenly places" (Eph. 6:12).

So we pray that God will renew the wonders He worked of old. Smite afresh, we implore, the forces of Jabin and Sisera (cf. Judg. 4). Give us Gideon again, we plead, to crush those Midianites. Let Oreb and Zeb, Zebah and Zalmunna fall anew in defeat (cf. Judg. 7; 8). May their blood blemish the streams of Kishon, and their bodies lie once more on the dung heap at Endor. Against these demonic enemies of God and His people, we pray with the warrior's fervor, anger, and zeal.

PSALM 83 (84)

Several of the psalms are inscribed as being "of the sons of Korah," an inscription apparently designating one of the choirs in Israel's ancient temple (cf. 2 Chr. 20:19). In fact, some of the psalms so designated are much preoccupied with that temple, whether as a place to be longed for (Psalms 41; 42), or as a haven of experienced security (Psalms 45; 47).

Psalm 83 (Hebrew 84), another such psalm "of the sons of Korah," combines both of these sentiments. It commences on the note of longing: "How beloved Your tabernacles, O Lord of hosts. My soul longs and faints for the courts of the Lord. My heart and my flesh have rejoiced in the living God." Immediately, however, the tone is transformed into one of secure resting in God's presence: "For the sparrow has found herself a haven, and the turtledove a nest for herself, where she may lay her young—even Your altars, O Lord of hosts, my King and my God." Sharing the psalmist's view of its symbolic propriety, generations of both Jews and Christians have loved this ancient poetic record about Palestinian birds constructing their nests in the wall niches of Solomon's temple. This is the endearing sight that prompts one to speak of "*my* King and *my* God."

But Solomon's famous construction, we know, was a figure passing away, for now "a greater than Solomon is here" (Matt. 12:42). The true and lasting temple of God, the term of our longing and the abode of our rest, is Christ the Lord. He is "greater than the temple" (12:6). So in this psalm we pray: "Give regard, O God, our Protector, and gaze on the face of Your Christ."

This image of Jesus as God's true temple, which provides the proper Christological key to Psalm 83, is indicated in the Gospel of John. Fairly early in that Gospel, when Jesus speaks of the destruction of the temple, the evangelist notes: "But He was speaking of the temple of His body" (John 2:21). This body of Christ, in the Johannine context, is His resurrected flesh and blood, the permanent and even physical abiding place of God's presence. John will say of heaven: "But I saw no temple in it, for the Lord God Almighty and the Lamb are its temple" (Rev. 21:22).

And because He is God's temple, God abides in Jesus. Jesus is the one place where we meet God, and we too abide in Jesus, being united to God in Him: "I do not pray for these alone, but also for those who will believe in Me through their word; that they all may be one, as You, Father, are in Me, and I in You; that they also may be one in Us, that the world may believe that You sent Me. And the glory which You gave Me I have given them, that they may be one just as We are one; I in them, and You in Me; that they may be made perfect in one" (John 17:20–23).

Such is the proper Christological context for our praying of Psalm 83. When we say to God, "Blessed are those who dwell in Your house; for ever and ever will they praise You," we are referring to the worship offered to the Father by those who abide in Christ, both on earth and in heaven.

So, does a man feel the pangs of his exile, being "absent from the Lord" (2 Cor. 5:6)? Let him cry out in the paths of his pilgrimage: "Blessed the man whose help is from You; he has arranged in his heart the steps of ascent, in the vale of tears, to the place that he determined." Let him pray: "O Lord God of hosts, listen to my prayer; give ear, O God of Jacob."

Or does a man want, with all his heart, "to be absent from the body and to be present with the Lord" (2 Cor. 5:8)? Let him put his trust in God, "for the Giver of the law will also give blessings." Let him bear in mind that "the Lord loves mercy and truth; God will give grace and glory."

Or do true disciples, grown weary on their pilgrimage, feel discouraged in the journey? Let them know that "they shall proceed from strength to strength. The God of gods shall be seen in Zion." Let them be assured that "the Lord will withhold no good things from those who walk in innocence."

Or do the travelers encounter those temptations attendant on their exile and "the sin which so easily ensnares us" (Heb. 12:1)? Let them never forget that "one day in Your courts is better than a thousand elsewhere." With all their heart and all their mind let them say: "I would choose to be ignored in the house of God rather than to lodge in the tents of sinners."

PSALM 84 (85)

"Unto us a Child is born," the lyric prophet wrote, "unto us a Son is given" (Is. 9:6). And he wrote these things with respect to the Incarnation of the divine Son becoming a human Child. Both aspects of this Christian mystery, which Isaiah perceived so lucidly (cf. John 12:41), were likewise seen by the Wise Men who came with adoration to welcome this Newcomer to the scene, the divine Son and human Child. St. Ambrose of Milan comments on these Wise Men: "When they looked upon the little one in the stable, they said: 'Unto us a Child is born.' And when they beheld His star, they exclaimed: 'Unto us a Son is given.' On the one hand, a gift from earth, and on the other a gift from heaven, for both are one Person, perfect in both respects, with no change in His divinity, and no diminution of His humanity. Only one Person did these Wise Men adore, and to one and the same did they present their gifts, showing that He who was beheld in the stall was the very Lord of the stars" (*De Fide* 3.8.54).

Psalm 84 (Hebrew 85) is a further canticle honoring both facets of the Incarnation, for the latter is that history-defining encounter of two worlds, wherein "the Lord will grant His mercy, and our earth shall give its fruit." "Truth has arisen from the earth," we pray in this psalm, speaking of the Child born unto us, "and righteousness has stooped down from the heaven," we go on, telling of the Son given unto us. This union is the sacrament of God become Man, in which "mercy and truth have met together; righteousness and peace have shared a kiss."

Thus, still following St. Ambrose, when mankind cried out in Psalm 84, "O Lord, show us Your mercy, and grant us Your salvation," it was a prayer for the Incarnation, in which "He, who is God's Son, is born as Mary's Child and given to us" (*op. cit.* 3.8.56).

Such, ultimately, is the meaning of the lines with which we begin this same psalm: "Kindly have You been to Your land, O Lord, bringing back the captivity of Jacob. You have forgiven Your people their iniquities; You have covered all their sins. An end have You given to Your anger; You abandoned the fury of Your wrath." All these blessings of reconciliation between two realms were accomplished, when the Father sent His only-begotten Son, "that in the dispensation of the fullness of the times He might gather together in one all things in Christ, both which are in heaven and which are on earth—in Him" (Eph. 1:10).

In this mystery of God's reconciliation, then, is fulfilled the prophecy of our psalm: "For His salvation is near to all those who fear Him, so that glory may inhabit (*kataskenosai*) our earth." This glory inhabiting our earth is what was first seen when "the Word became flesh and dwelt (*eskenosen*) among us, and we beheld His glory, the glory as of the only begotten of the Father, full of grace and truth. . . . No one has seen God at any time. The only begotten Son, who is in the bosom of the Father, He has declared Him" (John 1:14, 18).

The Father sent His Son in response to the most profound aspirations of men's hearts, because Isaiah spoke for all mankind when he pleaded: "Oh, that You would rend the heavens! / That You would come down" (64:1). Driven from God's presence in paradise and retained in bondage to unclean spirits by reason of transgression, the human race with Adam and Eve cried out in our psalm: "Convert us, O God of our salvation, and turn Your fury from us. Will You be angry with us forever? Or from generation to generation prolong Your wrath? O God, You will convert us and restore us to life, and Your people shall rejoice in You."

Christ, then, "is our peace" (Eph. 2:14), and likewise our "righteousness and sanctification and redemption" (1 Cor. 1:30). It is of these things that our psalm says: "Righteousness shall go before Him, and He will set His footsteps in the way." This is the Christ who "came and preached peace to you who were afar off and to those who were near" (Eph. 2:17). This the Christ, "being both begotten of the Father before all ages, and created from the Virgin in these final times" (Ambrose, *op. cit.* 3.8.60).

We pray with confidence, then, in the words of our psalm: "I shall hear what the Lord God speaks within me, for peace will He speak to His people, and to His saints, and to those who turn their hearts to Him."

PSALM 85 (86)

O LORD, INCLINE YOUR EAR

❧

Psalm 85 (Hebrew 86) is another psalm of the Lord's suffering and death. As such it contains His prayer to the Father for deliverance, especially from that "last enemy" which is death (cf. 1 Cor. 15:26). Thus Jesus pleads: "Incline Your ear, O Lord, and hear me, for I am poor and needy. Guard my soul, for I am holy. O God, save Your servant, who sets His hope on You. Have mercy on me, O Lord, for I cry to You all the day long. Gladden the soul of Your servant, for to You, O Lord, have I lifted up my soul. . . . O God, transgressors are risen against me, and the assembly of the strong has sought out my soul, nor have they set You before them."

Among the important themes in these lines, one will observe our Lord's deliberate identification with the poor and needy. As a poor man, without wealth and the power that wealth can afford, Jesus is unjustly condemned by those who, for their own reasons, have decided that He must die. Sold and purchased for a price, found guilty by a fixed jury on the testimony of perjured witnesses, condemned by an intimidated judge, our Lord makes Himself one with all those myriad human beings who suffer persecution, even death, by those willing and powerful enough to inflict it.

However, even when He says of Himself that "the Son of Man has nowhere to lay His head" (Matt. 8:20), it is important to remember that the poverty of Christ is more than a mere social and economic condition. Rather, it is integral to His being God's *servant*: "O God, save Your *servant*, who sets His hope on You. . . . Gladden the soul of Your *servant*." In various places in the Gospels Jesus refers to Himself as the servant, most especially in the setting of His sufferings: "For even the Son of Man did not come to be served, but to serve, and to give His life a ransom for many" (Mark 10:45). It is well known, of course, that in such statements our Lord was showing Himself to be "the servant of the Lord" spoken of repeatedly in the second part of Isaiah.

The *poverty* of our Lord is also the metaphor for His assumption of our fallen flesh, when, not considering His equality with God a thing to be grasped at, He "emptied Himself" and assumed the "form of a servant" (Phil. 2:5–10, RSV). As St. Paul elsewhere teaches: "For you know the grace of our Lord Jesus Christ, that though He was rich, yet for your sakes He became poor, that you through His poverty might become rich" (2 Cor. 8:9).

Another key idea in this psalm is that of our Lord's holiness: "Guard my soul, for I am holy," He pleads. Two things should be said of this holiness of Christ. First, it is like no other holiness on earth. It is not, as with the rest of mankind, a derived and relative holiness, because Christ, being God incarnate, is the font and principle of man's holiness. In comparison with even the holiest of others, consequently, the holiness of Christ is not simply one of superior degree, for His holiness is not an effect but a cause. Christ is holy, not as a result or consequence, but by way of premise and principle. He is "the Holy one of God" (John 6:69, NIV). Whoever else is holy, is holy because of Christ. Such is the sense of that line in the Great Doxology where we say to Him: "You alone are holy . . . Jesus Christ."

Second, the holiness of Christ, considered especially in the context of His Passion and death, has to do with sacrificial consecration. It is in going to the Cross that Jesus prays: "And for their sakes I sanctify Myself, that they also may be sanctified by the truth" (John 17:19). It is by the holiness of His priesthood and His sacrifice that we ourselves are redeemed and rendered holy, for the price of our redemption and our sanctification is "the precious blood of Christ, as of a lamb without blemish and without spot" (1 Pet. 1:19).

Even as He prays, in this psalm, for deliverance from His adversaries, Jesus also speaks with the assurance of that faith of which He is "the author and finisher" (Heb. 12:2). In His darkest hour He knows already the final outcome of the fight: "I lay down my life that I may take it again. No one takes it from Me, but I lay it down of Myself. I have power to lay it down, and I have power to take it again" (John 10:17, 18). This is the assurance in which Jesus makes His prayer during the Passion: "I will confess You, O Lord my God, with all my heart, and I shall glorify Your name forever. For great is Your mercy towards me, and You have delivered my soul from deepest Hades."

PSALM 86 (87)

HIS FOUNDATIONS ARE IN THE HOLY MOUNTAINS

Each time we celebrate those Sacred Mysteries that are the source of our identity as the Church, we arrive at a restrictive, very definite, and even defining point in the structure of that service: our common recitation of the Nicene Creed. By this component there is introduced into our worship a perceptible note of intolerance, a marked sense of selection and narrowing of sympathies. Indeed, were we to follow the letter of the rubric with respect to it ("Let all catechumens depart . . . The doors, the doors!"), no one would remain present in the church building, from this point on, except those who are to participate in the Body and Blood of the Lord. The Eucharist is a hidden, a secret ritual (*mysteria, arcana*) available only to the initiate. The altar is a family table, by which the family itself is strictly defined. Hence, the importance of the Nicene Creed at this point in the service. Traditionally understood, it is the Creed of Nicaea that distinguishes and identifies the Orthodox Church.

For this reason it is matter of no little irony that, when the Creed itself describes our Church, it employs the more ancient designation "catholic," an adjective indicating nearly the very opposite of anything restrictive or narrow. "Catholic" means "according to the whole" (*kat' holon*). It designates the fullness of the Church. This ecclesial fullness or amplitude is itself to be understood in a rather ample sense, for catholicity is a rich and manifold characteristic. It is the wholeness of the Church, rooted in her institutional access to the permanent outpouring of the Holy Spirit. Thus "catholic" describes the Church in the fullness of her being in the Holy Spirit, the life of divine grace, her sacraments and doctrine ("the *catholic* faith"), the historical integrity of her defining institutions. (It is instructive that, in our very first extant occasion of this expression, in the year 107, St. Ignatius of Antioch used it with respect to the office of bishop. When he said "catholic" in describing the Church, St. Ignatius clearly presumed that his readers knew exactly what the word meant. That is to say, long before there was a canon of the New Testament, the Church was already understood to be "catholic.")

Now one of the most important aspects of "the fullness of her being" is the Church's role as the proper home of all the nations. Thus, catholic also means universal with regard to the Church's evangelical mission: "Make disciples of *all* nations." She is "catholic" in the sense that all mankind, and all the redeemable components of their cultures, are to find their own proper vocation and destiny around her eucharistic table.

But "catholic" remains a theological term, not a sociological description. Catholic does not mean that the Church is, in fact, universally extended in a geographical sense. No, already the Church was completely catholic on Calvary, when she consisted of only one apostle and a handful of faithful women. The Church does not become more catholic by incorporating more peoples into herself. Her universality is, on the contrary, an inalienable aspect of her theological being; she is more than a "multinational corporation." Her universality is not a quantitatively measurable trait. It says nothing about her size, for it is not the addition of the nations that universalizes the Church. On the contrary, it is the nations themselves that are catholicized by accepting her given catholic integrity, thereby being incorporated into that cosmic fullness (*pleroma*) which is "the rich and great mercy" in Christ.

Psalm 86 (Hebrew 87) is a meditation on the catholicity of Holy Church, that city of the Lord of whom it is said: "His foundations are in the holy mountains; the Lord loves the gates of Zion more than all the tabernacles of Jacob." This is the city of which we ourselves proclaim: "You are the dwelling of all who rejoice in you." In this psalm the Church is portrayed as the true mother of all the nations. It says that a birth certificate from Zion will be issued to the great cultural and political powers at both ends of the Fertile Crescent, Egypt ("Rahab," cf. Psalm 88:10; Is. 30:7) and Babylon. She includes the nations to the north (Tyre, or Phoenicia) and to the south (Ethiopia), and those migratory warriors of Philistia. Their very literature is now part of her heritage: "The Lord will narrate in the writing of the peoples and of these princes who were born in her."

PSALM 87 (88)

O LORD, GOD OF MY SALVATION

Psalm 87 (Hebrew 88) is possibly the most difficult of the psalms. In any case, it is arguably the darkest. It even stands among the most somber compositions in all of Holy Writ, comparable to the overcast pages of Job and Ecclesiastes.

It not being readily apparent, perhaps, how to reconcile such tenebrous tones with evangelical hope, some may even judge the sentiments of this psalm too dismal for it to serve as Christian prayer at all. Psalm 87 is not only darksome in its every line; almost alone among the psalms, it even ends on a dark note. Its final line says: "My friend and confrere have You kept afar from me; and my neighbors, because of my distress." Now, how can that sort of sentiment be the "last word" in a Christian prayer?

But then, on closer inspection, we may observe certain subtler features softening this impression of our psalm. For all its gloom and shadow, for example, is it without significance that Psalm 87 begins by thus addressing the Almighty: "O Lord, the *God of my salvation*"? The intimacy and quiet hope of this address put one in mind of Psalm 21, in which the crucified Jesus, asking why God has forsaken Him, nonetheless continues to call Him "*my* God, *my* God."

Three further comments seem appropriate regarding this umbrageous aspect of Psalm 87. First, one must bear in mind that, like all of the Bible, it comes to us from the Holy Spirit. If death is portrayed in this psalm as a very bad thing, then the Holy Spirit wants us to regard death as a very bad thing. One occasionally meets pagans and unbelievers who avow that they are not afraid to die. Well, this psalm suggests that maybe they should be. In line after line of Psalm 87, a writer under the guidance and impulse of the Holy Spirit says, in the sharpest terms, that death is a most terrifying prospect. Moreover, in prescribing this psalm to be prayed each morning at the very beginning of the day, among the "Hexapsalmos," Holy Church must think it important that we commence our day with this thought of death in mind.

Second, bearing in mind that our fear of death is a reaction of the fleshly man, the "old Adam," still active within us, we should be mightily consoled to think that the Holy Spirit, in this psalm, has made such generous provision for this fleshly side of ourselves. The Holy Spirit, that is to say, gives our fleshly fear its due. If we yet feel this fear of death, the Holy Spirit is careful for this fear to find expression in prayer. Here is the tender condescension of God, that He provides even that our fallen nature may voice itself to Him in supplication and the lowly fealty of our very fear.

Third, Jesus took on Himself, not our pristine, unfallen nature, but our nature as tainted at the ancient tree and throughout the rest of our history. So the fear of death expressed in this psalm is certainly a fear that Jesus felt. If, in addition, as Holy Scripture indicates in so many places, death is but the outward expression of sin and our alienation from God, then a deeper understanding of sin must surely imply a more profound understanding of death. And who understood sin more than Jesus? Likewise was His perception of death vastly more ample and accurate than our own. And, as He knew more about the power of death than any of the rest of us, there is every reason to believe that He felt this fear of death more than the rest of us possibly could.

Finally, it is an ironic feature of liturgical and homiletic history that one expression from this psalm has been consistently used by the Church to refer to the death of Jesus, not as a term of doom but as an emblem of the high triumph and validation inherent in His Cross. That expression is "free among the dead." In the mystic vision of Holy Church, Jesus was indeed "free among the dead" in the sense that death had no dominion over Him. He was "free" with respect to death, inasmuch as it could not hold Him fast. Reaching to seize Jesus in the moment of His final breath, death found itself, instead, cast down and trampled by the rush of His abundant life crashing into that realm where the grave, hitherto undisputed, had so long held sway. Every antagonist fell beneath His mighty, grinding tread.

And forthwith striding to the nether world, Jesus "went and preached to the spirits in prison, who formerly were disobedient" (1 Pet. 3:19, 20). To demonstrate, moreover, that our Lord was truly free among the dead, "the earth quaked, and the rocks were split, and the graves were opened; and many bodies of the saints who had fallen asleep were raised; and coming out of the graves after His resurrection, they went into the holy city and appeared to many" (Matt. 27:51–53).

PSALM 88 (89)

Psalm 88 (Hebrew 89) is composed of three parts. The first has to do with God's activity in the creation of the heavens and the earth, the second with His covenant and promise with respect to the house of David, and the third with certain crises of history that threaten that covenant and put its promise at peril. All three themes are organically connected.

To see how these three realities are joined within the Christian mystery, we may begin with a text from St. Clement of Alexandria around the year 200. He wrote that "the ancient and catholic Church stands alone in essence and idea and principle and preeminence, gathering together, by the will of the one God, through the one Lord, into the unity of the one faith, built upon the appropriate covenants, or rather the one covenant given at different times, all those who are already enlisted in it, whom He foreordained, having known from the foundation of the world that they would be righteous" (*Stromateis* 7.17.107). In sum, all of God's dealings with this world are of whole cloth, including the grace of creation. All the historical covenants are expressions of the one covenant. From the beginning of time there has been only one God, one Lord, one faith.

The mystery of Christ was already present, then, when the voice of God called out into the aboriginal darkness of non-being, "Let there be light." Christ is no afterthought in the divine plan; God has no relations with this world except in Christ. Even when the Father's voice imposed form over the chaos of nonexistence, it was the form contained in His Word, who is His Son. God's covenant with creation was the initial exercise in applied Christology.

The first part of our psalm, taking up the theme of this divine imposition of form over chaos, emphasizes the structural constancy of the universe, but already this cosmic theme is introduced in a setting best described as messianic. That is to say, already anticipating the psalm's second part, the permanence of the Davidic throne is related to the unvarying dependability of the heavenly bodies, for both things are given shape by God's holy word and sworn resolve: "For You declared: '*Mercy* shall be built up forever.' Your *truth* is prepared in the heavens: 'A covenant have I formed with my chosen ones; to David my servant I swore an oath: Forever will I provide for your seed; I shall establish your throne unto all generations.' The heavens will confess Your wonders, O Lord, and Your *truth* in the church of Your saints."

Now, as Christians, we know that God's solemn promise to David, with respect to the everlasting stability of his throne, is fulfilled in the kingship of Christ, for the Son of David now sits forever enthroned at God's right hand, executing both prophecy and promise. Only in Christ do we find the key to the mystery of this psalm: "Once I swore by My holiness, nor would I ever lie to David. His seed shall abide forever, and his throne as the sun in My sight, and like the moon forever established, a faithful witness in heaven."

The theological bond, then, joining the creation to David, is Christ: "God . . . has in these last days spoken to us by His Son, whom He has appointed heir of all things, through whom also He made the worlds. . . . But to the Son He says: 'Your throne, O God, is forever and ever.' . . . And: 'You, Lord, in the beginning laid the foundation of the earth, / And the heavens are the work of Your hands'" (Heb. 1:1, 2, 8, 10). The regal, messianic covenant of sonship is related to the fixed structure of the very world, because both realities are rooted in Christ. As font and inner form, He is their common warrant.

In fact, nonetheless, both things, God's creation and His covenant, appear ever under threat throughout history, which theme brings us to the third part of our psalm. In this section we pray repeatedly for God's vindication of the messianic covenant, which man in his rebellion endeavors ever to overthrow. Indeed, in our own times this struggle seems to have intensified and entered a new phase. After deism, rejecting God's messianic covenant with us in Christ, strove to content us solely with the rational structure of creation, it was only a short time before creation itself came under siege. Now we live in a world where even the clearest manifestations of intelligent order are routinely dismissed as chaos, so grievously has the human spirit lost its use of reason.

One especially observes the recurrence of two expressions in this psalm: mercy (five times) and truth (seven times).

PSALM 89 (90)

LORD, YOU HAVE BEEN OUR REFUGE

For many centuries Psalm 89 (Hebrew 90), the only one of the psalms to be ascribed to Moses, has been associated with the beginning of the day, especially with the beginning of the workday. In the East this psalm is assigned to Prime, or First Hour, the prayer to be recited at sunrise. In the West Psalm 89 was traditionally prayed on Thursdays at Matins, the hour of dawn. Moreover, in the Western monastic tradition the closing lines of this psalm were daily chanted by the monks in their "chapter prayers," right after Prime (First Hour) and just before going out to the morning labor: "Look upon Your servants and upon Your works, and direct their sons; and may the splendor of the Lord our God be upon us, and establish the works of our hands for us." The recitation of this verse at the commencement of the workday, just as the full sun begins to shed its brilliance upon the world, is a needed reminder that the goal of all Christian labor on this earth is the manifestation of the glory of God: "Let your light so shine before men, that they may see your good works and glorify your Father in heaven" (Matt. 5:16). All of our daily labor is to become the medium for the showing forth of the divine splendor.

Surely new though each day is, we do not really start it from scratch, for each day begins with the memory of days gone by: "Lord, you have been our refuge from one generation to the next. Before the mountains were brought forth, or ever You had formed the earth and the world; You are, even from everlasting to everlasting."

One recalls Isaac Watts's paraphrase of this line in his famous hymn based on Psalm 89: "O God, our help in ages past, / Our hope for years to come, / Our shelter from the stormy blast, / And our eternal home. / . . . Before the hills in order stood, / Or earth received her frame;/ From everlasting Thou art God, / To endless years the same."

God is eternal, but man is frail. Even as we go forth to our daily labor, we know that work is now onerous because we are fallen creatures. Even as we endeavor to labor in such a way as to manifest the glory of God, the difficulty of the work itself, along with the weariness that attends it, bears witness to the Fall of our first parents and the curse laid upon our race—that we labor until we die: "Cursed is the ground for your sake; / In toil you shall eat of it / All the days of your life. / . . . / In the sweat of your face you shall eat bread / Till you return to the ground, / For out of it you were taken" (Gen. 3:17–19).

Psalm 89 likewise gives voice to the sentiments of a folk thus cursed: "You turn man to destruction, and say: 'Return, O children of men'. . . . You carry them away like a flood, like a dream. In the morning they are like grass that grows up; in the morning it thrives and flourishes, but in the evening it is cut down and withers."

The flow of the years, the passage of days into nights, conducts us all to death. Even as we go forth to our labor at the beginning of the day, it is without guarantee of returning home at its end: "For we have been consumed by Your anger, and by Your wrath we are terrified. You have set our iniquities before You, our secret sins in the light of Your countenance. For all our days are passed away in Your wrath; we finish our years like a sigh." Once again, Isaac Watts paraphrased our psalm: "Time, like an ever-rolling stream, / Bears all its sons away; / They fly, forgotten, as a dream / Dies at the opening day."

The eternal God, however, is outside of time, abiding beyond the vicissitudes of this earth. To Him the passage of time seems no more than an instant: "For a thousand years in Your sight are like yesterday when it is past, and like a watch in the night." Watts translated this line in the stanza that reads: "A thousand ages in Thy sight / Are like an evening gone, / Short as the watch that ends the night, / Before the rising sun."

Second Peter 3:8 quotes this same line of our psalm to remind Christians that God is not subject to our own sense of time: "But, beloved, do not forget this one thing, that with the Lord one day is as a thousand years, and a thousand years as one day."

God's treasure here below is borne in vessels of clay, for of the mire He made us to be the very bearers of His glory. Because we are also creatures of the Fall, our own tilling of the soil—that is to say, our labor to support our lives in this world—is infected with the forces of death. At the same time, by reason of our incorporation into Christ, our daily labor may also share in the firstfruits of redemption, our glorification as God's children. Our daily work, done for the sake of His glory, may become the medium by which that glory is rendered manifest.

PSALM 90 (91)

HE WHO DWELLS IN THE HELP OF THE HIGHEST

Psalm 90 (Hebrew 91) has always ranked among the more favorite and popular psalms of the Christian people, a fact that surely has something to do, in the East, with its being the opening psalm of the funeral service in the Orthodox Church.

It is also one of the very few psalms about which everyone in antiquity agreed that it should be prayed each day of the week. For all that, Christians have shown themselves less sure about exactly when, during the course of the day, this psalm should best be prayed.

Two specific periods during the day—the night and the noontide—are indicated in the psalm itself: "You shall fear no terror *of the night*, nor the arrow that flies *by day*; neither the thing that prowls in the *darkness*, nor the attack of the *noonday* devil."

Christians in the East, because of the references to daylight and high noon, picked this psalm to be prayed daily at the sixth hour, a custom that prevails to the present time. According to Saint John Cassian in the early fifth century, some of the monastic elders of the East understood the "noonday devil" of this psalm to be a special temptation to spiritual weariness and dejection, that mysterious despondency and distress of heart known in ascetical literature as *akedia* (*The Institutes* 10.1).

Christians in the West, on the other hand, more struck by the references to darkness and the night, chose Psalm 90 to be prayed each evening at the canonical hour of Compline. One finds this usage in the sixth-century monastic Rule of St. Benedict and in the traditional Roman breviary.

In either case, however, one observes the sustained persuasion that this psalm has to do with divine protection from satanic attack, speaking of deliverance from several sorts of demons: the noonday devil, the "thing" that prowls in the darkness, the "evil" that will not come nigh us, the "scourge" that shall not approach our dwelling, "the asp and the adder" that we will step upon, "the lion and the dragon" that we will trample underfoot.

With respect to the demons there is nearly no end of diversity. Again we read in Cassian: "Their variety is such that it would take a long time if we wanted to search all the Scriptures and to go through them individually, seeing which ones are designated by the prophet as onocentaurs, which as satyrs, which as sirens, which as enchantresses, which as screechers, which as ostriches, and which as urchins, which is the asp and which the adder in the psalm; which is called a lion, which a dragon, and which a scorpion in the Gospel; which is the prince of this world, and which are referred to by the Apostle as the rulers of this darkness, and which as the spirits of evil" (*Conferences* 7.32.4).

The satanic assault on our lives is manifold. "A thousand shall fall at your side," says our psalm, "and ten thousand at your right hand." Our experience of temptation, that is to say, very much like our experience of divine grace, is of variant texture, and there should be a corresponding variety in how we deal with it.

The great diversity among the demons is best explained, perhaps, by the fact that each of them is a fallen angel. When God made the myriads of angels, He created them to manifest the vast variations of His own splendor. The angels are thus so diverse among themselves that Thomas Aquinas even speculated that each angel is a separate species. And the demons, because they are fallen angels, represent a like diversity, as John Milton so marvelously portrayed at the beginning of *Paradise Lost*. Indeed, one even suspects that each of the fallen angels fell in a distinct and different way.

Whatever may be the case in the latter respect, there is no doubt that the demons attack our souls with a great assortment of temptations and trials, described in Holy Scripture with manifold symbols and metaphors. Once more Cassian explains: "We must not think that these names are given to them by chance or haphazardly. Rather, by using the names of these wild animals . . . the ferocity and rage of those other beings is denoted. . . . Thus one is called a lion because of his wild fury and raging ferocity, another an adder because of the mortal poison that kills before it is noticed, and still another an onocentaur or an urchin or an ostrich because of the subtlety of its malice" (*Conferences* 7.32.5).

Subtlety? Of course, and also irony, for Psalm 90, so descriptive of demonic attack, is the one psalm actually used and quoted by Satan to tempt our Lord (cf. Matt. 4:6)!

PSALM 91 (92)

IT IS GOOD TO ACCLAIM THE LORD

Psalm 91 (Hebrew 92) has been a morning psalm for a very long time. Besides its use on the Sabbath, as indicated in its title, we know from the Mishnah that this psalm was daily sung in the temple during the libation that accompanied the morning sacrifice of a lamb. Thus, while the priest poured the drink offering of one-quarter of a hin of wine into the fire of this morning sacrifice (cf. Ex. 29:40), the choir chanted: "It is good to acclaim the Lord, and to sing to Your name, O Most High; to declare Your mercy in the morning." Then, because the same sacrifice of a lamb would be made toward the end of the day, the psalm goes on to remember, "and Your truth in the night."

That liturgical setting of Psalm 91 in the ancient temple goes far to explain its traditional use in the Church. From times past remembering, the sixth-century Rule of St. Benedict testifies to the primitive Christian custom of chanting this psalm at daybreak on Friday, the true Pascha and Atonement Day, on which the Lamb of God took away the sins of the world. Thus, the "mercy" declared "in the morning" bears a most specific sense, for our Friday is both Yom Kippur and Passover, the day of that "darkness over the whole earth," the three hours of that ninth plague immediately prior to the atoning death of the Firstborn, the sprinkling of that paschal blood without which there is no remission.

Prayed on Friday mornings, as the ancient Western monastic rule prescribed, this psalm reminds the Church why it is no longer necessary to make the daily offering of lambs in the temple, for those sacrifices had only "a shadow of the good things to come, and not the very image of the things" (Heb. 10:1). With respect to those quotidian lambs offered of old, we are told that "every priest stands ministering daily and offering repeatedly the same sacrifices, which can never take away sins" (10:11). But, with respect to the Lamb in the midst of the Throne, we are told that "this Man, after He had offered one sacrifice for sins forever, sat down at the right hand of God . . . For by one offering He has perfected forever those who are being sanctified" (10:12–14). This is the true Lamb to whom we chant: "You are worthy to take the scroll, / And to open its seals; / For You were slain, / And have redeemed us to God by Your blood" (Rev. 5:9).

Continuing this psalm, we glorify the things that God does and His wisdom in their doing: "How magnified are Your works, O Lord, how exceedingly deep Your thoughts." Once again, these praises of God bear specific reference to the things of our redemption. The "works" of God have to do with the sending of His Son (cf. John 3:17; 6:29), the giving of His Son (3:16), the handing over of His Son (Rom. 8:32), "the exceeding greatness of His power toward us who believe, according to the working of His mighty power which He worked in Christ when He raised Him from the dead and seated Him at His right hand" (Eph. 1:19, 20).

The exceedingly deep thoughts of God, likewise, have to do with the mystery of Christ, the profound counsel of our redemption, "the wisdom of God in a mystery, the hidden wisdom which God ordained before the ages for our glory, which none of the rulers of this age knew" (1 Cor. 2:7, 8). It is in the blood of Jesus that these exceedingly deep thoughts of God are made manifest to our minds, for "in Him we have redemption through His blood, the forgiveness of sins, according to the riches of His grace which He made to abound toward us in all wisdom and prudence, having made known to us the mystery of His will" (Eph. 1:7–9). God's exceedingly deep thoughts, of which our psalm speaks, have to do with the "mystery [of Christ], . . . which in other ages was not made known to the sons of men, as it has now been revealed by the Spirit" (3:3–5).

In speaking of these exceedingly deep thoughts of God, concealed from the wicked but perceived by the just man, our psalm resonates with the language of the Old Testament wisdom literature, describing the just as trees "who are planted in the house of the Lord" and who "will flourish in the courts of our God." Contrary to what nature might cause us to expect of the palm and the cedar, the just man is a house plant. He flourishes *within* the Church, the courts of eternal wisdom, the temple where God's exceedingly deep thoughts are rendered lucid to the pure of heart. This is the "wisdom . . . from above" (James 3:17), "all the treasures of wisdom" (Col. 2:3), "the mystery of the gospel" (Eph. 6:19).

PSALM 92 (93)

THE LORD IS KING; HE IS CLOTHED WITH SPLENDOR

Three psalms (92, 96, 98) begin with the line, "The Lord is King." In each case the expression is actually a verb in both the Greek (*ebasilevsen*) and Hebrew (*malak*), but it is translated here as a noun in order to give clearer attention to the image of "king" (*basilevs, melek*) suggested in the underlying verbs. Proper English usage has no verb "to king," and the usual substitution, "to reign," fails to convey that image adequately.

Psalm 92 (Hebrew 93) is a brief but rich composition, resonating large biblical themes in its every line: "The Lord is King; He is clothed with splendor. In might has the Lord adorned and girded Himself. The world He made firm, that it be not shaken. Your throne is prepared from everlasting; You are from all eternity. The rivers rise in flood, O Lord, the rivers lift their voices, with the voices of many waters. Marvelous these swellings of the sea; marvelous the Lord on high. Your testimonies have proved exceedingly faithful. Holiness befits Your house, O Lord, unto length of days." Among the manifold liturgical settings of this theophanic psalm, its weekly use at Saturday Vespers is the one that comes most readily to mind.

Perhaps its most significant use, however, and arguably the most striking, is as the first psalm at the Ninth Hour (None) and again at Great Vespers on January 6, the feast of the Lord's Theophany. In that context Psalm 92 serves as a meditation on the various Gospel readings of Jesus' Baptism in the Jordan River. Thus, the Lord's kingship, His clothing in splendor and girding in might, is manifested in the Holy Spirit's descent upon Him in the form of a dove, and is revealed in the Father's voice calling Him "My beloved Son."

It is in His Baptism that Holy Church is granted the vision of the Lord Christ's deepest identity. In this sacramental revelation of His oneness with the Father and the Holy Spirit, we know Him to be "from all eternity" and acknowledge His throne "prepared from everlasting." Moreover, when we say to our Lord: "From all eternity *You are*," we are taking up what He spoke of Himself from the burning bush: "I am Who am." As He is proclaimed in the nimbus with which sacred iconography normally adorns His head, Jesus is *Ho On*, "He Who is," the truly existing One, the very source of all being, and more especially of our own. Eight times in the Gospel of St. John, therefore, Jesus speaks of Himself with this same identifying reference, the absolute *Ego eimi*, the "I am" of Mount Sinai (John 6:20; 8:24, 28, 58; 13:19; 18:5, 6, 8).

Identified here, then, as divine and eternally preexisting, Jesus also shares in the work of Creation, for "all things were made through Him, and without Him nothing was made that was made" (John 1:3). "By Him," furthermore, "all things were created that are in heaven and that are on earth . . . All things were created through Him and for Him. And He is before all things, and in Him all things consist" (Col. 1:16, 17). It is the very eternity of His throne that establishes the fixed character of creation. Thus we pray of Jesus in this psalm: "The world He made firm, that it be not shaken. Your throne is prepared from everlasting."

The very undulations of Jordan, too, rise flooding to acclaim Him, raising their voices and rendering marvelous the swellings of the sea. These are the world's baptismal waters, made holy at the touch of Christ, who steps out into the stream in order to fulfill all righteousness (cf. Matt. 3:15). In the liturgical texts for the Theophany feast, this fulfillment of all righteousness is accomplished by the Lord's trampling down of the demonic dragon concealed in the depths, "rescuing the world from his traps and granting eternal life."

And what, in response, do these waters say for themselves? "I cannot bear a consuming fire. Therefore do I marvel at Your exceeding condescension, for I am not accustomed to wash the Pure One, nor have I learned to purify the Sinless One."

The waters that lift up their doxological voices, therefore, are the sacramental waters of our rebirth. It is in these waters that God's people are washed and made holy. The Holy Trinity, revealed in the Baptism of Jesus, is the mystery of our incorporation into the Church, for we are baptized in the name of the Father, and of the Son, and of the Holy Spirit. In these waters we become God's very house, and holiness befits His house unto length of days.

PSALM 93 (94)

A GOD OF VENGEANCE IS THE LORD

A literal translation of Psalm 93 (Hebrew 94) would begin: "A God of vengeances is the Lord; the God of vengeances has plainly spoken," nor is the plural "vengeances" in this first line less striking for being somewhat clumsy. As the rest of the psalm goes on to show, what is intended here is not simply God's general disposition for setting things straight, but the individual acts of judgment by which He does so.

God's avenging justice with respect to the misdeeds of history, that is to say, is directed against man's single and specified acts of injustice, some of which are enumerated: "They have humbled Your people, O Lord, and Your inheritance have they oppressed. They have slain the widow and the orphan, and the foreigner have they slaughtered. . . . They shall hunt down the soul of the righteous man, and the blood of the innocent will be condemned."

It is common nowadays, alas, to imagine that the final divine avenging of the persecuted righteous is simply an "Old Testament idea," whose time is now past in our New Testament dispensation of (alleged) indiscriminate love and universal nonjudgmentalism. This is not true; the New Testament proposes a softening of our hearts, not our heads, nor was it an Old Testament figure who put to us the question: "And shall God not avenge His own elect who cry out day and night to Him, though He bears long with them? I tell you that He will avenge them speedily" (Luke 18:7, 8).

God's resolve seems really quite unaltered from one testament to the next with respect to "vengeances." If the Lord did, somewhere along the line, modify His views about the propriety of executing vengeance on the earth, He failed to share the news with the Apostle John, for the latter mentions a "voice from heaven" proclaiming of Babylon: "Her sins have reached to heaven, and God has remembered her iniquities. Render to her just as she rendered to you, and repay her double according to her works; in the cup which she has mixed, mix double for her" (Rev. 18:5, 6). Indeed, God "has avenged on her the blood of His servants shed by her" (19:2). So much for the alleged updating in the divine program.

Psalm 93, before going on to speak of trust in God, which is the real theme, devotes some lines to an exhortation to "fools." This noun is understood in the sense of the Bible's wisdom literature: men unprincipled and morally obtuse, those who recognize no objective ethical structure within the world, nor any final sanctions to avenge that structure. These moral fools are exhorted to take thought at least for probabilities: "Understand, you fools among the people, and engage your minds at last, you dolts. Does He who implanted the ear not hear? Will He who fashioned the eye not see? Shall not He reprove who instructs the nations, and who teaches men knowledge?"

The appeal here is quite marvelous in its juxtaposition of sensory and moral perception. The intricate construction of man's ears and eyes, their irreducible complexity manifestly directed to the grasping of empirical information, is no accident, no result of cosmic happenstance. How, then, is it conceivable that man's moral sense, as innate and inalienable to his nature as his seeing and hearing, is not also directed to a truly existing moral truth?

It is this native sense of moral truth, a truth fixed eternally in the structure of reality, that gives man a fundamental hope. It is this moral hope that tells man he is more than an animal, for an animal can no more reflect on the moral structure of the world than it can speculate on the intentionality of its eyes and ears. This innate moral sense in man's mind remains the foundation of what Aristophanes called "the great hopes (*elpidai megistai*)." Pindar, for his part, said that man faces old age with the companionship of "hope, which principally governs the fickle mind of mortals."

Among the final articles of the Nicene Creed we affirm that God is discriminating: "He will come again in glory to judge." If this assertion were not true, the rest of the Creed would be worthless, for this assertion proclaims the vindication of our moral sense, the innate source of our hope. According to our psalm, it is this hope that God finally justifies. "The Lord has become my refuge," we pray near the end, "and my God the helper of my hope (*ho Theos mou eis boethon elpidos mou*)."

PSALM 94 (95)

OH COME, LET US EXULT IN THE LORD

Psalm 94 (Hebrew 95) has for many centuries been used as one of the first psalms with which to begin the Christian day. It commences, after all, with an invitation to the praise of God: "Oh come, let us exult in the Lord, let us shout with joy to God, our salvation. Let us come with confession before His face, and shout to Him in joy with psalms. . . . Come, let us adore and fall down and weep before the Lord who made us."

All of these sentiments will mark our prayer during the course of the Christian day: joy and exultation, exclamation and resounding praise, humble adoration, weeping before the Lord, sometimes in sorrow for our sins, sometimes in the joy of His redeeming grace.

Because we belong to God in two ways, the psalm gives a double reason for our worship: creation and election.

First, creation; the whole of created order belongs to God—"for in His hand are all the ends of the earth, and the heights of the mountains are His; for the sea belongs to Him, and He made it, and to the dry land His hands gave form." Our worship is rooted in God's sustained act of creation, by which we, and all things, have our being. (Being, and not just naked existence. We are not existentialists. We do not believe ourselves supplied merely with a generic, undetermined existence, but endowed, rather, with a specific, identified and summoned "being" that forms the foundation and context of our destiny.) God is the resident Landlord of all the earth. Wherever we go upon the earth this day—whether the mountains, the sea or the dry land—it all belongs to the God in whom we live and move and have our being (Acts 17:28).

Second, our special divine election; we Christians belong to God in a most particular way, for He has called and chosen us in Christ: "for He is the Lord our God, and we are the people of His pasture and the sheep of His hand." Our worship is thus rooted in our identity as the Chosen People of God: "Blessed be the God and Father of our Lord Jesus Christ, who has blessed us with every spiritual blessing in the heavenly places in Christ, just as He chose us in Him before the foundation of the world, that we should be holy and without blame before Him in love" (Eph. 1:3, 4). Our worship rests in who we are by reason of our election.

This is all a very consoling doctrine, of course, but our psalm also sees in it a component of danger—namely, the frightful possibility of failure in this matter of our "being in Christ," should memory fade and heart be hardened. Since God has chosen us, we are summoned to choose God, and because our future turns largely on the freedom of our choice, it is by no means inevitable that we will, in the end, be faithful to the invitation of our destiny. Thus, there is an explicit and real warning in this psalm, a warning born of bitter historical memory: "Today, if you hear His voice, harden not your hearts as at the offense on the day of temptation in the desert, where your fathers tempted Me and put Me to the test and beheld My works. Forty years I was offended with that generation and said: 'They always wander in their hearts, and they have not known My ways,' so I swore in My wrath: 'They shall not enter into My rest.'"

Although the specific instance of infidelity here being recalled was the people's unbelief at the rock of Kadesh (Num. 20), God's complaint is more general and takes in the entire forty years during which His unfaithful people wandered in the desert. Almost none of that generation entered into the Promised Land. Our psalm stands as a warning that all of us are capable of a like infidelity and hardness of heart. What happened in the desert to Israel of old can also happen "today." The day of decision is always "today."

This is likewise the point of the earliest Christian interpretation of this psalm, found in chapters 3 and 4 of Hebrews, a work addressed to a Christian congregation which, the author feared, was in serious danger of falling away from the faith. After quoting the above lines of our psalm, the author goes on to comment: "Beware, brethren, lest there be in any of you an evil heart of unbelief in departing from the living God; but exhort one another daily, while it is called 'Today,' lest any of you be hardened through the deceitfulness of sin. . . . Therefore, since a promise remains of entering His rest, let us fear lest any of you seem to have come short of it. For indeed the gospel was preached to us as well as to them" (3:12, 13; 4:1, 2). The psalm's warning, then, is always a matter of "today," as we begin our daily worship.

PSALM 95 (96)

We know that Psalm 95 (Hebrew 96) was among the psalms chosen to be sung when the Ark of the Covenant was placed in the new tabernacle that David had constructed for it in Jerusalem (cf. 1 Chr. 16:23–33). This piece of information is valuable because it sets Psalm 95 in at least one of its interpretive contexts in biblical history: God's enthronement as King in the worship of His holy people. Inasmuch as the Lord's symbolic enthronement "between the cherubim" in the Holy of Holies was one of the more important Old Testament institutions preparatory for His definitive *presence* in the human race by reason of the Incarnation, the deeper meaning of this psalm is likewise to be sought in its relationship to God's Word that "became flesh and dwelt [or tabernacled] among us" (John 1:14).

This psalm, then, and all other Old Testament references to God as King are prophecies fulfilled in the Kingship of Jesus the Lord, who declared to the local representative of the Roman Empire, "You say rightly that I am a king" (John 18:37).

Thus, our psalm commands, "Announce among the nations that the Lord is King." Truly, this is the sum and essence of everything the Church was given to proclaim, not only to the Roman Empire, but to all the nations of the earth at all times: "Let all the house of Israel know assuredly that God has made this Jesus . . . both Lord and Christ" (Acts 2:36). The word "Christ" here, of course, is a translation of the Hebrew expression "anointed one," which referred to Israel's anointed king. In the context of Peter's sermon, Jesus is made Lord and King by His Resurrection from the dead (cf. 2:22–32).

It is in the mystery of His Resurrection, then, that Jesus the Lord fulfills the prophetic dimension of that symbolic enthronement of God in Israel's ancient Holy of Holies. Psalm 95, which was sung to celebrate that figurative enthronement, finds its intended completion in Jesus' victory over death. This is the truth of that invitation of its first line: "Sing to the Lord a new song; sing to the Lord, all the earth." It is a "new song" exactly as this term is used of the anthem sung to the victorious Lamb in Revelation 5:9; it is a "new song," because henceforth humanity is dealing with a wholly new reality. And it is "all the earth" that is summoned to sing this new song, for the Resurrection of Christ establishes His kingship, not only over human hearts, but also over the nations. It is precisely the nations that are called to sing the new song.

Indeed, the universal Kingship of the risen Christ is the root and warrant of the entire mission of the Church to the nations: "*All* authority has been given to Me in heaven and on earth. Go *therefore* and make disciples of *all* the nations" (Matt. 28:18, 19). The first component justifies the second. These two sentences are related as premise and inference. *Because* He has received all authority in heaven and on earth, we *therefore* go forth to make disciples of all nations. The proclamation elicits the universal evangelical mandate.

Therefore, the Resurrection of Christ is the foundation of the Church's missionary imperative. The first sermon of the Church, that of Simon Peter at nine o'clock on Pentecost morning, was a sermon entirely about the Lord's Resurrection. It may thus be summarized: "Announce among the nations that the Lord is King."

Of course, the Resurrection of Jesus our Lord provides the theological context for understanding all of Holy Scripture (cf. Luke 24:25–27, 44–46). Moreover, this Christological fulfillment is the basis of the Church's proclamation "to all nations" (24:47). The Lamb's victory is what authorizes Him "to open the scroll and to loose its seven seals" (Rev. 5:5), thus leading to the acclamation of "every tribe and tongue and people and nation" (5:9), and "every creature which is in heaven and on the earth and under the earth and such as are in the sea, and all that are in them" (5:13).

What is true of all inspired Scriptures seems especially applicable to Psalm 95 and its call to the nations to enter the Church in praise of the risen Christ: "Confession and beauty are before Him; holiness and splendor stand in His sanctuary. Bring to the Lord, you families of nations, bring to the Lord glory and honor; bring to the Lord the glory due His name. Bring sacrifices, and process into His courts. Worship the Lord in His holy court."

PSALM 96 (97)

THE LORD IS KING, LET THE EARTH BE GLAD

Psalm 96 (Hebrew 97) is one of those Old Testament texts explicitly interpreted for us in the New Testament. The Epistle to the Hebrews, telling how "God, who at various times and in various ways spoke in time past to the fathers by the prophets, has in these last days spoken to us by His Son," went on to tell of the reverence and service shown to this Son by the holy angels as He entered into the world through the Incarnation: "But when He again brings the firstborn (*prototokos*) into the world, He says: 'Let all the angels of God worship Him'" (1:1, 2, 6). This quotation is, of course, from Psalm 96, which the author of Hebrews here interprets with reference to that ministry of the angelic hosts to the incarnate Lord. The relationship of the angels to Christ is the dominant motif of the first chapter of Hebrews.

The Gospels also treat explicitly with this theme. Matthew, for instance, tells of the ministry of the announcing angel just prior to the birth of the first-begotten (*prototokos*) (1:20–25, with some manuscript variants on verse 25). Similarly, Luke describes how the Mother of Jesus placed the first-begotten (*prototokos*) in a manger, His entry into the world then being announced by the angels (2:7–13).

The ministry of the angels in the life of Jesus is a standard motif in the Gospels, especially near their beginnings and final pages. Thus, in the Gospel of Mark the service of the angels to Jesus at the commencement of His ministry (1:13) finds its parallel later on at the empty tomb (16:5). The Gospel of Matthew is structured within a similar parallelism (1:20; 28:2). Luke, on the other hand, not only has this identical diptych framing his work (1:26; 24:4), but he also introduces the ministry of an angel into the context of the Lord's Passion, the angel of the agony (22:43).

Nor is this theme of angels in relationship to Christ our Lord alien to the thought of St. Paul. When, in Colossians, the Apostle refers to Jesus as the first-begotten (*prototokos*), he goes on immediately to speak of His relationship to the angelic powers: "For by Him all things were created that are in heaven and that are on earth, visible and invisible, whether thrones or dominions or principalities or powers" (1:15, 16).

Thanks to its being quoted by the Epistle to the Hebrews, then, we know the theological context in which the early Christians prayed Psalm 96, which was understood by them as referring to the Incarnation of the First-begotten.

The appearance of the King into this world brings joy to the whole earth: "The Lord is King, let the earth be glad; let the many islands rejoice." Indeed, this is the very message of the angels at the birth of the Lord: "Do not be afraid, for behold, I bring you good tidings of great joy which will be to all people. For there is born to you this day in the city of David a Savior, who is Christ the Lord" (Luke 2:10, 11). The universality of His Kingship includes both men and angels.

The Incarnation means, first of all, that God is forever "present" to creation, especially humanity, in a new way. There is now a most special sense in which man stands before Him, since He has joined Himself inseparably to our nature, divinity and humanity united indissolubly in a single Person. "God *with us*" is how the Gospel of Matthew begins, and "Behold, I am *with you* all days" is how it ends.

Our psalm is likewise preoccupied with the presence of God in our midst: "Fire will go before Him. . . . The mountains melted like wax from before the face of the Lord; from before the face of the Lord, all the earth. The heavens declared His justice, and all peoples have seen His glory." The threatening brightness of God's presence puts one in mind of John's inaugural vision of Christ at the beginning of Revelation. One will also be reminded of the bright cloud of the Lord's Transfiguration on the mountain by a line of this psalm: "Clouds and darkness are round about Him."

God's appearance in this world, says our psalm, is the source of joy for those who wait for Him in purity of life: "Light has risen for the just man, and gladness for those upright in heart. Rejoice in the Lord, you just ones, and confess the memory of His holiness." Men and angels join together in common adoration at God's supreme manifestation in the incarnate Son.

PSALM 97 (98)

SING TO THE LORD A NEW SONG, FOR THE LORD
HAS DONE WONDROUS THINGS

The latter part of Isaiah, in which the dominant theme is Israel's return from the Babylonian Captivity, speaks several times of God's "arm," a metaphor especially used in conjunction with the noun "salvation" and the adjective "holy" (Is. 40:10; 51:9; 52:10; 53:1; 59:16; 63:5). This robust image of God's arm, which had first appeared in the Bible in the context of the people's deliverance from Egypt (cf. Ex. 6:6; 15:16), was thus applied to their return from exile in Babylon. In each case, the redemption of the oppressed was ascribed to the holy flexing of God's muscle, as it were, on their behalf.

It is significant that the Mother of God summoned this same metaphor to describe God's definitive historical intervention on behalf of His people: "Holy is His name, / And His mercy is on those who fear Him, / From generation to generation. / He has shown strength with His arm" (Luke 1:49–51). God's arm in these contexts is an image of His "power according to the Spirit of holiness" (Rom. 1:4), "the power of God to salvation" (1:16).

The same reference to God's holy, salvific arm appears several times in Psalms, one example being the opening of Psalm 97 (Hebrew 98): "Sing to the Lord a new song, for the Lord has done wondrous things; His right hand and His holy arm have wrought salvation."

God's salvation is not simply a thing announced, but a "wrought" reality. In saving us, God truly *does* certain deeds, "wondrous things," by which we are redeemed. God saves man by the forceful intrusion of His holiness into man's history. God's arm is a metaphor of this irrupting redemptive holiness. In the "wondrous things" of the Incarnation, the Atonement, the Resurrection, God's arm invades the processes of human destiny with the outpouring of His own life. Man's life is thereby given access to the incorruptible life of God.

This, says our psalm, is the substance of the Gospel proclaimed to the nations and peoples of the earth: "The Lord has made known His salvation; unto the nations has He revealed His righteousness. All the ends of the earth have seen the salvation of our God."

The substance of the Gospel, then, is not some theory about God or even some set of norms by which man is to live. At root, the Gospel has absolutely nothing in common with even the highest religious speculations, such as those of the Upanishads, Pythagoras, Heraclitus, Lao Tzi, or the Buddha. In the strictest possible sense, beyond all human reckoning or expectation, the Gospel is a "new song," a radically different voice on the human scene. It is the revelation of God's holy arm taking charge of man's history. It is that redemptive, holy activity by which "He has shown strength with His arm." It is "the power of God and the wisdom of God" (1 Cor. 1:24).

Such is the meaning of Theophany, literally "the appearing of God" in man's history. This appearing of God is not a general and pervasive luminosity to which the human race has a ready and easy access. It is, on the contrary, most particular, very specified with respect to time and place. God has become incarnate only once. Only once has the price of our sins been paid. Only once has He "appointed a day on which He will judge the world in righteousness by a Man whom He has ordained." Moreover, "He has given assurance of this to all by raising Him from the dead" (Acts 17:31). Only once has God done all of these "wondrous things."

Our psalm speaks likewise of this latter judgment of the world by one Man whom He has ordained. "For He comes to judge the earth," it says, "He will judge the world with righteousness, and the peoples with uprightness." All of human history will, at the last, be summoned before the same Judge whom God has ordained, giving "assurance of this to all by raising Him from the dead." This single, unique standard of the final judgment is likewise a component of the Gospel itself: "When the Son of Man comes in His glory, and all the holy angels with Him, then He will sit on the throne of His glory. *All the nations* will be gathered before Him" (Matt. 25:31, 32).

Particular in the time and place of its appearance, the Gospel of Jesus Christ is nonetheless universal as the canon and measure of man's destiny, being solely the source of the "knowledge of salvation" (Luke 1:77).

PSALM 98 (99)

THE LORD IS KING, LET THE PEOPLES RAGE

In the Liturgy of St. Basil we pray the Father to "receive from the hands of us sinners these gifts" that we present before Him that they may become, by the outpouring of the Holy Spirit, the Body and Blood of Jesus Christ. We ask Him to "behold this our worship and receive it" as He received the sacrifices of various priestly figures in Holy Scripture. In making this petition to the Father, we believers seek inclusion in a high company of men to whom God, when they called upon Him, paid special attention. Among these latter we particularly mention "the priestly offices of Moses and Aaron, the peace-offerings of Samuel."

To seek a fellowship in worship with the likes of Moses, Aaron, and Samuel is a bold thing indeed. With respect to the first of these, we are told: "So the Lord spoke to Moses face to face, as a man speaks to his friend" (Ex. 33:11). And of the second we read that "Aaron lifted his hand toward the people, blessed them, and came down from offering the sin offering, . . . and fire came out from before the LORD and consumed the burnt offering" (Lev. 9:22, 24). Finally, with respect to Samuel, we learn that "he called upon the mighty Lord, when his enemies pressed upon him on every side, when he offered the suckling lamb. And the Lord thundered from heaven, and with a great noise made His voice to be heard" (Ecclesiasticus 46:16, 17).

These three men all worshipped the Lord in His tabernacle, whether in the desert or at the shrine of Shiloh. All three, that is to say, stood in the presence of the Lord's "mercy seat" atop the Ark of the Covenant, overshadowed by the wings of the cherubim, behind the veil, within the Holy of Holies.

Psalm 98 (Hebrew 99) is among those psalms that speak of the Lord's symbolic enthronement in that holy place: "The Lord is King, let the peoples rage; He thrones upon the cherubim, let the earth be shaken."

This psalm also speaks of the worship offered to the Lord in that holy place by the same three men of whom we have been speaking: "Moses and Aaron among His priests, and Samuel among those who call on His name, they called upon the Lord, and He answered them. He spoke with them in the pillar of cloud, for they guarded His testimonies and the precepts that He gave them. O Lord, our God, You answered them."

We Christians pray, then, to be admitted, reverently, to the realm of holiness, as were God's servants of old; "let us have grace, by which we may serve

God acceptably with reverence and godly fear" (Heb. 12:28). Thus we pray in this psalm: "The Lord is great in Sion, and He is exalted over all peoples. Let them confess Your great name, for fearsome it is, and holy. . . . Exalt the Lord our God, and bow down before His footstool, for He is holy."

Psalm 98 also warns that the praise and adoration of God may not be separated from the doing of His will in holy obedience. As we read above with regard to His three ancient servants, "they guarded His testimonies and the precepts that He gave them." Were these men obedient at all times? Perhaps Samuel was, for the Bible speaks of no disobedience on his part, and "all Israel from Dan to Beersheba knew that Samuel had been established as a prophet of the Lord" (1 Sam. 3:20). However, Holy Scripture makes no secret of the failings of Moses and Aaron (cf. Ex. 32; Num. 20). Our psalm likewise speaks of God's reproving and forgiving the failings of these two servants: "You were gracious to them and corrected all their misdeeds."

In another and deeper sense, nonetheless, our own boldness of worship before the Lord may be said to surpass that of Moses, Aaron, and Samuel. They stood and ministered before a "real presence" of God, certainly, but it was enshrined in a tabernacle made with human hands. The true Holy of Holies, however, that to which we ourselves draw near, is in "the greater and more perfect tabernacle not made with hands, that is, not of this creation" (Heb. 9:11). The true "mercy seat" (*hilastrion*) where God meets us is Christ our Lord (cf. Rom. 3:25, textual variant), who "has not entered the holy places made with hands, which are copies of the true, but into heaven itself" (Heb. 9:24). For us to worship in the name of Jesus means to "come boldly to the throne of grace, that we may obtain mercy and find grace to help in time of need" (4:16).

PSALM 99 (100)

SHOUT FOR JOY TO THE LORD, ALL THE EARTH!

Psalm 99 (Hebrew 100) falls into a class of canticles traditionally known as the "invitatory," a summons to come into God's presence with confession and praise: "Shout for joy to the Lord, all the earth! Serve the Lord with gladness, and come into His presence with exultation. Know that the Lord Himself is our God. He it is that made us, and not we ourselves; we are His people and the sheep of His pasture. Enter His gates with confession, and His courts with hymns. Confess Him! Give praise to His name! For the Lord is gracious; His mercy is everlasting, and His truth stands fast to all generations."

Psalm 99 has not traditionally served as the regular invitatory psalm of the Christian Church, however, for a very simple reason. That is, much of it is virtually identical with some lines of Psalm 94. This latter, probably because of the prominence it receives in the New Testament (cf. Heb. 3 and 4), has always been the Church's invitatory "of choice." So Psalm 99, beyond its place in the weekly sequence of the Psalter, has been accorded no special role by liturgical custom, except for its occasional use as the Prokeimenon, or Gradual. Nonetheless, if one is looking for an easily memorized psalm with which to begin a short time of daily prayer, one could hardly find a better than Psalm 99.

The correct praise of God in this psalm, as truly in all of Holy Scripture, is inseparable from our relationship to Him in covenant. He is "our God," as distinct from simply "God." And we are "His people," as distinct from just a bunch of folks. This mutual belonging to one another is the whole business of the covenant. "I will be their God, and they shall be My people," the Lord says through Jeremiah (31:33) in a passage later quoted by Hebrews (8:10). This, one may take it, is the source of the joy in our psalm.

This "belonging," nonetheless, our mutual relationship to God, is not a purely individual thing. True it is, of course, that He "calls his own sheep *by name* "(John 10:3), nor is one disposed to give that important fact less than its proper emphasis. The Good Shepherd did die for each one of us (cf. Gal. 2:20), so each of us can address Him as "my God," which in the psalms we rather often do. In the present psalm, on the other hand, the accent seems rather to fall on the human community created by God's covenant; we speak of ourselves as "the sheep of His pasture." It is precisely the pasture that we belong to; it is the flock that we are members of. Which is to say that the mystery of Holy Church is ever at the heart of our prayer, no matter how individual the setting or intimate the sentiments.

Furthermore, even beyond the catholicity of the Church, this psalm's invitation to worship is directed to the very catholicity of the world. "Shout for joy to the Lord, *all the earth!*" we say. When the people of God, "the sheep of His pasture," assemble to rejoice in His presence and enter His courts with praise, there is always an evangelical summons implied in the action. We believers are priests; we stand in, as it were, on behalf of the whole world. No one is to be excluded from our prayer, because no one is excluded from the heart of Christ. Even as He chose us "out of every tribe and tongue and people and nation," He appointed us intercessors on their behalf; that is, He made us "priests to our God" (Rev. 5:9, 10).

And as the call to God's worship is universal throughout space, its basis is universal throughout time, for our prayer is founded on the mercy and truth of God. "For the Lord is gracious," we say, "His mercy is everlasting, and His truth stands fast to all generations." To "enter His gates with confession" is always timely, but it is never time-bound. To come "into His courts with hymns" is to step into the realm of eternal mercy and eternal truth.

As we worship, this mercy and truth of God are matters of our *knowledge*. "*Know* that the Lord Himself is our God," we say. According to Jeremiah (31:34) and Hebrews (8:11, 12), near the texts cited above, this knowledge of God pertains to the covenant itself: "All shall know Me, from the least of them to the greatest of them. For I will be merciful to their unrighteousness." Revelation does not give us only knowledge *about* God, but the personal knowledge *of* God. This knowledge of God is that to which we give voice when we "come into His presence with exultation."

PSALM 100 (101)

MERCY AND JUDGMENT WILL I CHANT TO YOU, O LORD

Psalm 100 (Hebrew 101) is a hymn of dedication and promise on the part of God's servant, and its reference to the punishment of evildoers has prompted some critics to see in it the kind of righteous political program possibly associated with a royal enthronement. Indeed, the psalm is ascribed to David.

Along with such a political reading of the text, nonetheless, this psalm applies also to the humbler, yet perhaps more substantial task of the governance of one's own home. Twice here we find the expression "my house"—"I have walked in the innocence of my heart, in *the midst of my house*" and "The man who practices arrogance will not lodge in *the midst of my house*." This psalm may be read, then, as a text concerned with the godly governance of a man's household.

A house is an intentionally structured reality; it is quite different from dwelling in a cave or abiding under the branches of a tree. A house is designed; it is shaped according to a pattern, and the integrity of the house depends on its adherence to principles and laws. And what is true of the house is true likewise of the household, which is also structured according to principles and laws.

A household, moreover, is "hierarchical," a Greek word indicating that its structure, its ordering, is sacral and stands under the aegis of heavenly prerogative. Founded on divinely sanctioned authority, families are hierarchical realities. Family homes are eminently prescriptive institutions, the loci of inherited wisdom and the transmission of identity and culture. It is in homes that we learn to speak, and therefore to think. It is in homes that we learn to relate to other people and are thus cultured into human beings.

Proper, godly governance of one's house is called "economics," another Greek word that literally means "house law." Perhaps most often understood nowadays solely in terms of the material resources of a household, economics certainly means a great measure more. A house is a human institution, after all, and a properly human existence involves dimensions far beyond the maintenance of physical and material conditions. If man is truly to be man, he does not live by bread alone. Indeed, with respect to those material and physical things needed for the household, our unique Economist affirmed that, if we will seek first the Kingdom of God and His justice, all these other things would be given to us as well. The standing or falling of houses has less to do with the material than with the moral, for the pursuit of justice is the true foundation of a house.

So, what sorts of things are banished from this well-ordered house? "Transgressions" (*parabaseis*) and "any unlawful deed" (*pragma paranomon*). And who will not be welcomed in this house? The one "who slanders his neighbor in secret." And just who will not be invited to sit at table in this house? "The man of proud eye and greedy heart." This is not, in other words, an "open house"; the door thereto is narrow, and there are specified conditions for entrance. A house is a measured structure, and there is no such thing as measure without the acceptance of limits.

The house in this psalm is also, of course, the house of God, the great hall of the supper of the Lamb, to which, once again our Economist tells us, many are called but few are chosen. This psalm describes what it means not to be clothed in that proper wedding garment, the wearing of which saves a man from being ejected into the outer darkness: "No perverse heart has been my companion. . . . The man who speaks unjust things will not abide before my eyes."

If the door to the house is narrow, so is the way that leads to life. Twice this psalm speaks of walking "in the blameless path" (*en hodo amomo*). Indeed, this is how the psalm begins: "Mercy and judgment will I chant to You, O Lord. I will sing (*psalo*), and I will understand (*syneso*) in the blameless path." In this line we are presented with a reliable pattern for prayer and the life of virtuous striving. The singing here has specific reference to psalmody, which is to be done, says our psalm, with understanding (cf., too, 1 Cor. 14:15—"I will also sing with the understanding."). And whence comes this understanding? From walking blamelessly. The path to the understanding of prayer is the narrow way of virtuous struggle.

PSALM 101 (102)

OH LORD, HEAR MY PRAYER

Psalm 101 (Hebrew 102), the fifth of the traditional "penitential psalms," is structured on a contrast, pursued through two sequences. The first half of the first sequence is all "I"—I am miserable, I am sad, my heart withers away like the grass in the heat, I lie awake at night, I feel like a mournful bird, I mingle my drink with tears, my days flee like the shadows of an evening, and so forth. Life being rough, a goodly number of our days are passed with such sentiments, so it is usually not difficult to pray this part of the psalm.

The second half of the first sequence arrives with the expression, "but You, O Lord," which is just as emphatic in the Hebrew (*we'attah Adonai*) and the Greek (*sy de Kyrie*). "You" is contrasted with "I." God is not like me; God is almighty and does what He wants and does not die. God is enthroned forever, and His name endures from generation to generation. God will arise and deliver His people.

The second and shorter contrasting sequence repeats the first. Once again, as at the beginning, there is the sense of our human frailty, our shortened days, our strength broken at midcourse. To this is contrasted the eternity of God; His years endure unto all generations. Thus, both sequences in this psalm form contrasts between the permanence of God and the transience of everything created.

Two further things should be said about Psalm 101, the first Christological and the second ecclesiological.

First, Christology. The God addressed here is Christ our Lord, a point made clear in Hebrews 1, which quotes this psalm as a prayer to Christ. The author had just quoted Psalm 44 about the permanence of Christ's throne ("Your throne, O God, is forever and ever . . ."), a verse strikingly similar to a verse in Psalm 101 ("But You, O Lord, are enthroned forever . . ."). Quoting the other psalm seems to lead naturally to quoting this one, and the author of Hebrews proceeds to do so, still addressing it to Christ: "You, Lord, in the beginning laid the foundation of the earth, / And the heavens are the work of Your hands. / They will perish, but You remain; / And they will all grow old like a garment; / Like a cloak You will fold them up, / And they will be changed. / But You are the same, / And Your years will not fail" (Heb. 1:10–12).

In Psalm 101, then, as read through New Testament eyes, the God who made the heavens is Christ our Lord. This idea is thematic in the first chapter of Hebrews, which begins by affirming that "God . . . has in these last days spoken to us by His Son, whom He has appointed heir of all things, through whom also He made the worlds" (vv. 1, 2). To the impermanence of the heavens, then, is contrasted the permanence, and therefore complete dependability, of Christ: "Jesus Christ is the same yesterday, today, and forever" (Heb. 13:8). Heaven and earth will pass away, but His words will never pass away.

"You are our God, and we know no other than You," we pray to Jesus each Sunday at the time of Holy Communion. We Christians acknowledge no divinity apart from the God revealed in Jesus Christ. The universe is without explanation except in Him. He is the very coherence of all creation. The world has no center apart from Him, "for by Him all things were created that are in heaven and that are on earth, visible and invisible . . . and He is before all things, and in Him all things consist" (Col. 1:16, 17). The permanent, the creating God addressed all through Psalm 101 is the very one revealed in the Gospel.

Second, ecclesiology. This is a psalm about the Church. Both of its sequences are completed by celebrating the hope of God's people, their deliverance from shame and from captivity, the rebuilding of Jerusalem, the proclamation of God's name in Sion, the gathering of the nations unto the service of God. This psalm gives voice to the hope of the Church.

It also prays for the swift vindication of that hope: "You will arise and have mercy on Sion, for the time, the right time, has come." If this is indeed "the church of the living God, the pillar and ground of the truth" (1 Tim. 3:15), the one source of her stability is that same Lord who spread out the heavens and will, at the end, fold them up like a cloak. The single permanent institution in this world is that consecrated people that God has chosen for His own inheritance. God shares His permanence with the Church.

PSALM 102 (103)

☙

Psalm 102 (Hebrew 103) is another of those psalms in which the believer addresses mainly his own soul. It both commences and ends with the invitation: "Bless the Lord, O my soul."

This psalm is an outstanding illustration of that special quality of Christian prayer that we may call the interiorization of sacred history, that dimension of the Bible that Saint John Cassian calls its "third sense."

A word of explanation may be in order here. The "second sense" of Holy Scripture (following Cassian's schema) is its relationship to our Lord Jesus Christ, in whom the Bible is "fulfilled." He is the exegetical key. He is the Lamb who opens the seven seals of its mysteries (Rev. 5). Any reading of Holy Scripture, then, that attempts to bypass its fulfillment in Christ will attain only to the letter that kills, not the Spirit that gives life.

But we Christians, precisely because we are "in Christ," also read the Bible as our own book. The Bible is the word directed to our hearts, the perfect law of liberty that reflects our own natural faces (James 1:23–25). The lengthy story of God's dealings with His people is the history of our own souls. "For whatever things were written before were written for our learning, that we through the patience and comfort of the Scriptures might have hope" (Rom. 15:4). "When you pray," wrote St. Jerome, "you speak to the Bridegroom; when you read the Bible, He speaks to you." The reading of Holy Scripture is thus a privileged locus of the Christian's dialogue with the Lord. For the soul in Christ, the Bible is preeminently the book of the heart, where we study our own history and come to know our own identities in Christ. This "third sense" of Scripture corresponds to what Bernard of Clairvaux meant when he called the Bible "the book of experience." It means that we do not correctly interpret the Bible except in permitting the Bible to interpret us.

One observes in Psalm 102 this great effort to take into one's own heart God's manifold acts of mercy all through the history of the Bible. This is the God "who made His ways known to Moses, His deeds to the children of Israel." This is the historical God of the covenant and the commandments: "The mercy of the Lord is from everlasting to everlasting on them that fear Him, and His righteousness unto children's children; to such as keep His covenant, and to those who remember His commandments to do them." It is to this interiorization of the commandments, this "remembrance" of the everlasting covenant, that this psalm summons the soul: "Forget not all His benefits; He forgives all your iniquities."

This inner knowledge of the forgiving mercy of God is the substance of the covenant that we have with God in Christ: "For this is the covenant that I will make with the house of Israel after those days, says the LORD: I will put My laws in their mind and write them on their hearts. . . For I will be merciful to their unrighteousness, and their sins and their lawless deeds I will remember no more" (Jer. 31:33, 34; Heb. 8:10, 12). This knowledge of the true God is inseparable from the forgiveness of our sins: " . . . To give knowledge of salvation to His people / By the remission of their sins" (Luke 1:77).

In Psalm 102, then, the soul is called to the contemplation of God's infinite, forgiving mercy: "The Lord is merciful and gracious, slow to anger, and plenteous in mercy. . . He has not dealt with us according to our sins, nor rewarded us according to our iniquities." Indeed not, for "while we were still sinners, Christ died for us" (Rom. 5:8).

This is a psalm appropriately to be prayed in front of an icon of the Cross, for only in the crucified Jesus is it truly fulfilled. The four dimensions of the Cross, its length and breadth, its height and depth, are the dimensions of God's mercy: "For as the heaven is high above the earth, so great is His mercy toward them that fear Him; as far as the east is from the west, so far has He removed our transgressions from us." This *hesed* or mercy of God is not a hazy benevolence. It has a definite history that climaxes in specific acts of salvation: "For Christ also suffered once for sins, the just for the unjust, that He might bring us to God" (1 Pet. 3:18). And again, "By this we know love, because He laid down His life for us" (1 John 3:16).

This is a psalm, then, to be kneaded carefully into the leaven of the soul, for it is concerned with the blood-forgiveness we receive in Christ our Lord. It may especially be recommended as part of one's regular thanksgiving after the sacrament of Confession.

PSALM 103 (104)

BLESS THE LORD, O MY SOUL

౸

The Eastern tradition of the Orthodox Church begins Vespers each evening with the recitation of Psalm 103 (Hebrew 104), a usage amply justified by some of its lines: "The moon You made to mark the seasons; the sun knows the time for its setting. You made the darkness, and it is night, when the wild beasts prowl in the forest."

On the other hand, the sixth-century Rule of Saint Benedict assigned Psalm 103 to be prayed in the West at the early hour of Saturday mornings, a usage also justified in the text: "The sun rises, and [the lions] gather together, lying down to rest in their dens, while man goes forth to his work, and to his labor until the evening."

Nonetheless, there is evidence that at one time the West too had recited Psalm 103 at Vespers, at least on Sundays. For many centuries and, indeed, well into the second half of the twentieth century, the brief "responsorial" chanted after the Bible reading at Western Vespers on Sundays was a verse from this psalm: "How magnified are Your works, O Lord; in wisdom have You made them all." Almost certainly this verse was vestigial testimony that the whole psalm was sung at this point during an earlier period of liturgical history.

Though prayed in the lengthening shadows of evening, Vespers itself has always been thought of rather as an hour of light than of darkness, a perspective inspired both by the special quality of the gloaming and sunset and by the ritual lighting of the candles. This note of vesperal light is obvious in the traditional hymnody of both the East and the West. One thinks, for instance, of the ancient vesperal hymns *Phos Hilaron* ("O Gladsome Light") in the East and *Lucis Creator Optime* ("Most Good Creator of the Light") in the West. An early line of our psalm strengthens the same impression: "You are clothed in praise and majesty, adorning Yourself in a garment of light."

Psalm 103 is likewise one of those psalms for which the New Testament provides at least a partial interpretive key. An early verse of it is quoted in Hebrews with respect to the angels: "Who makes His angels spirits, / And His ministers a flame of fire" (1:7). This line of the Psalter is interpreted just a few verses later: "Are they not all ministering spirits sent forth to minister for those who will inherit salvation?" (1:14).

Psalm 103 is not difficult. Indeed, the flow of its poetry has made it a favorite, and it is no surprise that the Church has long tended to pray it daily.

The psalmist meditates on the various "days" of Creation, starting with the vast expanse of the heavens, then the ministry of the angels, then the earth and its myriad phenomena, the various plants and diverse animals, from sparrows and rabbits to deer and lions, and not excluding man, always with an emphasis on God's generous provision for the needs of all: "Expectantly do all things look to You, to give them their food in due season. You give, and they gather in. When You open Your hand, all things are filled with goodness."

Psalm 103 combines considerations of the natural order with those of human commerce, suggesting a "cooperation" between God's work and man's. This perspective is true with regard to both the land ("You make grass to grow for the cattle, and vegetation for the service of man—to make bread spring from the earth, and wine to gladden his heart, and oil to shine on his face, and bread to strengthen his heart") and the sea ("Here is the sea, great and wide, holding creatures without number, living things both great and small. Here too go the ships to and fro, and the great sea serpent that frolics therein"). Man's own labor is matched by that of other creatures in nature, such as the hunting of the lions and the nest-building of the birds.

Toward the end our psalm speaks of God's Holy Spirit at work in the world: "You will send forth Your Spirit, and they shall be created, and You will renew the face of the earth." Perhaps inspired by this psalm, the poet G. M. Hopkins saw the sun's daily rising as a sign that "the Holy Ghost over the bent / World broods with warm breast and with ah! bright wings."

His older contemporary, J. H. Newman, especially liked the line about man going "forth to his work, and to his labor until the evening." This was the text of his very first sermon, and it later became also the text for his last sermon as an Anglican, "The Parting of Friends."

PSALM 104 (105)

CONFESS TO THE LORD, AND CALL UPON HIS NAME

It is common to think of the Greeks as the first people to arrive at the notion of "history," understood as the ability to perceive and narrate a single, coherent texture of many diverse events united by patterns of cause and effect. Thus, in the very first work to be called *Historiai*, in the fifth century before Christ, Herodotus was able to unite into a single interpretive picture the diverse accounts of several peoples and empires on three continents, over several centuries, as they came to bear on the Persian invasion of Asia Minor and Greece. Herodotus, therefore, is commonly called the world's first historian.

In fact, however, since at least the reign of Solomon five centuries earlier, Israel had already demonstrated an analogous ability to trace coherent, interpretive patterns uniting historical events over an even longer period of time. These discerned patterns, further elaborated by later inspired authors, eventually became the panoramic vision of biblical history.

In Greek history, as in the formal Greek science that was beginning about the same time, the perspective was what we may call secular, in the sense that the empirical data were arranged into intelligible patterns requiring no transcendent or divine explanation. Much as the modern social sciences attempt to adopt the methodology of the physical sciences, so ancient Greek historiography tended to follow certain perspectives and procedures developed for Greek physical science. In this way both Greek history and Greek science represented a break with traditional mythology, which had endeavored to interpret observable phenomena by recourse to religious explanation.

In Israel's historiography, on the other hand, all was theology. The unifying theme was God's governance of events through various interventions, whether by perceived phenomena (miracles, apparitions, direct speech) or by that subtle, secret influence of divine activity that we have come to call God's providence. It was to this latter that St. Paul referred when he wrote: "And we know that all things work together for good to those who love God, to those who are the called according to His purpose" (Rom. 8:28).

One small biblical exercise in the narrative tracing of such a pattern is Psalm 104 (Hebrew 105), the first of three consecutive psalms structured on detailed historical narrative. While their varying constructions show no original relationship joining them, the first two are arranged in the Psalter in such a way as to suggest an overlapping sequence. Thus, Psalm 104 begins with

Abraham and ends with the Sinai covenant, while Psalm 105 begins with the Exodus and ends with the period after the Conquest.

Even the most casual reader will also note the similarities of Psalm 104 with Psalm 77 with respect to historical outline. These differ from one another considerably in inspiration, however. That earlier psalm especially emphasizes the repeated infidelities of the people, whereas Psalm 104 concentrates entirely on praising God for His providential directing of Israel's history.

Following the primitive schema preserved in Deuteronomy 26:1–9, the narrative of Psalm 104 breaks into three parts: the Patriarchs, the sojourn in Egypt, and the Exodus, all of them joined by the themes of God's fidelity to His covenant promises and His active providence in fulfilling them.

While the whole psalm deals with God's providence on behalf of all the people, the second section, dealing with the sojourn in Egypt, also includes what we may think of as "individual" providence. What the Bible portrays as God's care for the history of the whole people of Israel is shown also to be at work in the life and destiny of a single man. It is the awesome story of Joseph and God's care for him through many trials. Sold by his brothers into Egypt, falsely accused and unjustly imprisoned, forsaken for twenty years, the faith of Joseph was still able to say, at the end: "God sent me before you to preserve life. . . . God sent me before you. . . . But as for you, you meant evil against me, but God meant it for good" (Gen. 45:5, 7; 50:20). Joseph's faith in God's providence, even as he was proved by steel and fire, is preserved also in this psalm: "[God] sent a man before them, Joseph, sold into slavery. They humbled his feet with fetters; his soul was shackled in iron. Until his word came to pass, the word of the Lord seared through him."

PSALM 105 (106)

CONFESS TO THE LORD, FOR HE IS GOOD

৯৯

Whereas Psalm 104 uses historical narrative as an outline for the praise of God for His deeds of salvation, Psalm 105 (Hebrew 106) uses it as the structure of a sustained confession of sins and ongoing motive for repentance. The praise of God in this psalm, then, springs from the consideration of God's fidelity to His people notwithstanding their own infidelities to Him: "Praise the Lord, for He is gracious, for His mercy endures forever!"

The examples of the people's continued sin are drawn from the accounts of the Exodus and the Desert Wandering, a period of such egregious unfaithfulness that only a few of that entire generation were finally permitted to enter the Promised Land. The examples are detailed: the constant murmuring against the Lord both in Egypt and in the desert, the rebellion of Dathan and Abiron, the cult of the golden calf, the succumbing to temptation from the Moabites and other moral compromises with the surrounding nations, child-sacrifice to Moloch, and so forth. In all of these things God nonetheless proved His patience and fidelity to the people of His covenant: "Who will tell the mighty deeds of the Lord, or make all His praises heard?"

This poetic narrative, which summarizes much of the Books of Exodus and Numbers, deals with the period of the Desert Wandering as a source of negative moral example: "Don't let this happen to you." Such is the approach to that period through much of biblical literature, from Deuteronomy 33 to 1 Corinthians 10.

The value of this perspective is that it tends to discourage a false confidence that may otherwise deceive the believer. Never has there been missing from the experience of faith the sort of temptation that says: "Relax! God has saved you. You are home free. Once saved, always saved. Don't worry about a thing. Above all, no effort."

This temptation was recognized by certain discerning men in the Bible itself. Thus, the Prophet Jeremiah saw it working insidiously in the hearts and minds of his contemporaries near the end of the seventh century BC. They reasoned among themselves that God, because of His undying promise to David, would never permit the city of Jerusalem, to say nothing of His temple, to fall to their enemies. After all, had not the Lord, speaking through Isaiah a century earlier, promised King Hezekiah that such a thing was unthinkable? And had not the Lord, at that time, destroyed the Assyrian army as it besieged the Holy City? Even so, reasoned Jeremiah's fellow citizens, there was no call now to fear the armies of Babylon. Thus, fully confident of divine deliverance, they permitted themselves every manner of vice and moral failing. After all, once saved, always saved. Much of the message of Jeremiah was devoted to demolishing that line of thought.

The identical sort of temptation seems likewise to have afflicted the first readers of Hebrews, whose author also took the period of the Desert Wandering as exemplifying their moral dilemma. Repeatedly, then, he cautioned those early Christians of the genuine danger of stark apostasy facing those who placed an unwarranted, quasimagical confidence in their inevitable security. This entire book is devoted to warning believers that "it is a fearful thing to fall into the hands of the living God" (10:31).

The gravity of this temptation, of course, arises from its resting on a solid truth. God *is* faithful to His promises; He will never abandon those who place their confidence in Him. The danger here is not that of excessive trust in God's fidelity, but of not guarding sufficiently against man's infidelity. Just as the Galatians were warned against forsaking the Gospel of pure grace, they were also instructed that "God is not mocked; for whatever a man sows, that he will also reap" (Galatians 6:7).

Even the believers at Philippi, though manifesting no discernible disposition to false confidence, were admonished to work out their salvation with fear and trembling (Phil. 2:12).

And even as the Ephesians were reminded of being sealed and rendered secure "with the Holy Spirit of promise, who is the guarantee of our inheritance" (Eph. 1:13, 14), they were earnestly exhorted not to "grieve the Holy Spirit of God, by whom you were sealed" (4:30).

The history of Israel in the desert of old, a sustained account of such grieving, is the theme of Psalm 105.

PSALM 106 (107)

Psalm 106 (Hebrew 107) describes a series of adversities suffered by God's servants, along with His continued intervention to deliver them from all such troubles. It is an historical meditation for attaining contemplative wisdom; its final line asks, "Who is wise and will guard these things, and will understand the mercies of the Lord?"

Among the distresses of God's servants, as our psalm narrates them, we may identify two sections, one near the beginning and one close to the end, as dealing with the sufferings associated with the wandering of the people in the desert.

Between these two sections are three others that describe a situation of imprisonment or bondage, a sickness, and a storm at sea. All of these depictions are colorful and detailed. Two refrains bind all the parts together: "Then they cried to the Lord in their tribulation, and He delivered them from their every distress," and "Let them confess the Lord for His mercies, and His wonders to the sons of men." These various afflictions may be understood literally or by way of metaphor, or as combinations of these.

Thus, for instance, when two sections of our psalm speak of suffering in a waterless, trackless wasteland, this may be understood as referring to the return from the Babylonian Exile as well as to the earlier wandering of the Exodus generation. It may also include any experience of being lost and trying to find one's way back home. Thus, it may describe the journey of a reckless son lost in a distant country and already given up for dead (Luke 15:13, 24). This son, in turn, may be Jacob exiled in Harran, where the drought consumed him by day, and the frost by night, and sleep departed from his eyes (cf. Gen. 31:40). And it may likewise be any one or all of us, exiled from the Garden and wandering away from the face of God. This part of the psalm, then, is a parable of ourselves "without Christ, being aliens from the commonwealth of Israel and strangers from the covenants of promise, having no hope and without God in the world" (Eph. 2:12).

Similarly, the psalm's next part, dealing with bondage or imprisonment, may refer to Joseph sold into slavery, fettered in a foreign land and presumed already to have perished (Gen. 37). Or it may be descriptive of Micaiah (1 Kin. 22:26, 27), or Jeremiah (chapters 37—39), or John the Baptist (Matt. 11; 14), or the Apostle Paul (Acts 23—26). And it may refer to our spiritual captivity, of which Jesus said that He came to set the oppressed at liberty (Luke 4:18).

Then there is the section of the psalm describing conditions of sickness, which is potentially manifold in its applications. This could be a prayer during the deathly illness of King Hezekiah, for instance, or the affliction of the paralytics of Capernaum (Mark 2) and Bethesda (John 5), or the woman with chronic bleeding (Mark 5), or the lame man at the gate called Beautiful (Acts 3). To Jesus, after all, they brought "all sick people who were afflicted with various diseases and torments, and those who were demon-possessed, epileptics, and paralytics; and He healed them" (Matt. 4:24). And the Lord's healing especially concerns the forgiveness of sins (cf. Mark 2:5; John 5:14). This part of the psalm, then, is also a metaphor of our own various illnesses.

Likewise, when our psalm speaks of enduring a storm at sea, it may refer to the storm suffered by the shipmates of Jonah, or St. Paul, or the disciples on the Lake of Gennesaret, while Jesus yet slept in the stern of the boat. The fierce storm of this story may also indicate all of us as "children, tossed to fro and carried about with every wind of doctrine, by the trickery of men, in the cunning craftiness of deceitful plotting" (Eph. 4:14). Many and diverse are this world's storms and hurricanes.

Our psalm is addressed to "those redeemed by the Lord" (*hoi lelytromenoi hypo Kyriou*). Its historical meditation, that is to say, is directed to those who stand already "within" that history, the beneficiaries of its blessing. This is the Church, made up of "those whom He redeemed out of the hand of the enemy and assembled out of the lands."

Our psalm summons such as us to meditate on what the Lord has done in our midst and on our behalf, "that we might know the things that have been freely given to us by God" (1 Cor. 2:12). Psalm 106 is a call to that profound effort of thought and praise.

PSALM 107 (108)

MY HEART IS PREPARED, O GOD

Psalm 107 (Hebrew 108) is composed of two parts, both of which we have already met in two other psalms. Thus, the first half of Psalm 107 is also found in Psalm 56, and its second half is found in Psalm 59. The references to the dawn and awakening make Psalm 107 most suitable for morning prayer.

The line of this psalm most often heard is "Be exalted, O God, above the heavens, and may Your glory be over all the earth." Nor is it surprising that this line is repeated several times on the feast of the Lord's Ascension into heaven.

Moreover, no matter what the feast or season, this same line of Psalm 107 is prayed in every celebration of the Divine Liturgy. As the priest nine times censes the Blessed Sacrament remaining in the chalice after the congregation has received Holy Communion, prior to its removal to the table of preparation, he thrice proclaims: "Be exalted, O God, above the heavens, and may Your glory be over all the earth." The priest then says, "Blessed is our God," and turning around he blesses the congregation with the Holy Communion, singing out "always, now and ever, and unto ages of ages." To which the people answer "Amen" and continue singing with joy, "Let our mouths be filled with Your praise, O Lord, that we may sing of Your glory; for You have permitted us to partake of the holy, divine, immortal, and life-creating Mysteries. Establish us in Your holiness, that all the day long we may meditate upon Your righteousness. Alleluia, alleluia, alleluia." Such is the Church's solemn response to this line of Psalm 107.

In view of the explicit application of our psalm in this formal eucharistic setting, it does not seem unreasonable to understand this verse and this setting as a key to interpreting the psalm as a whole. This is a prayer appropriately filling our mouths as we leave the Lord's house, going forth to His service in the world: "I shall confess You, O Lord, among the peoples, and I will sing to You among the nations. . . . That Your loved ones may be delivered, save with Your right hand, and hearken to me. . . . And will not You, O God, go forth with our host? O, give us help from our affliction, for vain is deliverance by man."

Holy Communion is our strength for combat in the cause of sanctification. Our mouths, which we pray God to fill with His praise, are yet moist with the Blood of redemption. "Establish us in Your holiness," we pray, for through the Holy Communion we become "partakers of His holiness" (Heb. 12:10), that very "holiness, without which no one will see the Lord" (12:14). Therefore, the priest closes the post-Communion litany by chanting, "for You are our sanctification."

But this holiness, freely conferred in the Sacred Mysteries, must be further *established* in the governance of our lives, for it will be tried in combat throughout the rest of the day. Thus, that same litany prays "that this whole day may be perfect, holy, peaceful, and sinless," and the priest, in the collect that follows it, beseeches God, "Make straight our path; establish us all in Your fear. Guard our life, make firm our steps."

This is a *holy* warfare, for it is fought by a holy people: "In God shall we do valiantly, and He will bring our oppressors to naught." Through us, made holy with His sanctification, will the Lord throughout the day arise and divide Shechem, and measure out the valley of Succoth, taking possession of Gilead and Ephraim, Manasseh and Moab. By reason of our sanctification in the Holy Eucharist is the rest of the world, through our lives, to be sanctified. Especially are we to conquer the reputedly impregnable fortress of Edom, those very gates of Hades that the Lord says will not be able to withstand the onslaught of the Church's faith in Him (cf. Matt. 16:18).

So we pray, "Let our mouths be filled with Your praise, . . . that all the day long we may meditate upon Your righteousness." This is the daily praise of which our psalm says: "My heart is prepared, O God, my heart is prepared; I shall praise and sing in my glory." It is with this *prepared* heart, rendered pure and fit for God's praise by the assiduous effort of inner struggle, that we will meditate all the day long on His righteousness, for higher than the heavens is His mercy, and His truth above the clouds. He goes forth with us against our foes.

PSALM 108 (109)

BE NOT SILENT TO MY PRAISE, O GOD

Some modern folk evidently find Psalm 108 (Hebrew 109) difficult to pray. For instance, in the schema of the Psalter found in the prayer book currently used by the Episcopalians, the entire central section of this psalm, roughly half of it, is listed as optional.

Episcopalians, however, may not be the only ones troubled by the difficulty of praying this psalm. The sentiments contained in it, after all, seem so violent and vengeful, so greatly at odds with the sorts of feelings that one would prefer to have during prayer. For example: "When he is judged, let him be found guilty, and let his prayer become sin. . . . Let the iniquity of his fathers be remembered before the Lord, and let not the sin of his mother be blotted out." This is rough stuff, and what Christian can pray such things?

The real problem, nonetheless, is not with the psalm, but with ourselves. We modern Christians are far too disposed to establish our personal sentiments, our own spontaneous feelings, as the standard for our prayer. Thus, if the words of a particular prayer (in this case, a psalm inspired by the Holy Spirit) express emotions and responses with which we do not "feel" comfortable, we tend to think that we are being insincere in praying it. Contemporary Christians have made a virtual fetish of spontaneity in worship, and sincerity nowadays is measured by pulse rhythm. One would think that our Lord had said: "I have come that you may have sincere and heartfelt emotions, and have them more abundantly."

It is a big mistake to adopt this attitude, for it places even the authority of God's inspired Word under the tribunal of our subjective sentiments. Is it not obvious that to set up our own feelings as the measure of our worship is utterly arrogant? The proper standard for the worship of God is already established in His unfailing Word, and no one will pray as he should unless he submits his prayer entirely to the authority of that Word. Otherwise there is a real danger that our worship will express only the unredeemed sentiments of unrepentant hearts.

If we are going to pray as Christians, it is essential that we submit ourselves unreservedly to the authority of the Holy Spirit who speaks in the inspired words of the psalms. In the present case, this will likely mean ignoring our feelings on the matter and going on to understand exactly what this psalm does, in fact, say.

One of the things that our Lord did during the forty days between His Resurrection and Ascension was to explain to the nascent Church the correct interpretation of the Old Testament (cf. Luke 24:25–27, 32), including the psalms (vv. 44, 45). Moreover, it is recorded that the true meaning of our present psalm, Psalm 108, was one of the subjects that explicitly preoccupied the Apostles during those ten days that they spent in prayer in the upper room awaiting the coming of the Holy Spirit. Indeed, in our limited record of those ten days, this psalm is one of two passages of Holy Scripture actually quoted on their lips.

Recall that the sole task appointed to the Church during that brief period of preparation was the choice of a successor to Judas Iscariot (Acts 1:15–26), and Simon Peter, as he summoned his fellow Apostles to that task, announced that they were, in fact, fulfilling a prophecy contained in Psalm 108. He quoted our present psalm with reference to the fallen Judas: "For it is written in the Book of Psalms: 'Let his dwelling place be desolate, / And let no one live in it'; and, 'Let another take his office'" (v. 20).

In the calamitous career of Judas Iscariot, then, we have the interpretive key and context to this very disturbing Psalm 108. It is a sustained reference to that most unfortunate man of whom Truth Himself said: "It would have been good for that man if he had never been born" (Mark 14:21).

It is no wonder that this psalm is unsettling, for it is concerned with the danger of damnation. During the several minutes that it takes to pray through this psalm, we are brought face to face with the real possibility of eternal loss and reminded that "it is a fearful thing to fall into the hands of the living God" (Heb. 10:31). No one enjoys being warned that the apostasy of Judas could be chosen by any one of us. Yet, the story pointedly appears in all four Gospels. Over and over, eight times, the New Testament stresses that the betrayer arose from among the chosen, "one of the Twelve." Such too is the distressing, but very necessary, sane, and sobering thought raised in this important psalm.

PSALM 109 (110)

THE LORD SAID TO MY LORD

I have always been fond of the traditional Western practice of praying Psalm 109 (Hebrew 110) as the first psalm of Vespers on Sundays. It may be only a matter of comforting custom, early memories, and deep sentiment on my part, but for me the proper way for Christians to begin Sunday evening is by lighting some candles and then chanting, in the solemn seventh tone, "The Lord said to my Lord, 'Sit at My right hand . . .'"

In all of the Psalter, is there a line more precious and beloved than this? No other line of the Book of Psalms enjoys, in the New Testament, a prominence equal to these opening words of Psalm 109. In the traditions reflected in the Synoptic Gospels, for example, Christians remembered that Jesus had quoted this verse in controversy with some of His rabbinical opponents (cf. Matt. 22:44; Mark 12:36; Luke 20:42) and that the context for His citation was the decisive and great kerygmatic question of the Lord's identity: "What do you think about the Christ? Whose Son is He?" (Matt. 22:42). In these few words of the Psalter, "The Lord said to my Lord," Christians learned that Jesus is not only David's descendant but also his preexisting Lord. He is the Son, not only of David, but of God.

Having mysteriously addressed the identity of Christ, this same line of our psalm goes on to speak of His triumph and enthronement, with the solemn proclamation: "Sit at My right hand." These majestic words were quoted in the first sermon of the Christian Church, that of Pentecost morning at the third hour (cf. Acts 2:34), and became the foundation of some of the most important Christological and soteriological statements of the New Testament (cf. Mark 16:19; Rom. 8:34; Eph. 1:20; Col. 3:1; Heb. 1:3; 8:1; 10:12; 12:2.).

In this one line of the psalm, then, we profess, in summary form, those profound doctrines at the foundation of our whole relationship to God—the eternal identity of Jesus Christ, His triumph over sin and death, and His glorification at God's right hand: "God . . . has in these last days spoken to us by His Son, . . . who . . , when He had by Himself purged our sins, sat down at the right hand of the Majesty on high" (Heb. 1:1–3).

Our psalm immediately goes on to speak of those who oppose the triumph of Christ: "'. . . till I make Your enemies Your footstool.' The Lord shall send the rod of Your strength out of Zion. Rule in the midst of Your enemies." Once again, in the writings of the New Testament these few words were quoted to lay the basis for the Christian interpretation of history and eschatology (cf. Acts 2:35f, 36 1 Cor. 15:25; Eph. 1:22; Heb. 10:12, 13; and perhaps 1 Pet. 3:22).

The reference to "Zion" evokes remembrance of the history of that ancient city, also known as Salem and Jerusalem, and the figure of her earliest recorded king, Melchizedek. He was not only the king of Jerusalem but also her "priest of God Most High" (Gen. 14:18), and it is with reference to that mysterious priesthood of Melchizedek that Psalm 109 speaks of the priesthood of Jesus: "The Lord has sworn and will not relent, 'You are a priest forever according to the order of Melchizedek.'"

No other commentary on these words surpasses their theologically rich elaboration in Hebrews 7, which sees the priesthood of Melchizedek as a type or foreshadowing of the eternal priesthood of Jesus, speaking of our Lord's glorification above the heavens, at God's right hand, our permanent intercessor at the Throne, the one Mediator between God and man: "For this Melchizedek, king of Salem, priest of the Most High God, . . . first being translated 'king of righteousness,' and then also king of Salem, meaning 'king of peace,' without father, without mother, without genealogy, having neither beginning of days nor end of life, but made like the Son of God, remains a priest continually. . . . And it is yet far more evident if, in the likeness of Melchizedek, there arises another priest who has come . . . according to the power of an endless life. For He testifies: 'You are a priest forever / According to the order of Melchizedek.' . . . But He, because He continues forever, has an unchangeable priesthood. Therefore He is also able to save to the uttermost those who come to God through Him, since He always lives to make intercession for them. For such a High Priest was fitting for us, who is holy, harmless, undefiled, separate from sinners, and has become higher than the heavens" (vv. 1–3, 15–17, 24–26).

PSALM 110 (111)

I WILL CONFESS YOU, O LORD, WITH ALL MY HEART

At Rome during the earliest centuries it was the custom of the Christians at Sunday Vespers to sing "Alleluia" in response to each verse of the "Alleluia Psalms" (110 to 117) as these were chanted by a deacon or cantor. When did they start doing this?

For all we know, this Roman usage could very well go back all the way to Saints Peter and Paul. Indeed, it would not be surprising, for our earliest information on the subject comes from about AD 210; that is to say, only a century and a half after these same apostles evangelized and organized the church at Rome. Writing at that time, St. Hippolytus, a local priest, included this practice as part of the primitive customs handed down in that city. In short, the praying of the "Alleluia Psalms" at Sunday Vespers was already regarded, at the very beginning of the third century, as ancient, venerable, and even apostolic.

In the sixth century the Rule of St. Benedict, which often depends on earlier Roman usage, prescribed some of these same psalms, specifically Psalms 110 to 112, to be prayed at Sunday Vespers following Psalm 109. This old practice remained in force in all Western monasteries from the sixth century until Vatican II just a few years ago.

Thus, the first of these psalms, Psalm 110 (Hebrew 111), has long been associated in the West with Sunday evenings. For reasons easily perceived in various lines of the psalm, this is a time most appropriate. It is especially fitting, for example, that on Sunday evening we should sing out: "He has sent redemption unto His people; He has commanded His covenant forever. Holy and awesome is His name."

Why is this line especially fitting at that particular time? Well, Sunday evening is the quiet closing of a small weekly cycle commemorating the redemption that God "sent" unto His people in the death and Resurrection of Christ. That cycle began on Wednesday, when we observed a regular fast day to recall that dreadful Wednesday on which Judas sold the Lord for thirty pieces of silver. Then, on Thursday, Friday, and Saturday, we again bore in mind the events of the Lord's suffering, death, and burial. Just as every Sunday is Pascha, each Friday is Holy Friday, the day on which the Bridegroom is taken away, so on that day too we observed a fast (cf. Mark 2:20).

Finally, on Sunday morning we weekly celebrate, especially in Orthros and the Divine Liturgy, our Lord's Resurrection. On all these days, then, we observe a weekly round, as it were, of the redemption that God has sent unto His people, and we once more recall that redemptive "sending" on Sunday evening by praying this psalm.

Similarly, we who receive Holy Communion on Sunday morning will remember that event with gratitude during the evening's psalmody. Our psalm, in that line quoted above, speaks explicitly of the Lord's prescriptive institution of the Holy Eucharist: "He has commanded His covenant (*diatheke*) forever." The Lord gave this command when, speaking of the "new covenant (*diatheke*) in My blood," He told the Church: "Do this in remembrance of Me" (Luke 22:19, 20). This memorial of the new covenant is the Holy Eucharist which the Lord left us as both gift and precept.

Another verse of Psalm 110 also speaks of this gift and command: "The merciful and compassionate Lord made *memorial* of His wonders—He gave food to those who fear Him; He shall forever be mindful of His covenant (*diatheke*)." This is the covenant food of His Body and Blood as the perpetual memorial of the wonders of His saving work on our behalf and for our benefit. Truly, "He has sent redemption unto His people." Psalm 110 closes Sunday evening, then, by once again bringing to remembrance the redemptive wonders wrought in our midst.

Ultimately, of course, this liturgical "remembrance" is God's more than ours. While it is true that we call to mind "all those things that have come to pass for us," the memorial of the covenant is infinitely more than the human effort of recollection. Indeed, our own remembrance would count for nothing except for God's. As our psalm says, "*He* shall forever be mindful of His covenant." This same Lord, who looks at the rainbow and thereby remembers His eternal covenant with Noah (Gen. 9:13–16), looks likewise upon His people as they fulfill His eucharistic mandate in the sacrament of Christ's Body and Blood. God looks, and God "remembers."

PSALM 111 (112)

Psalm 111 (Hebrew 112) may be regarded as a companion psalm of the one immediately before it. In structure, the two are identical acrostics, each composed of twenty-two half-lines that begin with the twenty-two letters of the Hebrew alphabet in succession.

More than merely juxtaposed and similarly constructed, however, these two psalms are also joined by a common theme—wisdom, and especially wisdom's relationship to obedience and the fear of the Lord. Thus, Psalm 110 closed with its famous statement about how the path to wisdom commences: "The fear of the Lord is the beginning of wisdom, and all who practice it have a good understanding." Psalm 111 immediately takes up the challenge, as it were, of this proclamation. "Blessed is the man that fears the Lord," it says, "he will greatly delight in His commandments."

Biblical "fear of the Lord," which is the beginning of biblical wisdom, is not a psychological state marked by terror or timidity. Perhaps the correct idea is better conveyed by the word "reverence." Still, the fear of the Lord is far more than the cultivated sentiment of reverence. It is, rather, a resolved dedication of oneself to the accomplishing of God's will through the industry of obedience. As the psalm says, it is something to be *practiced*. The wisdom promised in Holy Scripture is derived from reverent obedience to God. Since this is a motif found here in two consecutive psalms, it merits a more elaborate explanation.

Much of contemporary religion is based on the dichotomy between *Law* and *Gospel*, which are usually contrasted to the advantage of the latter. Law, according to this popular distinction, has to do with fear and the performance of duty and is regularly thought of as an inferior, even servile, state. Gospel, on the other hand, is commonly conceived in terms of God's free gift, conferred without respect to human merit or work, and having as a chief effect man's deliverance from the burden of Law.

Now, though the foregoing distinction between Law and Gospel is not without foundation in Holy Scripture and is, indeed, useful to clarify many important aspects of theology, it hardly provides an adequate paradigm for the whole of Christian thought and experience. With respect to the "fear of the Lord," for example, which is a motif common to these two psalms, that distinction between Law and Gospel proves to be quite inadequate. It is not hard to see why. If the fear of the Lord means reverent obedience to His will, the paradigm Law-or-Gospel will almost certainly put this obedience in the former category, Law. Thus, obedience would be something associated with duty, perhaps even servile duty. What, after all, could obedience have to do with *Gospel*?

Unfortunately, this line of thought is rather common. For instance, one may read modern commentaries on the Sermon on the Mount, premised solely on that foregoing dichotomy between Law and Gospel, that treat even the prescriptions of our blessed Lord Himself as simply points of *Law*, promulgated for the purpose of teaching frail and failing man his need for a Gospel of grace that will deliver him from such Law. That is to say, Jesus gave us these commandments on the Mount precisely that we might fail to obey them! Now this is a preposterous interpretation. If Jesus' Sermon on the Mount can find no place under the heading of *Gospel*, one is at a loss to say what can.

But the Gospel itself includes a call to a life of obedience (cf. Rom. 6:16; 15:18; 1 Pet. 1:2). In fact, the very act of faith, which is man's correct response to the Gospel, involves a certain kind of obedience. It is called the *hypakoe pisteos*— "obedience of faith" (Rom. 1:5; 16:26; cf. Acts 6:7). Obedience to God's will, moreover, is the living out of our faith.

And it is this reverent obedience, called the fear of the Lord, that leads to wisdom. Such is the burden of both these psalms.

The deeper message of these psalms, however, is Christological before it is moral, for our righteousness is ever a sharing in the righteousness of Christ. That is to say, the wise man, who fears the Lord and greatly delights in His commandments, is, in the first place, Jesus the Savior. He it is, described here as generous and just and unshaken, as leaving a seed powerful on the earth, as being had in eternal remembrance.

PSALM 112 (113)
PRAISE THE LORD, YOU SERVANTS
☙

It is not often the case, perhaps, that a single psalm serves to summarize an entire book of the Bible, but Psalm 112 (Hebrew 113) does seem to be one such. Virtually every line of this psalm resonates with ideas from the Gospel of St. Luke. Indeed, Psalm 112 may be read as a prayerful compendium of that Gospel. Conversely, Luke's Gospel itself may be used to illustrate the psalm.

The imagery of Psalm 112 is structured on the polarity of "high and low." "The Lord is exalted over all the nations," it says, "above the heavens is His glory." And, it asks, "Who is like the Lord our God, who dwells on high?" Yet, of this same high Lord it is also said that "He watches over what is humble, in heaven and on earth. He lifts up the beggar from the earth, and the needy He raises from the dunghill, in order to sit him down with princes, with the princes of His people."

Such a motif is introduced early in Luke—specifically in the *Magnificat*, where our Lady proclaims that God "has regarded the lowly state of His maidservant. . . . He has put down the mighty from their thrones, / And exalted the lowly" (Luke 1:48, 52). This theme is then developed on numerous pages of Luke. For instance, his clearest example of God's lifting up a needy man from a dunghill and putting a mighty one down from his throne, is doubtless the parable of Lazarus and the rich man (16:19–31).

Likewise, if we seek an illustration of God's raising a beggar from the earth in order to sit him down with princes, we will find none better than the Lukan parable of the young, runaway son graciously restored to his father's house after living in great poverty (15:11–32). And as the poor Lazarus on his dunghill is contrasted with the rich man in his palace, so the younger brother is contrasted with the older, self-righteous brother. Similarly, the humble publican in the temple, who goes down to his house justified, is contrasted with the haughty Pharisee, who spends his prayer time feeling good about himself (18:9–14).

Moreover, Luke preserves this theme in his version of the Beatitudes. Unlike their straightforward presentation in Matthew 5, Luke's version places each "blessed" in opposition to a corresponding "woe," further illustrating the same contrast. As the Virgin Mary had proclaimed that God "filled the hungry with good things, / And the rich He has sent away empty" (1:53), so Luke's Beatitudes announce both "Blessed are you who hunger now" and "Woe to you who are full" (6:21, 25).

And just as there is a "Blessed are you poor," so is there a "woe to you who are rich" (6:20, 24). Luke illustrates this "woe" by the parable of the rich man's barns (12:13–21) and this beatitude by his emphasis on the preaching of the Gospel to the poor (4:18; 7:22). Luke's examples of such humble folk, exalted by the Gospel, include the likes of the shepherds of Bethlehem (2:8–18), Simeon and Anna (2:25–38), the newly bereaved widow of Nain (7:11–15), the sinful but repentant woman (7:36–50), the Samaritan leper (17:11–19), Zacchaeus of Jericho (19:1–10), the penurious widow in the temple (21:1–4), Joanna and various other women disciples (8:1–3; 23:27–31; 23:55—24:10), the thief on the cross (23:39–43), and the two disciples on the road to Emmaus (24:13–35). To the lowly such as these our psalm says: "O children, praise the Lord! Praise the name of the Lord. Blessed be the name of the Lord, from henceforth and forevermore. From the rising of the sun to its setting, may the name of the Lord be praised."

Speaking of those humble whom God exalts, Psalm 112 ends with the related image of the barren woman to whom the Lord unexpectedly grants the blessing of offspring: "The barren woman He settles in a home, as the joyful mother of children." This final image in our psalm, exemplified in such biblical women as Sarah, Rebecca, Rachel, and Hannah, is the very one with which Luke commences. As a kind of foretaste of all the blessings narrated in his Gospel, Luke begins with the story of the barren Elizabeth, who miraculously becomes the mother of John the Baptist. This wonder of the Lord, in turn, prepares for the still greater miracle of the Virgin Mary's own conception of God's Son. Thus, Elizabeth and then Mary initiate and model Luke's sustained theme of the raising of the lowly.

PSALM 113A (114)

WHEN ISRAEL WENT FORTH FROM EGYPT

For purposes of our thinking about it here, let us call the first part of Psalm 113 "Psalm 113a" and treat it as a separate psalm. (In the Hebrew Psalter, it is Psalm 114.) Even though it appears in our canonical Greek Psalter as part of a longer psalm, a close inspection of its eight lines shows that it was not originally such, and, as I propose to demonstrate, it makes a great deal better sense if we read these lines as an integral composition on their own.

We may read it thus: "When Israel went forth from Egypt, the house of Jacob from a barbarous people, Judah was made His sanctuary, and Israel His domain. The sea beheld and fled, and Jordan turned back at the sight. The mountains skipped like rams, and the little hills like lambs. Why, O sea, did you flee, and why, O Jordan, turned you back? Why this skipping like rams, you mountains, and why, little hills, like lambs? From the face of the Lord was the earth disturbed, from the face of the God of Jacob, who turned the stone to flooding pools, and the flint into fountains of water."

From the perspective of style, this psalm is a perfect illustration of Hebraic parallelism, a feature found in so much of the Bible's poetry and the aphorisms of its wisdom literature. The references to Egypt/barbarous people, mountains/hills, stone/flint, rams/lambs, sanctuary/domain, are synonymous parallels, in that they are roughly repetitious. They serve the function of slowing down our prayer, making us take a calmer, more contemplative pace.

Others of the parallelisms here, Red Sea/Jordan and Judah/Israel, are merismatic, the merismus being a device of dividing a whole into representative components and addressing them separately. This serves the function of making our prayer more discursive and analytical. Our psalm combines both techniques very effectively.

In all such cases, the intent of the literary construction is to slow down our reading of the poem, making us go over everything twice, forcing the mind to a second and more serious look at the line, prolonging our prayer, obliging us not to go rushing off somewhere. Such poetry is deeply meditative, and the reader who resists its impulse will find himself with acid indigestion of the mind, serious "heartburn" in a most radical and theological sense.

There are two events described in this psalm, the turning back of the Red Sea at the Exodus, and the identical phenomenon of the Jordan River at Israel's entrance into Canaan. These two occasions, which are also juxtaposed in Joshua

4:23, form the psalm's twin poles, Israel's departure from Egypt and her entrance into the Promised Land. Between these two events lie the giving of the Law and the forty years' wandering of God's people in the wilderness. Whereas the two poles of that crucial period, the Red Sea and the Jordan, are marked by God's removal of the waters from their native settings, the time in between them is marked by God's miraculously given water for His people wandering through the dry sands of the desert.

God, in short, reverses the expected course of things. He makes wet places dry, and the dry places wet. As for mountains and hills, what could be better symbols of stability, standards of the normal and expected? Mountains and hills, it would seem, are not easily moved. Nonetheless, God moves them, as was demonstrated in the earthquake shaking Mount Sinai when the Law was given. Because of the face of the Lord, that face that Moses prayed to behold on Sinai, the mountains and the hills jumped around like sheep, as it were, the normal and expected state of things becoming unstrung before the awesome face of God. Hills go skipping about!

Everything is set on its head. It is this complete dominion of the Lord that is manifested in His great acts of redemption: the Exodus, the giving of the Law, the desert wandering, Israel's crossing the Jordan's rocky bed into the land flowing with milk and honey.

There have been several occasions, in these ponderings on the psalms, to point out that Holy Scripture often identifies the Church in terms of Israel's experience in the Red Sea, at Sinai and in the desert, and in the crossing of the Jordan. The pattern is quite standard in the New Testament, and readers of the multiplication of the loaves, 1 Corinthians, and Hebrews will recognize this at once. Psalm 113a, then, is very much a psalm about ourselves and our life in Christ.

PSALM 113B (115)

Psalm 113b, the second and longer part of Psalm 113 in the Orthodox Psalter (Septuagint and Vulgate), is Psalm 115 in the inherited rabbinical text. It begins with the verse, "Not unto us, O Lord, not unto us, but to Your name give glory."

One way of approaching this psalm is through the consideration of space. It speaks of heaven, earth, and the nether world, and all of these references are related to the question, posed in an early verse, about where God is to be located: "So where is their God?"

This question, posed by the unbelievers as a mockery ("Why should the Gentiles say"), is answered by the psalmist: "But our God is in heaven." The affirmation here is not merely spatial, so to speak, for he goes on immediately to draw an inference that becomes a theme of the psalm: God "*does* whatever He pleases." The verb, to "do" or "make" (*'asah* in Hebrew) appears now for the first time and may be seen as a key to the psalm's meaning. This psalm is about a God who *does* things.

Nothing more is said about space until a dozen verses later, when the psalmist speaks of "the Lord, who *made* heaven and earth." The word "made" here is *'oseh*, the active participle of the same verb as before; it could be translated even as a substantive—God is a *doer*. The Lord *does* things.

Here, then, is heaven once more, not simply a spatial reference but a symbol of God's omnipotence. Just as, earlier, "heaven" had to do with God's activity ("He does whatever He pleases"), so now the reference to God's activity leads back immediately to the thought of heaven: "The heaven, even the heavens, are the Lord's."

In contrast to heaven there is the earth: "But the earth He has given to the children of men." God is in heaven; He is omnipotent. Men dwell on earth; they are not omnipotent. Indeed, they will die and "go down into silence," and this brings us to the psalm's final reference to space—the nether world, where the "dead do not praise the Lord." The "sons of men" are, in themselves, but creatures of a day. They are unlike God, for there are very strict limits to what they can do. And that was exactly the note on which our psalm began: "Not unto us, O Lord, not unto us, but to Your name give glory."

In contrast to God, what can men, on their own, *do*? They can make idols. In fact, left to themselves, making idols is exactly what they will do.

These idols he calls "the work of men's hands," the noun "work" translating here *ma'aseh*, a Hebrew passive participle of the same verb we have been examining all along. That is to say, idolatry is the only thing that the children of men, left to their own devices, can *do*. Once again, then, we continue the theme of man's utter weakness contrasted with God's omnipotent activity: "Not unto us, but to Your name give glory."

The psalmist seems to enjoy meditating on the futility of these idols, "the work of men's hands," for he spends considerable effort in describing their impotence. Using the mystical number seven, a standard biblical symbol of perfection, he goes on to tell what these idols cannot *do*: (1) "They have mouths, but they *do not* speak;" (2) "Eyes they have, but they *do not* see;" (3) "They have ears, but they *do not* hear;" (4) "Noses they have, but they *do not* smell;" (5) "They have hands, but they *do not* handle;" (6) "Feet they have, but they *do not* walk;" and (7) "*Nor do* they mutter through their throat." There you have it. These idols, "the work of men's hands," are perfectly imperfect. They are infinitely nothing; there is simply no limit to their imperfection and nothingness.

And what becomes of the men who devote their lives to the making of these idols? They too become nothing: "Those who make them are like them; so is everyone who trusts in them." The makers of idols (which includes any one of us who insists on going his own way) will, in the end, have nothing to show for their efforts and their lives: "The dead do not praise the Lord, nor any who go down into silence." The silence of the idols becomes the unending silence of eternal loss. Those who make them become like them.

The children of men, therefore, must not put their trust in the works of their own hands, which are destined to perish with them. Where, then, put our trust? "O Israel, trust in the Lord . . . O house of Aaron, trust in the Lord . . You who fear the Lord, trust in the Lord; He is their help and their shield."

PSALM 114 (116A)

I HAVE LOVED

What is given in the traditional Hebrew Psalter as Psalm 116 is listed as two discrete compositions in our canonical Greek version, where they appear as Psalms 114 and 115. In these ponderings they will be treated as two distinct psalms, following (as usual) the Greek text and numbering.

It is instructive to compare the symmetric openings of these psalms, for each begins with a simple verb in the aorist tense, active voice, first person singular. Thus, Psalm 114 commences: "I have loved" (*egapesa*), and Psalm 115 begins "I have believed" (*epistevsa*). We should also observe that the verb in each case is without a direct object. This lack of direct objects, following what are normally transitive verbs, gives them here what we may call a more general tone. Not specified by particular objects, the "loving and believing" spoken of in these psalms point rather to an abiding intention of soul.

The voice in both these psalms is that of Christ our Lord; it is He who says, "I have loved" and "I have believed." Loving and believing, that is, are not simply religious requirements laid on the Christian conscience; they are, first of all, characteristics modeled in Christ the Lord. All love and all belief begin in Jesus. Any loving and any believing that we others may accomplish is an inner participation in His loving and His believing, for His loving and His believing form the font of our salvation.

When, in Psalm 114 (Hebrew 116a), Jesus says, "I have loved," the rest of the psalm shows that its special setting is the mystery of His suffering and death endured for the sake of our salvation in loving obedience. Firstly, Jesus did all these things because of His love for the Father: "But that the world may know that I love the Father, and as the Father gave Me commandment, so I do" (John 14:31).

Secondly, Jesus did all of these things because He loved us. Thus, St. Paul refers to our Lord simply as "Him who loved us" (Rom. 8:37). And because He loved us, Jesus gave Himself up to death on the Cross: "The life which I now live in the flesh," wrote St. Paul, "I live by faith in the Son of God, who loved me and gave Himself for me" (Gal. 2:20). This self-offering of Jesus was the supreme proof of His love for us: "And walk in love, as Christ also has loved us and given Himself for us" (Eph. 5:2). So, in this psalm, which is especially concerned with the mystery of His sufferings, Jesus our Lord begins His prayer: "I have loved."

The Savior goes on to speak of the supplication that He offered in the context of His sufferings, beseeching God that, if possible, the cup might be taken away: "The sorrows of death encompassed me; the hazards of Hades found me out. Affliction have I found and sorrow, and I called on the name of the Lord: 'O Lord, deliver my soul.'"

Then, abruptly and dramatically, the tone of the prayer changes to a hope nearly realized, as though His suffering's supplication had been answered already: "Merciful is the Lord, and righteous. And God has mercy on us; the Lord stands guard over infants. I was humbled, and He saved me. Return, my soul, to your rest, for the Lord has been good to you. For He delivered my soul from death, my eyes from tears, my feet from stumbling. Well-pleasing will I be in the sight of the Lord, in the land of the living."

This and so many other psalms testify that the Lord's Passion was a sustained act of worship. This interpretation of His death was perfectly obvious to the early Christians, who said of Christ that "He offered up Himself" (Heb. 7:27), and who spoke of "the offering of the body of Jesus Christ once for all" (10:10), and who described His self-oblation as "an offering and a sacrifice to God for a sweet-smelling aroma" (Eph. 5:2).

This is the language of the temple and of the sacrificial worship, and we are probably so accustomed to hearing it that we have lost all sense of how terribly strange and improbable it must have sounded when the Christians first began to speak this way of the unjust death inflicted on a just man. This event outsiders would have considered as, at best, a great tragedy, but for the Christian mind the death of Jesus was not a mere miscarriage of human justice; it was the supreme act of worship that endowed all mankind with God's justice. It was the single deed of such condign and consummate devotion as to render possible humanity's access to God for all time and into eternity.

PSALM 115 (116B)

I HAVE BELIEVED

The Gospels of Matthew (20:20–23) and Mark (10:35–40) record the occasion on which James and John, the two sons of Zebedee, approached the Lord requesting that they be given the seats at His right and left hands on the day of His enthronement. Their request is ironical in the extreme, for Jesus had just that minute foretold in vivid detail the suffering and death awaiting Him at Jerusalem (Matt. 20:17–19; Mark 10:32–34). Not a single word stands between His pronouncement and their request; preoccupied with their own selfish interests, the two brothers obviously had not been paying attention to the Lord's message of the Cross.

By way of response to their inappropriate request, Jesus then puts a further question to them: "Can you drink the cup of which I am to drink?" The cup to which He refers is, of course, the cup of His own suffering and death— the cup of which He later prays: "Remove this cup from Me." It is the very chalice of His coming Passion and death. This is the cup that the two brothers must be prepared to drink.

From another perspective it is also the cup of the Holy Communion, that cup of which Jesus says, "Take this, all of you, and drink of it, for this is the cup of My blood." This cup contains that very price poured forth for our salvation, because: "The cup of blessing which we bless, is it not the communion of the blood of Christ?" (1 Cor. 10:16). This is the cup that gives shape and contour to the lifegiving blood that paid for our redemption. The drinking of this cup of salvation is itself a proclamation of the mystery of the Cross, "for as often as you eat this bread and drink this cup, you proclaim the Lord's death till He comes" (11:26).

Thus, in the question that the Lord puts to the two sons of Zebedee— "Can you drink the cup of which I am to drink?"—He establishes the essential relationship between our reception of the Holy Communion and our dedication to follow Him along the way of the Cross. The question points at once to His gift and our duty, for the Eucharist means the two things inseparably. Like the mystery of the Cross itself, drinking the cup involves both God's grace and man's commitment.

Earlier Christian writers, when they came to comment on this theme in the Gospels of Mark and Matthew, rather often had recourse to Psalm 115 (Hebrew 116, second half): "What shall I render to the Lord for all His benefits to me? I will take up the cup of salvation and call upon the name of the Lord. I will fulfill my commitment to the Lord, now in the presence of His people. Precious in the sight of the Lord is the death of His saints."

This "cup of salvation," wrote Origen in the third century, is the cup of martyrdom, the Christian's supreme identification with the death of the Lord. This is the cup of which venerable Polycarp, the Bishop of Smyrna, had prayed from his pyre of martyrdom nearly a century earlier: "I bless Thee that Thou hast granted me this day and hour, that I might receive a portion amongst the number of martyrs in the cup of Thy Christ."

The identical interpretation of Psalm 115 is found all through patristic and medieval writers, East and West: Athanasius, Basil, Didymus the Blind, Theodoret of Cyr, John Chrysostom, Jerome, Augustine, Cassiodorus, Haymo of Halberstadt, Gerard of Cunard, Thomas of Chobham, and so forth, as well as several liturgical texts.

For the Tradition of the Church, "the cup of salvation" in Psalm 115 refers to the Holy Eucharist in its fullness, the wide dimensions of which include at once the grace of God ("all His benefits to me"), the cup of blessing ("and call upon the name of the Lord"), the baptismal vows ("I will fulfill my commitment to the Lord"), the gathering of the Church ("now in the presence of all His people . . . in the courts of the house of the Lord, in the midst of you, O Jerusalem"), the vocation to martyrdom ("Precious in the sight of the Lord is the death of His saints"). Psalm 115 is prayed from within the very heart of the Christian mystery.

According to Matthew 26:30, Jesus and the disciples sang hymns at the end of the Last Supper. Since this latter was a Passover Seder (Luke 22:15), we know that their singing involved the Hallel psalms, 112—117 (Hebrew 113—118), prescribed for that liturgical context, including of course the lines here under consideration.

Thus, in the very setting of the Institution of the Holy Eucharist, just before He went forth to the Garden of Gethsemane to accept the cup from the hand of His Father, Jesus stood with James, John, and the other disciples, singing: "What shall I render to the Lord for all His benefits to me? I will take up the cup of salvation and call upon the name of the Lord. I will fulfill my commitment to the Lord, now in the presence of His people. Precious in the sight of the Lord is the death of His saints."

PSALM 116 (117)

PRAISE THE LORD, ALL YOU NATIONS

❧

Psalm 116 (Hebrew 117) is the shortest of the psalms: "Praise the Lord, all you nations; extol Him, all you peoples. For His mercy is confirmed upon us, and the truth of the Lord abides forever."

In the terms of its address, the initial line of this psalm touches two poles of a tension, as it were. The first pole, that of universality, is indicated by the repetition of the word "all." No nation or people is to be excluded from the praise of God. "Go therefore," says our Lord, "and make disciples of *all* the nations" (Matt. 28:19). That is to say, the Church is to be absolutely universal with respect to her geographical extension; there is a radical sense in which she is to recognize no national borders.

The other pole of the address, indicated by the words "nations" and "peoples," is what we may think of as regional, perhaps even provincial. That is to say, within the universality of the Church, respect is accorded to the distinct and distinguishing forms of individual races and other ethnic groupings. These are called to the praise of God within the particularities of their own history and culture, especially through their inherited languages.

The word "nations" in this psalm does not mean the modern "countries" as political units. In the psalm's context, indeed, the term has no *political* meaning at all, even though ethnic divisions are very often embodied in political structures. Standing as a synonymous parallel to "peoples," the word "nations" in this psalm has a general reference to those various distinctions among human beings that are determined by geography, language, specific histories, and other cultural patterns. The sense is conveyed by Daniel's exhortation that "all peoples, nations, and languages should serve Him" (Dan. 7:14).

The history of evangelism is replete with examples of the ways in which particular peoples found their own cultural histories perfected by the proclamation of the Gospel. A number of the Greek Fathers, for instance, were well aware that the particular genius of their "ethnic" history prepared the way for the coming of the Gospel. Similarly, the Christian Latin apologists never tired of observing that the Gospel perfected the great classical norms of Roman culture. There are myriad similar examples of this persuasion throughout history.

In the psalm's context, this diversity of the nations and the peoples is not limited simply to an evangelistic program. It is particularly related, rather, to the praise of God, or worship; ethnic identity must receive a liturgical as well as an evangelistic form, for it is properly in worship that a people's culture is centered and sanctified. "Praise the Lord, all you nations" is a command weighted with immense significance for a people's poetic language, music, architecture, art, and other cultural expressions.

And why do the nations (*ethnoi*) and the peoples praise the Lord? "For His mercy (*eleos*) is confirmed upon us, and the truth of the Lord abides forever." When St. Paul quotes the first half of our psalm in Romans 15:11, it is in support of his large argument "that the Gentiles (*ethnoi*) might glorify God for His mercy (*eleos*)" (15:9).

God's mercy is here described as "confirmed (*ekrataiothe*) upon us." This means that mercy has taken a defined and permanent form. Mercy here is not a mere sentiment; it is something fixed within the structure of salvation.

And what, exactly, is this fixing and specifying of the mercy of God? It is the Incarnation of Christ, the hypostatic union of divinity and humanity in the one Person of Jesus Christ. For the Incarnation "abides forever." God and man were made one in a specific historical act, God's irrevocable adoption of our humanity when "the Word became flesh and dwelt among us" (John 1:14). "His mercy is confirmed upon us" in the "one Mediator between God and men, the Man Christ Jesus" (1 Tim. 2:5).

This permanent confirmation of God's mercy upon us means that Jesus "is the Mediator of the new covenant" (Heb. 9:15; 12:24), that "He is also Mediator of a better covenant, which was established on better promises" (8:6). Similarly, that "truth of the Lord," which is said here to abide forever, is not some general, abstract metaphysics; it is that personal truth who told us, on the very night that He established the new covenant, "I am . . . the truth" (John 14:6).

PSALM 117 (118)

Besides being the last psalm of the sixteenth Kathisma, Psalm 117 (Hebrew 118) has long been favored, in both the East and the West, as the major psalm for Sunday Matins. This is the psalm that speaks of "the day that the Lord has made," encouraging us to "rejoice and be glad in it," and Sunday is preeminently that day wherein we most fittingly sing: "God is the Lord, and He has given us His light." In the ancient liturgical Tradition of the Church, Psalm 117 is the psalm that sets the tone for Sunday morning worship.

Every Sunday morning is full of the great Pascha surprise: "Yes, and certain women of our company, who arrived at the tomb early, astonished us. When they did not find His body, they came saying that they had also seen a vision of angels who said He was alive" (Luke 24:22, 23). And our response to this message from the Myrrhbearing Women? "Oh, give thanks to the Lord, for He is good! For His mercy endures forever. Let Israel now say, 'His mercy endures forever.' Let the house of Aaron now say, 'His mercy endures forever.' Let those who fear the Lord now say, 'His mercy endures forever.'"

Sunday morning is the hour of victory, at which we of the Eastern Church normally read one of the Gospel accounts of the Resurrection. Such is the usual and proper context for this psalm. Still bearing in His flesh the wounds of the Passion, the risen Jesus comes to His Church in the vibrancy of His conquest over sin, Satan, and death: "I called on the Lord in distress; He answered me and set me in a broad place. . . . All nations surrounded me, but in the name of the Lord I will destroy them. They surrounded me, yes, they surrounded me, but in the name of the Lord I will destroy them. They surrounded me like bees; they were quenched like a fire of thorns; for in the name of the Lord I will destroy them. You pushed me violently that I might fall, but the Lord helped me. The Lord is my strength and song, and He has become my salvation."

Every Sunday morning is the Church's jubilant celebration of the Resurrection of Christ. Joining the Myrrhbearing Women who discovered His empty tomb, we raise our voices to greet the new dawn with shouts of exaltation: "The voice of rejoicing and salvation is in the tents of the righteous; the right hand of the Lord does valiantly. The right hand of the Lord is exalted; the right hand of the Lord does valiantly." The message of Sunday morning is that the forces of death have not prevailed: "I shall not die but live, and declare the works of the Lord. The Lord has chastened me severely, but He has not given me over to death."

We Christians have every right to find in Psalm 117 the expression of our paschal joy. Even the children of Israel had recourse to a line of this psalm to greet the Lord on His triumphal entry into Jerusalem: "Blessed is he who comes in the name of the Lord." This line of our psalm, moreover, we sing at a central point in every celebration of the Divine Liturgy by way of greeting the Lord's arrival on the eucharistic altar: "Blessed is he who comes in the name of the Lord."

And whence did we Christians derive the idea that Psalm 117 is a psalm about Christ? From a very good source, actually—Christ Himself. Our Lord quoted a line of this psalm to His enemies by way of interpreting His parable of the wicked vinedressers: "Have you not even read this Scripture: 'The stone which the builders rejected / Has become the chief cornerstone. / This was the Lord's doing, / And it is marvelous in our eyes'?" (Mark 12:10, 11). Using a play on words, Jesus here identifies Himself as both the Son (*ben*) and the Stone (*'eben*) of His story about the drama of His death and divine vindication. The Lord's parable of the wicked vinedressers is thus the interpretive key to this psalm.

It is in the Resurrection that we perceive that the "stone which the builders rejected has become the chief cornerstone." The detailed accounts of the Lord's Passion are descriptions of His rejection by the builders, while the Gospel stories of the risen Jesus are the narratives of "the Lord's doing" that is so "marvelous in our eyes."

Psalm 117 is the canticle of the empty tomb. It is to the risen Jesus that we sing, with the Myrrhbearing Women: "You are my God, and I will praise You; You are my God, and I will exalt You." It is to the risen Jesus that we say with Mary Magdalene: "Rabboni!" It is to the risen Jesus that we address the words of the Apostle Thomas: "My Lord and my God." Truly, in the Resurrection we see clearly that "God is the Lord, and He has given us light."

PSALM 118 (119)
BLESSED ARE THE BLAMELESS IN THE PATH

The longest of the psalms, of course, is Psalm 118 (Hebrew 119), constructed of twenty-two stanzas of eight lines each. While there are several other psalms that are called "alphabetical," in the sense that each verse, or pair of verses, begins with the next sequential letter in the Hebrew alphabet, Psalm 118 is alphabetical in a more extreme way. In this instance every verse in each stanza begins with the same letter of the alphabet. Thus, in the first stanza, each of the eight verses commences with the first Hebrew letter, *aleph*. Each line of the second stanza begins with *beth*, and so on, through all twenty-two letters of the alphabet.

(This rather artificial arrangement may not be, in every instance, the most inspired, or inspiring, device of poetic construction, but it certainly does challenge the skills of the poet. For example, the seventh letter of the alphabet is *wav*, but strictly speaking no word in Hebrew actually begins with the letter *wav*. So what to do? Well, in fact there is a way of making a Hebrew word begin with *wav*; that is, by adding wav as a prefix meaning, roughly, "and." This is exactly what the psalmist did. In the Hebrew text every line of the seventh stanza commences with "and." The older translations used by the Church followed suit; each line in the Greek text begins with *kai*, and each Latin line begins with *et*. English translations on the whole, however, tend to ignore it.)

If the artificiality of this alphabetic arrangement is not the stuff of powerful poetic impulse, it does serve, nonetheless, an important theological purpose. Psalm 118 is concerned entirely with the Law of God, the Torah, and its structural use of the alphabet serves here the purpose of asserting that the Law of God is the inner core and essential substance of human language. This is a very deep reflection. Language is the gift of God. Its primary function, in the Bible (cf. Gen. 2:19, for example), is the formation of thought in accord with reality, and the world's deepest created reality, according to the rabbis, is the Torah, the eternal Law of God, on which the inner being of all created reality is based. The eternal Law of God, the Torah, reflects in turn the very being of God, and the final purpose of language is to lead man's thought to the knowledge of God. Language and Torah, thus, are inseparable. In Psalm 118 Law and Word tend to be used interchangeably.

The Christian will, of course, want to assert something further. The Christian will insist that the eternal Law is really derived from God's eternal thought, and that God's eternal thought is His Word, that same Word that for us men and for our salvation came down from heaven. The Torah, that is to say, speaks of Christ; the Law of God points to Christ and is fulfilled in Christ. The final purpose of language is that men may know Christ. He is, after all, the Word, the very Word that was in the beginning. He is the alpha and the omega, the beginning and end of language (cf. Rev. 1:8; 21:6; 22:13), both human and divine.

Christ, as the Latin Fathers called Him, is the *verbum abbreviatum*, God's Word abbreviated, in the sense that all that God has to say is summed up in Christ. Christ is likewise the goal of man's own language, because the purpose of human language is that men may know the truth, and Christ is the truth, the very truth that makes true all things that are true.

All through this psalm, then, the Law of God is described as the path to knowledge of the truth. It is the Law of God that "is a lamp unto my feet," that "gives light to my eyes," "my meditation all the day," "sweeter than honey to my mouth," and "better unto me than thousands of gold and silver."

There are several possible ways of praying this psalm. For example, one may pray it as the prayer of Jesus to His Father, filled with the resolve to do in all things the Father's will, the faithful Servant of God, obedient unto death; in the psalm Jesus appears as the model and author of our own faith.

Or one may pray Psalm 118 as a psalm about Jesus Himself, each of the psalm's testimonials to the Law, the precepts, the commandments, etc., referring to Him of whom the Law itself prophesies and in whom it is fulfilled. Thus, every line speaks of Jesus.

Almost every line also, if one looks closely, is structured on an I-You polarity: "*I* keep *Your* precepts," "*You* hold *me* up," "teach *me Your* statutes," "*You* have taught *me*," and so on. The entire psalm thus becomes a sustained I-You prayer, verse by verse.

PSALM 119 (120)

TO THE LORD I CALLED IN MY DISTRESS

Psalm 119 (Hebrew 120) is the first of fifteen consecutive psalms known as the "songs of ascent." Though the origin of the expression is not entirely certain, a very probable interpretation takes this title to mean that these particular psalms were chanted by pilgrims to Jerusalem as they drew near and began to ascend the heights on which the Holy City is settled. Truly, quite a number of lines in these psalms are readily understood in such a context. In any case, these fifteen form a distinct collection within the Psalter.

Eastern Orthodox Christians will recognize them as the usual psalms at midweek Presanctified Liturgy during Great Lent. In the Western monastic tradition, moreover, the first nine of these "songs of ascent" were invariably among the earliest to be learned by heart. From Tuesday through Saturday each week, these nine psalms, broken into three groups of three, were recited at the third, sixth, and ninth hours of the daily office. As these canonical hours were often prayed by the monks during short "rest breaks" while at work in the woods or fields, it was necessary that they be memorized.

Thus Psalm 119 was on most days the first psalm of the canonical hour of Tierce, or Third Hour, and immediately followed a short hymn to the Holy Spirit (*Nunc Sancte nobis Spiritus*), who is most appropriately invoked at the day's "third hour" (cf. Acts 2:15).

We know that the Church in the upper room, as she anticipated the arrival of "the Holy Spirit of promise" (Eph. 1:13) from on high, "continued with one accord in prayer and supplication" (Acts 1:14), nor is it difficult to hear this psalm arising from her mouth as she waited: "To the Lord I called in my distress, and He answered me. O Lord, deliver my soul from wicked lips, and from a deceitful tongue."

Lies and deception lay all about the Church on that morning. Already, for instance, the rumor was started that the disciples had stolen the dead body of Jesus from the grave while the soldiers slept (cf. Matt. 28:11–15). And as for the body of believers, already "we know that it is spoken against everywhere" (Acts 28:22). But soon would arrive that Holy Spirit to confront their accusers and "convict the world of sin, and of righteousness, and of judgment" (John 16:8).

Meanwhile the Church answers her calumniators in prayer: "What further would you have, or what more be given you, a deceitful tongue? The warrior's sharp arrows, with coals of desolation? Ah me, that my sojourn (*paroikia*) is prolonged, and I have made my home among the tents of Kedar. So much the sojourner (*paroikesen*) is my soul. Peaceful, I spoke peace to those who hated me. When I addressed them, they warred against me without cause."

The poetic imagery of these lines is dense. "The warrior's sharp arrows, with coals of desolation" probably means the incendiary arrows that destroy civilizations. The "tents of Kedar" refers to a warlike tribe in the Arabian desert and should be taken as a metaphor for surrounding hostility.

Used for many centuries by pilgrims marching to Jerusalem, this is a psalm about a "sojourn." Indeed, the word for "sojourn" in this psalm, *paroikia*, is the root of our English word "parish," meaning a congregation of pilgrims. It is the Church that is in exile, on pilgrimage, here in this world, encompassed by calumny and malice.

The First Epistle of Peter may serve as a kind of commentary on Psalm 119. Indeed, St. Peter actually uses the word "sojourn" with reference to the Church; "conduct yourselves throughout the time of your stay here [or "sojourn" (*paroikia*); see textual note] in fear" (1 Pet. 1:17), he exhorts "the pilgrims of the Dispersion in Pontus, Galatia, Cappadocia, Asia, and Bithynia" (1:1). Their situation is exactly that of our psalm. Peter calls them "sojourners (*paroikous*) and pilgrims" (2:11). He also mentions that these *pilgrims of the Dispersion* are being tempted, "grieved by various trials" (1:6), constantly reproached by those outside as evildoers (2:12, 20; 3:16; 4:14, 16). But by doing good, Peter assures them, they will "put to silence the ignorance of foolish men" (2:15). For their model, he holds out to them the suffering of Christ, "who, when He was reviled, did not revile in return; when He suffered, He did not threaten" (2:23). "Therefore let those who suffer according to the will of God commit their souls to Him" (4:19).

PSALM 120 (121)
I HAVE RAISED MINE EYES TO THE MOUNTAINS

Psalm 120 (Hebrew 121) may be prayed as a man's dialogue with his soul. As an internal discussion, the soul speaks both for itself and to itself, the pronouns alternating constantly between first and second person: "I have raised mine eyes to the mountains, from where my help shall come. My help is from the Lord, who made heaven and earth. He will suffer not your foot to slip, nor will your Guard succumb to slumber. Behold, the Guardian of Israel sleeps not, nor slumbers. The Lord will be your Guard. At your right hand will the Lord be your security. The sun will not burn you by day, nor the moon assail you by night. The Lord shall guard you from every evil. The Lord will guard your soul. The Lord will guard your coming in and your going out, henceforth and forever more."

The thoughts in Psalm 120 are clearly those to which the believing mind will cleave, especially in times of trial, when spiritual help is most needed. Whether as participle or finite verb, references to God's "guarding" me appear six times in this psalm's eight verses. God's protection of me is complete (". . . shall guard you from *every* evil"), because He "neither sleeps nor slumbers." This thoroughness of God's protection is emphasized by the twin polarities of sun by day/moon by night and coming in/going out.

For all that, the protection that God provides for me is not a merely individual blessing. This is not a psalm about "God and me." I may pray this psalm and lay claim to its blessings, rather, by reason of my adherence to His Chosen People, the Church. I am a sheep of His flock. My personal confidence in God's guardianship stands within a context determined by His covenanted interventions in human history. The Lord is the Guardian of my soul because He is "the Guardian of Israel." I may trust in Him, because He has made me too a child of Abraham.

This truth tells me, likewise, the meaning of these mountains to which "I have raised mine eyes" and "from where my help shall come." These mountains are my fixed foundations, the everlasting hills of my hope. Let these mountains ever serve, too, as bulwarks to my soul. Let me look upon them always. May the eyes of my soul never stray from gazing toward these mountains, because upon them "the Guardian of Israel neither sleeps nor slumbers."

Indeed, let me, even now, turn my thoughts to these godly mountains of my deliverance. Let me think of high Moriah, the mountain where the Lord provides. Let me climb with Abraham and wood-bearing Isaac to the altar of sacrifice. Let my help come to me, too, from mighty Sinai, in covenant and Law. Let me ascend with Moses and Elijah to stand before Your face. Likewise, Lord, make me ever mindful of the mountain where You dispel satanic thought with the keen sword of Deuteronomy. Oh, suffer not that handsome blade to sleep within my hand. Again, in blessed assurance, let my help come from the mountain where You proclaim blessed the poor in spirit. And kindly count me, Sir, among their number. Yet again, may my help come to me from the holy mountain where "such a voice came to Him from the Excellent Glory: 'This is My beloved Son'" (2 Pet. 1:17). With Simon, make me contemplate the glorious cloud, and with the Sons of Thunder. Oh, most certainly, let my help be established on forlorn Golgotha, whose dark ninth plague foreshadows, for three hours, the earthquake and the slaughter of the Firstborn. With Your Mother, let me stand, and the close companions of her sorrow. Ah, but let my help, too, be found on that mountain from which the Eleven are sent forth to make disciples of all nations, for how beautiful on the mountains are the feet of those who proclaim peace and bring good tidings. And now let my help come to me from mystic Nebo, where I may gaze, as the morning mist begins to clear, across the green, tree-lined Jordan to my wide inheritance. May I not perish, I pray, amidst the sons of Ammon, nor the children of Moab. And at the last, dear Lord, let me stand with John on that great and high mountain, to see the great city, Holy Jerusalem, descending down from heaven, her light like a most precious stone, like a jasper clear as crystal, and with streets of gold, like transparent glass. That city is the final Israel, whose Guardian "neither sleeps nor slumbers." And until that day, Lord, teach me always to raise my eyes to these mountains, "from where my help shall come."

PSALM 121 (122)

I WAS ELATED WHEN THEY SAID TO ME

Just as the previous psalm "of ascent" raised our eyes to those mountains from which our help shall come, Psalm 121 (Hebrew 122) now shows us that Holy City on the top thereof, the perfecting goal of our pilgrimage: "I was elated when they said to me, 'We shall go unto the house of the Lord!' In your very courts our feet were standing, O Jerusalem. Jerusalem! fashioned as a city, the abode of shared communion. For unto her have the tribes ascended, the tribes of the Lord, as a testimony unto Israel, to confess the Name of the Lord! For in her were set the thrones for judgment, thrones over the house of David. Oh, pray for the peace of Jerusalem, and the prosperity of those who love you. May there be peace in your power, and prosperity in your towers of strength. For the sake of my brethren and my loved ones, I have discoursed of your peace. For the sake of the house of the Lord our God, I have been zealous for your good."

This is a psalm about Jerusalem, obviously, but what Jerusalem? Surely not any city we may find on a map. And certainly not that rebellious city, "not willing" to repent, that killed the prophets and stoned those who were sent to her (Matt. 23:37). Most emphatically not that city "where also our Lord was crucified" (Rev. 11:8). Nor, indeed, that city where the eagles gathered together, as around a carcass, nor one stone thereof was left upon another (Matt. 24:2, 28).

Jerusalem in Psalm 121 is, rather, the city on high of which it was written, "the Jerusalem above is free, which is the mother of us all" (Gal. 4:26). It is the city concerning which it is said to us: "But you have come to Mount Zion and to the city of the living God, the heavenly Jerusalem" (Heb. 12:22). It is the city whose name is emblazoned on our brows, "the New Jerusalem, which comes down out of heaven from My God" (Rev. 3:12).

But if this Jerusalem is, firstly, the Church in heaven, it is also the Church on earth, and these two are the one reality that our psalm calls "the abode of shared communion." Moreover, just as all things are defined by relation to the purposes for which they exist, the Church on earth receives her very identity from the Church in heaven. She exists on earth only with a view to heaven; heaven alone holds the key to her being, for God already "raised us up together, and made us sit together in the heavenly places in Christ Jesus" (Eph. 2:6). Our psalm captures both these aspects of Jerusalem. She is the goal of those tribes ascending unto the house of the Lord and, even now, the courts where our feet are standing.

How, then, should we understand this "peace of Jerusalem" for which we pray? Again, two senses seem intended. The most obvious is to understand Jerusalem as the beneficiary of this peace, meaning "pray that Jerusalem will have peace," pray that the Church on earth will enjoy tranquility, in which to serve God with an undisturbed and quiet mind. Surely this is an appropriate prayer, and the traditional texts of our worship abound with examples of it. Thus, we pray for "the peace of the whole world, for the good estate of the holy churches of God, and for the union of all men."

But praying for "the peace of Jerusalem" bears an even deeper meaning, for Jerusalem's very name indicates peace. Thus, an ancient hymn of Holy Church speaks of the *urbs Jerusalem beata, dicta pacis visio*—"blessed city Jerusalem, called the vision of peace." The "vision" here, of course, is that of St. John who, in prophecy, beheld the final descent of this city to a renewed earth (Rev. 21:2, 10). Taken in this sense, to "pray for the peace of Jerusalem" means to pray that, even now, we may enjoy, in measure, the peace of eternal life. This prayer, too, it is most appropriate to make. Truly, we pray it first. Even before praying for the peace of the whole world and the good estate of the holy churches of God, we are careful to pray "for the peace from above and for the salvation of our souls." For the one is the wellspring of the other. The peace for which we pray is not that which the world gives (or, more often, fails to give). It is the peace with which the risen Lord greets us when, ever again, He enters through the locked doors (for such is the meaning of "The doors, the doors!"), and breathes His Holy Spirit upon us, and tells us to touch our fingers to the everlasting wounds.

PSALM 122 (123)

TO YOU HAVE I LIFTED UP MY EYES

In the canonical text of Holy Scripture used by the Holy Orthodox Church (as distinct from the truncated Protestant Bibles read by most English-speaking Orthodox Christians), the Book of Daniel commences with a dramatic, fast-moving narrative about a wise and beautiful woman named Susannah. It is the unforgettable story of the two lustful elders who attempted to seduce this virtuous lady by threats, their perjured testimony against her when she refused their lecherous advances, the death sentence imposed for the adultery they alleged against her in revenge, and the dramatic emergence of the young Prophet Daniel to vindicate the woman's innocence and confound her accusers.

The third-century Alexandrian exegete, Origen, drew attention to a particular detail in the story by way of illustrating an ironical contrast between Susannah and her accusers. These latter, Origen observed, when they begin to lust after the woman, are described in this way: "Thus they perverted their own minds and turned away their eyes from looking up to heaven, and they rendered not just judgments." In striking contrast to them, it is written of the accused Susannah that she simply "looked up with tears to heaven, because her heart trusted in the Lord" (*Commentary on John*, 28.5).

Unjust men, that is to say, do not look up to heaven, for heaven sees into their hearts and condemns them. Those who trust in God, however, always look up to heaven, for heaven alone is the final foundation of their hope. It is ever to heaven that the just man raises his eyes in trust.

Because of young Daniel's forensic intervention, Susannah's unjust, mendacious trial ended in her righteous vindication. Not so the unjust, mendacious trial of Stephen. Here no Daniel rose to redeem the moment and restrain the impulses of the multitude in their fury, for "they cried out with a loud voice, stopped their ears, and ran at him with one accord; and they cast him out of the city and stoned him" (Acts 7:57, 58). Stephen himself, nonetheless, raising his eyes exactly as did Susannah, "gazed into heaven and saw the glory of God" (7:55). With the just man it is ever thus. Condemned and contemned upon the earth, he lifts his vision and sets his sights on high, trusting in the God who reads hearts and recognizes those who belong to Him.

This trustful raising of the eyes to heaven is very much a component of prayer in the Book of Psalms. "My eyes are ever toward the Lord," says Psalm 24, and in Psalm 140 we read: "For to You, O Lord, Lord, are my eyes."

245

Psalm 122 (Hebrew 123) forms a sort of meditation on the raising of our eyes in prayer: "To You have I lifted up my eyes, You that dwell in heaven. Behold, as the eyes of servants are on the hands of their masters—as the eyes of a handmaid regard the hands of her mistress—so our eyes look to the Lord our God, till He take compassion on us. Have mercy on us, O Lord, have mercy on us, for overmuch have we been filled with scorn; overmuch has our soul been sated—a reproach to the prosperous, a disgrace to the proud."

It is to "You that dwell in heaven" that we lift up our eyes. This line resounds with the opening of the Lord's Prayer, "Our Father, who art in heaven." Indeed, even the Hebrew sound of "You that dwell in heaven" (*hayoshbi bashamaim*) resembles the opening of the Lord's Prayer translated into Hebrew (*abinu shebashamaim*). The physical heavens above us are but a reflection and a veil of the real heaven. Our communication is with the real heaven, where Stephen beheld Jesus standing at God's right hand. Whether or not, at any given moment, we actually raise our eyes to the visible vault above us, the inner eyes of the heart nonetheless "look to the Lord our God, till He take compassion on us."

And why do servants and handmaidens look to the hands of their masters and mistresses? Very simply, for direction, for the smallest gesture of command, for any faint indication of preference. That is to say, with a view to ready obedience in their service. And for this reason do we too raise our eyes to God, that we may be prompt to the doing of His will on earth, as it is done in heaven. Like Susannah and Stephen, we live for God and in hope of His approval. With respect to men on earth, it may always be the case that we are "a reproach to the prosperous, a disgrace to the proud." To this we are indifferent; for us it is sufficient to detect but the slightest sign of God's redemptive will.

PSALM 123 (124)

The Bible is a book of salvation. Its dominant theme, above all things, is deliverance. Its varied components, written and edited in different cultural settings over many centuries and in places as diverse as Mesopotamia and Rome, are collected into one volume under a single unifying head: soteriology, the study of salvation.

The God of the Bible is the God of deliverance. He is the saving Lord, the God who rescues His servants from a great variety of perils, including an imminent destruction at the Red Sea, the repeated threat of annihilation by multiple foreign armies, a menacing giant in the Valley of Elah, the conspiracy of Absalom and the counsel of Ahithophel, the search parties of Jezebel, the dungeon of Malchiah, the plot of Haman, the intrigue of Sanballat, Aretas guarding the walls of the Damascenes, wild beasts at Ephesus, tribulation on the island that is called Patmos, and a host of other hazards.

Most of all, this God "has delivered us from the power of darkness and conveyed us into the kingdom of the Son of His love, in whom we have redemption through His blood" (Col. 1:13, 14). This is the God who says to us: "Do not be afraid, but speak, and do not keep silent; for I am with you, and no one will attack you to hurt you" (Acts 18:9, 10). He is the God who saves, for the servants of this saving God seem forever in danger, finding themselves in a fiery furnace and a den of lions, "in journeys often, in perils of waters, in perils of robbers, in perils of my own countrymen, in perils of the Gentiles, in perils in the city, in perils in the wilderness, in perils in the sea, in perils among false brethren; in weariness and toil, in sleeplessness often, in hunger and thirst, in fastings often, in cold and nakedness" (2 Cor. 11:26, 27).

Thus, a common experience narrated in Holy Scripture is what, in our current idiom, is known as "the close call," the sense we have of having almost perished, of being snatched from destruction at the final moment, as it were. And Psalms tells us repeatedly to confess that experience of the "close call," to make such confession an integral part of our prayer: "Let Israel now say."

Thus we pray in Psalm 33: "Oh magnify the Lord with me, and let us exalt His name together. I sought the Lord, and He heard me, and delivered me from all my fears." Or again, Psalm 117: "Let Israel now say, 'His mercy endures forever.'" And Psalm 128: "'Many a time have they afflicted me from my youth,' let Israel now say."

Deliverance from a "close call" is the resonating message of one of the loveliest of the psalms, Psalm 123 (Hebrew 124): "'Had the Lord not been among us,' let Israel now say, 'had the Lord not been among us, when men rose up against us, they would have swallowed us alive. When their fury raged against us, the water would have engulfed us. Our soul would have passed through a torrent, our soul would have passed through the overwhelming water.' Blessed be the Lord who did not give us over as a prey unto their teeth. Our soul, like a sparrow, was delivered from the snare of the fowler. The snare was thrown, but we were delivered. Our help is in the name of the Lord, the Maker of heaven and earth."

The specific images of danger in this psalm are the engulfing flood and the bird-snare. The Bible's best example of the first, of course, is the peril of Israel at the Red Sea in Exodus, an image destined to assume archetypal significance all through Holy Scripture (e.g., 1 Cor. 10:1, 2). Another is the deluge in Genesis 6—8, which, like the crossing of the Red Sea, became a type of our deliverance through baptism (cf. 1 Pet. 3:20, 21). The image of the engulfing waters is especially prominent in Isaiah (cf. 8:8; 30:28; 59:19, etc.).

The second image of danger, the bird-snare, is also found in the most notable of the psalms of deliverance, Psalm 90: "He will deliver you from the snare of the fowler, and the deadly pestilence." In Proverbs 6:5 it symbolizes moral danger.

And how powerful is the God who protects us? Well, says our psalm, He made heaven and earth. This expression appears earlier in the psalms of ascent (Psalm 120:2), and the context in both cases is God's help (*he boetheia*). Because God's power is absolute, and His resolve unconditional, our safety is beyond doubt.

PSALM 124 (125)

Whereas the previous psalm had described God as "among us" (*en hemin*), Psalm 124 (Hebrew 125) speaks of Him as surrounding us (*kyklo*). In both cases the reference is to the Lord's protection of His people, a security symbolized in the elevated, walled city of Jerusalem.

Thus does Psalm 124 speak of this security: "Those who trust in the Lord are like Mount Zion, nor will he be shaken who abides in Jerusalem. Mountains are round about her, and the Lord surrounds His people, henceforth and forevermore. The Lord will not suffer the rod of sinners over the inheritance of the righteous, lest the righteous reach out their hands unto evil. Do good, O Lord, to the good, and to the upright in heart. But those who stray aside to evil ways the Lord will exile with the workers of iniquity. Peace be upon Israel."

This last blessing, "peace be upon Israel," which also closes Psalm 127, is part of the prayer that the Apostle Paul offers for the Church at the end of his argument in Galatians: "And as many as walk according to this rule, peace and mercy be upon them, and upon the Israel of God" (6:16). This is the peace that comes of living, by faith, under the protection of God.

This protection and this peace, however, are essentially matters of the spirit. One of ancient Israel's great mistakes, exemplified during the lifetime of Jeremiah and vigorously condemned by him, was to regard these blessings of protection and peace in a political sense, as though Jerusalem benefited from some kind of automatic geopolitical immunity from harm, no matter how wicked its ways and unrighteous the lives of its inhabitants.

Indeed, even when the Lord did grant political protection to Jerusalem, as in the case of the Assyrian invasions near the end of the eighth century (during the ministry of Isaiah), the purpose of such intervention was spiritual. No matter how destructive the Assyrian army, the worship of Assyrian gods was far worse.

Likewise, in our psalm the reason that "the Lord will not suffer the rod of sinners over the inheritance of the righteous" is a concern "lest the righteous reach out their hands unto evil." The Lord's concern, that is to say, is chiefly for the safety of our souls. He extends no promises of protection nor guarantees of peace except "to the good, and to the upright in heart."

Life in God's Church is no different. The protection He promises us is a matter of the spirit, not necessarily a deliverance from those who can kill the body. On the contrary, the Lord solemnly assured us, "In the world you will have tribulation" (John 16:33), the particulars of which are spelled out in several places. For example, "But before all these things, they will lay their hands on you and persecute you, delivering you up to the synagogues and prisons. You will be brought before kings and rulers for My name's sake" (Luke 21:12).

Thus, when Jesus promises us, "not a hair of your head shall be lost" (21:18), His promise must be understood in some sense compatible with the various persecutions predicted in the same context. There is no such notion in the Bible as a "pretribulation rapture" that would spare the faithful from the manifold sufferings that come upon the whole world. Nor should the Lord's assurance, "not a hair of your head will perish," be understood as a protection against baldness. All these things are matters of the spirit.

In the context of our psalm, then, the promise of divine protection is not disassociated from a moral concern. Should the inhabitants of Zion "stray aside to evil ways," the Lord will not protect them. On the contrary, He will "exile" them; He will lead them away (*apaksei*) "with the workers of iniquity."

To abide in Zion, therefore, to confide in those blessed mountains round about her, is a task as well as a grace. And how does the Lord Himself describe this task? "Abide in My love. If you keep My commandments, you will abide in My love, just as I have kept My Father's commandments and abide in His love" (John 15:9, 10). And again, "If you love Me, keep My commandments" (14:15). And again, "For this is the love of God, that we keep His commandments" (1 John 5:3). To abide in the love of God, manifested in the observance of His commandments, is to dwell in Jerusalem. Such a dweller will never be shaken, promises our psalm.

PSALM 125 (126)
WHEN THE LORD BROUGHT BACK THE CAPTIVITY OF ZION
※

Through ancient Israel's history, but especially during times of extraordinary trial, men of historical understanding looked to God's salvific interventions in the past in order to draw hope for the immediate future. For example, we saw how Psalm 88 meditated at length on the Lord's redemptive, covenanted choice of David and his royal household in order to draw strength and inspiration during a period in which that household appeared to stand in great peril. In a similar way, several passages in the middle section of Isaiah look back to Israel's deliverance from Egypt as a kind of foreshadowing of Israel's coming deliverance from captivity in Babylon.

In later periods, but especially during Israel's humiliating subjugation to the Seleucid throne at Antioch (the time of the Maccabees), the vision of faith once again gazed backwards to that deliverance from Babylon in order to find hope that God would once again redeem His people from their oppressors. In all these cases, the argument ran along the following lines: "If God has done such and such a thing on our behalf, then surely He will do this and that as well." This is essentially the argument that St. Paul uses to inspire Christian hope. We may summarize his thesis thus: "If God has redeemed us in Christ, then He will also give us all other things necessary." This seems a fair paraphrase of his words: "If God is for us, who can be against us? He who did not spare His own Son, but delivered Him up for us all, how shall He not with Him also freely give us all things?" (Rom. 8:31, 32).

Psalm 125 (Hebrew 126) is one of those texts that looks back to Israel's deliverance from Babylon in order to plead for a new deliverance. "When the Lord brought back the captivity of Zion," it begins, "we were like men in rapture."

This last expression needs and will profit from further comment. The Hebrew of the traditional rabbinical text here reads *keholmim*, "like dreamers." That is to say, the experience of salvation has a kind of dreamlike quality. Those who are saved must pinch themselves, as it were, to make sure it is really happening. God's redemption of us from bondage and oppression is so marvelously incomprehensible; it is "too good to be true." The sheer joy of the thing encourages unbelief, as it were. Thus, when they were faced with the risen Jesus standing before them in His glorified flesh, the Apostles "did not believe for joy, and marveled" (Luke 24:41). The whole thing seemed like a dream. Likewise, when the angel of the Lord delivered the Apostle Peter from Herod's prison, his sensations spoke of something nearly unreal, a sort of fantasy. Indeed, he "did not know that what was done by the angel was real, but thought he was seeing a vision" (Acts 12:9). This is the impression conveyed in the rabbinical text of our psalm with respect to God's deliverance.

The canonical Greek text, however, reads somewhat differently here. It suggests that the earlier Hebrew expression was not "like dreamers" (*keholmim*,), but "like those consoled" (*kenihamim*). Thus, the Latin Vulgate reads *sicut consolati.*

Why, then, do I translate it here as "like men in rapture"? "Those consoled," I believe, is too weak to render the stronger nuances of the Greek *parakeklemenoi.* Surely, one of the basic meanings of the verb *parakaleo* is "to console." To read our psalm within the full contextual field of Holy Scripture, however, it is theologically useful to consider other nuances of this word. *Parakaleo* also means to fill with encouragement and even excitement.

Parakaleo is formed of the same two roots as the marvelous noun *parakletos*, the name that Christ our Lord gave to the Holy Spirit (John 14:16, 26; 15:26; 16:7). What is being spoken of here in our psalm is that "state of mind" given by the Holy Spirit. When the Lord turned back our captivity, says Psalm 125, we were "parakleted." The Holy Spirit, that is to say, took command of our hearts and minds. Becoming children of God, we are led by the Spirit of God (Rom. 8:14). Surely there is something dreamlike in this experience, as we have seen, but the proper state of Christian consciousness is a great deal more. It is full conviction in the Holy Spirit (1 Thess. 1:5). It is insight and wisdom given in faith. It involves the utter transformation of thought and perception. It is the true knowledge of the God who transcends all our knowledge. It is the enraptured mind.

PSALM 126 (127)

UNLESS THE LORD SHOULD BUILD THE HOUSE

Among the "psalms of ascent," chanted by Israel's pilgrims as they climbed the final steps up Mount Zion on their pilgrimage to the temple, Psalm 126 (Hebrew 127) is the only one ascribed to Solomon. The latter being the Bible's preeminent wise man, this detail may serve to direct our attention to certain "wisdom themes" in the psalm, and, in truth, these are readily discerned. Most particularly there is the theme of the wise householder.

A man did not normally make this pilgrimage to Jerusalem alone, but in the company of his family (cf. Luke 2:41). Indeed, this customary pilgrimage was a significant way of giving a godly identity to a man's family. It was itself an exercise of "edification," this word taken in its etymological sense of building or constructing an "edifice." An important purpose of the pilgrimage was that of "building the house," the latter term understood as "home" or "household." Like everything else a family does together, the regular pilgrimage was an exercise in house-building. In fact, this is a psalm about the proper maintenance of the household and, by extension, the city. Any simple reading of, say, Proverbs will show that these preoccupations very much constitute a wisdom theme.

Now the message of Psalm 126 is that all human effort directed toward such wise pursuits must be founded on a firm trust in God's grace and assistance. Thus, our psalm begins: "Unless the Lord should build the house (Hebrew *bayit*, Greek *oikos*), in vain have the builders toiled. Unless the Lord should guard the city, in vain did the guardian keep watch."

In our present state these tasks, construction and vigilance, are matters of great toil, of course, and frequently of frustration and sadness, because we are children of fallen Adam, who discovered his daily labor impeded by thistle and thorn. Thus, our psalm addresses those "who eat the bread of grief"—that is to say, ourselves, descendants of that man to whom the Lord said, "In the sweat of your face you shall eat bread" (Gen. 3:19). We are heirs of that Eve to whom it was declared, "I will greatly multiply your sorrow and your conception; / In pain you shall bring forth children" (3:16).

No matter with how much discipline and industry we labor for our family's bread, the bread itself is always God's gift, a truth we acknowledge each day when we pray, "Give us this day our daily bread." Likewise, the wearisome toil of the Apostles, fishing all night to no avail, is followed by the sudden and unexpected catch at the Lord's bidding (cf. Luke 5:5, 6; John 21:3–6). No human effort can hope for much apart from the graciousness of God.

It was important for the fishermen Apostles to learn this truth deeply, for it would have special application to the ministry of the Church. The labor of evangelism, for instance, depends entirely on the grace of God, for it is the Lord who day by day adds to our number such as are being saved (cf. Acts 2:47). The Apostle Paul thus described the ministry at Corinth: "I planted, Apollos watered, but God gave the increase." Then, shifting his metaphor to the one used in our psalm, he went on to assert, "For we are God's fellow workers; you are God's field, you are God's building (*oikodome*)" (1 Cor. 3:6, 9).

Then our psalm, pushing the point still further, reflects on the irony that one of the most important blessings of human house-building takes place in bed. It is in the bed, after all, in the context of rest and sleep, that children are conceived. Thus, God's great gift, the gift of children, appears to have more to do with human rest than with human toil. So, after speaking of the loss of sleep involved in keeping a night vigil over the city, the psalm goes on to say that, without the Lord's assistance, "in vain do you wake early, rising up after resting, you that eat the bread of grief, when He gives sleep to those He loves. Behold, sons are the inheritance of the Lord, the reward of the fruit of the womb."

There is no room for a planned parenthood in this psalm. Conceived in the context of rest, children are purely the gift of God. These are the arrows of a man's quiver, says our psalm, waxing ever bolder in poetic image. They will be his stay and support when he sits and deliberates with his neighbors in the gate of that city over which the Lord maintains a constant vigilance. This is what it means to construct a home.

PSALM 127 (128)

There are passages in the Gospels which, were they to be interpreted in isolation, would seem to suggest a relatively unenthusiastic, or at least very qualified, view of marriage and the family. In St. Luke's Gospel we are warned, for example, that marriage itself may prove to be an impediment to one's entry into the Kingdom (14:20). Another passage in Luke speaks about leaving one's father and mother, and even one's wife, for the sake of the Kingdom of God (18:29), hardly a strong endorsement of the family. In the Gospel of St. Matthew, there is a recommendation about making oneself a eunuch for the sake of the Kingdom (19:12). While this expression is to be understood as a metaphor, it still does not reflect especially well on the married state. After all, eunuchs tend not to be solid family types. Moreover, in St. Paul's First Epistle to the Corinthians, the high level of eschatological expectancy among the early Christians was the context in which he argued for the preference of celibacy over the state of marriage (7:25–38). Perhaps more than one reader of the New Testament over the centuries has felt obliged to ask if it really has anything encouraging to say about marriage except for its symbolic, sacramental application (cf. Eph. 5:32).

We should not reach any hasty conclusions on the basis solely of the foregoing evidence, however. On the contrary, the New Testament indicates in a number of places that the experience of the Church is very much joined to the experience of the household. Indeed, entire households adopted the Christian faith of the heads of the household, as in the cases of a centurion at Capernaum (John 4:53), another centurion at Caesarea (Acts 11:14), a businesswoman and a jailer at Philippi (Acts 16:15, 31), a synagogue leader at Corinth (Acts 18:8). It was in such "core families," doubtless, that the great majority of the second, or at least the third, and later generations of Christians were born. That is to say, in spite of the many obvious exceptions, whether because of monastic dedication or the plain circumstance that a person has remained single, for most Christians the Gospel life has meant being a member of a Christian household. In other words, most Christians have been sanctified, made holy, through the varied relationships and obligations established by the sacrament of marriage and the begetting of children.

In this connection, the theme of the believer's family, so prominent in Psalm 126, is even more dominant in Psalm 127 (Hebrew 128): "Blessed are all who fear the Lord, those who walk in His ways. The fruits of your labors will you eat; you are blessed, and it will be well with you. Your wife shall be like a vine, flourishing within the walls of your house, your sons like olive shoots about your table. Behold, thus shall be blessed the man who fears the Lord. The Lord bless you from Zion, and may you see the good things of Jerusalem, all the days of your life. May you see your children's children. Peace be upon Israel."

This psalm, which begins with a beatitude and ends with a blessing, is modest in its hopes. It does not wish for wealth, or power, or prestige. There is nothing here about "getting ahead." The psalm speaks, rather, of eating the fruits of one's own labors (in idiom, literally, the labors of one's fruits). It is not a wish for easy money, but for such resources as come from hard employment. Indeed, the word used here is not the usual one designating work; it is, rather, the plural form of *ponos*, which means labor in the sense of very arduous tasks, even pain. In fact, in most versions of Revelation 16:10 and 21:4, *ponos* is translated as "sorrow." Once again, as in the previous psalm, the image evoked here is that of the fallen Adam, bending over his hoe to deal with the uncooperative soil. Yes, this is the blessing of our psalm, the simple joy of maintaining one's own life, even at subsistence level.

And also the life of one's family. A man's wife and his children are blessings from God, here described with the metaphors of fruitful plants. The blessing of this psalm is the happiness found in the life of work and the circle of the family, all the way to old age and the vision of grandchildren. God, says our psalm, blesses His reverent ("all who fear the Lord") and obedient ("those who walk in His ways") servants with these benedictions. Such things pertain to the peace of Jerusalem.

PSALM 128 (129)

MANY TIMES HAVE THEY WARRED AGAINST
ME FROM MY YOUTH

According to Holy Scripture, the lot of the true Israel in this world involves a great deal of grief from those distressed by the very thought of God and offended at the occasional recollection of His claims. Often enough, persecution ensues: "Yes, and all who desire to live godly in Christ Jesus will suffer persecution" (2 Tim. 3:12).

Psalm 128 (Hebrew 129) speaks of the history of this persecution and the Lord's constant deliverance of His people in the face of it: "'Many times have they warred against me from my youth,' let Israel now say, 'many times have they warred against me from my youth, but they could not prevail against me.' The sinful contrived behind my back, perpetual in iniquity; but the righteous Lord broke the necks of the sinful."

This persecution is described as a warfare—"they *warred* against me." The Greek verb here is *epolemesan*, a close inspection of which will remind one of the cognate word, "polemics." Ours being a fallen world, life in the service of God provokes any amount of such polemics. As we have had occasion to reflect many times in these pages, the Book of Psalms is a prayer book for warriors.

And when began this persecution of—this polemic against—God's people? "From my youth" would seem to place the beginnings of the experience pretty far back in Israel's memory. Perhaps one might think of the early oppressions by the Egyptians (Ex. 1:14), or the Moabites (Judg. 3:14), or the Canaanites (4:3), or the Midianites (6:6), or the Ammonites (10:9; 1 Sam. 11:2), and so on. The polemic against the righteous, however, goes back further still. "From my youth" would seem to include even the murder of righteous Abel (Gen. 4:8), who, we are told, "offered to God a more excellent sacrifice than Cain, through which he obtained witness that he was righteous" (Heb. 11:4). Indeed, Christ our Lord apparently took "from my youth" to begin at that exact point, for He spoke of "all the righteous blood shed on the earth, from the blood of righteous Abel to the blood of Zechariah, son of Berechiah" (Matt. 23:35). And in this same context the Lord further prophesied that this persecution, this relentless polemic, will continue yet: "I send you prophets, wise men, and scribes: some of them you will kill and crucify, and some of them you will scourge in your synagogues and persecute from city to city" (23:34).

For all that, says our psalm, "they could not prevail against me." Indeed, they cannot prevail, whether by "persecutions, afflictions, which happened to me at Antioch, at Iconium, at Lystra—what persecutions I endured. And out of them all the Lord delivered me" (2 Tim. 3:11). Therefore, we take heart from this repeated experience of God's deliverance: "We are hard pressed on every side, yet not crushed; we are perplexed, but not in despair; persecuted, but not forsaken; struck down, but not destroyed" (2 Cor. 4:8, 9).

Our psalm ends with a threefold imprecation against the persecutors, which is perhaps one of the most ironic pieces of poetry in the whole Book of Psalms. It compares the sinful to the dried-up grass on a mud roof, but instead of simple passing mention of this metaphor, our psalm pauses to let us meditate more deeply on its implications. Such dried-out grass, we reflect, never becomes part of the harvest. No reaper will gather it; it will never be bundled nor baled, and for that reason it will never be the occasion for the customary blessing mutually extended by the laborers at the time of harvest (cf. Ruth 2:4). This is a truly remarkable section of poetry, dwelling on various benedictions that are never to be. Such is the everlasting loss of the sinful that waged war on Israel from his youth. The imprecations are entirely negative; the hatred of holy Zion leads to the loss of a blessing that need not have been lost. The shallow roots wither; there is no harvest for it; the voice of blessing will never again be heard: "Let them be ashamed and confounded, all those who hate Zion. Let them become like the grass on the rooftops, all dried out before the plucking. The harvester took it not in hand, nor did the bundler take it to his bosom. Neither did the passersby say, 'The Lord's blessing be upon you; we bless you in the name of the Lord.'"

PSALM 129 (130)

OUT OF THE DEPTHS HAVE I CRIED TO YOU, O LORD

֍

Throughout Christian history, Psalm 129 (Hebrew 130) has been one of the psalms most frequently prayed. Indeed, this psalm having long been designated for daily recitation in both the East and the West, there are undoubtedly thousands of Christians even now who know it by heart.

Named by its Latin opening words, *De Profundis*, Psalm 129 has always been considered an appropriate supplication on behalf of the souls departed. Thus, for many centuries in Western monasticism it was recited not only at Tuesday Vespers as part of the weekly course of the Psalter, but at least two more times each day, specifically for the deceased faithful: at the end of the regular monastic "chapter meeting" in the morning, and again after the day's principal meal.

In the Orthodox East, Psalm 129 is not only recited within the course of the weekly Kathisma, but it is chanted each evening at Vespers between Psalms 141 and 116, during the great censing. Thus, as the day gathers to a close and the shadows lengthen, Holy Church, having prayed at the appointed intervals throughout the day, now appropriately says to the Lord: "My soul has waited on Your word. My soul has hoped on the Lord, from the morning watch till nighttime. From the morning watch, let Israel hope on the Lord."

Perhaps this same sense of deepening eventide is further conveyed in the opening line of our psalm, "*Out of the depths* have I cried to You, O Lord; Lord, listen to my voice. Let Your ears be attentive to the voice of my prayer." Certainly this line reechoes the opening line of Psalm 140, which begins the sequence of the psalms of the censing: "Lord, I have cried to You; give heed to me. Attend to the voice of my prayer, when I cry unto You."

And as the day ends, most of us are aware of various ways in which, during the course of it, we have failed of the grace of God, perhaps permitting some root of bitterness to spring up and trouble us, whereby many are defiled (Heb. 12:15). We end our day, therefore, by remembering God's mercy: "If You, O Lord, should count our sins, O Lord, who could stand it? But with You there is appeasement. For Your name's sake have I waited for You, O Lord. My soul has waited on Your word."

And if with such sentiments we end the day, how fitting it is that we should so end our lives, hoping solely in the goodness of God and awaiting the visitation of His mercy. These lines indicate why we also pray this psalm for those who have passed from us.

And what is this "word" from God for which we wait at the end of the day? Is it, perhaps, "Today you will be with Me in paradise"? Surely the thief hanging on the Lord's right hand was waiting for such a word, knowing that if the Lord should count our sins, who could stand it? Some mysterious movement of grace in his soul, however, prompted him to hope that with the Lord there is appeasement.

"Rich mercy" is one of the loveliest expressions characteristic of the vocabulary of Orthodox worship. In various troparia, antiphons, litanies, etc. we continually speak of God's "rich mercy." The image of abundant, overflowing mercy is preeminently biblical, of course. For example, one thinks of Ephesians 2:4, where St. Paul speaks of "God, who is rich in mercy." And of Christ he writes: "In Him we have redemption through His blood, the forgiveness of sins, according to the riches of His grace" (1:7). And somewhat later he says that God will "show the exceeding riches of His grace in His kindness toward us in Christ Jesus" (2:7).

Each evening Psalm 129 likewise speaks of this abundant, redemptive mercy of God: "For with the Lord there is mercy, and with Him is copious redemption; and He shall redeem Israel from all his iniquities." This merciful redemption is that of the "evening sacrifice," which we daily remember at Vespers, that salvific raising of Christ's hands in prayer on the Cross when He paid the purchase of the world. It was in the evening sacrifice, offered while the world was plunged in a darkness that started at noon, that the Father "delivered us from the power of darkness and conveyed us into the kingdom of the Son of His love, in whom we have redemption through His blood, the forgiveness of sins" (Col. 1:13, 14). This is the vesperal mercy and the copious redemption in which, at the end of the day, we place all our hope.

PSALM 130 (131)

O LORD, MY HEART IS NOT ARROGANT

St. Paul warned the Christian congregation at Rome, "Think not haughty thoughts (*me hypsela phronei*), but fear" (Rom. 11:20, author's translation). This is nearly a quotation from Proverbs: "Do not be thinking (*phronimos*) about yourself, but fear God" (3:7, author's translation).

Perhaps the Apostle had some special concern for the brethren in the imperial capital in this respect, for he mentioned the matter again after only a few verses, using a complex wordplay that tends to elude adequate translation: "For I say through the grace given to me, to everyone who is among you, not to think too highly (*me hyperphronein*), above what he ought to think (*phronein*), but to think (*phronein*) unto sensible thought (*sophronein*)" (Rom. 12:3, author's translation). When he warns against thinking "too highly," St. Paul is not referring to exalted thought in general, but to such pretensions as serve mainly to exalt the thinker. His caution is directed against engaging in sentiments and perspectives that chiefly promote one's self-importance.

From such texts one gains the impression that there must have been Christians at Rome who were "giving themselves airs," as we say, indulging in the sorts of reflections that made them feel superior to others. This impression is further confirmed only a few verses later when St. Paul tells those Romans, "Be mindful (*phronountes*) of one another, not setting your mind on high things (*me ta hypsela phronountes*), but associating with the humble. Do not be mindful (*phronimoi*) about yourselves" (12:16, author's translation).

The church at Rome was not the only one to be afflicted with this problem. A good measure of St. Paul's correspondence with the church at Corinth seems likewise to have been preoccupied with a group in that place which boasted of a spiritual "knowledge" (*gnosis*) not enjoyed by the rest of the congregation. To such as these St. Paul was obliged to insist that "Knowledge puffs up, but love edifies. And if anyone thinks that he knows anything, he knows nothing yet as he ought to know" (1 Cor. 8:1, 2). Since St. Paul himself, when he founded the church at Corinth, had deliberately forsworn any attempt to appeal to a merely human yearning for wisdom (cf. 2:1–5), those Corinthians guilty of this fault may well have been brought to conversion by the efforts of the evangelist Apollos, whom we know to have been an especially learned man (cf. Acts 18:24—19:1). We also know that there was a group at Corinth whose members actually claimed, "I am of Apollos" (1 Cor. 1:12), a claim that apparently caused the man himself no little embarrassment (cf. 16:12).

Opposite to the uppish ideas against which St. Paul warns some of the Roman and Corinthian Christians are those sentiments found at the beginning of Psalm 130 (Hebrew 131): "O Lord, my heart is not arrogant, my eyes are not haughty. I have not pursued high matters, nor marvels far above me."

It would be easy to interpret such texts, and to view such a problem, as part of the ongoing moral concern for humility and intellectual modesty that has burdened the history of philosophy for many centuries. Indeed, the entire legacy of Socrates was built over the graves of the Sophists, whom Socrates proved to be not nearly so wise as they pretended.

Holy Scripture's call for humility of the mind, however, involves a great deal more than cultivating a modest epistemology, a proper respect for the limits of human thought. The human race surely did not require a special divine revelation to discourage it from thinking too highly of its mental powers. China, India, Egypt, Greece, Rome, and other places all provided sages to spread that important message to us.

No, the true foundation for intellectual humility involves a great deal more than an acceptance of human limitations. It requires Christ. Indeed, faced with God's wisdom in Christ, philosophy's sane quest for mental modesty seems, itself, dreadfully presumptuous. It is the deep humility of the Truth Himself, the source of all truth, that provides adequate ground for man's proper humility of the mind.

It is from Christ that our minds are fed with the milk of divine truth. Apart from Him we can do nothing, we can know nothing. Thus our psalm goes on to pray: "Were I not humble-minded, but had exalted my soul, like a child deprived of its mother's milk—let that be as the recompense of my soul."

PSALM 131 (132)
O LORD, REMEMBER DAVID
≈

As Israel's mounting pilgrims neared the top of Mount Zion and beheld the glory of the temple in greater detail, they sometimes spoke thus to one another: "See what manner of stones and what buildings!" (Mark 13:1). They doubtless also reflected, some of them, on how that temple came to be on Mount Zion, and such reflections perhaps go far to explain why Psalm 131 (Hebrew 132) is found toward the end of these "psalms of ascent." This psalm is concerned, after all, with David's role in the construction of Jerusalem's temple.

As the pilgrims remembered King David in the context of the temple, they prayed that the Lord would do so too: "O Lord, remember David and all his self-abasement—how he swore unto the Lord, and vowed an oath to the God of Jacob." And exactly what were the terms of David's oath? "The shelter of my house I shall not enter, nor mount to lie upon my bed; neither close my eyes to sleep, nor let my eyelids drop in slumber, nor give repose unto my brow—till I should find the Lord a place, a shelter for the God of Jacob."

There are several details in these lines most striking and worthy of comment. First, there is a pronounced delay in the pace. The verses move very slowly and deliberately, as though David were quite tired. Each movement is detailed: entering the house, climbing the steps to go to bed, closing the eyelids and resting the eyes, letting the head sink into the pillow. It is the entire process of relaxing and falling asleep. But the irony, of course, is that David is *not* going to do any of these things! He looks longingly, as it were, at a coveted chance to rest, but he forswears indulging it, until he accomplish this great task of building the Lord a temple.

Second, the reason prompting David to make this vow is that the Lord Himself does not yet have a dwelling comparable to David's own. (The same word, *skenoma*, translated here as "shelter," is used to speak of both David's house and the Lord's.) Although the narrative descriptions of David's resolve (cf. 2 Sam. 7:1–13; 1 Chr. 22:7; Acts 7:46) do not speak specifically of an oath in this respect, we know that David was disturbed by the circumstance that his own dwelling was so much superior to the Lord's desert tabernacle (2 Sam. 7:2). This sentiment of deep piety in David's soul is what our psalm calls his *praütes*, meekness or self-abasement.

Third, we are well advised not to interpret literally every detail of our psalm's description of David's oath. Otherwise we might conclude that David never again went to bed, since he did not, in fact, build the temple. Nonetheless, there is good reason to believe that David sometimes went to bed toward the end of his life (cf. 1 Kin. 1:1–4)!

In ascribing this large role to David in the construction of Solomon's temple, Psalm 131 is in harmony with the perspective in 1 Chr. 28 and 29, where David is described as making the necessary preparations for the building and conferring on Solomon the mandate to build it. The affinities between Psalm 131 and the theology of the Chronicler are further indicated by the latter's recording Solomon quoting a verse from this psalm: "Arise, O Lord God, to Your resting place, / You and the ark of Your strength" (2 Chr. 6:41). (It is at this point in the psalm, Orthodox Christians will recognize, that the Blessed Sacrament is moved from the altar to the table of oblation during the Presanctified Liturgy during Great Lent.)

The psalm goes on to tell of God's answer to David's plan, which involved a special covenant with David's family. If David had thought to build God a house (*bayit*), God would build David a *bayit*, in the sense of a household dynasty. The latter would be divinely protected forever: "For David's sake, Your servant, scorn not the face of Your anointed (*christos*). The Lord has pledged His truth to David, which He will never nullify: 'From your very body's fruit, will I set a man upon your throne.'"

In this perspective, the proper place for the temple is Jerusalem precisely because it *is* David's city. That is to say, the *place* of God's covenant is the House of David, so the temple is designated as God's house *because* of His covenant with David. After saying that David's "sons shall sit upon your throne forevermore," Psalm 131 goes on immediately to speak of the temple: "For the Lord selected Zion for Himself; He has chosen her for His own dwelling: 'This is My resting place forever; here will I dwell, for I have chosen her.'"

The Church reads all such texts as prophecies, of course, finding their fulfillment solely in Christ our Lord. He is at once the new Temple and that very son of David who gives defining substance to God's covenant sworn to the son of Jesse. When we pray this psalm, it is entirely with reference to its fulfillment in Jesus, *the* Anointed One and *the* Temple.

PSALM 132 (133)

BEHOLD HOW GOOD AND DELIGHTFUL A THING

୶

Psalm 132 (Hebrew 133) is arguably among the loveliest of the small compositions in Holy Scripture: "Behold how good and delightful a thing, for brothers to abide as one; like balsam on the head, descending down on the beard, the beard of Aaron, descending to the hem of his robe; like the dew of Hermon, descending on the mountains of Zion. For there the Lord decreed blessing, life for evermore."

This translation preserves a delicate but structurally important feature of both the Hebrew and the canonical Greek texts; namely, the psalm has only one finite verb, and it is found in the final line: "decreed" (*eneteilato, tsivvah*). The blessing in this psalm is a matter of God's command and ordinance.

Now the blessing (*evlogian, berakah*) decreed of the Lord is everlasting life (*zoen heos tou aionos, haiim 'ad ha'olam*), and He decreed it in the holy mountains of Zion. This is Jerusalem, which appears in the final chapters of Revelation as the home of those brothers who abide as one. This is the ultimate meaning of "good and delightful." It is eternal life.

The place of the Lord's decree, "there," is accented in both the Greek (*ekei*) and the Hebrew (*sham*). The blessing of this psalm is not some sort of general benediction poured out at random; it is specified, rather, with respect to place. It is defined and fixed in the institutions of the holy city of Jerusalem, especially in the priesthood, most particularly the high priesthood of Aaron. That is to say, the blessing decreed by the Lord is related to the consecration of that priesthood by which the people of God is defined as a priestly people and holy nation.

The emphasized "there" of the last verse stands in structural parallel and contrast with the earlier sense of "here" conveyed by the "behold" (*idou, hinneh*), with which the psalm begins. The poem commences, then, with the atmosphere and feeling of presence. Accordingly, there are no verbal sentences; the action in these early verses is entirely conveyed, as in both the Hebrew and Greek, by an infinitive, "to abide," and the threefold repetition of a single participle, "descending."

Moreover, this steady descent is described so as to suggest the slow flowing down of a consecratory blessing, and the same words for "descending" are used for both the priestly oil and the dew of Hermon in both the Greek (*katabainon*) and the Hebrew (*yored*). This sustained blessing is also conveyed by the advancing flow of the ointment, poured out in consecration on the high priest's head, then oozing down to saturate his priestly beard, before flowing onto the hem of his priestly vestment. The "oil" of the Hebrew (*shemen*) is enriched and sweetened to "balsam" (*myron*) in the Greek text.

The high priest's beard is mentioned twice in connection with this bountiful anointing, portraying the accumulated saturation of the blessing into this supreme symbol of his manhood. (Indeed, Holy Scripture is very strict on the point. The priest may not shave his beard, and the man who can't grow a beard cannot be a priest.)

Beneath the beard of the high priest there hangs from his neck a pectoral of stones on which are engraved the names of Israel's twelve tribes. When he comes to appear before the Lord, Aaron thus bears all of Israel upon his breast, directly in the path of the descending ointment of his sacerdotal consecration. The whole people of God is rendered holy in his priesthood. The oneness celebrated in this psalm is the unity of God's people gathered in worship with their priest.

This pervasive saturation is high and exotic poetry, of course. Indeed, the picture of the heavy dew descending all the way from Mount Hermon, up in Syria, down to Jerusalem in Judah can only be introduced in a poetic context already conditioned by the psalm's earlier and more plausible images.

The priesthood of Aaron is, moreover, the ministry preparatory to the definitive priesthood of our Lord Jesus Christ. It is He who ever lives to make intercession for us (cf. Heb. 7:25). "For brothers to abide as one" is the blessing given to the Church, described in St. Paul's epistles as the "body of Christ" and in St. John's Gospel as the vine with its branches. Our unity is in Christ, and more specifically in that unchangeable priesthood by which He ministers in heaven on our behalf, the one mediator between God and man. *There* the Lord decreed blessing.

PSALM 133 (134)

In certain times of festival it was apparently the custom for ancient Israel to spend the night, or part of the night, in worship. Thus, we read in Isaiah, "You shall have a song / As in the night when a holy festival is kept" (30:29). It is not difficult to imagine that the last of the "psalms of ascent," Psalm 133 (Hebrew 134), was used on such occasions: "Behold, now, bless the Lord, all you servants of the Lord, who stand in the house of the Lord, in the courts of the house of our God. By night lift up your hands unto the holy place and bless the Lord. May the Lord bless you from Zion, the Maker of heaven and earth."

It will come as no surprise that this psalm has a long usage in the Church as part of the day's final canonical hour, Compline. For example, in the monastic Rule of St. Benedict in the sixth century, this is the last psalm prescribed for recitation at that hour.

Near the beginning of the Book of Psalms, Psalm 5 had spoken of "standing" before the Lord in the morning hours; that psalm has always been favored at that time, whether for Matins or First Hour (Prime). Now the present psalm, traditionally prayed at Compline, speaks again of "standing" before God during the night (cf. 1 Chr. 23:30).

Virtually all physical postures, of course, are fitting for prayer. One of these, kneeling, has long been thought especially proper for certain prayers (cf. 2 Chr. 6:13; Dan. 6:10; Luke 22:41; Acts 7:60; 9:40; 21:5). A lesser variant of it is the genuflection (cf. Is. 45:23; Rom. 14:11; ; Eph. 3:14; Phil. 2:10). Even more intense than kneeling is the full prostration (cf. Matt. 28:9; Rev. 4:10; 5:8), sometimes moderated to a simple bow (cf. 2 Chr. 29:30). Sitting seems to be a prayer-posture particularly fitting for settings of contemplative quiet (cf. Luke 8:35; 10:39). Many, too, have found walking to be a fine way of communing with the Lord (cf. Luke 24:13–17), nor should even lying on one's bed be excluded from among the acceptable postures of prayer (cf. Psalms 4:4; 62:6). If Holy Scripture does anywhere explicitly speak of prayer while hanging upside down, I have not yet discovered the text, but my search goes on.

Of all positions to be adopted for prayer, however, the most favored in the Orthodox Church has been that of steady standing, which singularly combines the features of dignity, attentiveness, readiness, obedience, and vigilance. Outside of those seasons and occasions that call for kneeling or prostration, standing is our most normal position for prayer when we worship, whether alone or with one another in church.

Prayer at night is much recommended in Holy Scripture, especially under the aspect of vigilance. Thus, we are told that we should be watching for the Bridegroom who comes at midnight (Matt. 25:6, 13). The spirit of such prayer is well summarized in the troparion of Bridegroom Matins: "Behold, the Bridegroom comes at midnight, and blessed is the servant whom He shall find wakeful. But he whom He finds neglectful is truly unworthy. Behold, therefore, my soul, beware, lest you fall into deep slumber, and the door of the kingdom be closed against you, and you be delivered over to death."

Since the Lord Himself gave us such warning, it is not surprising that He spent nights or parts of nights in prayer (cf. Mark 1:35; Luke 6:12). Likewise, midnight prayer seems to have been well established in the apostolic band (cf. Acts 16:25). Night was a special time to speak with the Lord (cf. John 3:2). Moreover, the earliest Christians seem to have spent each Saturday night in prayer, holding vigil in preparation for the celebration of the Divine Mysteries on Sunday morning. Besides the description in Acts 20, we also have, from the first decade of the second century, the report on the Christians written by Pliny to Trajan.

If prayer at night is particularly necessary, it is because the demons seem to be especially active after dark. One observes how "night" becomes a symbol of the hour of dark powers in the Gospel of St. John (cf. 3:19, 20; 9:4; 11:10; 13:30). Similarly, the other Gospels speak of keeping vigilance with Jesus during His nocturnal agony.

Prayer at night pertains only to this world, however, for there will be no night in heaven (cf. Rev. 21:25).

PSALM 134 (135)
PRAISE THE NAME OF THE LORD

It is the liturgical tradition of the Church to chant Psalm 134 (Hebrew 135) and Psalm 135 in sequence. In the West, particularly in traditional monastic usage, these were sung on ordinary Wednesdays at Vespers, which was simply the place where they happened to fall in St. Benedict's weekly distribution of the Psalter. In the East, on the other hand, the favored place of these two psalms is on the solemn feast days of the Church, when they together form the central core of Matins. This liturgical combination is called the *polyeleion,* meaning "many mercies," a title derived from that constantly repeated line in Psalm 135, "His mercy endures forever."

Inasmuch as these two psalms summon the memory of God's deeds of merciful intervention as the basis for His praise, it seems entirely proper that they be sung on the Church's special feast days, which commemorate various aspects of His saving work in our Lord Jesus Christ.

In the New Testament, after all, God's redemptive interventions in the history of ancient Israel are viewed as prophetic foreshadowings of our true salvation in Christ. Thus, the Lord's election of Israel (cf. Ex. 19:5; Deut. 7:6) is the foreshadowing and firstfruits of the Church. That is to say, Israel herself was "chosen" as God's people only in view of Christ, who is the theological root of our own election (*ekloge*—cf. Rom. 9:10–13; 11:5, 6; 2 Pet. 1:10).

Thus, it is of our own election in Christ that we sing in Psalm 134—and most specifically on the great feast days of the Church—"For the Lord has chosen Jacob for Himself, Israel for His own possession."

This election of the Church is not an afterthought in salvation history. It is what God had in mind, rather, *from the very beginning* of His choices. Abraham, Isaac, David, whoever was chosen, was chosen for the sake of Christ, and we ourselves are chosen in Christ. As in Psalm 134, this awareness of God's choice *from the beginning* of biblical history is the font and motive of that very thanksgiving that identifies the Church. Thus wrote St. Paul: "But we are bound to give thanks to God always for you, brethren beloved by the Lord, because God *from the beginning chose you* for salvation through sanctification by the Spirit and belief in the truth, to which He called you by our gospel, for the obtaining of the glory of our Lord Jesus Christ" (2 Thess. 2:13, 14).

Moreover, this "election" is a reality "known" to the Church, a component of the Church's self-awareness. This does not mean, as some later Christians wrongly argued, that each individual Christian can infallibly foreknow his final perseverance in grace, as though the Christian becomes incapable of apostasy and final loss. Ultimate perseverance is not a matter of our infallible knowledge. If this were so, the Bible would contain none of its dire warnings against apostasy and final loss. What this truth means, rather, is that the Church herself is infallibly aware of being God's own Chosen People, His elect in Christ.

And this knowledge is real knowledge. Thus, within the opening lines of the earliest book of the New Testament, St. Paul tells the newly converted Thessalonians that they should be "knowing, beloved brethren, your election (*eklogen*) by God" (1 Thess. 1:4).

It is no accident, then, that in Psalm 134, the memory of our election is immediately followed by an assertion of our knowledge of God: "For I know that the Lord is great, and our Lord above all gods."

What was true of ancient Israel's election by God is likewise true of His other interventions on Israel's behalf; they were all foreshadowings of His salvific deeds in Christ in these final times. Thus, Israel's redemption from Egypt, explicitly commemorated in our psalm, was the foreshadowing of His over-throw of the demonic pharaoh to whom the human race, without Christ, is held in the vilest bondage. Likewise, the God-given conquest of the Promised Land by the Chosen People, along with the defeat of the various threatening nations, was the prefiguration of our entrance into the realm of eternal life through the vanquishing of the many spiritual enemies who impede our path. Every day, but especially on the great feast days of the Church, we celebrate our victory over the likes of Sihon and Og and our entrance into the land of milk and honey.

PSALM 135 (136)

CONFESS TO THE LORD, FOR HE IS GOOD

Because the line "for His mercy endures forever" appears in each of its twenty-six verses, Psalm 135 (Hebrew 136), combined with Psalm 134, is known in the Orthodox worship as the *polyeleion*, or "manifold mercy." In the East, where it is part of the nineteenth Kathisma, it is also an individual Matins psalm, used on Sundays between the "Lord is Light" and the troparion of the Resurrection. In the West, on the other hand, it was traditionally assigned to Wednesday Vespers, normally in the third tone, with its refrain used as an antiphon. Indeed, this psalm fits any and all contexts, and the litany-like refrain makes it one of easiest psalms to memorize and sing spontaneously on every occasion.

After three introductory verses that call for the praise of God, one may distinguish three stanzas in this psalm. Stanza 1, verses 4–9, we may think of as the "cosmic stanza," because it deals with God's work of Creation described in the opening verses of Genesis. This stanza is structured on four verbs (descriptive participles in Hebrew): "does great wonders . . . made the heavens . . . laid out the earth . . . made great lights." Verses 8 and 9 are a continuation of verse 7 ("the sun to rule by day . . . the moon and stars to rule by night") and bring the "cosmic" portion of the psalm to a close.

But Creation is the stage on which God makes history, so in stanza 2, verses 10–22, we move from Genesis to Exodus. This we may think of as the "history stanza," containing material from the Books of Exodus, Numbers, and Joshua. In this stanza likewise there is a fourfold series of verbs (again, descriptive participles in Hebrew), this time mainly in pairs, that describe God's redemptive activity for His people: (1) "struck Egypt . . . and brought out Israel;" (2) "divided the Red Sea . . . and made Israel pass through;" (3) "overthrew Pharaoh . . . led His people through the wilderness;" (4) "struck down great kings . . . slew famous kings . . . and gave their land as a heritage."

Finally, stanza 3, verses 23–26, speaks of God's continuing care for His people down through the ages. He is not simply a God of the past, but of "us," the present generation of believers. The last part of the psalm is about here and now: "remembered us in our lowly estate . . . rescued us from our enemies . . . gives food to all flesh."

Thus, Psalm 135 pursues a threefold theme: creation, deliverance, and the continued care of the redeemed. In this respect, the triple structure of our psalm is identical with that of the Nicene Creed: God made us, God saved us,

God stays and provides for us all days unto the end. In the Creed, this structure is explicitly Trinitarian: "one God, the Father Almighty, the Creator . . . one Lord, Jesus Christ . . . the Holy Spirit, the Lord and Giver of life."

Thus, there seems to be a special propriety in the Eastern custom of chanting this psalm at Sunday Matins, in the context of the weekly Resurrection Gospel (the eleven Eothonia). Sunday is the first day of Creation, the day of the paschal deliverance, and the day of Pentecost, the outpouring of the abiding Spirit in the Church. In the East every Sunday is the feast of the Holy Trinity.

Psalm 135 insists, literally in every verse, that the root of all of God's activity in this world, beginning even with the world's creation, is mercy—*hesed*. This mercy is eternal—*le'olam*—"forever." Mercy is the cause and reason of all that God does. He does nothing, absolutely nothing, except as an expression of His mercy. His mercy stretches out to both extremes of infinity. "For His mercy endures forever" is the palimpsest that lies under each line of Holy Scripture. Thus, too, from beginning to end of any Orthodox service, the word "mercy" appears more than any other word. The encounter with God's mercy is the root of all Christian worship. Everything else that can be said of God is but an aspect of His mercy. Mercy is the defining explanation of everything that God has revealed of Himself. Every Orthodox service of worship, from Nocturnes to Compline, is a *polyeleion*, a celebration of God's sustained and abundant mercy. What we touch, or see, or hear, or taste—from the flames that flicker before the icons and the prayers our voices pour forth, to the billowing incense and the mystic contents of the Chalice—all is mercy. Mercy is the explanation of every single thought that God has with respect to us. When we deal with God, everything is mercy; all we will ever discover of God will be the deepening levels of His great, abundant, overflowing, rich and endless mercy. "For His mercy endures forever" is the eternal song of the saints.

PSALM 136 (137)

BY THE RIVERS OF BABYLON

It is probably easier to identify the original setting of Psalm 136 (Hebrew 137) than of any other psalm. The opening lines give it away: "By the rivers of Babylon, there we sat and wept, when we remembered Zion. On the willows in the midst of it, we hung up our harps." This is a psalm of exile, and the setting is the Babylonian Captivity of the sixth century before Christ.

That exile of ancient Israel in Babylon is usually dated from 586 BC, the year that Jerusalem actually fell and was destroyed (cf. 2 Kin. 25:1–11), to 538, when Cyrus the Mede, having conquered Babylon the previous year, permitted the exiles to return to Jerusalem (cf. Ezra 1:1–4). It is useful to bear in mind, nonetheless, that some Jews, the Prophet Ezekiel among them, had already been taken to Babylon as hostages eleven years earlier (cf. 2 Kin. 24:10–16). Moreover, not all of the captives were able to return home, and their descendants remain in the territory of Babylon to this day.

Babylon was a land of great rivers, tributaries and canals. Indeed, the Greeks referred to that territory as Mesopotamia, "the midst of the rivers," a name reminiscent of the opening Greek words of our psalm, *epi ton potamon*. The major rivers of that region are the Tigris and Euphrates, but mention is made of other waterways. For example, the Prophet Ezekiel wrote of his inaugural vision "by the River Chebar" (Ezek. 1:1–3), a reference to the Kabari Canal that flowed out of the Euphrates, through the city of Babylon, and then back to its mother river. Such canals were essential to the mercantile economy of the Babylonian Empire. Another of these was known to the Greeks as the Eulaeus Canal, near the city of Susa. It was the site of an ecstatic vision given to another of Israel's prophets, Daniel, who refers to it as the River Ulai (Dan. 8:2). Daniel also had a vision beside the great Tigris (10:4).

In sum, the reference to the "rivers of Babylon" in the first line of our psalm is very important as an historical fact. We shall see presently that it is also important as a literary and theological image.

The exiles in Babylon have hung up their musical instruments on the weeping willow trees, sad, homesick, and dejected. Apparently, moreover, they were being taunted by their captors: "For those who took us captive sought from us some lyrics, and they who enslaved us asked to hear a song. 'Sing for us,' they said, 'from the canticles of Zion.'"

And just how can this be done? That is, "How shall we sing a song of the

Lord in a land far away?" Impossible? Well, not entirely. It is a striking irony of Psalm 136 that, having asserted the impossibility of singing a song of Jerusalem in the foreign land of Babylon, we nonetheless go on to do so! "Should I forget you, O Jerusalem, let my right hand be enfeebled! May I choke on my tongue, if I fail to think of you! If I do not hold Jerusalem as the wellspring of my joy."

This is a psalm of two cities, Babylon and Jerusalem, nor were Ezekiel and Daniel the last visionaries to write of them. The beloved John likewise beheld both of these cities in mystic vision. The first, Babylon, he describes as the "great harlot who sits on many waters" (Rev. 17:1), the source of her great wealth and power. "The waters which you saw," he was told, "where the harlot sits, are peoples, multitudes, nations, and tongues" (17:15). Such are the rivers where we sit and weep, when we remember Zion.

Babylon represents both exile and oppression, for John was told: "And the woman whom you saw is that great city which reigns over the kings of the earth" (17:18). Our psalm looks forward to the final downfall of that city, which St. John goes on to describe as the throwing of a millstone into the sea (18:21). On the willows of Babylon we did hang our harps, as though in prophecy of that day when the sound of the harp would be heard there no more (18:22). Should anyone feel daunted by the violent feelings that Psalm 136 entertains with respect to Babylon, let him consult the rejoicing of the saints over the fall of Babylon in John's mighty vision: "Rejoice over her, O heaven, and you holy apostles and prophets, for God has avenged you on her!" (18:20).

And Jerusalem, the wellspring of our joy? Her too John beholds, likewise as a woman, the Bride of the Lamb, the Holy City, descending out of heaven. It is the city where singing and harps are heard forever, our exile over at last (21:9, 10).

PSALM 137 (138)

The word "context" is an expression most worthy of reflection. Though often used as a synonym for "setting" or "situation," the word implies a good deal more than the mere surroundings or atmosphere of some object. "Context" obviously has to do with "text." To speak of something as having a context means, first of all, that the thing in question is being taken as a "text," a piece of writing, as it were, something with a meaning to be discovered. That is to say, it implies that the object in question is being considered under the aspect of its intelligibility, of its significance. To speak of the context of something, then, is to say that that something is being interpreted; it is being treated as a "text." Context, in short, is an instrument of interpretation. The interpretation of anything involves, among other aspects, an investigation of how the thing "fits in."

Psalm 137 (Hebrew 138) may be regarded as a meditation on the context of prayer; it is a serene reflection on what it means to speak to God. In approaching this psalm, it is useful to keep ready at hand the question, "What sorts of things are involved in prayer?" Thus, it begins, "I will confess to You, O Lord, with all my heart; in the sight of the angels will I sing to You, for You have heard all the words of my mouth."

What does it mean to pray? It is first of all a matter of the heart. The "confession" (*exsomologesomai*) of prayer is interior. Especially in this modern age of subjectivity, it would be easy to interpret this truth as implying that one's prayer is being made "with real feeling." Indeed, one meets many individuals who spend most of their prayer time attempting to "feel" the right sorts of things, so that prayer becomes an exercise in the cultivation of proper sentiments. Or worse, one meets those who have actually stopped praying because their hearts are "no longer in it," so that they do not "feel sincere." Alas, it is common these days to identify sincerity with emotional spontaneity. The word "heart," in the biblical and traditional vocabulary of prayer, bears no such meaning.

When we speak of prayer "from the heart" we mean, rather, from the very core of ourselves, the center of decision and resolve, a region vastly deeper than our emotions. It is at that level that God speaks to us. Truly, it is with a view to finding our hearts that we make the great efforts that prayer itself demands of us.

So when we begin to pray, we endeavor to involve, as best we can, our inner core of decision and resolve. To the extent that we can find them or know them at all, we turn our hearts to God, and we confess Him. We do it briefly; otherwise the very effort becomes a distraction from prayer.

From the context of our hearts, especially the placing of our minds within our hearts, we turn to God's "context"; that is to say, the holy angels. We place our hearts in His throne room; "in the sight of the angels will I sing to You." Strictly speaking, there is no such thing as "private prayer" in the Christian life. Our prayer to God is always sustained by the angelic presence. Even so was the prayer of Christ our Lord (cf. Luke 22:43–45).

The next dimension of prayer's context is direction: "Toward Your holy temple shall I bow down, and Your holy name will I confess, for You have magnified Your holy name above all things." As all regular visitors to Holy Scripture know, the true temple of God is Jesus Christ our Lord. He is the definitive abiding-place where mankind finds God. The goal of prayer, after all, is the union of God and man, so the proper foundation of prayer is the Incarnation, in which God and man are joined definitively. It is "the synthesis achieved by God, which carries the name of Jesus Christ" (Hans Urs Von Balthasar). The Christian religion knows nothing of prayer outside of Christology.

This principle is likewise the meaning of the words that follow: "Your holy name will I confess, for You have magnified Your holy name above all things." It is in God's magnification of the name of Jesus that all Christian prayer is safely placed. The fundamental confession that we make in our hearts is "Jesus is Lord!"

The name and Lordship of Jesus is the very substance of our prayer. When, in a later line, our psalm speaks of the salvific stretching forth of God's hand, we do well to keep in mind that this is done only in the name of Jesus (cf. Acts 4:30).

PSALM 138 (139)

LORD, YOU HAVE SEARCHED ME AND KNOWN ME

With some exceptions, the psalms are generally not to be recited very fast. Indeed, the structure of some of them shows that considerable care has been taken to slow the pace down. There is a pronounced disposition to say many things twice or more, for instance, so that the mind is not permitted to race on to the next idea right away.

Psalm 138 (Hebrew 139) may serve to illustrate this extensive characteristic. The Psalmist could have written, very simply, "Lord, Your knowledge of me is total." This brief statement would have said, in essence, what the first strophe of this psalm does say: "Lord, You have searched me and known me. You know my sitting down and my rising up; You understand my thoughts from afar. You encompass my paths and my lying down and are acquainted with all my ways. A word is not yet on my tongue, but You know it already."

Here, instead of one verb to describe God's knowledge of the heart, the author uses six. Obviously he wants to dwell on the thought; he is not anxious to leave it. He wants the conviction to sink deeply into his soul that God knows him through and through, so he comes at the idea from a variety of angles and aspects—search and know, sitting down and rising up and lying down, paths and ways, thoughts and words.

The psalm continues in the same vein: "You have beset me behind and before, and laid Your hand upon me." He is not content to say that this idea is transcendent; he must say it twice: "Such knowledge is too wonderful for me; it is high, I cannot attain to it."

The dominant sense of this psalm is similarly conveyed in an ancient Latin prayer that Archbishop Cranmer translated for the beginning of the Anglican Holy Communion service: "Almighty God, unto whom all hearts are open, all desires known, and from whom no secrets are hid . . ." Observe that the same idea is pronounced three times. This sense of God's thorough knowledge of us is not something that one wants to let go of. Like a diamond, it is turned in the light, to be seen from several angles, but it is always the same diamond, and the facets of it are interrelated.

And because God's knowledge of us is complete, it is impossible to escape His gaze. Once again the poet uses several lines to meditate on this fact, moving in several directions, as it were: "If I ascend to heaven [up!], You are there. If I make my bed in the netherworld [down!], behold, You are there. If I take

277

the wings of the morning [east!] and dwell at the uttermost parts of the sea [west!], even there Your hand shall lead me, and Your right hand hold me."

Here we are, ten verses into the psalm, and so far there is only a single idea. The poet is still not finished with it, however. He now switches from space imagery to symbolisms of light: "If I say, 'Surely the darkness will cover me,' even the night will be a light around me. Yea, the darkness hides me not from You, but the night shines as the day; to You the darkness and the night are both alike." Once again he has repeated the same motif several times. God's knowledge of our hearts is not an idea that he is disposed to let go of.

After these images of space and light, the psalmist moves to a consideration of time. He goes back to his very roots of being, his mysterious formation in the womb: "For You take hold of my inner parts; You covered me in my mother's womb." Is that sufficient? Oh, no. He must say it all again: "I will praise You that I am awesomely and wonderfully put together; marvelous are Your works, and my soul knows it well." Then, using a bold comparison of his mother's womb to the depths of the earth, he goes on to reflect on his own gestation as a prelude to his coming life: "My substance was not hidden from You, when I was being formed in secret, and strangely put together in the depths of the earth. You saw my substance, as yet unfinished, but all my days were written in Your book before a single one of them came into being." Even in the deepest past, God knows the future.

Then there is a quick twist. The tone of the psalm has, hitherto, been calm and contemplative, but we suddenly learn that there is trouble afoot: "Surely You will slay the wicked, O God; depart from me, therefore, you bloody men." This dramatic mention of enemies makes us realize that, even while making this deep meditation on a single theme, the poet is somehow fighting for the very life of his soul. He resolves this problem by placing his soul ever more deeply under the gaze of God: "Search me, O God, and know my heart; try me, and know my thoughts."

The psalm's final strophe thus indicates that this whole effort takes place in a situation of strife and conflict. His quest is for salvation, and salvation consists in God's salvific knowledge of us: "If anyone loves God, this one is known by Him" (1 Cor. 8:3); "Then I shall know just as I also am known" (13:12). So the believer seeks refuge in God's saving knowledge of him and ends by praying that God will ever lead him "in the path eternal."

PSALM 139 (140)

SAVE ME FROM THE EVIL MAN, O LORD

⚬

The four canonical Gospels, composed by individual evangelists writing within the contextual experience and concerns of local congregations at specific times, are each marked by easily discerned differences in emphasis and perspective.

We may take the Gospel of Mark by way of illustration. According to the unanimous testimony of all the second-century writers who commented on the subject, the setting of Mark's composition was the Neronic persecution of the church at Rome in the aftermath of the fire of July, AD 64. The raw ferocity of Nero's oppression of the Roman Christians, whom he blamed for that fire, was a source of wonderment even to the pagan historians, Tacitus and Suetonius. In was during that period that the Apostle Peter was executed by crucifixion on Vatican Hill, and his associate Mark, summarizing the preaching of the chief of the Apostles, addressed his work to that congregation enduring severe hardship and death. These facts easily account for the singular emphasis on the message of the Cross which is a distinguishing characteristic of Mark's Gospel.

Casting a massive shadow over all of Mark's work is the darkly rising Cross. After chapter one, nearly every scene in Mark betrays some shaded reference to the Lord's coming Passion and death. At the beginning of chapter two, for instance, there begins a series of five controversy stories, in which the Lord's enemies start to show themselves and challenge Him. Already in 2:7 Jesus is accused of blasphemy, which becomes the point on which He will eventually be condemned to death in 14:64. At the end of these five initial controversy stories we are told that "the Pharisees went out and immediately plotted with the Herodians against Him, how they might destroy Him" (3:6). That early and evil resolve will be played out through the rest of the narrative. The first reference to the Lord's betrayal by Judas occurs in 3:19, followed immediately by the malicious accusation of the scribes that Jesus was in league with the devil (3:22). And so on. The theme of the Cross never leaves Mark, intruding a somber hue into the contours of its every scene.

Psalm 139 (Hebrew 140), which the Christian liturgical tradition uniformly places toward the end of each week, may be prayed by us believers as the deep supplication of Christ our Lord, who lives, ministers, and prays through these various scenes in Mark's story.

Jesus' doom has early been decided. Already His enemies are joined in league. His betrayer has by now been identified. The nocturnal shadows close about Him. Jesus prays: "Save Me from the evil man, O Lord; from the unjust man deliver Me, from those who think injustice in their hearts, whose days are spent contriving strife. Their tongues they sharpen like a snake, the serpents' poison lies behind their lips."

Scene by scene, the story moves forward to the Cross. The parable of the sower speaks of those who are "outside" (Mark 4:11, 12) and even of persecution (4:17). Jesus is ridiculed (5:40) and held without honor (6:3, 4), and tells of those who refuse to listen (6:11). To foreshadow the Lord's coming death, His forerunner is beheaded (6:14–29). Almost the whole of Mark's chapter 7 is a sustained argument with Jesus' enemies. He continues to pray: "Guard Me, O Lord, from the sinner's hand; save Me from unrighteous men, who plot to trip My every step. The proud have laid a snare for Me; they spread their nets to catch My feet; along My path they set a trap."

After another warning about His plotting enemies (8:15), there follow the Lord's three predictions of His coming sufferings (8:31; 9:31; 10:33, 34), interspersed with a discourse on taking up the cross (8:34–38), a reference to His being reviled (9:12), and a prophecy of the coming persecutions (10:30). He speaks to Zebedee's sons of the impending cup that He must drink (10:38, 39), while His adversaries seek to implement their murderous resolve against Him (11:18). There follow five more stories of controversy (11:27—12:34), and at last the conspiracy of Jesus' enemies with His betrayer (14:10, 11), leading to His trial and death. Still, our Savior prays, "For to the Lord I said, 'You are My God; O Lord, give heed to the voice of My prayer. Lord, Lord, My salvation's strength, who sheltered My head on the day of strife.'"

PSALM 140 (141)

O LORD, I HAVE CRIED UNTO YOU

≈

Secure and unmistakable is the place of Psalm 140 (Hebrew 141) in the history of Christian worship. It is preeminently the psalm of Vespers. Thus, in the ancient Western monastic tradition, Psalm 140 was appointed for Vespers on Thursday evenings, and a single line of it ("Let my prayer arise in Your sight as the incense") was sung on most nights as the versicle following the vesperal hymn (the "Ambrosian").

In the East the whole of Psalm 140 is still appointed each evening to accompany the great censing at Vespers, a custom that makes it one of the psalms most familiar to Orthodox Christians. Truly, few biblical texts have been more often set to haunting, solemn melodies than the opening lines of this psalm: "O Lord, I have cried unto You. Hear me. Give ear to the voice of my prayer, when I cry unto You. Let my prayer arise in Your sight as the incense, and the lifting of my hands as the evening sacrifice."

Perhaps even more dear to Orthodox Christians is the second chanting of these verses during the solemn censing of the altar after the Old Testament readings during the Vesperal Presanctified Liturgy of Great Lent. In this setting the words are used as an antiphonal refrain after each of the psalm's following verses: "Set a watch, O Lord, before my mouth, and a guarding door about my lips. Incline not my heart to evil words, to make excuses for my sins. Nor with men who do evil, not even the best of them, will I be joined." These lines seem especially fitting to the Lenten season, when particular effort is spent with respect to the custody of the mouth. The Prayer of St. Ephrem, also associated closely with Lent, strikes the same theme.

Because of its reference to the evening sacrifice, one would like to believe that Psalm 140 was used in the ancient Jerusalem temple to accompany that daily rite (cf. Ex. 29:39) and especially the offering of incense as the high priest lit the lamps each evening (30:8). Nonetheless, even though Psalm 133 will refer to the raising of the hands during the nocturnal prayer in the temple, there is no solid evidence that Psalm 140 was used in the setting of the daily evening sacrifice in Old Testament times.

Nonetheless, our psalm's references to those vesperal rituals are clear enough, both the rising incense smoke and the evening sacrifice. Each of these deserves further comment.

First, the Old Testament's "evening sacrifice" was a type of and preparation for that true oblation rendered at the evening of the world, when the Lamb of God, nailed to the Cross, lifted His hands to the Father in sacrificial prayer for the salvation of mankind. This was the true lifting up of the hands, the definitive evening sacrifice offered on Golgotha, by which God marked His seal on human destiny.

Whenever, then, we Christians raise our hands in prayer, as St. Paul tells us to do (cf. 1 Tim. 2:8), it is to symbolize that our prayer, our entire relationship to God, is founded in the power of the Cross. We are thereby proclaiming that we have no access to God except through the Cross of the Lord. The raising of our hands in prayer is acceptable to God only because of its relationship to that true evening sacrifice through which we draw near.

Thus, Tertullian tells the newly baptized to "spread your hands for the first time in the house of your mother" (*On Baptism* 20). "We not only raise them," he says, "we spread them out; and, taking our model from the Lord's Passion, we confess to Christ in prayer" (*On Prayer* 14.). Likewise, commenting on that text of 1 Timothy referenced just above, St. Ambrose asks, "What is it to lift pure hands?" And he answers: "Must you not, in your prayer, show to the nations the cross of the Lord" (*On the Sacraments* 17).

Second, the rising incense smoke as symbolic of prayer is most vividly portrayed in the vision of the heavenly throne room in Revelation: "Then another angel, having a golden censer, came and stood at the altar. He was given much incense, that he should offer it with the prayers of all the saints upon the golden altar which was before the throne. And the smoke of the incense, with the prayers of the saints, ascended before God from the angel's hand" (8:3, 4).

In short, the hour of Vespers daily unites us to two places: the throne room of the Lamb and the hill on which He took away the sins of the world.

PSALM 141 (142)

cℛ

Psalm 141 (Hebrew 142) is normally joined to Psalm 140 each evening at Vespers during the great censing. Their themes and images are very similar.

Psalm 141 is a prayer of desolation and loneliness: "With my voice have I cried to the Lord, with my voice have I prayed to the Lord. Before Him will I pour out my prayer; my desolation shall I declare in His presence. Even as my spirit takes its leave of me, You are the knower of my paths. In the way wherein I walk, have they concealed a snare for me. I looked to my right hand and beheld, but no one there acknowledged me. Flight itself fled from me; there was no patron for my soul. I cried to You, O Lord, I said, 'You are my hope, in the land of the living my inheritance.' Attend to my entreaty, for I am greatly humbled. Deliver me from my pursuers, for they are mightier than I. From the dungeon free my soul, unto the praising of Your holy name. The righteous shall await me, until You recompense me."

Following an impulse early found in biblical history, an unknown hand added a note to the title of this psalm, describing it as the prayer (*tefilla*) offered by David "when he was in the cave." As, in his younger years, he was being pursued by Saul, David probably concealed himself in several caves, there being no shortage of them in the Judean desert. First Samuel 22 tells of his seeking refuge from Saul in "the cave of Adullam," and two chapters later there is a dramatic description of David's concealment from Saul in a cave near Engedi by the Dead Sea. Perhaps these are the scenes that the scribal hand intended. Anyway, it is easy to think of this psalm as inspired by such experiences in the life of David. Or to imagine David praying it later on when he was fleeing from Absalom.

Holy Scripture contains no end of stories in which this would have been an appropriate psalm to pray. One thinks of Jacob fleeing from Esau, walking alone from Beersheba up to Haran at the top of the Fertile Crescent. Such a prayer could have been made just before he laid his head on the stone at Luz: "I cried to You, O Lord, I said, 'You are my hope, in the land of the living my inheritance.' Attend to my entreaty, for I am greatly humbled."

Or the mind may jump forward to his son, Joseph, sold into slavery by his own brothers, falsely accused and thrown into prison, with no friend in this world. This could be the vesperal prayer of Joseph: "I looked to my right hand and beheld, but no one there acknowledged me. Flight itself fled from me; there was no patron for my soul."

The sentiments of this psalm fit well what we know of the prophetic career of Elijah, living in secrecy in the desert, then making the long trek down to Sinai, pursued by the forces of Jezebel, to meet the Lord at the mouth of the ancient cave: "Even as my spirit takes its leave of me, You are the knower of my paths. In the way wherein I walk, have they concealed a snare for me."

Surely this psalm graced the lips of Jeremiah, cast into the well, and drawn out of it only to be imprisoned until the fall of Jerusalem: "From the dungeon free my soul, unto the praising of Your holy name. The righteous shall await me, until You recompense me."

No effort is needed to hear this prayer welling up from the throat of Job, as he sat on his dung heap, bereft of every earthly consolation: "With my voice have I cried to the Lord, with my voice have I prayed to the Lord. Before Him will I pour out my prayer; my desolation shall I declare in His presence."

When we think of those unjustly accused who may have prayed this psalm, various characters come to mind from the Book of Daniel, such as Susannah, the three youths in the furnace, and the Prophet himself. And if this psalm is a fitting supplication for those in prison, then the Prophet Micaiah and John the Baptist are to be counted among those who may have prayed it. Likewise the Apostles Peter, Paul ("in prisons more frequently"), and John.

But most of all, and adding superabundant dignity to the rest, there is Christ our Lord, the Man of sorrows and acquainted with grief, abandoned by His closest friends, betrayed by one of them and denied in public by another, but finding His sole refuge in the Father.

PSALM 142 (143)

In the tradition of the East, Psalm 142 (Hebrew 143) is recited each morning as the final part of the Hexapsalmos (literally, six psalms) near the beginning of Matins. Traditionally in the West, this psalm is prayed at Matins on Saturdays. In both cases it is obviously thought to be a good psalm with which to begin the day. Thus we pray: "Make me to hear Your mercy in the morning, for I put my hope in You."

And as we begin the day with this prayer, we are especially concerned with the governance of God's Holy Spirit: "Your good Spirit will lead me in the right land," we pray with assurance. This governance of the Holy Spirit is essential to who we are, because "as many as are led by the Spirit of God, these are sons of God" (Rom. 8:14). Thus, we pray in this psalm: "Make known to me the way in which I should walk, for to You do I lift up my soul."

In the Bible, walking under the guidance of the Holy Spirit is especially contrasted with walking "according to the flesh," a contrast elaborated in Galatians: "I say then: Walk in the Spirit, and you shall not fulfill the lust of the flesh. For the flesh lusts against the Spirit, and the Spirit against the flesh; and these are contrary to one another, so that you do not do the things that you wish. But if you are led by the Spirit, you are not under the law." The Apostle then goes on to provide contrasting lists of "the works of the flesh" and "the fruit of the Spirit," closing his contrast with the exhortation: "If we live in the Spirit, let us also walk in the Spirit" (Gal. 5:16–25).

It is particularly to be observed here that St. Paul's treatment of the governance of the Holy Spirit is developed in a context of struggle, of resistance to temptation. Being led by the Spirit of God is not an easy thing, for there are spiritual enemies at work to subvert our efforts. In the same respect Psalm 142 also speaks of this experience of conflict with enemies of the soul: "For the enemy has afflicted my soul; he has humbled my life in the earth; he has placed me in the deep shadows, like the dead of the ages."

The Holy Spirit is distinct from our own human spirits. Indeed, this psalm speaks of the human spirit as "anxious" and "failing." To our frail human spirit, the Holy Spirit is a fountain of renewing hope, inasmuch as "the Spirit Himself bears witness with our spirit that we are children of God, and if children, then heirs—heirs of God and joint heirs with Christ, if indeed we suffer with Him, that we may also be glorified together" (Rom. 8:16, 17). Such is the ongoing, daily struggle and suffering with which Psalm 142 is concerned.

At the same time, the very foundation for all this ascetical struggle is grace, not law. Such is certainly the teaching of Galatians 5 and Romans 8 that serves to throw proper light on Psalm 142, in which we pray God, "Hear me in *Your* righteousness," not our own, and then go on to plead: "Enter not into judgment with Your servant, for no living being will be justified before You."

Mother Church is careful to bring this truth to our minds in a special way during Lent, when our ascetical struggle is the toughest and most demanding. Thus, she has us begin the season with the somber assessment of ourselves in the Great Canon of St. Andrew, and each Sunday we pray, in the epiklesis of the Liturgy of St. Basil: " . . . not through our own righteousness, for we have done no good deed upon earth, but because of Your mercies and compassions . . ." Nothing is further from the true religion of Christ than self-justification and "feeling good about ourselves." The one thing obvious about the man of prayer in Psalm 142 is that he appears not to entertain a very positive self-image.

This psalm also speaks of praying with arms raised in cruciform, which early Christian art and literature show to have been the believers' preferred posture of prayer: "I spread out my hands to You."

One may also pray this psalm in a purely Christological sense and reference, with particular attention to the Sabbath rest of Jesus in the grave, awaiting the Sunday Resurrection. Almost every line takes on an enhanced poignancy in that context, which may well have inspired the West (particularly the Rule of St. Benedict) to assign this psalm for Saturday mornings.

PSALM 143 (144)
BLESSED BE THE LORD MY GOD
%

Among the most difficult verses of Holy Scripture are those that speak of the "thousand-year reign of the saints," in Revelation 20. Being difficult, the interpretation of those verses has also spawned considerable disagreement, even in the early years of the Church. For example, in the mid-second century St. Justin the Martyr, who took those verses in a rather literal sense, also testified that not all Christians agreed with him on the point.

In more recent centuries, the interpretation of those references to a millennium was joined to various speculations about the "rapture" (cf. 1 Thess. 4:17) of believers, an interpretive approach arguably disadvantaged by its combination of two obscurities in order to arrive at a third.

Another interpretation of the "millennium," less sensational—and therefore less appealing to those who prefer sensations—draws attention to two other large theological truths by way of exegetical principle: first, that the Kingdom of Christ is not a kingdom of this world (John 18:36); and second, that Christ already reigns in His Church, the house of Jacob, the saints who even now confess His name among the nations (Luke 1:33). This is the reign of grace (Rom. 5:17, 21). And we believers already reign with Him, for we are already kings, and our reign has even now commenced (Rev. 5:10). All this is to say that the millennium is a theological dimension of the present hour, "these last days" (Heb. 1:2).

I take Psalm 143 (Hebrew 144) to be a description of the present reign of Jesus our Lord, the Son of that very David to whom it is ascribed. By this I do not mean Christ's reign solely in heaven, where He is enthroned at the right hand of the Power. This is not a psalm about heaven; it contains too much indication of conflict for this to be the case.

This psalm has in mind, rather, the reign of Christ over the faithful on earth, His dominion over our hearts. This is a psalm about life here below; heaven is the place above the present fray. It is the place from whence we hope to receive our help: "Lord, bow the heavens and descend; touch the peaks, and make them smoke. Flash forth Your lightning bolts and scatter them. Let fly Your missiles, and dismay them. From high above extend Your hand. Snatch me up and rescue me, from the flooding waters' torrent, from the hand of foreign sons."

On earth the reign of Christ in His saints is an experience of the both war and peace, which two components dominate, respectively, the first and second halves of our psalm.

Inasmuch as "all who desire to live godly in Christ Jesus will suffer persecution" (2 Tim. 3:12), the Christian life is properly thought of as combat. Thus, Jesus, as King, is also a military leader, God's final answer to that ancient petition "that our king may judge us and go out before us and fight our battles" (1 Sam. 8:20). Thus, in this psalm we bless Him for teaching our hands to do battle and our fingers to make war, and for delivering us from the evil sword. In the words of the traditional Latin anthem, *Christus vincit, Christus regnat, Christus imperat*—"Christ conquers, Christ reigns, Christ rules." Such were the words sung by the martyrs, their blood poured out for Caesar's pleasure. Those men, women, and children were not in doubt as to the identity of the true King.

Thus, the Christ who appears in the first half of our psalm is the One described by St. John: "Now I saw heaven opened, and behold, a white horse. And He who sat on him was called Faithful and True, and in righteousness He judges and makes war. His eyes were like a flame of fire, and on His head were many crowns. . . . He was clothed with a robe dipped in blood, and His name is called The Word of God. And the armies in heaven, clothed in fine linen, white and clean, followed Him on white horses" (Rev. 19:11–14).

But Christ is also the Prince of Peace, the latter being the theme of the second half of our psalm. This part describes "the blessings of those whose God is the Lord." However literally or figuratively we are to understand the sons like ripened shoots, the daughters like pillars in a temple, the full storehouses, the many sheep and fattened cattle, they all refer to the tranquility and prosperity of a well-governed realm. Such is the Kingdom of the Christ celebrated in this psalm.

PSALM 144 (145)
I WILL EXTOL YOU, O MY GOD AND KING
℘

In traditional Christian usage, some lines of Psalm 144 (Hebrew 145) have made it a prayer popular and suitable for grace before meals: "The eyes of all men hope in You; in fitting season You give them food. Unfolding forth Your hands, You fill all living things with blessing." This first line is translated very literally from the Greek text, for there is unusual force in portraying "hope" as an act of the eyes themselves.

This psalm of most exuberant praise is also the last one composed (in the original Hebrew) as an alphabetic acrostic, and perhaps it is the one that best illustrates the intent of that rhetorical medium. To begin each successive line of a psalm with the next letter of the alphabet is not simply a cute literary trick (as it is in, say, those two marvelous pages of *Bleak House*, where Charles Dickens rings the changes on the characters Boodle, Coodle, Doodle, Foodle, Goodle, and so forth, followed by Buffy, Cuffy, Duffy, etc.). In the Book of Psalms this device serves, rather, to state an aspiration to a truth—namely, that God is to be praised by every sort of sound, that every conceivable formulation of our throat and tongue and lips is to be directed to the divine glory, that no kind of intonation should be deprived of His presence.

And Psalm 144 conveys this verity in grand style. Indeed, this psalm so overflows with rich, resonating magnificence that it is nearly a crime simply to recite it. The very luxury of the sounds needs to be tasted, the mouth and throat filled by its glory. I confess that for many years I have habitually sung this psalm in the shower (always in the eighth tone).

The dominating ideas appear repeatedly, variously combined and in end-less replications: benediction, magnificence, glory, abundance, majesty. To speak of "restraints" imposed on this psalm by reason of its acrostic form (as one curiously benighted commentator does) is a judgment belied by every line. There are no discernible restraints in this most prodigal of psalms. Psalm 144 is sumptuous and extravagant. It is an earthly taste of the very joy of heaven.

The previous psalm, as we saw, was much taken up with the image of Christ as King, a theme that Psalm 144 is pleased to carry forward: "I will extol You, O my God and King; Your name will I bless forever, and from age to age! Every day will I bless You and praise Your name, always and for ever and ever. Great is the Lord, and greatly to be praised; there is no measure to His majesty. . . . O let them bless You, Lord, all Your works, and let Your saints extol You!"

They shall tell the glory of Your kingdom, and Your sovereignty (literally "dynasty," *dynasteia*) will they proclaim, that the sons of men may know Your might, and the glory of the magnificence of Your kingdom. An eternal kingdom is Your kingdom; Your authority holds sway, from age to age."

Psalm 144 is the voice of the new life within us, that life of which Jesus said, "I have come that they may have life, and that they may have it more abundantly" (John 10:10). Each mounting crescendo of this psalm abounds with the life of the victorious Christ: "Generation after generation will praise Your deeds, and make declaration of Your might. The magnificence of the glory of Your holiness they will tell, and Your wonders will they proclaim. They will speak the power of Your fearsome deeds, and expound on Your magnificence. They will herald the remembrance of Your goodness, and in Your righteousness will they exult."

The God praised in this psalm is praised chiefly for His great and rich mercy: "Compassionate is the Lord and merciful, longsuffering and abounding in mercy. Gracious is the Lord to all alike; His compassions rest on all His works."

The Kingdom of Christ is not of this world; it is truly eternal and transcendent and belongs to heaven. Accordingly, the words and sentiments of our psalm repeatedly raise the mind above earthly things to the realm of eternal life. Several expressions of eternity appear in its lines: "from age to age," "for ever and ever," and so forth. Its emphasis thus goes beyond specific and individual deeds. Accordingly, it is one of a short series of psalms, near the end, that forms a final doxology to the whole Psalter. It is used invariably toward the end of the week, at Saturday Matins in the East, at Vespers on Friday and Saturday in the Benedictine Rule.

PSALM 145 (146)

PRAISE THE LORD, O MY SOUL

In the Slavic liturgical tradition Psalm 145 (Hebrew 146) is very often chanted early in the Divine Liturgy, right after the Great Litany, a custom recommending itself in a dozen points of propriety. How fitting, after all, to commence the Holy Eucharist with a list of the great messianic signs: "The Lord sets free the prisoners; the Lord enlightens the blind; the Lord straightens up those bowed down; the Lord loves the righteous; the Lord protects the strangers; He will adopt the orphan and the widow, but the way of sinners He will overthrow."

This list from Psalm 145 is not unlike our Lord's own description of His ministry: "The blind see and the lame walk; the lepers are cleansed and the deaf hear; the dead are raised up and the poor have the gospel preached to them" (Matt. 11:5). Such are the great messianic signs prophesied in Isaiah: "'Behold, your God will come with vengeance, / With the recompense of God; / He will come and save you.' / Then the eyes of the blind shall be opened, / And the ears of the deaf shall be unstopped. / Then the lame shall leap like a deer, / And the tongue of the dumb sing" (35:4–6).

This is not the only such list of messianic signs in Isaiah. Indeed, the Lord commences His ministry at Nazareth by publicly reading yet another of them: "The Spirit of the Lord is upon Me, / Because He has anointed Me / To preach the gospel to the poor; / He has sent Me to heal the brokenhearted, / To proclaim liberty to the captives / And recovery of sight to the blind, / To set at liberty those who are oppressed." This Isaian prophecy, Jesus announced, was being fulfilled in His own ministry (Luke 4:18–21; cf. Is. 49:8, 9; 61:1).

These miracles and wonders that marked the work of Jesus among men were at once the fulfillment of prophecy and signs of the divine presence. They are integral to the proclamation of the Gospel itself, which is concerned with "how God anointed Jesus of Nazareth with the Holy Spirit and with power, who went about doing good and healing all who were oppressed by the devil, for God was with Him" (Acts 10:38). They were not, therefore, merely incidental to Jesus' revelation and redemption.

First, revelation. The miraculous healings and other signs done by Jesus are revelatory of the presence of God: "So the multitude marveled when they saw the mute speaking, the maimed made whole, the lame walking, and the blind seeing; and they glorified the God of Israel" (Matt. 15:31).

Second, redemption. The miraculous signs in the earthly life of Jesus, but most especially His healings, are directly related to the mystery of the divine atonement. All of the Lord's various restorations and acts of therapy were both the foreshadowing and the firstfruits of that definitive curing of the human race accomplished on the Cross. In testimony to this truth, Matthew even cites one of the Isaian Suffering Servant songs in reference to the healing miracles of Jesus: "When evening had come, they brought to Him many who were demon-possessed. And He cast out the spirits with a word, and healed all who were sick, that it might be fulfilled which was spoken by Isaiah the prophet, saying: 'He Himself took our infirmities / And bore our sicknesses'" (Matt. 8:16, 17; Is. 53:4).

The use of the list of messianic signs from Psalm 145 at the beginning of the Divine Liturgy in the Slavic tradition is a very rich theological statement, asserting that the Holy Eucharist is supremely the *locus* of the messianic presence and activity among us. It announces, as surely as in the beginning of His earthly ministry in the synagogue at Nazareth, that Jesus is among us, in fulfillment of prophecy, doing the work of God on our behalf and unto our blessing. In the worship of the Church, and most prominently in the Divine Liturgy, Jesus of Nazareth stands in our midst as the healer, the restorer, the raiser-up of mankind. It is He, says Psalm 145, "who made heaven and earth, the sea and all that is in them, standing guard over truth forever, doing judgment for the oppressed, and giving food to the hungry." Even more than of the earthly ministry of Jesus must it be said of the Lord's eucharistic presence: "Then Jesus went about all the cities and villages, teaching in their synagogues, preaching the gospel of the kingdom, and healing every sickness and every disease among the people" (Matt. 9:35).

PSALM 146 (147A)

Psalms 146 and 147 in the Greek Bible form a single psalm in the traditional rabbinical text. Because of this arrangement, the disparity of numbering between the two versions of the Psalter, which began back at Psalm 9, is finally resolved. In the Eastern weekly cycle of the Psalter, both psalms are prayed at Saturday Matins. In the monastic cycle of the West, they are the final two psalms of Saturday Vespers.

Psalm 146 (Hebrew 147a) is the second of the six "Alleluia" psalms that close the canonical Psalter.

A good interpretive key to this psalm is provided by the line that says of God that "He counts the multitude of the stars, and calls them all by name." The parallel text that jumps to mind is in Genesis 15:5, where God tells Abraham, "Look now toward heaven, and count the stars if you are able to number them." And to what point? The Lord goes on, "So shall your descendants be."

The context of this promise is God's covenant with Abraham, who as yet had no offspring and was married to a woman past the time of bearing children. God's promise had to do with a numerous progeny who would share in the covenant with Abraham. Indeed, it would be a universal covenant, embracing all those who, from every nation, would share in the faith of Abraham. He would become the "father of many nations" (Gen. 17:4). Thus, St. Paul described Abraham as "the father of us all" (Rom. 4:16–18).

Our psalm's reference to the multitude of the stars, then, points to the numerous children of Abraham, for they are the Church, which takes Abraham's faith as the model for all times. Prophesying this truth, St. John the Baptist declared that "God is able to raise up children (*banim*) to Abraham from these stones (*abanim*)" (Matt. 3:9). These stones are we who believe with the faith of Abraham, "living stones, . . . being built up a spiritual house" (1 Pet. 2:5).

These are the stones—whether set on the breastplate of the high priest (cf. Ex. 28:17–21) or standing by the baptismal waters of the Jordan (cf. Josh. 4:3–7)—that represent the fullness of the people of God.

Such is the burden of that line of our psalm that says, "The Lord builds up Jerusalem; He will gather the dispersed of Israel." In the Psalms, Israel is the Church, and of her building up we are told that "the Lord added to the church daily those who were being saved" (Acts 2:47).

And as they are added to the Church, what are these "dispersed of Israel" described as doing? Listen to one who saw it: "And they continued steadfastly in the apostles' doctrine and fellowship, in the breaking of bread, and in prayers. . . . So continuing daily with one accord in the temple, and breaking bread from house to house (*kat' oikon*), they ate their food with gladness and simplicity of heart" (Acts 2:42, 46). All of these things pertain to the building up of Jerusalem. The apostolic doctrine and the liturgical prayers of the Church, including this psalm, are here placed into the context of the Holy Eucharist, for it is in the Holy Eucharist that the Lord builds up Jerusalem and gathers together the dispersed of Israel: "For we, though many, are one bread and one body; for we all partake of that one bread" (1 Cor. 10:17).

This Jerusalem is the house of reconciliation and healing. "Every broken heart He heals," says our psalm, "and bandages their every wound. . . . The Lord lifts up the meek." In order to gather together the dispersed of Israel, the Lord sent forth His disciples with the command: "Go out quickly into the streets and lanes of the city, and bring in here the poor and the maimed and the lame and the blind. . . . Go out into the highways and hedges, and compel them to come in, that my house may be filled" (Luke 14:21, 23).

These are "the children of God who were scattered abroad" (John 11:52). These are the very stones that God has raised up as children to Abraham. These are the promised multitude of stars, each one of which He calls by name. As they approach to share His Bread, Jesus recognizes that "some of them have come from afar" (Mark 8:3). Indeed so, for they were "aliens from the commonwealth of Israel and strangers from the covenants of promise" (Eph. 2:12). But now in Christ they are brought near and made the children of Abraham, the very heirs of those covenants and that promise.

PSALM 147 (147B)

Among the parables of Jesus our Lord recorded in the Synoptic Gospels, hardly any receives as much attention, within the Gospels themselves, as that of the sower going out to sow his seed. The story is also allegorical with respect to its details, unlike most of the Lord's other parables. (There are other evident examples of dominical allegory, nonetheless, such as the parable of the two sons in Luke 15.) Moreover, the story is interpreted within the biblical text, again unlike most of the Lord's other parables. (Still, it is not entirely unique in this regard; cf. the parable of the tares in Matthew 13:37–43.)

In Mark, this parable of the fallen grain serves to introduce the theme of spiritual blindness (4:10–12), which becomes so dominant a motif in Mark, especially in the two parallel cycles about the bread (6:30—7:37 and 8:1–26). Thus, in the rich but subtle development of the Markan narrative, the theme of spiritual blindness grows more intense as the author shifts his imagery from grain to bread. Indeed, the rest of Mark's Gospel becomes an extended interpretation of the parable of the sower, as the different characters illustrate the varying soils.

In His parable of the grain as a symbol of God's Word, our Lord brings to fullness an image with some prior literary history. In Deuteronomy, for example, when bread from heaven feeds the people in the desert (where they were unable to grow grain) this bread serves as a metaphor for God's Word (8:3, quoted in Matt. 4:4 and Luke 4:4).

Likewise, in the last part of Isaiah there is a poetic meditation built around bread as an image of God's Word, this time through a consideration of the moisture that feeds the grain: "For as the rain comes down, and the snow from heaven, / And do not return there, / But water the earth, / And make it bring forth and bud, / That it may give seed to the sower / And bread to the eater, / So shall My Word be that goes forth from My mouth; / It shall not return to Me void, / But it shall accomplish what I please, / And it shall prosper in the thing for which I sent it" (55:10, 11). (The appeal of this latter text among the early Christians is suggested in 2 Cor. 9:10.)

Psalm 147 (Hebrew 147b) is part of the literary history that lies behind the Lord's parable of the sower. As the psalm begins, Holy Church is once again summoned to the praise of God: "Praise the Lord, Jerusalem! Exalt your God, O Zion! For He has enforced the bars of your gates, and has blessed your children within you." And how has God blessed those children abiding within the Church? "Within your precincts He sets His peace." (No translation can match the Hebrew text here: *hashsham-gebulek shalom.*)

But a city under siege, no matter how well guarded, will never survive without food. Thus our psalm continues, combining virtually all of the images we considered in the foregoing texts: "He feeds you with the fat of wheat. He sends His Word upon the earth; very quickly runs His Word. He spreads the snow like wool; He lays the frost like ash. Like crumbs of bread He spreads the crystals; who can endure to face the frost?" Here are images associated with the dropping of the manna in the desert, described in Exodus 16:14 as "fine as frost on the ground." As in the text of Isaiah studied above, it is from this winter snow and frost that the fat of the wheat will be nourished to feed God's people. Hence, the very snow symbolizes His Holy Word.

But first that snow must melt, and this too involves God's Word. Our psalm continues: "His Word will He send and melt them. His Spirit breathes, the waters flow." Yes, both His Word and His Spirit. God sends Them both into the world, and the living waters flow for His Church. That is to say, ourselves, "having our hearts sprinkled from an evil conscience and our bodies washed with pure water" (Heb. 10:22).

Such is the uniqueness of Holy Church, true Jerusalem, among the peoples of the earth. She, then, is the teacher of all the nations. After the foregoing poetic elaboration to describe the power of God's sustaining Word, our psalm abruptly closes on the thesis that God's blessing of revelation has been granted to the Church is a fashion most singular: "To Jacob He declares His Word, to Israel His judgments and decrees. Not so has He done to other nations, nor revealed to them His judgments."

PSALM 148
PRAISE THE LORD FROM THE HEAVENS

It is the universal custom of the Church to pray the last three of the psalms as a unit during Matins. In the West they traditionally follow the daily appointed psalmody and Old Testament canticle, all of these components joined with a single antiphon. In the East, where they are chanted with a separate antiphon ("Let everything that breathes praise the Lord"), and finished with special stikhera for each day, these three psalms come immediately prior to the Great Doxology. In both instances Psalms 148—150 form a sort of climax to the psalmody, which is exactly how they function in the Psalter itself.

Psalm 148 is a summons directed to all of creation to praise God, its constantly repeated exhortation being *allelu*, "praise ye." In structure and imagery Psalm 148 has great affinities to the Greek form of the hymn of the three young men in the fiery furnace in Daniel 3:52–90, and in the Western liturgical tradition this latter is very often, and always on Sundays, the Old Testament canticle immediately preceding this psalm itself.

Psalm 148, in calling on all creation to praise the Lord, also follows much the same sequence as the fiery furnace song in Daniel: heaven, sun, moon, stars, angels, waters above the heavens, followed by the various elements and formations on the earth, etc. A similar sequence is found in other biblical poetry, such as Job 28 and Sirach 43. The general format for this sequence is derived, of course, from the created order in Genesis 1. Indeed, the doctrine of creation is precisely the reason given for the praise: "Let them praise the name of the Lord, for He spoke, and they came to be; He gave command, and they were created. He established them forever and ever. He decreed His precept, and it will not pass away." One may pray this psalm, then, as Genesis 1 adapted to the form of praise.

But we are not simply Jews, and this praise must be properly Christian; that is to say, it must be prayer firmly anchored in the "fullness of time," the full Christian faith, most particularly faith in the Resurrection of our Lord Jesus Christ. Except for His Resurrection, after all, the whole created world is "subjected to futility," held in "bondage of corruption" (Rom. 8:20, 21; cf. Luke 4:6). It is only in Christ that the created order is put right and set on the path to transfiguration. When, in this psalm, we summon the whole created order to praise God, we are eliciting a Spirit-given impulse that lies already at the heart of the world, "for the earnest expectation of the creation eagerly waits for the revealing of the sons of God" (Rom. 8:19).

Such a consideration makes Psalm 148 especially appropriate for Sunday, which is at once the first day of creation and the "eighth day" of the new creation inaugurated by the Resurrection of our Lord. Truly the "Lord" being praised in each verse of this psalm is the risen Jesus, whose victory over death constitutes the final vindication of the created order itself. In short, all Christian consideration of the created world will instinctively regard it through the properly defining lens of the Resurrection.

If the whole world of spirit and matter is called upon to join in a common praise of God, this praise is concentrated in the Church, which is explicitly spoken of in the psalm's final lines: "This is the song for all His saints, the children of Israel, the people who draw near to Him."

In the Church creation itself finds its destiny and proper form through the Resurrection of Christ: "For by Him all things were created that are in heaven and that are on earth, visible and invisible . . . All things were created through Him and for Him . . . and in Him all things consist. And He is the head of the body, the church . . . . " (Col. 1:16–18).

Consequently, the more ample measure of this psalm is perhaps the "sign" of the Child-bearing Woman who appears in the heavens, for it is her forces that engage that old serpentine foe of the whole created world (Rev. 12). Should the moon, then, be admonished to acclaim the Lord? Doubtless so, for on the moon she abides who bears the Messiah. And should the sun be summoned to an outburst of blessing? Without question, for with the luster of the sun is that Lady invested. And the stars, will they be included in the heavenly song? Surely so, for the stars form the crown that garlands her brow. Prefigured and modeled on the very Mother of Jesus, she is that new Eve who appears in history as the last and the finest of all that God has made. It is her voice, finally, that fills all creation with the praise of God.

PSALM 149

A verse in the Greek version of Blessed Hannah's canticle reads: "The Lord has ascended into heaven and has thundered forth. He will judge the ends of the earth. And He will give strength to our kings and shall exalt the horns of His Christ" (1 Sam. 2:10). Eusebius of Caesarea saw in this line a reference to the Ascension of our Lord and the consequent proclamation of the Gospel throughout the world: "The Lord who descended from heaven, the very Word of God, again ascended to heaven and, ascending, He thundered forth with His divine power the evangelical message (*to evangelikon kerygma*), so that it might be heard throughout the whole world. He Himself will judge the ends of the earth and those who live therein, as He has received all judgment from the Father. But He has also given power to His disciples—even the Apostles and the prophets—that is to say, our kings, and He has exalted the horns of His Christ, that is, of His people so named because of their participation in Christ" (*Fragments from the Prophetic Selections* 1.18).

This exaltation of the saints in the victory of Christ, their evangelical struggle for the Gospel, and the ultimate judgment of the world thereby are the themes of Psalm 149. This is a psalm of triumph in warfare, specifically that warfare described in Ephesians 6, the battle "against principalities, against powers, against the rulers of the darkness of this age, against spiritual hosts of wickedness in the heavenly places" (6:12). As we have had occasion to observe so often in the psalms, combat and invocation, battle and blessing, are inseparable in the evangelical life. Therefore, we may take this same sixth chapter of Ephesians, a true warfare passage, to help us penetrate the meaning of Psalm 149.

To pray this psalm properly, we must be numbered among those warriors that it thus portrays: "The saints shall exult in glory; they will rejoice in their quarters. The exaltations of God are in their throats, and two-edged swords in their hands." The latter blade so described is, of course, "the sword of the Spirit, which is the word of God" (Eph. 6:17). It is part of that "whole armor (*panoplia*) of God" which the Apostle Paul tells us to put on that we "may be able to stand against the wiles of the devil, . . . [to] be able to withstand in the evil day, and having done all, to stand" (6:11, 13).

This double-edged sword of God's Word will be of scant use to us, nonetheless, if we are not further girded and more amply fortified. Thus, to guard the affections of our hearts, lest they wax wanton, we wear the breastplate of righteousness; to protect the reflections of our minds, lest they be distracted, we don the helmet of salvation; to be defended against the fiery shafts of satanic assault, lest we fall victim to their deceptions, we bear the shield of faith; and since our psalm summons us forth to "wreak vengeance among the nations and to reprove among the peoples, . . . to pass on them the judgment decreed," we shoe our feet with the preparation of the gospel of peace (6:14–17).

Above everything we continue "always with all prayer and supplication in the Spirit, being watchful to this end with all perseverance and supplication for all the saints" (6:18), because our prayer is never to be separated from the general struggle of the Gospel in this world. The saints are the one group of people on this earth who speak the final, decisive truth to its inhabitants through their perseverance in the evangelical life, testifying to the final exaltation of the meek and thereby rendering judgment on what the world fancies important. "Do you not know that the saints will judge the world?" St. Paul asked the saints at Corinth (1 Cor. 6:2).

Meanwhile, assured of the final outcome of the combat, and confident even now that "this will be the glory of all His saints," their song is a glorification of God for His ever-renewed wonders in the struggle: "Sing to the Lord a new song! Let His praise be sung in the church of His saints. Let Israel be glad in her Maker, and the sons of Sion exult in their King. Let them praise His name with dancing; and sing to Him with the timbrel and harp. For the Lord takes pleasure in His people, and will exalt the meek in salvation." All this dancing of the meek, all this music of the saints—what is it but a foretaste of the day when they "shall see His face, and His name shall be on their foreheads"? (Rev. 22:4).

PSALM 150

PRAISE THE LORD IN HIS HOLY PLACE

Among the wonders of our redemption, as described in Holy Scripture, is a mysterious transformation of certain human experiences, especially cultural forms, that are associated in their origin, or at least their earliest historical expression, with the Fall. That is to say, the new life in Christ includes His taking hold of and entirely remolding certain components of life that were not part of man's original, innocent state. Even as He vanquishes sin, God does not simply undo or reverse the effects of man's Fall. Rather, He assumes these same effects, particularly cultural effects, into a larger expression of man's ascent.

Perhaps the example most easily grasped is that of clothing. Man's sin created the problem of nakedness, and hence the solution of clothing, as described in the first book of the Bible. In the Bible's last book, nonetheless, when man's sin has in every last sense been conquered, we do not see the human race returned to the nakedness of its primitive, unfallen state. The new man in Christ is clothed. We are described as wearing the white robes of glory. Grace, that is to say, does more than reverse the effects of sin; it transforms the effects of sin. Our new innocence in Christ is not to be identified as simply the earlier innocence of Adam. The effect of sin is not merely removed; it is assumed into a more ample transformation.

What is said of clothing seems also true of what we may call "urban life." God did not, at the beginning, place man in a city, but in a garden. The city was fallen man's idea. The first city was founded by the first murderer. Indeed, the first city was founded by the first fratricide, a fact that becomes the most ironical of archetypes. The irony was certainly not lost on St. Augustine, who commented at some length on the manifest travesty that such a great enterprise of brotherly cooperation should be started by a man who killed his brother. In his lengthy *The City of God*, the saintly bishop of Hippo went on to compare Cain's founding of the city of Enoch (cf. Gen. 4:17) to the founding of the city of Rome by Romulus, who had killed Remus, his own brother. The second city mentioned in Holy Scripture, Babel, was likewise an expression of man's rebellion against God. Holy Scripture, in speaking of such things, only calls attention to a fact that any of us can observe with minimum effort—that cities can be unpleasant, dangerous, and even violent places to live.

Still, when the Bible's last book describes man's return to Paradise, the latter is portrayed, not only as a garden (cf. Rev. 22:2), but also as a city (21:2).

Once again, a cultural form associated with the Fall, from the very beginning, comes to embody the social dimensions of Christian redemption.

Much the same is to be said about instrumental music. Originally crafted by a descendant of Cain (cf. Gen. 4:21), musical instruments do not, perhaps, look very promising when first we learn of them. Moreover, there has often been something a bit problematic about such music, morally considered. When King Nebuchadnezzar employed "the sound of the horn, flute, harp, lyre, and psaltery, in symphony with all kinds of music" (Dan. 3:5) for his idolatrous purposes, it was not the last instance when instrumental music served to deflect men from the worship of the true God.

Yet, in fact, God rather early designated musical instruments as appropriate to His own worship in the tabernacle and the temple. And, once again, in the final book of the Bible we find heaven to be a place resonating with the sounds of trumpet and harp.

Moreover, as an added irony, instrumental music is eventually limited so exclusively to heaven that the damned are forever deprived of such music! The sinful descendants of Cain, the very inventors of harp and flute, will never hear them again, inasmuch as the "sound of harpists, musicians, flutists, and trumpeters shall not be heard in you anymore" (Rev. 18:22). These things are now reserved for the blessed.

Reflecting on that final hour of perfected humanity, the last of the canonical psalms, Psalm 150, calls forth the voices of all these instruments for the eternal worship of the true God. He is forever to be praised with the voice of the trumpet, the psaltery and harp, timbrel and dance, strings and bells, loud-sounding cymbals, cymbals of jubilation. "Let every breath praise the Lord."

PSALM 151
SMALL I WAS AMONG MY BROTHERS
❧

It is curious that, following the list of the musical instruments in Psalm 150, the Greek Bible includes an additional psalm that speaks of David's crafting such an instrument for the praise of God.

Psalm 151, though contained in the earliest extant manuscripts of the Septuagint and recommended by some of the Fathers, is not regarded in the Church as equal to the other 150 psalms. It is designated as *exsothen tou arithmou,* "outside the number." Indeed, in the West it is practically unknown, and among the Orthodox it is prescribed that this psalm "is never read in Church." Leaving aside the questions raised regarding its canonical status, it will be included here, nonetheless, as pertaining, in a limited fashion, to the traditional praying of the Psalter.

Psalm 151 reads this way: "Small I was among my brothers, the youngest son in my father's house, and a shepherd to my father's sheep. I used my hands to craft a lyre, and a lute I fashioned with my fingers. And who should tell this to my Lord? For the Lord will hear it for Himself. His messenger did the Lord commission, and took me from my father's flocks. With the oil of consecration he anointed me. Tall and handsome were my brothers, but the Lord took no delight in them. To face the foreigner I went forth, and he cursed me by his idols. But I seized his sword and beheaded him, and removed the reproach of Israel's sons."

This small psalm combines two occasions that 1 Samuel juxtaposes: David's anointing by Samuel in chapter 16, and his slaying of Goliath in chapter 17. Both of these deserve comment.

When Samuel was commissioned by the Lord to anoint a replacement for Saul on the throne of Israel, he was directed to the house of Jesse in Bethlehem. The new king would come from among Jesse's sons. Left to his own inclinations, we are told that Samuel would have chosen one of David's seven older brothers, all of them tall and handsome men. An inner voice, however, reminded the prophet that "the Lord does not see as man sees; for man looks at the outer appearance, but the Lord looks at the heart." At last, Jesse summons his youngest son, and him Samuel anoints. At exactly that point in the narrative the name of David very dramatically appears in Holy Scripture for the first time: "Then Samuel took the horn of oil and anointed him in the midst of his brothers; and the Spirit of the Lord came upon David from that day forward" (16:13).

In this story of David's divine election, the Bible resonates with a major theme: God's rather habitual choice of the younger son. Thus, Abel and Seth were chosen, not Cain; Isaac, not Ishmael; Jacob, not Esau. Between the sons of Joseph, himself a younger son, the Lord chose Ephraim over Manasseh, and so on. All of biblical literature was composed during periods when the law of primogeniture held sway, the law determining that the eldest son in a family would be the major inheritor of his father's fortune and blessing. In making His own choices, however, the God of the Bible pays not the slightest regard to that human law. Truly, God does not choose as man chooses. Romans 9—11 will meditate at length on this theological irony, and it will be reflected in our Lord's parable of the two sons in Luke 15.

The second scene recalled in this psalm, and mentioned in its title, is David's slaying of Goliath. Once again, this is a story of God's choice of a victor contrary to all human expectation. Moreover, David's fight with Goliath was really a battle of conflicting theologies, for each man represented powers much larger than himself. Indeed, in the dialogue between them, both men appeal to their differing theologies. "And the Philistine cursed David by his gods," we are told, and David responds, "But I come to you in the name of the Lord of hosts, the God of the armies of Israel, whom you have defied" (1 Sam. 17:43, 45).

The deeper meaning of this psalm is Christological, for in mystic image David represents Christ victorious over the demons. Indeed, when Jesus speaks of His own despoiling of "a strong man, fully armed" (Luke 11:21), the mind goes readily to the elaborate description of Goliath's armor in 1 Samuel 17.

But this psalm has, as well, a moral meaning for the Christian, inasmuch as David is a model of the humility and self-abasement to which God summons the friends of His Son.

NUMBERING OF THE PSALMS

SEPTUAGINT	HEBREW (KJ)
1–8	1–8
9	9–10
10–112	11–113
113	114–115
114	116 v. 1–9
115	116 v. 10–19
116–145	117–146
146	147 v. 1–11
147	147 v. 12–20
148–150	148–150

NOTES